The Possibility of the ICJ and the ICC Taking Action in the Wake of Israel's Operation "Cast Lead" in the Gaza Strip

Internationales und Europäisches Strafverfahrensrecht

Herausgegeben von Hans-Heiner Kühne und Robert Esser

Band 10

PL ACADEMIC RESEARCH

Oded Friedmann

The Possibility of the ICJ and the ICC Taking Action in the Wake of Israel's Operation "Cast Lead" in the Gaza Strip

A Jurisdiction and Admissibility Analysis

PL ACADEMIC RESEARCH

Bibliographic Information published by the Deutsche Nationalbibliothek
The Deutsche Nationalbibliothek lists this publication in the Deutsche Nationalbibliografie; detailed bibliographic data is available in the internet at http://dnb.d-nb.de.

Zugl.: Trier, Univ., Diss., 2012

Library of Congress Cataloging-in-Publication Data

Friedmann, Oded, 1978-
The possibility of the ICJ and the ICC taking action in the wake of Israel's operation „Cast Lead" in the Gaza Strip : a jurisdiction and admissibility analysis / Oded Friedmann.
pages cm. — (Internationales und Europäisches Strafverfahrensrecht ; Band 10)
ISBN 978-3-631-62936-9
1. Complementarity (International law) 2. Arab-Israeli conflict 3. Criminal jurisdiction. 4. Admissible evidence. 5. Gaza War, 2008-2009—Destruction and pillage. 6. International criminal courts. 7. International Criminal Court. 8. International Court of Justice. 9. Israel—Government policy—Gaza Strip. I. Title.
KZ7379.F75 2013
341.6'9—dc23

2013016129

D 385
ISSN 1611-275X
ISBN 978-3-631-62936-9

PL Academic Research is an Imprint of Peter Lang GmbH.

Peter Lang – Frankfurt am Main · Bern · Bruxelles · New York · Oxford · Warszawa · Wien

www.peterlang.de

ACKNOWLEDGMENTS

In December 2012, this book was accepted as a doctoral thesis by the University of Trier Law Faculty.

In addition to the in-depth and objective understanding of the historical "roots" of the ongoing Arab-Israeli conflict in the Middle East, the extensive researching and writing of this book provided me with a unique opportunity to analyze and understand the purpose and role of the ICJ and the ICC. Specifically, the way they function and act in particular cases, and their ability (or lack thereof) to investigate, prosecute and eventually prevent the most serious crimes of international concern. These insights provided the basis for the analysis of the highly complex and intriguing legal relationship between Israel, the state of the Jewish people, and the international courts, following Israel's operation "Cast Lead" in the Gaza Strip.

For this once in a lifetime, enriching experience I would like to thank a number of people. First and foremost, my doctoral adviser, Prof. Dr. Dr. h.c. mult. Hans-Heiner Kühne, who from the very beginning of our cooperation supported this project, providing indispensable academic guidance. I sincerely thank him for the warm and productive work environment, his genuine interest in my topic and the numerous suggestions and fruitful discussions.

I would also like to thank: Prof. Dr. Alexander Proelß, whose valuable comments as second reviewer of my doctoral thesis significantly contributed to its final form and content; the University of Trier Law Faculty's academic adviser, Ulrike Leich, for her crucial help and support, without which this project would never have started; my very good friend, Tilman Quarch, for his support, advice and countless discussions, especially during the difficult times every doctoral candidate experiences; and the management and staff of the Max Planck Institute for Foreign and International Criminal Law in Freiburg, where I researched this doctoral thesis and which I consider its intellectual home.

Finally, I would like to express my deepest gratitude to my parents, Relli and Menachem Friedmann, for their unconditional and boundless love, support and encouragement over the years. I cannot imagine better parents and this book is dedicated to them.

Tel Aviv, February 2013 Oded Friedmann

TABLE OF CONTENTS

LIST OF ABBREVIATIONS

Art.	Article
ASP	Assembly of States Parties
CCW	Convention on Certain Conventional Weapons
EU	European Union
ICC	International Criminal Court
ICJ	International Court of Justice
ICRC	International Committee of the Red Cross
ICTR	International Criminal Tribunal for Rwanda
ICTY	International Criminal Tribunal for the former Yugoslavia
IDF	Israel Defense Forces
MAG	Military Advocate General's Corps
MPCID	Military Police Criminal Investigation Division
PCIJ	Permanent Court of International Justice
PLO	Palestine Liberation Organization
UN	United Nations
UNESCO	United Nations Educational, Scientific and Cultural Organization
US	United States
WHO	World Health Organization

INTRODUCTION

1. The Gaza armed conflict of 2008/2009

The Gaza armed conflict between the State of Israel and Hamas, began on 27 December 2008 at 11:30 AM with the launch of a military offensive by the Israel Defense Forces ("IDF") against Hamas targets within the Gaza Strip. The offensive – known as Operation "Cast Lead" – consisted, at first, of aerial, naval and ground artillery fire (from outside Gaza) and was expanded to include a ground offensive on 3 January 2009.

Israel, which consistently maintained that the offensive was action taken in self-defense[1], set three objectives for its operation in Gaza: (i) Stopping the incessant rocket attacks aimed at Israeli civilians from Gaza, (ii) dealing Hamas a forceful blow, and (iii) fundamentally changing the situation in Gaza[2].

During and following Operation "Cast Lead", Israel was severely criticized by many in the international community for the force used by the IDF – especially in light of the fact that the conflict took place in the heart of one of the most densely populated areas in the world[3] – and the devastating results of the conflict. Such criticism eventually became very serious accusations of international law violations, which shall be discussed in further detail below.

On 18 January 2009 at 2:00 AM, the Israeli offensive ceased, with the last IDF soldiers leaving Gaza on 21 January 2009.

1.1. The situation in the region prior to the Israeli offensive

Israel has been engaged in an ongoing armed conflict with Hamas (and other militant Palestinian organizations) since the massive outbreak of armed terrorist violence and hostilities in October 2000 (known as the *Al Aqsa Intifadah*).

Mortars started to be fired from Gaza into and around Sderot – a town of some 20,000, about 1.5 km from Gaza – and nearby villages in 2001[4]. Crude

---

1 The State of Israel, *The Operation in Gaza, 27 December 2008 - 18 January 2009: Factual and Legal Aspects* (2009), para. 72.

2 Israel Ministry of Foreign Affairs, *Operation Cast Lead: Israel Strikes Back Against Hamas Terror in Gaza* (2009).

3 More than 1.5 million people populate the Gaza strip on a territory of barely 360 square kilometers.

4 From this point and until the beginning of the Israeli offensive in the Gaza strip, Hamas (and other militant organizations such as "Palestinian Islamic Jihad" and the "Popular Resistance Committees") launched more than 12,000 rockets and mortar rounds from

home-made Qassam rockets followed, initially with a maximum range of 3-4 km, but progressively upgraded to reach 12-15 km by 2005. In recent years, longer-range Qassam rockets fired from Gaza have begun to reach further into Israel, notably Ashkelon, a major town some 20 km north of Gaza with a population of 120,000. While most Qassam rockets initially fell to the south of the town, away from the populated areas, since early 2008 Grad-type rockets – apparently smuggled into Gaza – have reached the center and north of Ashkelon, as well as Netivot, some 20 km east of Gaza[5]. By late 2008, a total of one million Israeli civilians – almost 15% of Israel's population – were directly threatened, as some of Israel's largest cities, including Ashdod (with a population of 210,000) and Be'er Sheva (with a population of over 185,000), could be reached by rockets fired from Gaza. In addition to the civilian population, the increased range of the Hamas rockets directly threatened Israeli strategic installations, such as major electricity and gas storage Facilities[6].

In September 2005, Israel completed its disengagement from the Gaza Strip, which was approved by the Israeli Government on 6 June 2004[7]. The disengagement included a full withdrawal of Israeli settlers and armed forces from the Gaza Strip and led to controversy with regard to the legal status of the latter[8].

In January 2006, Hamas won the Palestinian parliamentary elections, securing 74 of the 132 seats in the Legislative Council[9]. This political victory did not improve the reality on the ground or change Hamas' agenda with regard to its cross-border attacks against Israel, which on 25 June 2006 reached a new cli-

---

the Gaza Strip at towns in Southern Israel. In all, 18 Israeli civilians, including four children, have been killed by rocket and mortar attacks from Gaza since June 2004, when the first fatality from such attacks occurred. Hundreds of other civilians have been injured, several very seriously.

5 Amnesty International, *Israel/Gaza – Operation 'Cast Lead': 22 Days of Death and Destruction* (2009), p. 69.

6 The State of Israel, *The Operation in Gaza: Factual and Legal Aspects*, *supra* note 1, para. 49.

7 The Independent Fact Finding Committee on Gaza to the League of Arab States, *No Safe Place* (2009), para. 19.

8 Despite the Israeli disengagement of 2005, Israel maintained effective control over the Gaza strip (including control over Gaza's six land crossings, complete control of Gaza's airspace and territorial waters, continued military incursions and rocket attacks, and control over the Palestinian population registry, which determines who may reside in Gaza and who may leave / enter the territory) and thus – in the eyes of many – continued to fulfill the *de facto* requirements of an occupying power.

9 The Independent Fact Finding Committee on Gaza to the League of Arab States, *supra* note 7, para. 23.

max, when Palestinian terrorists from Gaza attacked an Israeli army post on the Israeli side of the southern Gaza Strip border. During the attack the terrorists killed two IDF soldiers, wounded four others and captured the Israeli soldier Corporal Gilad Shalit[10]. Shalit has been held by Hamas incommunicado in an undisclosed location for 1941 days until his release – as part of a prisoner swap between Israel and the Hamas – on 18 October 2011.

The results of the Palestinian parliamentary elections led to a violent power struggle between the Fatah Group[11] – led by the President of the Palestinian Authority, Mahmoud Abbas – and Hamas. In June 2007, the latter violently seized control of the Gaza Strip by persecuting some of the leaders and members of Fatah and neutralizing the Palestinian Authority's military and political power in Gaza. The final result of this struggle was a Palestinian movement divided into two quasi-states or enclaves: a Hamas-controlled Gaza and a Palestinian Authority-controlled West Bank[12]. As a result of Hamas gaining control over the Gaza Strip, Israel imposed a blockade[13] on Gaza, limiting the quantity and type of goods that were permitted to be transferred from Israel into Gaza[14], in order to prevent the smuggling of arms and stop the firing of rockets and other attacks

10 The Israeli Government responded to this action on 27 June 2006 by launching Operation "Summer Rains". The two stated goals of the operation were to (i) secure the release of Corporal Shalit, and (ii) stop the ongoing rocket attacks from the Gaza Strip into Israel. Operation "Summer Rains" ended in September 2006. Two additional Israeli offensives into the Gaza strip followed Operation "Summer Rains": Operation "Autumn Clouds" (1-7 November 2006) and Operation "Warm Winter" (28 February to 3 March 2008). The goal of both operations was to put an end to the intensifying rocket attacks from the Gaza strip.

11 Fataḥ is a major Palestinian political party and the largest fraction of the Palestine Liberation Organization (PLO).

12 Cordesman, Anthony H., *The "Gaza War": A Strategic Analysis*, Center for Strategic & International Studies (2009), p. 6.

13 The scope and duration of the Israeli blockade on Gaza made it very controversial in the eyes of many in the international community. As a result, Israel has been accused of (i) collectively punishing the population of Gaza, (ii) flagrantly violating its obligations under the Fourth Geneva Convention, (iii) violating the Gaza population's basic rights regarding freedom of movement, adequate standard of living and work, and (iv) deliberately devastating the Gaza economy.

14 The blockade on the Gaza Strip led to a great increase in smuggling of goods into Gaza through tunnels under the Gaza-Egypt border. Over time, the underground tunnels became a lifeline for the Gaza economy and the only way to obtain certain products in the Gaza Strip. Several hundred tunnels run under the Gaza-Egypt border. The tunnels are owned by a number of local merchants and supervised by Hamas, which issues individual operating licenses and collects taxes from their use.

against Israel. The Israeli blockade on the Gaza Strip led to further intensification of rocket fire from Gaza into Israel, and on 19 September 2007, Israel's security cabinet declared the Gaza Strip a "hostile entity"[15] and announced it would begin cutting electricity and fuel to the Hamas-run territory in an effort to stop near-daily rocket fire into Israel.

On Thursday, 19 June 2008 at 06:00 AM, Hamas and Israel agreed to a six month ceasefire (*Tahadiya*)[16]. The (unwritten) agreement was negotiated indirectly through Egyptian good offices and was effected without the two parties ever meeting each other in direct talks and without either of them having to make any political concessions[17]. The ceasefire between Israel and Hamas did not last the agreed upon six months, as on 4 November 2008, Israel launched an incursion into Gaza, killing 6 and injuring 7 others[18]. As a result, Hamas renewed its rocket fire into Israel and on 19 December 2008 unilaterally[19] declared the end of the ceasefire.

1.2. The twenty-two day armed conflict between Israel and Hamas

The Israeli offensive in Gaza commenced on 27 December 2008 with aerial strikes against Hamas infrastructure, as well as rocket and mortar launching units. In addition to clear military objectives (such as command posts, training camps and weapons stores used in the planning, preparation, guidance and execution of attacks against Israel), the Israeli Air Force targeted Hamas infrastructure, which was occupied and used by the governmental / civilian arm of Hamas (the Palestinian Legislative Council, various ministries, administrative structures and civilian police stations)[20]. Despite coming under heavy international criti-

---

15 The Independent Fact Finding Committee on Gaza to the League of Arab States, *supra* note 7, para. 402; Israel Ministry of Foreign Affairs, *Security Cabinet Declares Gaza Hostile Territory* (2007).

16 The Independent Fact Finding Committee on Gaza to the League of Arab States, *supra* note 7, para. 35.

17 Halevy, Efraim, "Israel's Hamas Portfolio", *Israel Journal of Foreign Affairs* 2.3 (2008), p. 46.

18 The Independent Fact Finding Committee on Gaza to the League of Arab States, *supra* note 7, para. 23.

19 The State of Israel, *The Operation in Gaza: Factual and Legal Aspects*, *supra* note 1, para. 60.

20 The State of Israel, *The Operation in Gaza: Factual and Legal Aspects*, *supra* note 1, para. 235; Amnesty International, *supra* note 5, p. 9.

cism[21] for attacking these targets, the Israeli Government has maintained that despite its governmental and social function in the Gaza Strip, Hamas remains a terrorist organization and many of its alleged civilian elements are in reality active components of its terrorist and militant efforts[22]. With regard to the targeting of the Hamas civilian police force[23], Israel has argued that there is proof that Hamas' civilian police force was part of the organization's armed forces in the course of the conflict and, therefore, could be considered a legitimate military target under the Law of Armed Conflict[24].

On 3 January 2009, one week into the Gaza operation, the IDF commenced its ground operations as dozens of Israeli tanks took position in various locations inside the Gaza Strip – mostly in the east and north of Gaza. On 10 January 2009, the IDF expanded the ground maneuver by entering deeper into the urban areas of the Gaza Strip, in order to take control of and dismantle rocket launching sites positioned in those areas. In total, nine Israeli soldiers were killed[25] and 336 were injured during fighting in the Gaza strip[26].

During the Gaza armed conflict, the armed wing of Hamas (and other militant Palestinian groups) launched rockets and mortars[27] on a daily basis into towns and villages in southern Israel, as well as against Israeli military positions and patrols inside Gaza and along Gaza's perimeter. According to Israeli authorities, 571 rockets and 205 mortar shells landed in Israel during the 22 days of armed conflict, killing four (three civilians and one soldier)[28] and injuring 182

---

21 The Independent Fact Finding Committee on Gaza to the League of Arab States, *supra* note 7, paras. 458-464; Amnesty International, *supra* note 5, pp. 8-9.

22 The State of Israel, *The Operation in Gaza: Factual and Legal Aspects*, *supra* note 1, para. 235.

23 In the morning of 27 December 2008, some 240 Hamas police officers were killed in bombardments of police stations across the Gaza Strip in the first moments of Operation "Cast Lead" – including scores who were killed when the first Israeli air strikes targeted the police cadets' graduation parade in the central police compound in Gaza City.

24 The State of Israel, *The Operation in Gaza: Factual and Legal Aspects*, *supra* note 1, paras. 238-248.

25 Four of the IDF soldiers killed during the conflict were killed in two separate "friendly fire" incidents, which occurred on 5 and 6 January 2009 in northern Gaza.

26 Israel Ministry of Foreign Affairs, *IDF Operation in Gaza: Cast Lead* (2009).

27 The rockets fired by Palestinian armed groups include Grad or Katyusha rockets with a range of about 35 km, home-made short-range Qassam rockets and locally manufactured mortars. All are unguided projectiles, which cannot be directed at specific targets.

28 United Nations Fact-Finding Mission on the Gaza Conflict, *Human Rights in Palestine and Other Occupied Arab Territories*, UN Doc. A/HRC/12/48, 25 September 2009 (hereinafter "Goldstone Report"), para 31.

others. In addition, several civilian homes and other structures were damaged, some extensively[29].

1.2.1. Armed conflict in a densely populated area

Both Hamas and Israel have been the targets of wide spread, severe international criticism based on the methods they chose to deploy during the Gaza conflict, despite the fact that it took place in a very densely populated area.

Hamas was accused – both by Israel[30] and by members of the international community[31] – of gravely endangering Palestinian civilians by launching rockets from residential areas, locating military equipment in and near civilian homes / facilities and using empty homes, properties and other civilian facilities[32] as combat positions during armed confrontations with Israeli forces. As a result of such tactics, Hamas was accused of using the civilian population of Gaza as a "human shield"[33]. In addition, Israel has claimed to have seized information, which proves Hamas' tactic of booby trapping homes, roads and schools with mines and explosives, in order to inflict casualties on IDF forces – while ignoring the severe danger to the local civilian population[34].

The accusations against Israel, on the other hand, focused on its disregard for civilian lives and property, reflected in the severe force, methods and weapons it chose to use during the armed conflict with Hamas[35]. In addition, Israel was accused of deliberately causing a humanitarian crisis in the Gaza Strip, in order to increase the internal pressure on the Hamas leadership by collectively punishing Gaza's civilian population[36].

---

29 Amnesty International, *supra* note 5, p. 66.

30 The State of Israel, *The Operation in Gaza: Factual and Legal Aspects*, *supra* note 1, para. 141.

31 Amnesty International, *supra* note 5, pp. 3, 4, 74, 75.

32 Israel has presented proof for the fact that Hamas' main base of operations during the Gaza conflict was located inside Shifa Hospital in Gaza City.

33 The deliberate placement of civilians in or around combat targets to deter an enemy from attacking those targets.

34 The State of Israel, *The Operation in Gaza: Factual and Legal Aspects*, *supra* note 1, para. 181.

35 Goldstone Report, *supra* note 28, paras. 62, 593, 594, 1919.

36 Amnesty International, *supra* note 5, p. 51; The Independent Fact Finding Committee on Gaza to the League of Arab States, *supra* note 7, para. 435; Goldstone Report, *supra* note 28, paras. 1330, 1331.

1.2.1.1. The controversial use of white phosphorus and flechettes

During its Gaza offensive, the IDF made use of white phosphorus, which is a pyrophoric chemical (self-igniting at contact with air) intended primarily as an obscurant to provide cover for troop movements on the battlefield. It does so by releasing thick white smoke as it burns[37]. White phosphorus is extremely dangerous for humans, as it causes deep burns through muscle and down to the bone, continuing to burn until deprived of oxygen[38]. After the Gaza conflict has ended, Israel explained that the restrictions on the use of incendiary weapons under Protocol III to the 1980 Convention on Certain Conventional Weapons[39] ("CCW") were observed at all times. Furthermore, the small number of exploding munitions containing white phosphorous, which were used during the conflict, were fired only at open unpopulated areas and were used only for marking and signaling, not in an anti-personnel capacity[40]. With regard to smoke projectiles containing white phosphorous[41], Israel asserted that such projectiles contained relatively small amounts of white phosphorus and that they were used exclusively to create smoke screens for military requirements[42]. Despite the fact that the use of white phosphorus is not prohibited under International Humanitarian Law[43], Israel has been heavily criticized by many in the international community for its decision to use the dangerous chemical – in particular in light of the obvious disproportion between the risk the chemical posed to the civilian population in the conflict area and the military benefits it offered[44].

Flechettes (3.5 cm-long steel darts, sharply pointed at the front, with four fins at the rear[45]) are an additional weapon used by the IDF during the Gaza

---

37 It can also be used to mark targets, to "trace" the path of bullets and as an incendiary weapon. It can be dispersed by artillery shells, grenades, and rockets.

38 Amnesty International, *supra* note 5, p. 28.

39 Officially known as the United Nations Convention on Prohibitions or Restrictions on the Use of Certain Conventional Weapons which may be Deemed to be Excessively Injurious or to have Indiscriminate Effects as amended on 21 December 2001.

40 The State of Israel, *The Operation in Gaza: Factual and Legal Aspects*, *supra* note 1, para. 407.

41 The second and main type of munitions containing white phosphorous employed by the IDF during Operation "Cast Lead".

42 The State of Israel, *The Operation in Gaza: Factual and Legal Aspects*, *supra* note 1, para. 409.

43 Amnesty International, *supra* note 5, p. 31; Goldstone Report, *supra* note 28, para. 901.

44 Goldstone Report, *supra* note 28, para. 893.

45 5,000 to 8,000 of these darts are packed into shells, which are generally fired from tanks. The shells explode in the air and scatter the flechettes in a conical pattern over an area of about 300m x 100m.

armed conflict and severely criticized by members of the international community[46]. Due to the fact that flechettes are an area weapon – designated to be used against massed infantry attacks or squads of troops in the open – highly unsuitable for use in urban settings[47], the question of their use in the Gaza Strip has already reached the Israeli Supreme Court, sitting as the High Court of Justice, in 2002. The latter has ruled that flechettes were not covered by the CCW and, therefore, not illegal under the Law of Armed Conflict[48]. Despite the fact that International Humanitarian Law does not prohibit the use of flechettes in all circumstances, many members of the international community maintain that by using such weapon in predominantly civilian areas during the Gaza armed conflict, Israeli forces have violated customary international law[49].

1.2.1.2. The destruction of civilian property in the Gaza Strip

Although destruction of private civilian property and infrastructure is an inescapable by-product of every armed conflict, the IDF was severely criticized for the destruction and damage it caused in the Gaza Strip by demolishing civilian houses / structures, agricultural land and infrastructure[50]. This criticism was based on (i) the sheer scale of destruction caused, and (ii) the view that much of the destruction was wanton, deliberate and unnecessary[51]. Following the Gaza conflict, the State of Israel confirmed that extensive damage has been caused to private civilian property during the conflict, but claimed that the vast majority of IDF activities, which caused the destruction and damage, were demanded by the necessities of war and, thus, complied with the Law of Armed Conflict[52].

1.2.1.3. The humanitarian situation during the conflict

The fact that during a time of armed conflict – particularly when the combat operations take place in densely populated urban areas – the tragic suffering of the civilian population in the combat zone cannot be completely avoided is beyond dispute. The difference of opinion between members of the international com-

---

46 Amnesty International, *supra* note 5, p. 40.

47 *Ibid.*, pp. 38-39; Goldstone Report, *supra* note 28, paras. 903, 1924.

48 *Physicians for Human Rights v. OC Southern Command*, Israel Supreme Court, sitting as the High Court of Justice (27 April 2003).

49 Goldstone Report, *supra* note 28, para. 880; The Independent Fact Finding Committee on Gaza to the League of Arab States, *supra* note 7, para. 472; Amnesty International, *supra* note 5, p. 40.

50 The State of Israel, *The Operation in Gaza: Factual and Legal Aspects*, *supra* note 1, paras. 436, 439, 442.

51 Amnesty International, *supra* note 5, p. 55.

52 The State of Israel, *The Operation in Gaza: Factual and Legal Aspects*, *supra* note 1, paras. 437, 442.

munity and the Government of Israel relates to the question, whether the latter fulfilled its obligations regarding the humanitarian needs of Gaza's civilian population during the conflict. Many in the international community argue that the Israeli occupation of Gaza did not end with Israel's unilateral disengagement in 2005[53]. Thus, as an occupying power, Israel was duty-bound under the Fourth Geneva Convention[54] and to the full extent of the means available to it, to ensure the supply of foodstuff, medical and hospital items and other goods, to adequately meet the humanitarian needs of the population of the Gaza Strip without qualification[55]. Despite the fact that the quantity of humanitarian goods – particularly foodstuff – allowed into Gaza significantly increased during the military operations[56], the effects of the long-term Israeli blockade on the Gaza Strip[57] and the intense fighting led to a humanitarian crisis, in which everyone[58] suffered from the lack of basic necessities. The conditions of life created by Israel in the Gaza Strip led many to believe the humanitarian suffering of Gaza's civilian population was deliberate as part of Israel's war plan against Hamas[59].

Israel, on the other hand, argued that it implemented a far reaching effort to try to ensure that the humanitarian needs of Gaza's civilian population were met and that Hamas was the one interested in creating a humanitarian crisis in Gaza – as part of its war plan against Israel[60]. The Israeli humanitarian efforts in Gaza included (i) increasing and ensuring the supply of humanitarian aid, such as food, medical supplies and fuel, through the crossing points[61], (ii) coordination of evacuations[62] and other humanitarian movements within the Gaza Strip and

---

53 See *supra* note 8.

54 Fourth Geneva Convention relative to the Protection of Civilian Persons in Time of War (12 August 1949).

55 Goldstone Report, *supra* note 28, para. 28.

56 The average number of truckloads allowed into Gaza by Israel increased from 35 (before the conflict) to 122 (during the conflict).

57 On 31 December 2008, as a rare exception, Egypt opened the Rafah Crossing – Gaza's only border not with Israel – on a daily basis to allow injured from the Gaza Strip into Egypt and medical equipment from Egypt into the Gaza Strip. For other movement of people, the Rafah Crossing has been almost completely blocked during the conflict.

58 Amnesty International, *supra* note 5, p. 52.

59 See *supra* note 36.

60 The State of Israel, *The Operation in Gaza: Factual and Legal Aspects*, *supra* note 1, para. 277.

61 See *supra* note 56.

62 A special medical coordination center was set up in the Gaza Coordination and Liaison Administration ("CLA"), under the command of an officer with the rank of Major. The coordination center dealt with assistance to civilians in danger and with evacuation of

between Gaza and Israel[63], (iii) ensuring the functioning of essential infrastructure in the Gaza Strip[64], and (iv) unilaterally suspending military operations for at least three hours every day to enable the civilian population to re-supply and other humanitarian relief activities[65]. According to the Israeli Government, not only did Hamas not try to improve the humanitarian situation in Gaza, it actively took measures to prevent humanitarian relief from reaching its intended recipients[66]. Such measures included firing rockets into Israel during humanitarian pauses[67], attacking cross points into Gaza and hijacking humanitarian supplies once they crossed into Gaza[68].

---

the wounded and dead from areas of hostilities. In total, the center coordinated 150 different requests during the Gaza conflict and all professional decisions were made by a medical doctor.

63 During the Gaza conflict itself, the Gaza CLA operated a 24 hour operations room tasked with communicating with the IDF and international organizations to deal with real time problems and requests. The CLA coordinated close to 500 movements of international organizations' vehicles and convoys during the conflict. In addition, a special Humanitarian Coordination Center ("HCC") was established for enhanced coordination with representatives of the international organizations working in Gaza. Representatives of the United Nations OCHA, UNRWA, ICRC, WFP and other international organizations met on a daily basis with IDF representatives to coordinate the entry of humanitarian aid into Gaza.

64 The IDF maintained contact with the Palestinian Electricity, Water and Sewage and Communications Authorities in Ramallah and their crews in Gaza, in order to ensure the functioning of essential utilities during the Gaza conflict. The IDF also set up and manned an Infrastructure Coordination Center to monitor the situation in Gaza, identify needs and coordinate repairs where necessary.

65 The IDF began these "humanitarian pauses" on 7 January 2009.

66 The State of Israel, *The Operation in Gaza: Factual and Legal Aspects*, *supra* note 1, para. 195.

67 During the period between 8 and 17 January 2009, Hamas fired a total of 44 rockets and mortars at Israel during humanitarian pauses.

68 On 3 February 2009, the UNRWA reported that Hamas armed assailants seized by force 3,500 blankets and 406 food parcels from its distribution center at the Shati refugee camp. On 5 February 2009, the UNRWA suspended all imports of aid into the Gaza Strip after 10 truckloads of flour (equivalent to 100 tons) and rice (equivalent to 200 tons) imported from Egypt by the UNRWA were taken from the Palestinian side of the Kerem Shalom Crossing into Gaza. With regard to how Hamas used the hijacked supplies, a captured Hamas activist reported that Hamas sold the supplies (intended as free humanitarian aid) to the population of Gaza.

1.2.2. The aftermath of the armed conflict

The special circumstances of the Gaza Strip, in combination with the methods used by the IDF and Hamas during the conflict, led to very significant losses – both in terms of civilian lives and property.

Statistics regarding Palestinians killed during the Gaza armed conflict vary: Extensive field research performed by non-governmental organizations[69] places the number of Palestinians killed between 1,387 and 1,417[70]. Of those killed, the number of civilian non-combatants varies between 773[71] and 1,036[72]. Out of the civilian non-combatants killed, the number of women varies between 109[73] and 116[74] and the number of children varies between 313[75] and 348[76]. In addition some 5,000 Palestinians were injured during the conflict[77].

After it has completed its post-conflict investigation, the IDF reported different numbers regarding the civilian casualties of the Gaza conflict: According to the IDF, from the 1,166 Palestinians killed, 709 were identified as Hamas (and various other militant organizations) terror operatives and 295 were uninvolved Palestinians (162 additional men not yet identified). From those identified as uninvolved, 49 were women and 89 children (under the age of 16)[78].

In addition to the loss of life, the armed conflict between Israel and Hamas caused substantial destruction to homes and businesses across the Gaza Strip. According to information provided by non-governmental organizations and the United Nations ("UN") Development Programme, some 3,000 houses were

---

69 Such as: Palestinian Center for Human Rights (PCHR), Al Mezan Center for Human Rights, B'Tselem and Defence for Children International – Palestine Section.

70 Goldstone Report, *supra* note 28, para. 30.

71 B'Tselem – The Israeli Information Center for Human Rights in the Occupied Territories, *B'Tselem Publishes Complete Fatality Figures from Operation Cast Lead* (2009).

72 Al Mezan Centre for Human Rights, *Cast Lead Offensive in Numbers – Statistical Report on: Persons Killed and Property Damaged or Destroyed in the Gaza Strip by the Israeli Occupation Forces during Operation Cast Lead, 27 December 2008 - 18 January 2009* (2009), p. 7.

73 B'Tselem, *Complete Fatality Figures from Operation Cast Lead, supra* note 71.

74 Goldstone Report, *supra* note 28, para. 355.

75 *Ibid.*

76 *Ibid.*, para. 358.

77 Amnesty International, *supra* note 5, p. 6.

78 Israel Defense Forces, *Majority of Palestinians Killed in Operation Cast Lead: Terror Operatives* (2009).

completely destroyed and over 11,000 others damaged during the conflict[79]. In addition, some 700 private businesses (industry and trade)[80] and close to 60% of all agricultural land[81] were damaged or destroyed during the military operations in the Gaza Strip.

2. Purpose of the research

Once the hostilities between the IDF and Hamas forces ended and the former withdrew from the Gaza Strip, it became clear that the Gaza armed conflict of 2008/2009 was nothing like past military confrontations between the sides in terms of the death and destruction caused thereby. In light of this new level of deadly violence, the international community and numerous non-governmental organizations could not make do with criticizing or condemning the conduct of both sides during the conflict, but rather considered themselves obliged to actively investigate said conduct. Once these investigations have been concluded, numerous allegations of violations of the Law of Armed Conflict were made against the Hamas and (mainly) Israel – followed by calls that:

(i) Both sides investigate said allegations and, if appropriate, prosecute those responsible[82];

(ii) In the absence of good-faith investigations that are independent and in conformity with international standards having been undertaken within an agreed upon timeframe, the UN Security Council should refer the situation in Gaza to the Prosecutor of the International Criminal Court ("ICC"), pursuant to Art. 13(b) of the Rome Statute of the International Criminal Court ("Rome-Statute")[83];

(iii) Should the Security Council fail to do so – for the sake of accountability for victims and the interests of peace and justice in the region – the Prosecutor of the ICC should make the required legal determination regarding

---

79 Goldstone Report, *supra* note 28, para. 1242; The Independent Fact Finding Committee on Gaza to the League of Arab States, *supra* note 7, Executive Summary, para. 10; Amnesty International, *supra* note 5, p. 54.

80 Goldstone Report, *supra* note 28, para. 1228; Amnesty International, *supra* note 5, p. 61.

81 Private Sector Coordination Council Gaza Governorates, *Gaza Private Sector Post-War Status and Needs* (2009).

82 Goldstone Report, *supra* note 28, paras. 1773, 1774, 1836.

83 *Ibid.*, para. 1969.

the Palestinian Authority's declaration of acceptance of ICC jurisdiction under Art. 12(3) Rome-Statute as expeditiously as possible[84];

(iv) In addition to the ICC – as the enforcement mechanism most capable of responding to violations of international law – the UN General Assembly should request the International Court of Justice ("ICJ") to give an advisory opinion on the legal consequences for the State of Israel, following the IDF's three week military operation in the Gaza Strip[85].

The purpose of this research is to provide an in-depth analysis of each one of the above mentioned points, whereby the analysis shall focus solely on the procedural aspect of the possibility of Israel / Israelis facing legal consequences before the ICJ or the ICC, based on the serious allegations made against the conduct of the IDF during the Gaza armed conflict. Thus, there shall be no attempt to verify the correctness or legal accuracy of such allegations from a substantive perspective.

3. Summary of the research

This research is divided into three Chapters, reflecting the main legal challenges the State of Israel faced in light of the severe criticism and serious allegations voiced by many in the international community following Israel's Operation "Cast Lead" in the Gaza Strip.

Chapter One examines the possibility of the ICJ investigating alleged violations of international law during the Gaza armed conflict. Following a short introduction of the ICJ, the court's contentious jurisdiction in connection with the Gaza conflict is analyzed – focusing mainly on the consent requirement and the dependency of the court's jurisdiction *ratione personae* thereon. The Chapter then provides an analysis of the ICJ's advisory function – whereby, in addition to the court's advisory jurisdiction and the issue of possible circumvention of contentious jurisdiction prerequisites through the use of the court's advisory function, special emphasis is put on the legal effect and possible consequences of the ICJ advisory opinion.

Chapter Two examines the possible investigation / prosecution of Israeli military personnel and government officials by the ICC. The starting point in this chapter is an introduction to the ICC, which sheds light on the court's struc-

---

84 *Ibid.*, para. 1970; The Independent Fact Finding Committee on Gaza to the League of Arab States, *supra* note 7, Executive Summary, para. 40, Recommendation No. 4.

85 The Independent Fact Finding Committee on Gaza to the League of Arab States, *supra* note 7, Executive Summary, para. 40, Recommendation No. 1.

ture and its relation to the ICJ. This is followed by a detailed analysis of possible ICC jurisdiction over the events of the Gaza armed conflict. The latter consists of an overview of the following jurisdictional elements and an evaluation of whether they are fulfilled in the case at hand:

(i) ICC subject-matter jurisdiction – including genocide, crimes against humanity and, in particular, war crimes. Due to the fact that questions of substantive law are beyond the scope of this research, this analysis shall be limited to the question whether the allegations made against the IDF fulfill the requirements of the above mentioned crimes and, thus, fall within the subject-matter jurisdiction of the ICC;

(ii) ICC personal jurisdiction – pertains to the question of who may be brought to trial before the ICC;

(iii) ICC temporal jurisdiction – examines if / how such jurisdiction can be established in the case at hand in light of the fact that, principally, the ICC may exercise its jurisdiction only with respect to crimes committed after the entry into force of the Rome Statute for one of the states involved in the respective situation, and that none of the parties involved in the Gaza armed conflict have ratified the Rome Statute;

(iv) ICC nationality based jurisdiction – provides an overview of Art. 12(2)(b) Rome-Statute and examines Israel's dilemma between its genuine interest in the creation of the ICC and its objection to certain provisions in the Rome Statute – a dilemma that prevented Israel from ratifying the Rome Statute to this day;

(v) ICC territorial jurisdiction, in accordance with Art. 12(2)(alt. 1)(a) Rome-Statute – examines the lawfulness of the ICC having jurisdiction over nationals of states not party to the Rome Statute ("non-States Parties") as a result of the court's territorial jurisdiction, followed by an analysis of the legal history of the Gaza Strip, in order to determine whether the latter is / was under the sovereignty of a state, which became a State Party either prior to or during the Gaza armed conflict;

(vi) ICC *ad hoc* territorial jurisdiction, in accordance with Art. 12(2)(alt. 2)(a) and (3) Rome-Statute – this section, which constitutes the "heart" of this research, starts with an overview of Art. 12(3) Rome-Statute, including the procedural regime that applies when a non-State Party lodges a declaration under said provision and the actual object of such declarations – a discussion based on the risk of asymmetric liability. This is followed by an in-depth analysis of whether the Palestinian Authority's declaration under Art. 12(3) Rome-Statute fulfills the formal requirements of said provision – in particular that only "States" may accept ICC jurisdiction by lodging a declaration under Art. 12(3) Rome-Statute. The first possibility examined is the Palestinian Authority's declaration as that of a full-fledged state, in accordance with a literal interpretation of the term "State". In this analysis, the existence of a State of Palestine on the day the declaration was lodged is examined according to both the declarative and the constitutive theories of statehood. This is followed by the possibility of the Palestinian Authority's declaration as that of a quasi-state for the purpose of the Rome Statute only, in accordance with a teleological / functional interpretation of the term "State". In this analysis two main questions are addressed: First, can or should the teleological / functional approach be applied in the case at hand? Second, did the Palestinian Authority fulfill the requirements of a quasi-state for the purpose of the Rome Statute only on the day it lodged its declaration under Art. 12(3) Rome-Statute?

Chapter Two concludes by examining the two main factors the ICC must consider when dealing with individual participants in the Gaza armed conflict, namely (i) official capacity and immunity, and (ii) individual criminal responsibility of senior military commanders and non-military government officials.

Chapter Three completes the analysis of possible ICC investigation / prosecution of Israeli military personnel and government officials by examining the possible admissibility of cases related to the Gaza armed conflict before the ICC, in accordance with Art. 17 Rome-Statute. This section provides an overview of the principle of complementarity and the criteria, according to which the admissibility of cases before the ICC is determined. This is followed by an extensive analysis of whether, based on said criteria, the Prosecutor is expected to consider cases related to the alleged conduct of the IDF during the Gaza conflict admissible under Art. 17 Rome-Statute – based on the gravity of the alleged crimes and the investigatory steps Israel has already taken and is expected to take in the future.

The closing section of this research provides a summary of the main points examined therein and a final conclusion concerning the possibility of Israel / Israelis facing legal consequences before the ICJ or the ICC following the events and aftermath of the Gaza armed conflict.

Chapter One
THE POSSIBILITY OF THE INTERNATIONAL COURT OF JUSTICE INVESTIGATING THE ALLEGED VIOLATIONS OF INTERNATIONAL LAW DURING THE GAZA ARMED CONFLICT

1. The International Court of Justice

The ICJ (the "Court"), which is commonly referred to as the "World Court", is located in The Hague, The Netherlands. Founded in 1946 to replace the Permanent Court of International Justice ("PCIJ")[86], the ICJ ranks as the High Treasurer of the Rule of Law within the UN system[87], one of its main organs and its principle judicial organ[88]. Although the ICJ is not the legal successor to the PCIJ, it is in essence a continuation of the latter, with virtually the same statute and jurisdiction. There is also continuity of case law, as no distinction is made in ICJ jurisprudence between decisions rendered by the PCIJ and those rendered by the ICJ[89].

The Court is composed of fifteen judges of different nationalities, who are elected by the UN General Assembly and Security Council[90], and has a dual role: (i) To decide in accordance with international law legal disputes submitted to it by states, and (ii) to give advisory opinions on legal questions referred to it by duly authorized international organs and agencies. Accordingly, the jurisdiction of the Court falls into two distinct parts, namely, contentious and advisory. In either capacity, the ICJ operates in an intensely politicized environment and must, even under the best of circumstances, seek a balance between legal necessity and political feasibility, assertiveness and restraint, in order to secure the fickle confidence of states[91].

---

86 The PCIJ had functioned since 1922 and was dissolved after World War II.

87 Eyffinger, Arthur, "Legal and Political Acrobats – The Fate and Future of the International Court of Justice", *Harvard International Review* 27.1 (2005), p. 84.

88 Art. 92 UN Charter.

89 Bingbin, Lu, "Reform of the International Court of Justice – A Jurisdictional Perspective", *Perspectives* 5.2 (2004), p. 22.

90 Art. 3(1) and 4(1) ICJ-Statute.

91 Eyffinger, "Legal and Political Acrobats", *supra* note 87, p. 85.

There is no doubt that the ICJ has made a positive and substantial contribution to the relaxation of tension between states, the promotion of peace and the building of international law[92]. Nevertheless, the fact that (i) the Court's contentious jurisdiction is based on the consent of the respective parties[93] – which have the option to accept or decline the Court's jurisdiction and can do so under terms and conditions they determine themselves[94], and (ii) its advisory opinions are not binding[95], led many commentators over the decades to conclude that the ICJ has not quite fulfilled its potential or lived up to the high expectations from a "World Court"[96].

2. Possible ICJ contentious jurisdiction over the events of the Gaza armed conflict

In its capacity as the principal judicial organ of the UN, the main objective of the ICJ is to help achieve one of the primary aims of the UN, namely to bring about the (peaceful) settlement of international disputes – described by the PCIJ as a disagreement on a question of law or fact, a conflict, a clash of legal views or of interests[97] – in conformity with the principles of justice and international law[98]. The circumstances, under which the ICJ can exercise its contentious juris-

---

92 Amr, Mohamed Sameh M., *The Role of the International Court of Justice as the Principal Judicial Organ of the United Nations*, The Hague: Kluwer Law International (2003), p. 378; Sugihara, Takane, "The Judicial Function of the International Court of Justice with Respect to Disputes Involving Highly Political Issues", in: Muller, A.S., D. Raič and J.M. Thuránszky (eds.), *The International Court of Justice – Its Future Role after Fifty Years*, The Hague: Martinus Nijhoff Publishers (1997), p. 116.

93 Oda, Shigeru, "The Compulsory Jurisdiction of the International Court of Justice: A Myth? – A Statistical Analysis of Contentious Cases", *International and Comparative Law Quarterly* 49 (2000), p. 252.

94 Alexandrov, Stanimir A., "The Compulsory Jurisdiction of the International Court of Justice: How Compulsory is it?", *Chinese Journal of International Law* 5.1 (2006), p. 29.

95 Coleman, Andrew, "War Crimes and the ICJ's Advisory Jurisdiction", *Alternative Law Journal* 26 (2001), p. 35.

96 Eyffinger, "Legal and Political Acrobats", *supra* note 87, p. 84.

97 Tomuschat, Christian, in: Zimmermann, Andreas, Christian Tomuschat and Karin Oellers-Frahm (eds.), *The Statute of the International Court of Justice – A Commentary*, Oxford: Oxford University Press (2006), Art. 36, para. 9.

98 Eyffinger, Arthur, *The International Court of Justice, 1946 - 1996*, The Hague: Kluwer Law International (1996), p. 126.

diction in order to achieve this objective, shall be discussed in the following analysis.

2.1. The Court's personal jurisdiction (*ratione personae)*

2.1.1. Access to the Court

According to Art. 34(1) ICJ-Statute, "[o]nly states may be parties in cases before the Court". This important provision establishes a strict monopoly with regard to access to the Court's contentious jurisdiction and, thus, excludes any possibility of non-state entities – including both governmental and non-governmental international organizations[99] – being a party to a contentious case before the ICJ[100]. With regard to private persons, the ICJ is not a criminal court and as such does not have the competence to try individuals[101]. In the same way, no individual, whether a natural or a juridical person, may be a party or take any ancillary part in any contentious case before the Court[102].

Access to the ICJ requires that the statehood precondition – as the term is understood in the context and practice of the UN[103] – be supplemented by a legal link of the respective state to the ICJ Statute – whereby, principally, all (independent[104]) states can be parties to litigation before the ICJ[105], once such legal link has been established. UN member states enjoy automatic access to the Court, as according to Art. 93(1) UN Charter, "[a]ll Members of the [UN] are ipso facto parties to the Statute of the [ICJ]" – which in its Art. 35(1) provides that "[t]he Court shall be open to the states parties to the [ICJ] Statute".

With regard to states, which are not UN members / states parties to the ICJ Statute, the required legal link to the latter can be established in the following ways: First, according to Art. 93(2) UN Charter, non-member states of the UN may become a party to the ICJ Statute – on conditions of complete equality with

---

99 *Ibid.*

100 Dupuy, Pierre-Marie, in: Zimmermann, Andreas, Christian Tomuschat and Karin Oellers-Frahm (eds.), *The Statute of the International Court of Justice – A Commentary*, Oxford: Oxford University Press (2006), Art. 34, para. 1.

101 Iliopoulos, Katherine, *Will Anyone be Held Accountable for War Crimes in Gaza?*, The Crimes of War Education Project (2009); Coleman, *supra* note 95, p. 32.

102 Rosenne, Shabtai, *The Law and Practice of the International Court, 1920 - 2005*, Volume 1, Leiden: Martinus Nijhoff Publishers (2006), p. 590.

103 *Ibid.*, p. 588.

104 Eyffinger, *The International Court of Justice*, *supra* note 98, p. 126.

105 Rosenne, Shabtai, *The World Court – What it is and How it Works*, 2nd edition, Leyden: A.W.Sythoff (1963), p. 75.

UN members – if they accept the conditions laid down in each case by the UN General Assembly upon recommendation of the Security Council[106].

Second, Art. 35(2) ICJ-Statute empowers the UN Security Council to lay down the conditions under which the Court shall[107] be open to states, which are neither UN members nor contracting parties of the ICJ Statute under Art. 93(2) UN Charter[108]. These conditions have been adopted in UN Security Council Resolution 9 of 15 October 1946, which provides that the ICJ shall be open to a non-state party to the ICJ Statute, which (i) has deposited with the Registrar of the Court a declaration, by which it accepts the jurisdiction of the Court, and (ii) undertakes to comply in good faith with the decisions of the Court and to accept all obligations of a UN member under Art. 94 UN Charter. The mentioned declaration of acceptance of ICJ jurisdiction may be either particular – in respect of a specific dispute or disputes which have already arisen – or general – in respect of all disputes or of a particular class or classes of disputes which have already arisen or which may arise in the future[109]. In addition, a general declaration may take the form of a declaration of acceptance of the compulsory jurisdiction of the ICJ as contemplated in Art. 36(2) ICJ-Statute – which shall be addressed below.

In recent years, the question of access to the Court by non-states parties to the ICJ Statute has lost much of the practical importance it once might have had, as a result of the *de facto* universality of the UN[110].

2.1.2. The consent requirement

The fact that a state – whether or not a member of the UN – is a party to the ICJ Statute means that it is qualified to take part in litigation before the Court[111]. It does not mean the Court has the power or authority to render a binding decision on the substance or merits of a case concerning that specific state, as the ICJ derives its jurisdiction from the consent of the states that are party to each case[112].

---

106 *Ibid.*

107 Subject to the special provisions contained in treaties in force.

108 Zimmermann, Andreas, in: Zimmermann, Andreas, Christian Tomuschat and Karin Oellers-Frahm (eds.), *The Statute of the International Court of Justice – A Commentary*, Oxford: Oxford University Press (2006), Art. 35, para. 44.

109 UN Security Council Resolution 9 (15 October 1946), para. 2.

110 Zimmermann, *supra* note 108, Art. 35, para. 45; Rosenne, *The World Court – What it is and How it Works*, *supra* note 105, p. 76.

111 Rosenne, *The World Court – What it is and How it Works*, *supra* note 105, p. 76.

112 Orkand, Seth Benjamin, "Coming Apart at the Seamline – The Oslo Accords and Israel's Security Barrier: A Missed Opportunity at the International Court of Justice and the

Neither the UN Charter nor any general rule of contemporary international law imposes on states the obligation to refer their legal disputes to the Court[113]. For the latter to be able to exercise jurisdiction in a specific case, definite consent[114] – whether general or particular – on the part of the relevant states is required[115], so that no state can be made a party to contentious proceedings against its express will – or put positively, unless it has in some manner so consented[116].

There are two basic ways by which jurisdiction to decide contentious cases is conferred on the Court, or in other words, by which a title of jurisdiction may be created: (i) By specific agreement[117] between two or more states, or (ii) by unilateral declaration, emanating from a state and deposited with the Secretary-General of the UN, accepting the jurisdiction of the Court for defined types of legal disputes[118].

At least three systems of conferring Jurisdiction on the Court by way of international agreement can be distinguished: First, two or more states may conclude a special agreement (compromise) referring to the Court a defined issue[119]. Modern diplomatic requirements have introduced a refinement into the special agreement, which consists of a formal agreement between two states that a dispute exists and that it should be settled by the ICJ – without, however, defining the precise point in dispute, thus, allowing anyone of the involved parties to concretize it unilaterally. The value of this refinement is that through the agreement to invoke Court procedures, the later unilateral reference to the Court cannot be castigated as an inimical act. On the other hand, not defining the sub-

---

Israeli Supreme Court", *Gonzaga Journal of International Law* 10 (2007), p. 430; Fitzmaurice, Gerald, *The Law and Procedure of the International Court of Justice*, Volume 1, Cambridge: Grotius Publications Limited (1986), p. 111.

113 Rosenne, *The World Court – What it is and How it Works*, *supra* note 105, p. 73.

114 Art. 36(1) ICJ-Statute expresses in positive terms the fundamental rule that the Court's contentious jurisdiction to decide a particular case is based on the consent of the parties that it should do so. This is the statutory basis for the entire contentious jurisdiction of the Court.

115 Rosenne, *The Law and Practice of the International Court*, *supra* note 102, p. 590.

116 Eyffinger, *The International Court of Justi*ce, *supra* note 98, p. 126.

117 There are no formal requirements for an international agreement conferring jurisdiction on the Court, as the Court should be satisfied that the parties are in agreement regarding ICJ jurisdiction and not how that agreement is expressed. A question concerning the formal requirements of the agreement will only arise if one of the parties challenges the existence of such agreement.

118 Rosenne, *The World Court – What it is and How it Works*, *supra* note 105, p. 76.

119 Eyffinger, *The International Court of Justi*ce, *supra* note 98, p. 127; Rosenne, *The Law and Practice of the International Court*, *supra* note 102, pp. 643-644.

stance of the dispute accurately may prevent the Court from reaching a conclusive decision[120].

A second method of conferring jurisdiction on the Court is by a compromissory clause in a multilateral or bilateral treaty[121], according to which any disputes arising out of the application or interpretation of the treaty may be referred by any of the parties to the Court. In this case, the scope of the dispute that may be referred to the Court is defined in advance by reference to the treaty, while only the states, which are actual parties to the treaty, can be potential litigants[122]. If the unilateral institution of proceedings by application is permitted in the treaty, the compromissory clause establishes a form of compulsory jurisdiction, which is based on Art. 36(1) and not (2) ICJ-Statute. The implications of this are that the jurisdiction of the ICJ will not have the variable scope characteristics of the compulsory jurisdiction under Art. 36(2) ICJ-Statute, it will not be limited *a priori* to what Art. 36(2) ICJ-Statute classifies as a legal dispute and the Court shall be empowered to apply only the specific treaty and not the rules of customary international law[123].

Third, since the ICJ recognizes that its concern should be the substance of the agreement regarding its jurisdiction and not the form, in which it is expressed, state consent may be given informally even after the proceedings have commenced. The most common example for this is when the defendant pleads to the case on the merits while formally refusing to recognize the title of jurisdiction invoked by the plaintiff state. Once the issues on the merits have been joined, the defendant state cannot be heard to deny the jurisdiction of the Court[124].

Jurisdiction by unilateral declaration – frequently referred to as the compulsory jurisdiction or the system of the optional clause[125] – is embodied in Art. 36(2) ICJ-Statute, which provides that:

> [S]tates parties to the [ICJ] Statute may at any time declare that they recognize as compulsory ipso facto and without special agreement, in relation to any other state accepting the same obligation, the jurisdiction of the Court in all legal disputes concerning:
>
> a. the interpretation of a treaty;

---

120 Rosenne, *The World Court – What it is and How it Works*, *supra* note 105, p. 77.

121 Art. 36(1) ICJ-Statute.

122 Rosenne, *The World Court – What it is and How it Works*, *supra* note 105, p. 77.

123 Rosenne, *The Law and Practice of the International Court*, *supra* note 102, pp. 648-649.

124 Rosenne, *The World Court – What it is and How it Works*, *supra* note 105, p. 80.

125 *Ibid.*, p. 81.

b. any question of international law;
c. the existence of any fact which, if established, would constitute a breach of an international obligation;
d. the nature or extent of the reparation to be made for the breach of an international obligation.

Declarations under Art. 36(2) ICJ-Statute may be made unconditionally or subject to reservations[126], which are not incompatible with the purpose of the optional clause. Reciprocity is inherent in the system, so that where two declarations include different terms, jurisdiction exists only to the extent they coincide. In addition, such declarations may be limited or unlimited in time[127] and can be terminated by the declaring state – whereby difficulties arise with regard to the question when such termination takes effect[128]. In the *Nicaragua* case, the ICJ decided that declarations under Art. 36(2) ICJ-Statute cannot be terminated instantly, but only on a reasonable period of notice[129]. As a matter of procedure, Art. 36(2) ICJ-Statute declarations must be deposited with the Secretary-General of the UN, whereby no questions of form are prescribed. Once deposited with the Secretary-General, the declarations take effect immediately[130].

2.2. The Court's subject-matter jurisdiction (*ratione materiae)*

The existence of a dispute[131] is the primary condition for the Court to exercise its judicial function[132]. As the Court's jurisdiction extends only to disputes[133], proceedings aimed at obtaining an advisory opinion from the ICJ may not be instituted under the Courts contentious jurisdiction[134]. With regard to the nature of such disputes, the jurisdiction of the ICJ is confined to legal disputes as opposed

---

126 Eyffinger, *The International Court of Justice*, *supra* note 98, p. 130.
127 Art. 36(3) ICJ Statute.
128 Amr, *supra* note 92, pp. 188-189.
129 In this regard the Court referred to Art. 52 of the 1969 Vienna Convention on the Law of Treaties, which requires 12 months notice to terminate treaties.
130 Rosenne, *The World Court – What it is and How it Works*, *supra* note 105, p. 81.
131 See *supra* note 97.
132 Rosenne, *The Law and Practice of the International Court*, *supra* note 102, p. 506.
133 With regard to the legal questions involved in the relevant dispute, the Court's jurisdiction is limited by the *non ultra petita* rule, whereby the Court can answer only those legal questions submitted to it by the parties. The only exceptions to this rule are cases decided in accordance with Art. 53 ICJ-Statute.
134 Tomuschat, *supra* note 97, Art. 36, para. 8.

to political disputes[135]. The ICJ uses a wide interpretation of the term "legal dispute", namely, a dispute capable of being settled by the application of principles and rules of international law[136]. The list of specific types of legal disputes[137] – to which the Court's jurisdiction may apply – provided in Art. 36(2) ICJ-Statute has never played a role in practice, due to the extremely wide scope of the listed disputes and the overlap which exists between them[138].

Despite the clear and limited focus on legal disputes, the court is aware that political aspects may be present in any legal dispute brought before it, so that the fact that proceedings have been politically inspired as a means of exerting pressure on a state, does not affect the Court's jurisdiction[139]. The ICJ has been very clear regarding its view that no provision of the ICJ Statute contemplates that the Court should decline to take cognizance of one aspect of a dispute merely because that dispute has other aspects, however important[140]. In fact, the Court would emasculate itself if it refrained from agreeing to clarify the legal situation in disputes of great (political) importance for the peace and security of the world[141]. Only in one single instance has the ICJ refused to entertain a dispute for being unsuitable for judicial settlement. In the *Northern Cameroon* case, the Court felt that the developments on the ground could not be reversed, so that any adjudication would be devoid of purpose[142].

2.3. Implementation in the case at hand

Due to the fact that the ICJ has contentious jurisdiction to decide in a specific case, only if both its personal and subject-matter jurisdictions are given at the time proceedings are initiated (*ratione temporis*)[143], the question regarding possible ICJ contentious jurisdiction over the events of the Gaza armed conflict must be answered in accordance with this principle. Prior to discussing the first

135 *Ibid.*, para. 12.

136 *Ibid.*, para. 13.

137 Taken from Art. 13(2) Covenant of the League of Nations.

138 Tomuschat, *supra* note 97, Art. 36, para. 74.

139 Rosenne, *The Law and Practice of the International Court*, *supra* note 102, p. 506.

140 Case Concerning United States Diplomatic and Consular Staff in Teheran (*United States of America v. Iran*), ICJ (24 May 1980), para. 36.

141 Tomuschat, *supra* note 97, Art. 36, para. 14.

142 Case Concerning the Northern Cameroons (*Cameroon v. United Kingdom*), ICJ (2 December 1963), pp. 33, 38.

143 Sonntag, Michael, *Der IGH als Hauptrechtsprechungsorgan der UNO*, Johannes Kepler Universität Linz, Institut für Völkerrecht und Internationale Beziehungen (1998), p. 22.

requirement of the Court's personal jurisdiction, whereby only states may take part in contentious cases before the Court – which would require analysis of the highly controversial question regarding the legal status of Palestine / the Gaza Strip – the less controversial (legally more straightforward) question regarding Israel's consent to be made a party to contentious proceedings before the ICJ should be addressed.

2.3.1. Conferment of jurisdiction by way of international agreement

Neither prior to nor following the Gaza armed conflict, did Israel enter into a formal agreement with Palestinian representatives referring a possible legal dispute to the ICJ. None of the treaties and agreements concluded by Israel as part of the peace process with the Palestinians contain references to dispute resolution by the Court. In addition, no unilateral declaration by either Israel or the Palestine Liberation Organization ("PLO") provides for a compulsory settlement of a dispute by the Court[144]. Israel and the PLO have repeatedly agreed that their disputes should be settled by negotiation, with the possibility of an agreement that disputes be solved by arbitration. It is not just that Israel has not consented to the Court resolving – part or all of – its disputes with "Palestine"; it is that other mechanisms of dispute settlement more appropriate to the circumstances have been expressly preferred[145]. With regard to multilateral treaties, to which it is a party, Israel has not accepted the compulsory jurisdiction of the Court in any multilateral treaty since 1975. Although Israel has since then become party to a number of treaties that include the possibility of dispute settlement by the Court, such settlement is optional only. In other cases, Israel has attached reservations that expressly withhold consent to dispute settlement by the Court[146].

2.3.2. Conferment of jurisdiction by unilateral declaration (optional clause)

On 19 November 1985, Israel informed the Secretary-General of the UN that it was withdrawing the declaration of acceptance of the compulsory jurisdiction of the Court, which it had deposited on 17 October 1956 and modified on 28 Feb-

144 The State of Israel, *Written Statement on Jurisdiction and Propriety concerning the Request of the International Court of Justice for an Advisory Opinion on "the legal consequences arising from the construction of the wall by Israel"* (2004), para. 7.14.

145 *Ibid.*, para. 7.15; Orkand, *supra* note 112, p. 430.

146 The State of Israel, *Statement concerning the Request of the ICJ for an Advisory Opinion on the Wall, supra* note 144, para. 7.13.

ruary 1984[147]. In response, the Legal Counsel of the UN informed Israel that the Secretary-General had received the letter on 21 November 1985 and that the notification would take effect from that date[148]. Even if Israel had not withdrawn its declaration in 1985, the armed conflict in Gaza would not have been covered by Israel's optional clause declaration, as the latter included the following reservations:

> This Declaration does not apply to:
>
> (c) any dispute between the State of Israel and any other State whether or not a member of the [UN] which does not recognize Israel or which refuses to establish or to maintain normal diplomatic relations with Israel and the absence or breach of normal relations precedes the dispute and exists independently of that dispute;
>
> (e) [. . .] disputes arising out of, or having reference to, any hostilities, war, state of war, breach of the peace, breach of armistice agreement or belligerent or military occupation (whether such war shall have been declared or not, and whether any state of belligerency shall have been recognized or not) in which the Government of Israel is or has been or may be involved at any time[149].

2.4. Conclusion

As Israel explicitly objects to ICJ contentious jurisdiction with respect to any element of the Israeli-Palestinian conflict[150], the Court's personal jurisdiction in the case at hand must be rejected. Accordingly, it must be concluded that, due to a lack of jurisdiction, the events of the Gaza armed conflict cannot be the subject of contentious proceedings before the ICJ[151].

---

147 Orkand, *supra* note 112, p. 431.

148 The State of Israel, *Statement concerning the Request of the ICJ for an Advisory Opinion on the Wall, supra* note 144, para. 7.12.

149 *Ibid.*; Orkand, *supra* note 112, p. 431.

150 The State of Israel, *Statement concerning the Request of the ICJ for an Advisory Opinion on the Wall, supra* note 144, para. 7.11.

151 Some voices within the Arab world claim that the State of Israel may be held directly responsible for some members of the IDF allegedly committing acts of genocide during the armed conflict in Gaza. According to Art. 9 of the Convention on the Prevention and Punishment of the Crime of Genocide (to which Israel is a party), "[d]isputes between the Contracting Parties relating to the interpretation, application or fulfillment of the [. . .] Convention, including those relating to the responsibility of a State for genocide [. . .], shall be submitted to the International Court of Justice at the request of any of the parties to the dispute". Due to the fact that the prevailing opinion within the international

3. Possible ICJ advisory jurisdiction over the events of the Gaza armed conflict

Apart from deciding contentious cases between states, the ICJ has a second competence, namely an advisory one. The Court may give an advisory opinion on any legal question at the request of whatever body authorized to do so in accordance with the UN Charter[152]. The advisory opinion of the ICJ has been designed primarily to assist the UN Security Council and General Assembly in the discharge of their duties of conciliating and reporting upon disputes submitted to them, by affording them an authoritative legal opinion[153]. Despite providing a simpler[154] method of resolving international disputes and controversy, the ICJ advisory function is not a self-evident one for a court. Representatives of various legal systems, in which the idea is unknown or unpalatable, maintain that a court should restrict itself to rendering binding decisions on disputes[155].

3.1. Jurisdiction to give an advisory opinion

In its *Nuclear Weapons* opinion, the ICJ stated the three conditions, which must be satisfied, in order for the Court to have advisory jurisdiction: (i) The agency requesting the opinion from the Court must be duly authorized to do so, (ii) the opinion requested must be on a legal question, and (iii) such question must be one arising within the scope of activities of the requesting agency[156].

3.1.1. Bodies authorized to request an ICJ advisory opinion

According to Art. 96(1) UN Charter, the General Assembly and the Security Council are the UN organs, which are formally authorized to request – at their discretion[157] – the ICJ to give an advisory opinion[158] (Direct Authorization). Art.

---

community is that any genocide accusations against Israel are completely unfounded, there is no (realistic) chance of the Gaza conflict reaching the ICJ this way.

152 Art. 65(1) ICJ-Statute.

153 Singh, Nagendra, *The Role and Record of the International Court of Justice*, Dordrecht: Martinus Nijhoff Publishers (1989), p. 84.

154 *Ibid.*

155 Eyffinger, *The International Court of Justice*, *supra* note 98, p. 146.

156 Bingbin, *supra* note 89, p. 26.

157 Unless there is an explicit obligation upon the UN organs and agencies to request an opinion from the Court, these organs and agencies are the ultimate authority to evaluate the appropriateness and usefulness of a request.

96(2) UN Charter provides that other UN organs and specialized agencies[159], which may at any time be so authorized by the UN General Assembly, may[160] also request advisory opinions of the Court[161] (Indirect Authorization). In order to maintain the current political balance between the Secretary-General of the UN, on the one hand, and the UN General Assembly and Security Council, on the other, the former is not entitled to request ICJ advisory opinions[162]. Furthermore, in order to guarantee the clear separation between the Court's contentious and advisory jurisdictions, neither individual states nor groups of states are authorized to request an advisory opinion from the Court[163]. Finally, the ICJ has no power to give or to offer to give an advisory opinion *proprio motu*[164].

3.1.2. Advisory opinion concerning a legal question

Pursuant to Art. 96 UN Charter and 65(1) ICJ-Statute, the UN organ or specialized agency authorized to do so, may request an advisory opinion only on a "legal question"[165] – i.e. a question framed in terms of law, which raises problems of international law[166]. In many cases the basis of (external) objections to a request for an advisory opinion is that the question is based on political motives

---

158 A decision of the UN General Assembly to seek the advisory opinion of the Court does not require unanimity. Even though it was suggested that a request for an advisory opinion represents one of the "important questions" for which a two-thirds majority of the Assembly is necessary, it appears that in practice an advisory opinion can be sought on the basis of a simple majority. With regard to the Security Council, a proposal to seek an advisory opinion has to obtain the affirmative vote of nine members, including the concurring votes of the permanent members – Art. 27(3) UN Charter.

159 Such as: the International Atomic Energy Organization, Economic and Social Council, International Labor Organization, Food and Agricultural Organization, UNESCO, WHO, International Bank for Reconstruction and Development, International Development Association, IMF, International Maritime Organization, WIPO, UN Industrial Development Organization.

160 See *supra* note 157.

161 Frowein, Jochen Abr. and Karin Oellers-Frahm, in: Zimmermann, Andreas, Christian Tomuschat and Karin Oellers-Frahm (eds.), *The Statute of the International Court of Justice – A Commentary*, Oxford: Oxford University Press (2006), Art. 65, para. 12.

162 *Ibid.*, para. 13.

163 Rosenne, *The World Court – What it is and How it Works*, *supra* note 105, p. 90; Fitzmaurice, *supra* note 112, p. 115.

164 Amr, *supra* note 92, p. 79.

165 *Ibid.*, p. 84.

166 *Legal Consequences of the Construction of a Wall in the Occupied Palestinian Territories*, ICJ Advisory Opinion (9 July 2004), para. 37.

and, therefore, cannot be characterized as a "legal question" – in other words, the ICJ, as a legal organ, should not be asked to deliver advisory opinions on purely political questions, which should be settled by political means[167].

It is a fact that the very idea of giving advice to organs of the UN and specialized agencies will almost always carry a "political implication" with it[168]. In this regard, the Court has stated in its *Nuclear Weapons* opinion that "the political nature of the motives which may be said to have inspired the request and the political implications that the opinion given might have are of no relevance in the establishment of [the Court's] jurisdiction to give [. . .] an [advisory] opinion"[169]. It is not for the Court to delve into the motivation that leads a duly authorized organ to request an advisory opinion on a legal question falling within the jurisdiction of that organ, even when the question relates to an issue that involves important political facts or is itself essentially political[170]. Not only does the Court clearly believe that the fact that a legal question also has a political aspect does not suffice to deprive the legal question of its character as such and the Court of competence expressly conferred on it by its Statute[171], in its advisory opinion concerning the *Agreement between the WHO and Egypt*, the Court stated that "in situations in which political considerations are prominent it may be particularly necessary for an international organization to obtain an advisory opinion from the Court as to the legal principles applicable with respect to the matter under debate"[172]. Therefore, although states will continue to argue that certain questions put to the Court are mainly of a political nature, it is very difficult to see the Court ever finding that it has no advisory jurisdiction on the basis of such arguments. Rather, in such cases, the Court will focus on the legal aspects of such questions, while ignoring their political aspect[173].

Other objections to the Court's advisory jurisdiction are based on the claim that abstract, historical or academic questions presented to the Court do not constitute "legal questions". The question whether the Court should deal with ab-

---

167 Amr, *supra* note 92, p. 87.

168 Keith, Kenneth, "The Advisory Jurisdiction of the International Court of Justice: Some Comparative Reflections", *Australian Yearbook of International Law* 17 (1996), p. 54.

169 *Legality of the Threat or Use of Nuclear Weapons*, ICJ Advisory Opinion (8 July 1996), para. 13.

170 Amr, *supra* note 92, p. 89.

171 *Application for Review of Judgement No. 158 of the United Nations Administrative Tribunal*, ICJ Advisory Opinion (12 July 1973), para. 14.

172 *Interpretation of the Agreement of 25 March 1951 between the WHO and Egypt*, ICJ Advisory Opinion (20 December 1980), para. 33.

173 Frowein and Oellers-Frahm, *supra* note 161, Art. 65, para. 24.

stract questions was controversial in the past. On the one hand, it was contended that only opinions regarding abstract questions should be requested, as concrete differences were more appropriate for contentious procedures. On the other hand, it was argued that the role of the ICJ becomes a political or even legislative one if the questions asked do not concern concrete issues[174]. The Court does not consider that what is contended to be the abstract nature of the question posed to it raises an issue of jurisdiction. This became clear in the Court's *Nuclear Weapons* opinion, in which it stated that "to contend that [the Court] should not deal with a question couched in abstract terms is a mere affirmation devoid of any justification, [so] that the Court may give an advisory opinion on any legal question, abstract or otherwise"[175].

With regard to questions, which are purely academic or historical, the Court found in the *Western Sahara* opinion that the term "any legal question" was not to be interpreted restrictively and that "there is nothing in the [UN] Charter or [the ICJ] Statute to limit either the competence of the General Assembly to request an advisory opinion, or the competence of the Court to give one, to legal questions relating [only] to existing rights or obligations"[176].

Finally, some argue that for a question to constitute a "legal question" for the purpose of Art. 96(1) UN Charter and 65(1) ICJ-Statute, it must be reasonably specific[177]. This follows, in part, from the language of Art. 65(2) ICJ-Statute, which expressly requires "an exact statement of the question upon which an opinion is required", and, in part, from basic principles[178]. In this regard the Court pointed out that:

> [L]ack of clarity in the drafting of a question does not deprive the Court of jurisdiction. Rather, such uncertainty will require clarification in interpretation [on the part of] the Court. In the past, both the [PCIJ] and the present Court have observed in some cases that the wording of a request for an advisory opinion did not accurately state the question on which the Court's opinion was being sought, or did not correspond to the true legal question under consideration. [. . .] Consequently, the Court

174 *Ibid.*, para. 26.

175 ICJ, *Legality of the Threat or Use of Nuclear Weapons*, *supra* note 169, para. 15; Fitzmaurice, *supra* note 112, p. 116.

176 *Western Sahara*, ICJ Advisory Opinion (16 October 1975), para. 18; Frowein and Oellers-Frahm, *supra* note 161, Art. 65, para. 27.

177 This issue is not to be confused with the (above discussed) issue as to whether a question is unduly abstract, i.e. where the meaning of the question is certain but where it is said that it fails to relate to a specific situation.

178 The State of Israel, *Statement concerning the Request of the ICJ for an Advisory Opinion on the Wall, supra* note 144, para. 5.3.

has often been required to broaden, interpret and even reformulate the questions put [before it][179].

3.1.3. Competence to request an ICJ advisory opinion

The organization requesting an advisory opinion must not only be authorized to do so (as discussed above), but the request must also be in line with the requirements of Art. 96 UN Charter[180]. The latter makes a clear distinction regarding the power to request an advisory opinion between the UN General Assembly and Security Council, on the one hand, and other UN organs and specialized agencies, on the other[181]. According to Art. 96(2) UN Charter, other UN organs (other than the General Assembly and Security Council) and specialized agencies may request advisory opinions of the Court only "on legal questions arising within the scope of their activities" – i.e. activities expressly stated in their constituent instrument. This limit applies even if the General Assembly welcomes or supports a request that is considered beyond the scope of such activities[182]. Therefore, should a request for an advisory opinion come from one of the organizations mentioned in Art. 96(2) UN Charter, in addition to verifying that the requesting body is duly authorized to make such a request, the Court will examine the relevant rules of the organization, in particular its constitution, where the objectives and functions of the organization are spelled out, in order to delineate the organization's scope of activities or area of competence[183].

According to Art. 96(1) UN Charter, the UN General Assembly and Security Council may seek an advisory opinion "on any legal question", whereby no mention is made of such question falling within the scope of their activities[184]. The question whether the power of the General Assembly and Security Council to request advisory opinions is absolute and unlimited, continues to be the subject of debate[185], as even the Court's view in this regard remains unclear[186]. Fact is that both organs – especially the General Assembly – enjoy a vast scope of

---

179 ICJ, *Legal Consequences of the Construction of a Wall in the Occupied Palestinian Territories*, *supra* note 166, para. 38.
180 Frowein and Oellers-Frahm, *supra* note 161, Art. 65, para. 15.
181 Amr, *supra* note 92, p. 66.
182 *Ibid.*, p. 67.
183 *Ibid.*
184 Frowein and Oellers-Frahm, *supra* note 161, Art. 65, para. 16.
185 Amr, *supra* note 92, p. 69.
186 Frowein and Oellers-Frahm, *supra* note 161, Art. 65, para. 16.

activities, to the extent that it would be difficult to find any activity within the UN that falls outside their direct or indirect scope of activities[187].

3.2. International legal disputes and the circumvention issue

Due to the fact that it is possible for a state to propose a draft resolution – regarding the request for an advisory opinion from the ICJ – in the UN General Assembly and/or Security Council, which contains a question directly related to an ongoing situation or dispute between two or more states[188], the issue of the possible circumvention of contentious jurisdiction prerequisites through the use of the Court's advisory function must be addressed. It is of great significance for the advisory function's standing and legitimacy that it is not perceived to authorize the surreptitious introduction of compulsory jurisdiction to decide concrete disputes between states by devious means[189].

3.2.1. Advisory opinions regarding inter-state disputes

The question whether authorized organizations can ask for advisory opinions regarding international disputes – in addition to "legal questions"[190] – arises from the omission of the term "dispute" in Art. 96 UN Charter and 65(1) ICJ-Statute[191].

According to those who support the limitation of advisory opinions to "legal questions", the phrase "any dispute or question" in Art. 14 Covenant of the League of Nations offered an indirect method for settling international disputes without having the authority of a judgment and without obtaining the consent of the interested parties. In order to forestall such consequences, the drafters of the UN Charter and the ICJ Statute limited the power of request to a "legal question" only[192]. Advocates of this view further base their claim on the ICJ's *Peace Treaties* opinion, in which the Court referred to the difference between the wording of Art. 14 Covenant of the League of Nations, on the one hand, and the wording of Art. 96 UN Charter and 65(1) ICJ-statute, on the other[193].

---

187 Amr, *supra* note 92, pp. 69-70.
188 *Ibid.*, p. 93.
189 Rosenne, *The World Court – What it is and How it Works*, *supra* note 105, p. 89.
190 See *supra* note 166.
191 Amr, *supra* note 92, p. 84.
192 *Ibid.*, pp. 84-85.
193 *Ibid.*, p. 85.

Since the *travaux préparatoires* of the UN Charter and the ICJ Statute indicate that there was no intention of restricting the advisory competence of the Court to "non-contentious" cases only[194], the prevailing opinion within the legal community is that the omission of the word "dispute" is without significance and that the wording "legal question" is broad enough to include legal issues in dispute before the authorized organs[195].

In addition, the conclusion that the ICJ advisory function is restricted to "legal questions" only, seems inconsistent with the meaning of the following provisions:

(i) Art. 68 ICJ-Statute, which provides that "[i]n the exercise of its advisory function the Court shall [. . .] be guided by the provisions of the [ICJ] Statute which apply in contentious cases to the extent to which it recognizes them to be applicable"[196]. This provision, which derives from an amendment introduced in 1936 into the PCIJ Statute of 1929, was intended to take account of the fact that the Court may be called upon to give advisory opinions both in contentious and in non-contentious matters[197];
(ii) Art. 102(2) of the ICJ Rules of Court, which provides that the Court shall "above all consider whether the request for the advisory opinion relates to a legal question actually pending between two or more States"[198];
(iii) Art. 102(3) of the ICJ Rules of Court, which provides that Art. 31 ICJ-Statute shall apply when "an advisory opinion is requested upon a legal question actually pending between two or more States"[199].

In conclusion, the omission of the word "dispute" in Art. 96 UN Charter and 65(1) ICJ-Statute does not affect the power of the authorized bodies to request advisory opinions of the Court in respect of any inter-state dispute, as long as the question is of legal nature[200].

3.2.2. The advisory function and the requirement of consent

The combination between the conclusion that the ICJ can be requested to give an advisory opinion on a pending legal dispute between states, on the one hand, and the well-established principle of international law, whereby no judicial pro-

194 Singh, *supra* note 153, p. 93.
195 Amr, *supra* note 92, p. 85.
196 *Ibid.*; Singh, *supra* note 153, p. 93.
197 Singh, *supra* note 153, p. 93.
198 Amr, *supra* note 92, p. 85.
199 Frowein and Oellers-Frahm, *supra* note 161, Art. 65, para. 20.
200 Amr, *supra* note 92, p. 86.

ceedings relating to a legal question pending between states can take place without their consent[201], on the other, directly leads to the question, whether the contentious character of such cases should require the Court to obtain the consent of the interested parties prior to exercising its advisory jurisdiction – in order to prevent the circumvention of contentious jurisdiction prerequisites.

For many years it was believed that if a request for advisory opinion related to an existing dispute, the absent of consent of both parties to the dispute would act as to a bar to the Court considering and giving an advisory opinion in the matter[202]. According to this school of thought, the authorized bodies cannot request an advisory opinion from the ICJ concerning an international dispute without the consent of the disputant states, as allowing this would mean (i) abolishing a well-established principle of international law, namely, the necessity of the consent of the litigant states to refer their dispute to international adjudication, and (ii) introducing compulsory jurisdiction to the Court by the "back door" under the guise of advisory opinions, contrary to the UN Charter[203]. Advocates of this view also refer to Art. 68 ICJ-Statute, which provides that when the Courts exercises its advisory jurisdiction, it shall be guided by the provisions that govern contentious cases[204].

The authority usually quoted in connection with this view is the PCIJ *Eastern Carelia* opinion, in which the court stated that "no State can, without its consent, be compelled to submit its disputes with other States either to mediation or to arbitration, or to any other kind of pacific settlement"[205]. It was believed that the Court refused to give an advisory opinion in this case, as the question put to the Court was not one of abstract law, but directly concerned the main point of the controversy between the involved states (Finland and Russia), so that answering the question would have been substantially equivalent to deciding the dispute between the parties[206].

However, it has since become clear that the "*Eastern Carelia* Principle" is really quite limited and applies only to issues, which have only a bilateral nature and do not concern the international community of states, in particular the UN[207]. The refusal of the PCIJ to give an advisory opinion was due to the very

201 Singh, *supra* note 153, pp. 87, 90.
202 *Ibid.*, p. 87.
203 Amr, *supra* note 92, p. 93.
204 *Ibid.*
205 *Status of Eastern Carelia*, PCIJ Advisory Opinion (23 July 1923), para. 33.
206 Singh, *supra* note 153, p. 88.
207 In its advisory opinion concerning the *Wall*, the Court provided an explanation regarding its decision not to decline to give an advisory opinion with regard to the conse-

particular circumstances of the case, above all, the fact that the question directly concerned an already existing dispute, in which one of the sides (i) was neither a party to the PCIJ Statute nor a member of the League of Nations, and (ii) objected to the proceedings and refused to take part in any way[208]. The reason for the Court's refusal to reply to the request for advisory opinion was, therefore, the incompetence of the League of Nations Council to deal with the dispute. Thus, the Court was not saying that it could not give an advisory opinion in the absence of consent by Russia to its doing so; it was saying that it had been asked for the advisory opinion in the context of a dispute-settlement procedure, which was improperly set in motion in the absence of the consent of Russia. If this view of the matter is correct, it would appear to follow that had an advisory opinion been requested in the context of a procedure, which was not directed to the settlement of a dispute by the Council, the court would have been able to give an advisory opinion – despite the remaining fact that answering the question would have been substantially equivalent to deciding the dispute between the parties[209].

The question regarding the required consent of the interested parties for the ICJ's advisory jurisdiction was considerably clarified in the *Peace Treaties* opinion of 1950. In the latter, the Court dismissed the contention of Romania, Hungary and Bulgaria that the Court had no competence to give an opinion because they did not consent thereto. The Court concluded that (i) their contention confused the rules governing the Court's advisory jurisdiction with those governing its contentious jurisdiction, and (ii) the absence of a state's consent has no effect upon the Court's advisory jurisdiction – even when the request for the opinion relates to an inter-state dispute. The Court based its view on the nature of its advisory opinion, which has no binding force upon the interested states. Moreover, it pointed out that such advisory opinions are given directly to the requesting organ and not to the states concerned. Finally, the Court stated that

---

quences of the construction of a wall in the occupied Palestinian territory – despite the question referring to a bilateral matter between Israel and Palestine. According to the Court, given the powers and responsibilities of the UN in questions relating to international peace and security, the construction of the wall must be deemed to be directly of concern to the UN, so that the subject-matter of the General Assembly's request cannot be regarded as (only) a bilateral matter between Israel and Palestine: "The opinion is requested on a question which is of particularly acute concern to the [UN], and one which is located in a much broader frame of reference than a bilateral dispute".

208 Frowein and Oellers-Frahm, *supra* note 161, Art. 65, para. 36.

209 Singh, *supra* note 153, p. 89.

no state, whether a member or a non-member of the UN, can prevent the Court from replying to any request referred to it by a UN organ for whatever reason[210].

The relevance of the involved parties' consent to the Court's advisory jurisdiction was further examined by the ICJ in its *Western Sahara* opinion, in which Spain based its objection – to the Court's advisory competence as well as the propriety of its exercise[211] – on the fact that it did not give its consent thereto. The Court's response to Spain's objection[212] was based on the Court's view that the absence of an interested state's consent to the exercise of the Court's advisory jurisdiction does not concern the competence of the Court, but (only) the propriety of its exercise[213]. The Court stated that in certain circumstances, the lack of consent of an interested state may render the giving of an advisory opinion incompatible with the Court's judicial character – an instance of this being when the circumstances disclose that to give an opinion would have the effect of circumventing the principle that a state is not obliged to allow its dispute to be submitted to judicial settlement without its consent[214].

In the *Wall* opinion , the Court stated that despite having advisory jurisdiction, each time the Court is requested to give an opinion concerning an international dispute, it shall satisfy itself as to the propriety of the exercise of its judicial function – by reference to the criterion of "compelling reasons"[215]. The

---

210 Amr, *supra* note 92, pp. 95-96; Singh, *supra* note 153, p. 90; *Interpretation of Peace Treaties with Bulgaria, Hungary and Romania*, ICJ Advisory Opinion (30 March 1950), p. 71.

211 Singh, *supra* note 153, p. 91.

212 The Court rejected Spain's view, pointing out that in contrast to the *Eastern Carelia* case – where Russia was neither a member of the League nor a party to the PCIJ's Statute – Spain, as a member of the UN, had accepted the UN Charter and the ICJ Statute, whereby it had in general given prior consent to the Court's exercise of its advisory jurisdiction. Moreover, the Court noted that the question presented to it related mainly to the possibility of the application of the General Assembly's resolution, so that the aim of the question was to assist the Assembly in fulfilling its functions, namely the decolonization of the territories.

213 Singh, *supra* note 153, pp. 90-91.

214 ICJ, *Western Sahara, supra* note 176, para. 33.

215 Compelling reasons include: (i) The Court finds that giving an opinion might complicate the matter or create difficulties for another part of the UN in carrying out its responsibilities, (ii) the Court finds that giving an opinion would be contrary to (or infringe) its judicial character or affect its inherent capacity as a court of law and might damage the prestige of the Court, (iii) the Court finds that its opinion would be ineffective or without object – the Court's judgment must have some practical consequences in the sense that it can affect existing legal rights or obligations of the parties, thus removing uncertainty from their legal relations.

Court will accordingly examine in detail and in light of its jurisprudence each of the arguments presented to it in this regard[216].

In conclusion, the current prevailing opinion regarding the connection between the ICJ's advisory jurisdiction and the consent of the interested parties thereto is that the Court has (i) unlimited competence to give an advisory opinion on matters concerning international disputes[217] – not necessarily involving only states[218], and (ii) the discretion to decline to give an opinion[219] if a "compelling reason" in the specific case justifies such a decision.

3.3. The legal effect and consequences of the ICJ advisory opinion

In order to fully understand the role of the ICJ's advisory function in clarifying and, ultimately, solving international disputes, the issue of the advisory opinion's legal and non-legal effect, meaning and influence in practice must be addressed.

3.3.1. The binding effect of the advisory opinion

The majority of international legal experts agree that – unless there is a specific provision indicating otherwise[220] – the advisory opinions of the ICJ are not binding upon the requesting organs and, consequently, there is no obligation upon them to heed the Court's advice[221]. According to this view, advisory opinions and judgments of the ICJ differ in nature[222]. Whereas, according to Art. 59 ICJ-Statute, judgments of the Court – which are considered to be its original competence[223] – are binding between the litigant states in the particular case, advisory

---

216 ICJ, *Legal Consequences of the Construction of a Wall in the Occupied Palestinian Territories*, *supra* note 166, para. 45.

217 Singh, *supra* note 153, p. 91; Amr, *supra* note 92, p. 97.

218 In the *Wall* opinion, the Court incorporated a non-state party – Palestine and the Palestinian people – into its proceedings, not only as a participant, but as a main stakeholder.

219 The State of Israel, *Statement concerning the Request of the ICJ for an Advisory Opinion on the Wall, supra* note 144, para. 6.1.

220 Amr, *supra* note 92, p. 120.

221 *Ibid.*, p. 110; Frowein and Oellers-Frahm, *supra* note 161, Art. 65, para. 43; Eyffinger, *The International Court of Justice*, *supra* note 98, p. 146; ICJ Information Department, *Questions & Answers About the Advisory Procedure* (2010), p. 2.

222 Amr, *supra* note 92, p. 110.

223 *Ibid.*

opinions, as their name implies, are merely opinions and merely advisory[224]. This position was confirmed by the ICJ in its *Peace Treaties* opinion, in which the Court stated that within its advisory jurisdiction, the Court's reply to the question referred to it by an authorized organization is only of an advisory character and, "as such, [. . .] has no binding force"[225].

With regard to the effect of advisory opinions on individual states, the ICJ stated – in the same opinion – that "the Court's Opinion is given not to the States, but to the organ which is entitled to request it"[226]. The Court's clear view with regard to the addressee of its advisory opinion, in combination with the fact that even upon the intended addressee the opinion has no binding effect, leads to the conclusion that no individual state is legally obliged by the findings expressed in the Court's advisory opinion[227]. This conclusion is further supported by the poor "track-record" of UN member states with regard to compliance with ICJ advisory opinions[228].

3.3.2. Additional effects and consequences of the advisory opinion

Despite the lack of binding effect, it would be an error to conclude that ICJ advisory opinions are devoid of any legal value[229] and have no force at all[230]. While some go so far as to claim that, in practice, the Court's advisory opinions have the same value as its judgments, as they are "pronouncements" ruled by the Court regarding the applicable law in specific issues[231], the majority of international legal experts agree that, despite not having the formal authority of judgments, the persuasive character, moral consequences and substantive authority attached to pronouncements of the principal judicial organ of the UN and the highest international tribunal in the world, give ICJ advisory opinions great weight[232]. Accordingly, it seems desirable to elucidate how ICJ advisory opinions shape and affect international occurrences, while not being mandatory or compulsive for the requesting organ or the interested parties.

---

224 Fitzmaurice, *supra* note 112, p. 122.

225 ICJ, *Interpretation of Peace Treaties with Bulgaria, Hungary and Romania*, *supra* note 210, p. 71.

226 *Ibid.*

227 Fitzmaurice, *supra* note 112, p. 124.

228 Coleman, *supra* note 95, p. 35.

229 Amr, *supra* note 92, p. 110.

230 Fitzmaurice, *supra* note 112, p. 123.

231 Amr, *supra* note 92, p. 111.

232 Fitzmaurice, *supra* note 112, p. 124; Eyffinger, *The International Court of Justice*, *supra* note 98, p. 146; ICJ Information Department, *supra* note 221, p. 2.

First, the fact that the legal correctness of ICJ advisory opinions cannot be officially or formally questioned by the organs, to which they are rendered[233], may have a legal effect on the involved states, as UN organs (and other states) will be guided[234] in their actions by the opinion given[235]. The far-reaching legal consequences of the ICJ advisory opinion were clearly demonstrated in the *Wall* opinion, in which the Court found that the responsibility of Israel is engaged under international law[236], so that Israel has "an obligation to put an end to the violation of its international obligations flowing from the construction of the wall in the Occupied Palestinian Territory"[237]. The Court further found that Israel "has the obligation to make reparation for the damage caused to all the natural or legal persons concerned"[238]. These findings by the Court must, of course, be seen in light of the fact that the advisory opinion did not, as such, create a legal obligation for Israel. In the vast majority of cases the states directly concerned by an advisory opinion will rely on the non-binding effect and will not conform to the legal obligations explained as a consequence of the Court's evaluation of the legal situation[239]. The situation may, however, be completely different with regard to other states – as became evident by the Court's in-depth explanation regarding the legal consequences for such (other) states[240]. The Court explained that given the character and importance of the rights and obligations involved, "all States are under an obligation not to recognize the illegal situation resulting from the construction of the wall in the Occupied Palestinian Territory", and "not to render aid or assistance in maintaining the situation created by such construction". Furthermore, all states should, "while respecting the [UN] Charter and international law, see to it that any impediment, resulting from the construction of the wall, to the exercise by the Palestinian people of its right to self-determination is brought to an end". In addition, all states parties to the Fourth Geneva Convention are obliged "to ensure compliance by Israel with interna-

---

233 Fitzmaurice, *supra* note 112, p. 123.

234 Since the *Conditions of Admission of a State to Membership in the United Nations* opinion of 1948, the UN General Assembly has followed the practice of adopting resolutions concerning the advisory opinions given by the Court on request of the General Assembly.

235 Frowein and Oellers-Frahm, *supra* note 161, Art. 65, para. 44.

236 ICJ, *Legal Consequences of the Construction of a Wall in the Occupied Palestinian Territories*, *supra* note 166, para. 147.

237 *Ibid.*, para. 150.

238 *Ibid.*, para. 152.

239 Frowein and Oellers-Frahm, *supra* note 161, Art. 65, para. 54.

240 *Ibid.*, para. 55.

tional humanitarian law as embodied in that Convention"[241]. Finally, the Court was of the view that the UN, "especially the General Assembly and the Security Council, should consider what further action is required to bring to an end the illegal situation resulting from the construction of the wall"[242].

The issue of which counter-measures are lawful when the Court finds in an advisory opinion that a violation of obligations *erga omnes* has taken place, has not been fully settled in international law yet. However, it is clear beyond any doubt that such findings justify any state to take up that issue with the state concerned and to bring pressure on that state to conform with international law[243].

Therefore, since (i) no state could be seen as acting in violation of international law if it complies with the Court's advisory opinion[631], and (ii) a state referred to in an advisory opinion cannot reject as unlawful any statement by other states based on the Court's findings and explanations[244], one must conclude that despite the non-binding character of the ICJ advisory opinion, the latter clearly has legal effect in practice – based on its authority as a statements of law[245].

Second, in its capacity as the principal judicial organ of the UN, the Court is in the position to deal with and provide its findings regarding the most "burning" legal and political questions at any given time. This fact, in combination with the authority of the highest international tribunal in the world[246], results in advisory opinions, which have substantially influenced (i) the development of international law[247] – as clearly demonstrated in the *Genocide* opinion[248] of 1951 and the *Namibia* opinion[249] of 1971, and (ii) the approach and even rulings of domestic courts – as witnessed in the decision of the Israeli Supreme Court, sit-

---

241 ICJ, *Legal Consequences of the Construction of a Wall in the Occupied Palestinian Territories*, *supra* note 166, para. 159.

242 *Ibid.*, para. 160.

243 Frowein and Oellers-Frahm, *supra* note 161, Art. 65, para. 58.

244 *Ibid.*, para. 57.

245 Fitzmaurice, *supra* note 112, p. 123.

246 See *supra* note 232.

247 Frowein and Oellers-Frahm, *supra* note 161, Art. 65, para. 45.

248 *Reservations to the Convention on the Prevention and Punishment of the Crime of Genocide*, ICJ Advisory Opinion (28 May 1951).

249 *Legal Consequences for States of the Continued Presence of South Africa in Namibia (South West Africa) Notwithstanding Security Council Resolution 276 (1970)*, ICJ Advisory Opinion (21 June 1971).

ting as the High Court of Justice, in *Mara'abe v. The Prime Minister of Israel*[250], which was clearly influenced by the ICJ's *Wall* opinion[251].

3.4. Implementation in the case at hand

In order to assess whether the ICJ advisory function can play a role in clarifying the very complex legal situation following the Gaza armed conflict – and if so, to what extent – the following issues concerning the case at hand must be addressed based on the analysis above.

3.4.1. UN Security Council v. General Assembly

Shortly after the Gaza conflict came to an end, some members of the international community called on the UN General Assembly to request the ICJ to give an advisory opinion on the legal consequences of the Gaza conflict[252]. In addition, on 3 April 2009, the President of the Human Rights Council established the United Nations Fact-Finding Mission on the Gaza Conflict, headed by Justice Richard Goldstone, in order to investigate all violations of international human rights law and international humanitarian law that might have been committed at any time in the context of the military operations conducted in Gaza[253]. On 25 September 2009, the Fact-Finding Mission presented its report, widely known as the "Goldstone Report"[254], in which it recommended that: (i) In view of the gravity of the violations of international human rights and humanitarian law and possible war crimes and crimes against humanity, the UN Human Rights Council should request the UN Secretary-General to bring the fact-finding report to the attention of the UN Security Council under Art. 99 UN Charter[255], and (ii) the UN Human Rights Council should submit the fact-finding report to the UN General Assembly with a request that it should be considered[256].

On 16 October 2009, the Goldstone Report was endorsed by the UN Human Rights Council, which called upon all concerned parties, including UN Bodies, to ensure its implementation, and recommended that the UN General Assembly

---

250 *Mara'abe v. Prime Minister of Israel*, Israel Supreme Court, sitting as the High Court of Justice (15 September 2005).

251 Frowein and Oellers-Frahm, *supra* note 161, Art. 65, para. 66.

252 See *supra* note 85.

253 Goldstone Report, *supra* note 28, para. 1.

254 See *supra* note 28.

255 Goldstone Report, *supra* note 28, para. 1968.

256 *Ibid.*

consider the fact-finding report[257]. On 5 November 2009, the UN General Assembly endorsed the UN Human Rights Council's decision of 16 October 2009. The Assembly further requested the UN Secretary-General to transmit the fact-finding report to the Security Council, and called upon the Government of Israel to take all appropriate steps to undertake investigations, which are independent, credible and in conformity with international standards, into the serious violations reported by the Fact-Finding Mission, towards ensuring accountability and justice[258].

Based on the above, the findings of the Goldstone Report have been referred to both the UN Security Council and the General Assembly; this fact raises the question whether the UN General Assembly could, eventually, refer the investigation into the violations reported by the Goldstone Report to the ICJ, despite the matter being referred to the Security Council as well.

According to Art. 24(1) UN Charter, the UN Security Council bears "primary responsibility for the maintenance of international peace and security". Art. 12(1) UN Charter provides that "[w]hile the Security Council is exercising in respect of any dispute or situation the functions assigned to it in the [UN] Charter, the General Assembly shall not make any recommendation with regard to that dispute or situation unless the Security Council so requests". In its *Certain Expenses* opinion, the ICJ stated that Art. 24(1) UN Charter refers to a primary, but not necessarily exclusive, competence of the UN Security Council[259]. This is emphasized in Art. 14 UN Charter, which provides that the General Assembly does have the power, *inter alia*, to "recommend measures for the peaceful adjustment of any situation", whereby this power is limited by the provisions of Art. 12 UN Charter.

Both the UN General Assembly and Security Council initially interpreted and applied Art. 12(1) UN Charter to the effect that the Assembly could not make a recommendation on a question concerning the maintenance of international peace and security – including a request for an advisory opinion from the ICJ[260] – while the matter remained on the Council's agenda[261]. This interpretation

257 UN Human Rights Council Resolution S-12/1 (16 October 2009).

258 UN General Assembly Resolution 64/10 (5 November 2009).

259 *Certain Expenses of the United Nations (Article 17, Paragraph 2, of the Charter)*, ICJ Advisory Opinion (20 July 1962), p. 163.

260 Amr, *supra* note 92, p. 73.

261 ICJ, *Legal Consequences of the Construction of a Wall in the Occupied Palestinian Territories*, *supra* note 166, para. 27.

has, however, evolved over time[262], and, indeed, in the *Wall* opinion the Court noted that:

> [T]here has been an increasing tendency over time for the General Assembly and the Security Council to deal in parallel with the same matter concerning the maintenance of international peace and security. It is often the case that, while the Security Council has tended to focus on the aspects of such matters related to international peace and security, the General Assembly has taken a broader view, considering also their humanitarian, social and economic aspects[263].

In response to a question posed by Peru during the twenty-third session of the UN General Assembly, the Legal Counsel of the UN confirmed that the General Assembly interprets the words "is exercising the functions" in Art. 12(1) UN Charter as meaning "is exercising the functions at this moment"[264]. In addition, the Court has stated in this regard that a request for an ICJ advisory opinion by the UN General Assembly cannot, in itself, be considered a "recommendation" with regard to a "dispute or situation"[265].

In conclusion, in both scenarios concerning the UN Security Council and the Goldstone Report – i.e. a vote on the Goldstone Report is prevented or the veto right of one (or more) of the permanent members is used during a vote on the topic[266] – the UN General Assembly could refer the investigation into the violations reported by the Goldstone Report to the ICJ, despite the matter being on the agenda of the Security Council as well[267].

---

262 In 1961, The General Assembly deemed itself entitled to adopt recommendations in the matter of the Congo – Resolutions 1595 (XV) and 1600 (XV) – and in 1963, in respect of the Portuguese colonies – Resolution 1913 (XVIII) – while those cases still appeared on the Council's agenda, without the Council having adopted any recent resolution concerning them.

263 ICJ, *Legal Consequences of the Construction of a Wall in the Occupied Palestinian Territories*, *supra* note 166, para. 27.

264 General Assembly, 23rd Session, Third Committee, 1637th Meeting, A/C.3/SR.1637, para. 9.

265 ICJ, *Legal Consequences of the Construction of a Wall in the Occupied Palestinian Territories*, *supra* note 166, para. 25.

266 Many in the international community believe that the five permanent members of the Security Council share the (political) interest of preventing a vote on the Goldstone Report in the Security Council – partly for protecting Israel and partly due to fears of creating a precedent, which could be used against them in the future.

267 UN General Assembly Resolution 377 A (3 November 1950) provides that "if the Security Council, because of lack of unanimity of the permanent members, fails to exercise its primary responsibility for the maintenance of international peace and security in any case where there appears to be a threat to the peace, breach of the peace, or act of ag-

3.4.2. The discretion of the Court

Since the expected absence of Israel's consent would not affect the Court's advisory jurisdiction[268], prior to analyzing the existence of a possible "compelling reason", which could lead the Court to decline to give an opinion in the case at hand, one must bear in mind that the Court has always underlined that it must be mindful of its responsibilities as the principle judicial organ of the UN, so that it should not, in principle, refuse to give an advisory opinion when requested to do so by an authorized organization[269]. The Court's approach is confirmed by the fact that since the coming into force of the UN Charter, the Court has never declined to render an advisory opinion when requested to do so by an authorized organization[270]. The only time the Court refused to give an advisory opinion was in the case of the initial request for the *Nuclear Weapons* opinion. In that case, however, the Court's refusal was not based on its discretionary power to give advisory opinions, but was justified by lack of jurisdiction; the Court found that the World Health Organization ("WHO") was not empowered to seek an advisory opinion, as the matter fell outside the scope of its activities[271]. Accordingly, should the ICJ be requested to give an advisory opinion regarding the legal consequences of the Gaza armed conflict, the possibility of the Court declining such request based on its discretion to do so, is not to be expected.

3.5. Conclusion

In the event that (i) the UN General Assembly reaches the conclusion that the investigations conducted by Israel into the violations reported in the Goldstone Report cannot be considered independent or credible in accordance with international standards, and (ii) the case at hand has not reached / is not expected to reach the ICC, it is very much possible that, based on the Palestinian support and influence within the UN General Assembly[272], the latter will request the ICJ to

---

gression, the General Assembly shall consider the matter immediately with a view to making appropriate recommendations to Members for collective measures".

268 See *supra* note 213.

269 ICJ, *Legality of the Threat or Use of Nuclear Weapons*, *supra* note 169, para. 14.

270 Frowein and Oellers-Frahm, *supra* note 161, Art. 65, para. 31; Amr, *supra* note 92, p. 107.

271 Frowein and Oellers-Frahm, *supra* note 161, Art. 65, para. 31.

272 Lapidoth, Ruth, *Should the International Court of Justice Give an Advisory Opinion on Israel's Separation Fence?*, Jerusalem Center for Public Affairs (2004).

give an advisory opinion on the legal consequences of the Gaza armed conflict based on the findings of the Goldstone Report.

Despite its non-binding character and the fact that Israel has shown complete disregard for the ICJ in the past[273], such an advisory opinion could significantly influence:

(i) The post-conflict legal situation in the area – an ICJ advisory opinion could provide the, currently missing, authoritative view concerning the alleged Israeli violations of international law during the Gaza conflict, which could change / harden the international community's view and expectations from Israel with regard to ensuring accountability and justice. This, in turn, would significantly increase the pressure already put on Israel to investigate the allegations made against its armed forces and civilian leadership;

(ii) The manner, in which future armed conflicts are fought and managed by Israel, including: Changes in rules of engagement and standard procedures (on the military operational level), increased transparency during battle (real time information and explanations with regard to the necessity of military actions, in order to avoid future allegations) and changes in current procedures concerning the division of responsibility and protocoling of decision processes during battle (in order to prevent a negative impact on soldiers' and commanders' moral and motivation, as a result of uncertainty related to possible – national and international – legal proceedings following military operations)[274].

---

273 Bisharat, George E., *et al.*, "Israel's Invasion of Gaza in International Law", *Denver Journal of International Law and Policy* 38.1 (2009), p. 112.

274 Following its own investigations of the events of the Gaza armed conflict, the IDF issued new orders and operational guidelines designed to improve the protection of civilians and their property during combat, see Chapter Three – 3.1.3. An ICJ advisory opinion could possibly lead / force Israel to formulate and implement much farther-reaching orders and guidelines.

Chapter Two
POSSIBLE INVESTIGATION / PROSECUTION OF ISRAELI MILITARY PERSONNEL AND GOVERNMENT OFFICIALS BY THE INTERNATIONAL CRIMINAL COURT FOLLOWING THE GAZA ARMED CONFLICT

1. The International Criminal Court

1.1. Basic facts

The ICC is a permanent international institution established by treaty for the purpose of investigating and prosecuting individuals accused of committing "the most serious crimes of international concern"[275], namely genocide, crimes against humanity and war crimes[276]. Art. 5 Rome-Statute provides also for "aggression" as a crime[277] within the jurisdiction of the ICC, however, only after it has been defined and approved by the Assembly of States Parties ("ASP"), which is the management oversight and legislative body of the ICC[278].

The official seat of the ICC is at The Hague, The Netherlands (the host State), whereby its proceedings make take place anywhere[279].

The Rome Statute, which governs the ICC, was adopted on 17 July 1998 at the UN Diplomatic Conference of Plenipotentiaries on the Establishment of an International Criminal Court in Rome, Italy[280] (the "Rome Conference"). According to Art. 126(1) Rome-Statute, 60 ratifications of the Statute were required, in order for it to enter into force. The 60th instrument of ratification was deposited with the UN Secretary-General on 11 April 2002, when 10 countries

275 Art. 1 Rome-Statute.

276 Art. 6, 7 and 8 Rome-Statute, respectively.

277 In June 2010, the ICC's first review conference in Kampala, Uganda expanded the definition of the "crime of aggression" and the ICC's jurisdiction over it. The ICC will not be allowed to prosecute for this crime at least until the year 2017 – see also *infra* note 334.

278 ICC, *Establishment of the Court.*

279 Art. 3(1) and (3) Rome-Statute.

280 ICC, *Establishment of the Court.*

simultaneously deposited their ratifications[281]. On 1 July 2002 the Rome Statute entered into force[282]. As of December 2011, the Rome Statute has 120 States Parties, whereby 19 additional states have signed but not ratified the Statute.

The ICC is an independent organization, not part of the UN system[283]. As a treaty based institution, ICC obligations are binding only on its States Parties[284]. With the exception of the scenario, in which ICC jurisdiction is triggered by the UN Security Council, the ICC is not a supra-national body, but an inter-national body similar to others already in existence. However, when a situation is referred to the ICC by the Security Council and the latter decides to enforce the ICC's orders and judgments, the ICC becomes a derivative supra-national body by virtue of the Security Council's exercise of its powers pursuant to Chapter VII of the UN Charter[285].

The ICC is not a substitute for national criminal jurisdiction and does not supplant national criminal justice systems, but rather is complementary to them[286]. The ICC does no more than what each and every state in the international community can do under existing international law. It is the expression of collective action by States Parties, which established an institution to carry out justice for certain international crimes. The ICC is, therefore, an extension of national criminal jurisdiction, established by a treaty whose ratification under national law makes it part of the latter. Consequently, the ICC neither infringes upon national sovereignty nor overrides national legal systems capable of and willing to carry out their international legal obligations[287].

---

281 ICC, *Chronology of the International Criminal Court.*

282 According to Art. 126(1) Rome-Statute, the Statute shall enter into force on the first day of the month after the 60th day following the date of the deposit of the 60th instrument of ratification, acceptance, approval or accession with the UN Secretary-General.

283 International organizations provide important support to the ICC. Foremost among these is the UN. On 4 October 2004, the President of the ICC, Philippe Kirsch, and the Secretary-General of the UN, Kofi Annan, concluded the Negotiated Relationship Agreement between the International Criminal Court and the United Nations. This Agreement provides for institutional relations, cooperation and judicial assistance between the ICC and the UN, while reaffirming the independence of the court.

284 Except when ICC jurisdiction is triggered by the UN Security Council, in accordance with Art. 13(b) Rome-Statute, or a non-State Party, in accordance with Art. 12(3) Rome-Statute.

285 Bassiouni, M. Cherif, *The Legislative History of the International Criminal Court*, Volume 1, Ardsley: Transnational Publishers, Inc. (2005), p. 124.

286 Preamble para. 10, Art. 1 Rome-Statute.

287 Bassiouni, M. Cherif, *Introduction to International Criminal Law*, Ardsley: Transnational Publishers, Inc. (2003), p. 500.

1.2. The establishment of the ICC

The establishment of the ICC – arguably the most significant international institution since the creation of the UN[288] – which has been described as a "gift of hope to future generations, and a giant step forward in the march towards universal human rights and the rule of law"[289], took considerably longer than many had hoped[290]. The possibility of such a permanent court had been envisioned by the UN shortly after World War II and the Nuremberg Trials. In Resolution 260 of 9 December 1948, the UN General Assembly invited the International Law Commission to study the desirability and possibility of a permanent international criminal court. The Commission then codified the principles established in the Nuremberg Trials and prepared draft statutes for a permanent court. The intensification of the Cold War in the late 1940s quickly paralyzed the effort, which received renewed impetus in 1991 (after the end of the Cold War) when, in response to widespread atrocities in Rwanda and the former Yugoslavia, the UN Security Council established *ad hoc* criminal tribunals to try the perpetrators. By 1994 the International Law Commission submitted to the General Assembly its final draft statute for a permanent international court[291].

The process leading to the establishment of the ICC was driven by (i) the human rights agenda steadily taking center stage within the UN[292] – Art. 1(3) UN Charter, and the emergence of accountability and justice as values common to the international community[293], (ii) the consensus within the international community that impunity for those accused of the gravest crimes was unacceptable[294], and (iii) the fact that the pursuit of international criminal justice by means of international investigative commissions[295] and *ad hoc* international tri-

288 Schabas, William A., *An Introduction to the International Criminal Court*, 1st edition, Cambridge: Cambridge University Press (2001), p. 20.

289 Kofi Annan, at the signing of the Statute of the ICC in Rome, 18 July 1998.

290 Schabas, *An Introduction to the International Criminal Court*, 1st edition, *supra* note 288, Preface.

291 Abizadeh, Arash, "Introduction to the Rome Statute of the International Criminal Court", *World Order* 34.2 (2003), p. 19.

292 Schabas, *An Introduction to the International Criminal Court*, 1st edition, *supra* note 288, p. 20.

293 Bassiouni, *Introduction to International Criminal Law*, *supra* note 287, p. 498.

294 ICC, *About the Court*.

295 Such as: The 1919 Commission on the Responsibilities of Authors of War and on the Enforcement of Penalties, the 1943 United Nations War Crimes Commission, the 1946 Far Eastern Commission, the 1992 Commission of Experts Established Pursuant to Security Council Resolution 780 to investigate War Crimes and other Violations of International Humanitarian Law in the Former Yugoslavia, the 1994 Independent Commis-

bunals[296] was less than satisfying[297], as such efforts were often perceived as too focused on the defeated side and, in addition, were limited to certain conflicts, situations and territories.

1.3. The structure of the ICC

The ICC is composed of four organs: the Presidency, the Judicial Division, the Office of the Prosecutor and the Registry. The Presidency[298] is responsible for the overall administration of the ICC, with the exception of the Office of the Prosecutor, and for specific functions assigned to the Presidency according to the Rome Statute. The Presidency is composed of three ICC judges, elected to the Presidency by their fellow judges for a term of three years[299].

The Judicial Divisions consist of eighteen internationally respected judges, elected for a term of nine years[300]. The Judicial Division is organized into the Pre-Trial Division, the Trial Division and the Appeals Division. The judges of each Division sit in Chambers which are responsible for conducting the proceedings of the court at different stages. Assignment of judges to Divisions is made on the basis of the nature of the functions each Division performs and the qualifications and experience of the judge. This is done in a manner ensuring that each Division benefits from an appropriate combination of expertise in criminal law / procedure and international law[301].

The Office of the Prosecutor[302] is responsible for receiving referrals and any substantiated information on crimes within the jurisdiction of the ICC, for examining them and for conducting investigations and prosecutions before the court. The Office is headed by the Prosecutor, who is elected by the States Parties for a

---

sion of Experts Established Pursuant to Security Council Resolution 935 to Investigate Grave Violations of International Humanitarian Law in the Territory of Rwanda, the 2004 International Commission Established Pursuant to Security Council Resolution 1564 to Investigate Reports of Violations of International Humanitarian Law in Darfur.

296 Such as: The 1945 International Military Tribunal (IMT); the 1946 International Military Tribunal for the Far East (IMTFE); the 1993 International Criminal Tribunal for the former Yugoslavia (ICTY); the 1994 International Criminal Tribunal for Rwanda (ICTR).

297 Bassiouni, *Introduction to International Criminal Law*, *supra* note 287, p. 498.

298 Art. 38 Rome-Statute.

299 ICC, *Structure of the Court.*

300 Art. 36(9)(a) Rome-Statute; Philipp, Christiane E., "The International Criminal Court – A Brief Introduction", *Max Planck Yearbook of United Nations Law* 7 (2003), p. 331.

301 ICC, *Structure of the Court.*

302 Art. 42 Rome-Statute.

term of nine years (unless a shorter term is decided upon at the time of election)[303].

The Registry[304] is responsible for the non-judicial aspects of the administration and servicing of the court. The Registry is headed by the Registrar who is the principal administrative officer of the court. The Registrar exercises his/her functions under the authority of the President of the court. The Registrar is elected by the judges for a term of five years[305].

In addition to the four main organs, the ICC includes a number of semi-autonomous offices such as the Office of Public Counsel for Victims and the Office of Public Counsel for Defense. These offices fall under the Registry for administrative purposes, but otherwise function as wholly independent offices. The ASP has also established a trust fund for the benefit of victims of crimes within ICC jurisdiction and the families of these victims[306].

1.4. Applicable law

Art. 10 Rome-Statute, which contains the overarching principle with respect to the applicable law[307], requires the application of international law, the four sources of which are listed in Art. 38(1) ICJ-Statute[308]. Consequently, this also means that the Rome Statute must be interpreted in accordance with the 1969 Vienna Convention on the Law of Treaties. Furthermore, any provision in the Statute that conflicts or is inconsistent with general international law shall be subordinate to it, unless the provision is intended to be *lex specialis*, in which case it shall supersede other provisions and sources of international law. An exception to this exception is where the *lex specialis* is in contradiction with a peremptory norm (*jus cogens*) of international law[309] – in which case the latter prevails[310].

---

303 ICC, *Structure of the Court.*

304 Art. 43 Rome-Statute.

305 ICC, *Structure of the Court.*

306 *Ibid.*

307 Bassiouni, *Introduction to International Criminal Law, supra* note 287, p. 501.

308 (a) International conventions, whether general or particular, establishing rules expressly recognized by the contesting states, (b) international custom, as evidence of a general practice accepted as law, (c) the general principles of law recognized by civilized nations, (d) judicial decisions and the teachings of the most highly qualified publicists of the various nations, as subsidiary means for the determination of rules of law.

309 Art. 53 of the 1969 Vienna Convention on the Law of Treaties.

310 Bassiouni, *Introduction to International Criminal Law, supra* note 287, p. 502.

Art. 21 Rome-Statute, which adds specificity to the general provision of Art. 10 Rome-Statute, ranks the sources of applicable law as follows: (i) The Rome Statute, Elements of Crimes[311] and the Rules of Procedure and Evidence – as primary sources according to Art. 21(1)(a) Rome-Statute, and (ii) applicable treaties and principles and rules of international law, including established principles of the international Law of Armed Conflict – as secondary sources according to Art. 21(1)(b) Rome-Statute[312]. The apparent conflict between the ranking of sources of applicable law in Art. 10 Rome-Statute and the more specific aspects of Art. 21 Rome-Statute can be solved in accordance with the rules of treaty interpretation of the 1969 Vienna Convention on the Law of Treaties, which state that the intent of the parties is controlling. Since the drafters of the Statute did not intend to limit the well-established sources of international law referred to in Art. 10 Rome-Statute and contained in Art. 38(1) ICJ-Statute, one must conclude that the specificity contained in Art. 21 Rome-Statute is subordinate to the generality of Art. 10 Rome-Statute[313].

1.5. The ICC in relation to the ICJ

While the ICC was established for the purpose of investigating and prosecuting individuals who commit the most serious crimes of international concern, the ICJ's main functions are to (i) decide, in accordance with international law, such cases as are submitted to it by states[314], and (ii) give advisory opinions to the UN General Assembly, Security Council and other authorized organs and specialized agencies[315].

---

311 Pursuant to Art. 9 Rome-Statute, the ASP has adopted the Elements of Crimes, which purpose is to assist, rather than bind, the ICC in its interpretation and application of the definitions of crimes in Art. 6-8 Rome-Statute. The Elements of Crimes serve merely as guidelines for the ICC in determining individual criminal responsibility, whereby in the event of a conflict between the Statute and the Elements, the Statute will prevail. The Elements provide a description of the various material and mental elements constituting each ICC offence. Thus, notwithstanding their non-binding character, the Elements of Crimes may be expected to have an impact on the ICC's interpretation of the crimes within its jurisdiction.

312 Bassiouni, *The Legislative History of the International Criminal Court*, *supra* note 285, p. 163.

313 Bassiouni, *Introduction to International Criminal Law*, *supra* note 287, p. 502.

314 See *supra* note 98; Art. 34(1) ICJ-Statute.

315 See *supra* note 152.

Despite the clear distinction with regard to the purpose and functions of both institutions, concurrent jurisdiction (*ratione materiae*) between the ICC and the ICJ is possible[316]. Such a case could arise if at the time a certain individual is prosecuted before the ICC for crimes within the court's jurisdiction and a dispute – based on the same facts – is submitted against the individual's state to the ICJ. Due to the fact that (i) the ICC was established by treaty and is not a UN organ[317], (ii) the Rome Statute does not include particular findings of the ICJ as a precondition to the exercise of ICC jurisdiction[318], and (iii) the ICC can choose to apply ICJ decisions in contentious cases as principles and rules of international law[319] – although such decisions have no binding force except between the involved parties and in respect of the particular case, the ICC is not dependent on ICJ decisions and judgments. Therefore, when dealing with the same subject-matter, both courts are legally independent from each other[320]. This has been confirmed by the Appeals Chamber of the International Criminal Tribunal for the former Yugoslavia ("ICTY"), which has stated that "[i]n international law, every tribunal is a self-contained system (unless otherwise provided)"[321].

The fact that the rules of decision of the ICC and ICJ permit different results to be reached on similar facts[322] is perceived in different ways: On the one hand, those that do not consider this fact to be a serious problem argue that, technically, the ICC and the ICJ will not have concurrent jurisdiction in the vast majority of cases and that because the ICC is concerned with criminality of individuals and the ICJ with the responsibility of states, the two courts cannot burden a single entity with inconsistent rights or obligations[323]. On the other hand, some argue that the fact that differing tribunals have the power to define and apply a legal term such as "genocide" in different ways is very disturbing[324].

---

316 Boot, Machteld, *Genocide, Crimes Against Humanity, War Crimes: Nullum Crimen Sine Lege and the Subject Matter Jurisdiction of the International Criminal Court*, Antwerp: Intersentia (2002), para. 57.

317 See *supra* note 283.

318 Boot, *supra* note 316, para. 58.

319 Art. 21(1)(b) Rome-Statute; Sadat, Leila Nadya, *The International Criminal Court and the Transformation of International Law: Justice for the New Millennium*, Ardsley: Transnational Publishers, Inc. (2002), p. 274.

320 Boot, *supra* note 316, para. 58.

321 *The Prosecutor v. Dusko Tadic*, ICTY Appeals Chamber (2 October 1995), para. 11.

322 Gallant, Kenneth S., "The International Criminal Court in the System of States and International Organizations", *Leiden Journal of International Law* 16.3 (2003), p. 576.

323 *Ibid.*, pp. 576-577.

324 *Ibid.*, p. 577.

At the present time, if an inconsistency were to arise between statements of law made by the ICC and the ICJ, there is no mechanism in place for promptly liquidating the inconsistency. It would simply exist in the law until the normal processes of international law creation – especially the creation of customary law or the drafting or revision of multilateral treaties – could bring the law back into harmony[325].

2. Possible ICC jurisdiction over the events of the Gaza armed conflict

In addition to being a mechanism for helping prevent repetition of the massive atrocities to which the twentieth century was witness, the great significance of the ICC lies in the fact that it is the first permanent international court that recognizes the individual as the subject of international criminal law and, as such, seems philosophically to presuppose the notion of a global community[326] of which all human beings are subject, if not citizens[327]. The idea of the ICC aspires to a radical departure from the traditional model of humanity's political organization under international law – in which each member of a society of states enjoys supreme sovereign authority over its respective population and territory – to universal jurisdiction over individuals as such, across state boundaries[328]. The fact that many members of the international community did not agree with this idea[329] and did not aspire to achieve a global community, in which the sover-

---

325 *Ibid.*, p. 579.

326 The Preamble to the Rome Statute makes explicit reference to the "common bonds" that unite all peoples (para. 1) and to "the conscience of humanity" – a conscience deeply shocked by the "unimaginable atrocities" of the 20th century (para. 2).

327 Abizadeh, *supra* note 291, pp. 19-20.

328 *Ibid.*, p. 26.

329 At the Rome Conference, there was a range of views on the "preconditions" for jurisdiction, ranging from the exceedingly narrow proposal of the US, restricting the court's jurisdiction to nationals of States Parties, to a form of universal jurisdiction, by which the court would be able to prosecute any crime committed anywhere, providing that it could obtain custody over the offender. The most extreme view, in terms of favoring the jurisdiction of the court, came from Germany, and was often described as "universal jurisdiction". Germany argued that States Parties should be able to delegate to the court the jurisdiction that they are already entitled to exercise under customary international law. Thus, to the extent they may exercise jurisdiction over the "core crimes" of genocide, crimes against humanity and war crimes, wherever they are committed, they could also legitimately delegate this jurisdiction to an international tribunal of which they are

eignty and significance of the individual state are of subordinate significance, was the main reason why the provisions dealing with the jurisdiction of the ICC[330] were the most controversial and sensitive part of the Rome Statute negotiations[331]. The latter resulted in one of the most complex international instruments ever negotiated – a sophisticated web of highly technical provisions drawn from comparative criminal law combined with a series of more political propositions that touch the very heart of state concerns with their own sovereignty[332].

The requirements and circumstances, under which the ICC can exercise its jurisdiction – between the great expectations and deep suspicions it simultaneously faces[333] – shall be discussed in the following analysis.

2.1. ICC subject-matter jurisdiction (*ratione materiae*)

The subject-matter jurisdiction of the ICC is regulated in Art. 5(1) Rome-Statute, which provides that such jurisdiction shall be limited to the most serious crimes of concern to the international community as a whole, namely, the crime of genocide, crimes against humanity, war crimes and the crime of aggression[334].

---

members. Very much at the other extent was the position of the US, requiring consent of the state of nationality of the suspect in all cases, unless the jurisdiction of the court was triggered by the UN Security Council. The US argued that conferral of jurisdiction over nationals of non-States Parties would breach Art. 34 of the 1969 Vienna Convention on the Law of Treaties, which states that international treaties cannot be binding on third states.

330 This applied, to a certain extent, to all four components of jurisdiction – i.e. subject-matter jurisdiction, temporal jurisdiction, personal jurisdiction and territorial jurisdiction.

331 Williams, Sharon A. and William A. Schabas, in: Triffterer, Otto (ed.), *Commentary on the Rome Statute of the International Criminal Court – Observers' Notes, Article by Article* , 2nd edition, Munich: C.H.Beck (2008), Art. 12, para. 1.

332 Schabas, *An Introduction to the International Criminal Court*, 1st edition, *supra* note 288, p. 20.

333 Greenawalt, Alexander K.A., "Justice Without Politics? Prosecutorial Discretion and the International Criminal Court", *NYU Journal of International Law and Politics* 39 (2007), p. 584.

334 Despite the fact that the crime of aggression is listed in Art. 5(1) Rome-Statute as one of the core crimes under ICC subject-matter jurisdiction, the court remains (to date) unable to exercise its jurisdiction over this crime. Art. 5(2) Rome-Statute provides that the ICC shall exercise jurisdiction over the crime of aggression once a provision is adopted, which defines the crime and the conditions under which such jurisdiction shall be exercised. After years of preparatory work, the Review Conference of the Rome Statute

This limitation of ICC subject-matter jurisdiction to "the most serious crimes of concern to the international community as a whole" could be understood as a guiding principle for the work of the court as a whole. Accordingly, the threshold clause contained in Art. 8(1) Rome-Statute must be interpreted in line with Art. 5(1) Rome-Statute, so that individual war crimes, which are not committed as part of a plan or policy, shall only be prosecuted if they are of sufficient gravity to be of concern to the international community as a whole. In more general terms, the limitation in Art. 5(1) Rome-Statute can serve as a useful, legally binding, guiding tool for the Prosecutor when considering whether a specific crime falls within the jurisdiction of the ICC and justifies investigation[335].

The international dimension of the four crime categories mentioned in Art. 5(1) Rome-Statute is based on (i) the heinous nature of such crimes, which elevates them to a level, in which humanity as a whole is a victim – and therefore entitled (even required) to prosecute them[336], and (ii) the fact that very often such crimes remain unpunished, as they are perpetrated / supported by governments of states, to which the national courts – which would usually prosecute such crimes – belong as well[337].

The definitions of crimes, over which the ICC has subject-matter jurisdiction, reflect widely accepted international norms and are based on existing humanitarian treaty and customary international law. The growing consensus among legal experts is that the crime definitions in the Rome Statute reflect – for

---

(held in Kampala, Uganda between 31 May and 11 June 2010) adopted, on 11 June 2010, amendments to the Rome Statute, which include a definition of the crime of aggression and a regime establishing how the ICC will exercise its jurisdiction over this crime. Nevertheless, the relevance of the crime of aggression in connection with the Gaza armed conflict will not be discussed / analyzed in this research, as the conditions for entry into force of the amendments decided upon in Kampala provide that (i) the ICC may exercise its jurisdiction only with respect to crimes of aggression committed one year after the ratification / acceptance of the amendments by thirty States Parties, and (ii) the ICC will not be able to exercise its jurisdiction over the crime of aggression until a decision is taken by two-thirds of States Parties to activate the jurisdiction at any time after 1 January 2017.

335 Zimmermann, Andreas, in: Triffterer, Otto (ed.), *Commentary on the Rome Statute of the International Criminal Court – Observers' Notes, Article by Article* , 2nd edition, Munich: C.H.Beck (2008), Art. 5, para. 9.

336 Schabas, William A., *An Introduction to the International Criminal Court*, 3rd edition, Cambridge: Cambridge University Press (2007), p. 83.

337 *Ibid.*, p. 90.

the most part – the current state of customary international law[338]. Since, however, the correspondence between the Rome Statute and customary international law is not perfect, Art. 10 Rome-Statute addresses the concern that the crime definitions in the Rome Statute be taken as codification of custom, by providing that such definitions shall not be interpreted "as limiting or prejudicing in any way existing or developing rules of international law for purposes other than [the Rome] Statute"[339].

Despite the fact that there is no formal hierarchy among the four crime categories, there are suggestions within customary international law, the case law of international tribunals and the Rome Statute itself, that even among these "most serious crimes" some are more serious than others. Such an (informal) hierarchy could be based on the fact that (i) Art. 124 Rome-Statute allows new States Parties to "opt out" of ICC jurisdiction over war crimes for a period of seven years after the entry into force of the Statute for such states[340]. Since this possibility does not exist with regard to genocide and crimes against humanity, one could argue that war crimes are "less serious" than genocide and crimes against humanity, and (ii) two of the defenses codified in Art. 33(1) and 31(1)(c) Rome-Statute (superior orders and defense of property, respectively) are applicable only in the case of war crimes – implying that genocide and crimes against humanity are "more serious", as in such cases said defenses do not apply[341].

Although the crimes listed in Art. 5(1) Rome-statute are some of the worst imaginable, some argue that a number of very serious (treaty) crimes, relevant to the international community as a whole – such as terrorism and drug crimes – should have been on the list as well[342]. The reasons why such crimes have been rejected at the Rome Conference include (i) the fact that not all conventions, which provide the basis for such crimes, have found sufficient international ac-

---

338 The International Centre for Criminal Law Reform and Criminal Justice Policy, *International Criminal Court – Manual for the Ratification and Implementation of the Rome Statute*, 3rd edition (2008), p. 73.

339 Schabas, *An Introduction to the International Criminal Court*, 3rd edition, *supra* note 336, p. 85.

340 Elsea, Jennifer, *International Criminal Court: Overview and Selected Legal Issues*, New York: Novinka Books (2003), p. 17.

341 Schabas, *An Introduction to the International Criminal Court*, 3rd edition, *supra* note 336, p. 87.

342 Although not formally included as crime categories, some "treaty crimes" have found their way into the Rome Statute under the heading of crimes against humanity or war crimes. These include: The crime of apartheid – Art. 7(1)(j) Rome-Statute, and the intentional attacking of humanitarian assistance or peacekeeping personnel / equipment protected under the UN Charter – Art. 8(2)(b)(iii) Rome-Statute.

ceptance and, thus, could not be considered as reflecting customary international law[343], and (ii) the concern that inclusion of such crimes in the Rome Statute could interfere with existing international or transnational efforts to repress such crimes[344].

2.1.1. The crime of genocide

According to Art. 6 Rome-Statute, the crime of genocide requires the commission of one of the acts listed in Art. 6(a) - (e) "with the intent to destroy, in whole or in part, a national, ethnical, racial or religious group, as such"[345]. The term "genocide"[346] was coined by the Polish lawyer Raphael Lemkin during World War II to describe the crimes of the Nazi regime against the Jews. Lemkin defined genocide as different actions aimed at the destruction of essential foundations of the life of a group, guided by a plan to annihilate the group[347]. The list of protected groups in Art. 6 Rome-Statute – national, ethnical[348], racial[349] or religious groups – is exclusive, whereby membership in such groups is generally determined by birth and is of permanent and stable nature[350]. The targets of genocidal attacks are always individual members of protected groups. Despite the fact that Art. 6 Rome-Statute provides that the specific criminal acts must target the group or members thereof, the requirement is already fulfilled if a single member of the group is affected by the conduct[351].

---

343 Zimmermann, *supra* note 335, Art. 5, para. 1.

344 Schabas, *An Introduction to the International Criminal Court*, 3rd edition, *supra* note 336, p. 89.

345 Art. 6 Rome-Statute reproduces the exact text of Art. 2 of the 1948 Convention on the Prevention and Punishment of the Crime of Genocide, which is part of customary international law and *jus cogens*. In addition to the Rome Statute, the wording of Art. 2 Genocide Convention was also adopted into Art. 4(2) ICTY-Statute and Art. 2(2) ICTR-Statute.

346 The word is formed from the Greek *genos* (race) and Latin *caedere* (killing).

347 Werle, Gerhard, *Principles of International Criminal Law*, 2nd edition, The Hague: T.M.C. Asser Press (2009), para. 696.

348 Members of an ethnic group speak the same language, have the same customs and traditions, and share a common way of life. Common racial characteristics are not necessary for the existence of an ethnic group.

349 Members of a racial group exhibit the same inherited, visible physical traits – such as skin color or physical stature.

350 Elsea, *supra* note 340, p. 19; Werle, *supra* note 347, para. 707.

351 Werle, *supra* note 347, para. 725.

A high-level policy or overarching agreement / plan among various individuals to commit genocide is not required under Art. 6 Rome-Statute, so that an isolated individual – acting with the required specific intent – can be guilty of genocide[352]. The horrible nature and gravity of the crime of genocide is reflected in the mental element of Art. 6 Rome-Statute, which requires that the crime be committed with intent and knowledge – Art. 30(1) Rome-Statute, as well as with the specific intent to destroy, in whole or in part, a protected group, as such[353]. It is sufficient for the destructive intent to be present at the time of execution of the criminal act, so that no prior planning by the perpetrator is necessary[354].

The term "in whole or in part" was used in order to (i) differentiate between the crime of genocide and isolated acts of racially motivated violence[355], so that only the intent to destroy more than a small number of individuals from a certain protected group can qualify as genocide[356], and (ii) indicate that the perpetrator need not intend to destroy the entire group, but only a substantial part thereof[357]. The criterion "substantial" can be understood both quantitatively and qualitatively, so that both the intent to destroy a numerically significant part of the group and the intent to exterminate a representative part of the group (such as its intellectual leaders) are sufficient. The decisive question will always pertain to the effect the extermination of the specific part of the group was intended to have upon the existence of the group as a whole[358].

The addition of the term "as such" emphasizes the requirement that the criminal act be motivated specifically by the victim's membership in the protected group – a clear indicator of the perpetrator's interest in destroying the protected group, rather than the specific individual[359].

---

352 *Ibid.*, paras. 700, 743.

353 *The Prosecutor v. Radislav Krstic*, ICTY Appeals Chamber (19 April 2004), para. 134: "Convictions for genocide can be entered only where that intent has been unequivocally established".

354 Werle, *supra* note 347, para. 754.

355 The International Centre for Criminal Law Reform and Criminal Justice Policy, *supra* note 338, p. 74.

356 UN General Assembly Resolution 37/123 (16 December 1982), in which the massacres at Sabra and Shatila (between 300 – 1000 victims) were described as genocide, was fiercely criticized by many states for the misuse of the term "genocide".

357 Schabas, William A., in: Triffterer, Otto (ed.), *Commentary on the Rome Statute of the International Criminal Court – Observers' Notes, Article by Article* , 2nd edition, Munich: C.H.Beck (2008), Art. 6, para. 9.

358 Werle, *supra* note 347, para. 759.

359 *Ibid.*, para. 756.

2.1.2. Crimes against humanity

According to Art. 7(1) Rome-Statute, the term "crimes against humanity" shall be used to describe the inhumane acts listed in Art. 7(1)(a) - (k) Rome-Statute – when committed (i) "as part of a widespread or systematic attack directed against any civilian population", and (ii) "with knowledge of the attack". Crimes against humanity lie very much at the core of international criminal justice. They largely, if not entirely, encompass genocide, which is often viewed as an aggravated form of the crime against humanity of extermination or persecution. Moreover, to the extent that prosecuted war crimes involve atrocities perpetrated against civilians, they are also subsumed within the category of crimes against humanity[360].

The eleven criminal acts listed in Art. 7(1)(a) - (k) Rome-Statute were "borrowed" from many sources of international law – including the Nuremberg Charter, the Statutes of the ICTY and the International Criminal Tribunal for Rwanda ("ICTR"), and various human rights treaties, such as the 1984 Convention Against Torture[361] – whereby, as a result of changes and developments in international law over time, there are some differences between the definitions found in the Rome Statute and the original sources[362].

The first threshold, which elevates the listed criminal acts to the level of crimes against humanity, is the requirement that such acts be part of a "widespread or[363] systematic attack directed against any civilian population"[364]. The

---

360 Schabas, William A., *The International Criminal Court: A Commentary on the Rome Statute*, Oxford: Oxford University Press (2010), Art. 7, p. 144.

361 The Convention against Torture and other Cruel, Inhumane or Degrading Treatment or Punishment.

362 The International Centre for Criminal Law Reform and Criminal Justice Policy, *supra* note 338, p. 76.

363 The ICTY Trial Chamber stated that it is a well-established fact that the required attack against a civilian population is given if the acts occur either on a widespread basis or in a systematic manner (*The Prosecutor v. Dusko Tadic*, 7 May 1997, para. 646). Pre-Trial Chamber II of the ICC stated that the terms "widespread" and "systematic" are disjunctive, so that if the court is satisfied that the attack was "widespread", it need not also consider whether it was "systematic" (*The Prosecutor v. Jean-Pierre Bemba Gombo*, 15 June 2009, para. 82).

364 According to Art. 7(2)(a) Rome-Statute, the phrase "[a]ttack directed against any civilian population" means a course of conduct involving the multiple commission of acts referred to in Art. 7(1) against any civilian population, pursuant to or in furtherance of a state or organizational policy to commit such attack. The Elements of Crimes (crimes against humanity, Introduction, para. 3) provide that "policy to commit such attack" requires that the state or organization actively promote or encourage such an attack

term "widespread" refers to the large-scale nature of the attack, as well as to the number of victims it caused[365]. The attack must be massive, frequent and carried out collectively with considerable seriousness, and directed against a multiplicity of victims[366]. It can be carried out either over a large geographical area or in a small geographical area, but against a large number of civilians[367]. The term "systematic" pertains to the organized nature of the acts of violence and to the improbability of their random occurrence[368]. In the *Katanga* case, Pre-Trial Chamber I of the ICC defined the term "systematic" as "either an organized plan in furtherance of a common policy, which follows a regular pattern and results in a continuous commission of acts, or as patterns of crimes such that the crimes constitute a non-accidental repetition of similar criminal conduct on a regular

---

against a civilian population. The wording of Art. 7(2)(a) Rome-Statute and the relevant Elements of Crimes led some legal experts to believe that crimes against humanity require that the attack on the civilian population be both widespread and systematic – rather than one or the other. The prevailing opinion maintains that there is no requirement in customary international law that a crime against humanity be committed pursuant to or in furtherance of a plan or policy. The ICTY has stated very clearly that neither the attack nor the acts of the accused needs to be supported by any form of "policy" or "plan". Proof that the attack was directed against a civilian population and that it was widespread or systematic are the legal elements of the crime and their proof does not require to show that they were the result of a policy or plan. The existence of a policy or plan may be evidently relevant, but it is not a legal element of the crime (*The Prosecutor v. Dragoljub Kunarac, et al.*, ICTY Appeals Chamber, 12 June 2002, para. 98; *The Prosecutor v. Dario Kordic and Mario Cerkez*, ICTY Appeals Chamber, 17 December 2004, para. 98). Despite not being consistent with customary international law, the "policy requirement" in Art. 7(2)(a) Rome-Statute is not considered to be a substantial problem, as criminal acts that occur on a widespread or systematic basis, usually demonstrate a policy (whether formalized or not) to commit such acts (ICTY, *The Prosecutor v. Dusko Tadic*, 7 May 1997, *supra* note 363, para. 653). Therefore, the "policy requirement" is only meant to ensure that un-coordinated, spontaneous or isolated acts of violence are excluded from punishment under Art. 7 Rome-Statute (*The Prosecutor v. Germain Katanga and Mathieu Ngudjolo Chui*, ICC Pre-Trial Chamber I, 30 September 2008, para. 396).

365 *The Prosecutor v. Omar Hassan Ahmad Al Bashir*, ICC Pre-Trial Chamber I (4 March 2009), para. 81; The International Centre for Criminal Law Reform and Criminal Justice Policy, *supra* note 338, p. 75.

366 ICC, *The Prosecutor v. Jean-Pierre Bemba Gombo*, *supra* note 363, para. 83.

367 ICC, *The Prosecutor v. Germain Katanga and Mathieu Ngudjolo Chui*, *supra* note 364, para. 395; ICC, *The Prosecutor v. Jean-Pierre Bemba Gombo*, *supra* note 363, para. 83.

368 ICC, *The Prosecutor v. Omar Hassan Ahmad Al Bashir*, *supra* note 365, para. 81.

basis"[369]. In the *Al Bashir* case, the same Chamber considered an attack, which lasted well over five years and included acts of violence, which "followed, to a considerable extent, a similar pattern", to be systematic[370]. The requirement that the criminal acts be part[371] of a widespread or systematic attack is meant to exclude random or isolated acts of violence from the scope of Art. 7 Rome-Statute, as widespread or systematic attacks clearly demonstrate the existence of some kind of policy or plan, so that the criminal acts cannot be mere random or isolated acts of violence[372].

The widespread or systematic attack[373] must be "directed against any civilian population", whereby the civilian population must be the primary object of the attack and not just an incidental victim[374]. The term "civilian population" is defined in accordance with Art. 50 Additional Protocol I[375], which is said to reflect customary law[376].

The second threshold, which elevates the criminal acts listed in Art. 7(1)(a) - (k) Rome-Statute to the level of crimes against humanity, is the (subjective) requirement[377] that the criminal act be committed "with knowledge of the [widespread or systematic] attack". This requirement is further developed in the Elements of Crimes, in which the final element of each punishable act of crimes

---

369 ICC, *The Prosecutor v. Germain Katanga and Mathieu Ngudjolo Chui*, *supra* note 364, para. 397.

370 ICC, *The Prosecutor v. Omar Hassan Ahmad Al Bashir*, *supra* note 365, para. 85.

371 The commission of a single criminal act under Art. 7(1) Rome-Statute – such as one murder – can constitute a crime against humanity, if such criminal act is part of a widespread or systematic attack against a civilian population. Indicia for the required nexus between the single criminal act and the attack could include: Similarities between the single criminal act and other criminal acts occurring within the attack, the temporal and geographical proximity of the single act with the attack, and the nature and extent of the perpetrator's knowledge of the attack at the time he/she committed the single criminal act (ICC, *The Prosecutor v. Jean-Pierre Bemba Gombo*, *supra* note 363, para. 151).

372 See *supra* note 364.

373 The Elements of Crimes (crimes against humanity, Introduction, para. 3) provide that the criminal acts under Art. 7(1) Rome-Statute need not (necessarily) constitute a military attack – as an attack in the context of a crime against humanity is not limited to the use of armed force, but also encompasses any mistreatment of the civilian population; ICTY, *The Prosecutor v. Dragoljub Kunarac, et al.*, *supra* note 364, para. 86.

374 ICC, *The Prosecutor v. Jean-Pierre Bemba Gombo*, *supra* note 363, para. 76.

375 Additional Protocol I to the Geneva Conventions of 12 August 1949, relating to the Protection of Victims of International Armed Conflicts (8 June 1977).

376 ICTY, *The Prosecutor v. Dario Kordic and Mario Cerkez*, *supra* note 364, para. 97.

377 In addition to the specific criminal intent required for the underlying criminal act.

against humanity – often referred to as the "context element"[378] – reads: "The perpetrator knew that the conduct was part of or intended the conduct to be part of a widespread or systematic attack against a civilian population". The "context element" should not be interpreted as requiring proof that the perpetrator had knowledge of all characteristics of the attack or the precise details of the plan or policy of the state or organization. In the case of an emerging widespread or systematic attack against a civilian population, the intent clause of the last element indicates that this mental element is satisfied if the perpetrator intended to further such an attack[379]. The required "knowledge of the attack" could be inferred from factors, such as the functions of the accused when the crimes were committed, the responsibilities of the accused within the political or military hierarchy, the direct and indirect relationship between the political and military hierarchy, the scope and gravity of the acts perpetrated, the nature of the crimes committed and the degree to which they are common knowledge[380].

An individual who participates in crimes against humanity, but is unaware that they are part of a widespread or systematic attack on a civilian population may be guilty of murder and perhaps even of war crimes, but cannot be convicted by the ICC for crimes against humanity[381].

2.1.3. War crimes

Art. 8(1) Rome-Statute provides that the ICC shall have jurisdiction in respect of war crimes – traditionally defined as violations of the most fundamental laws and customs of war, which create direct criminal responsibility under international law[382] – "in particular when committed as part of a plan or policy or as part of a large-scale commission of such crimes". The use of the non-exclusive phrase "in particular" suggests that, unlike the case of crimes against humanity, ICC jurisdiction over war crimes is not strictly limited to such crimes committed as part of a plan or policy or on a large scale[383] – so that a single and isolated

---

378 Schabas, *A Commentary on the Rome Statute*, *supra* note 360, Art. 7, p. 155.

379 Elements of Crimes (crimes against humanity, Introduction, para. 2).

380 Schabas, *A Commentary on the Rome Statute*, *supra* note 360, Art. 7, p. 156; *The Prosecutor v. Tihomir Blaskic*, ICTY Trial Chamber (3 March 2000), para. 259.

381 Schabas, *An Introduction to the International Criminal Court*, 3rd edition, *supra* note 336, p. 104; Schabas, *A Commentary on the Rome Statute*, *supra* note 360, Art. 7, p. 155.

382 Werle, *supra* note 347, para. 929; The International Centre for Criminal Law Reform and Criminal Justice Policy, *supra* note 338, p. 76.

383 Cottier, Michael, in: Triffterer, Otto (ed.), *Commentary on the Rome Statute of the International Criminal Court – Observers' Notes, Article by Article* , 2nd edition, Munich:

case, such as rape or killing of a single person by a single perpetrator, could amount to a war crime[384]. As plan, policy or large-scale commission are by no means required elements of war crimes, Art. 8(1) Rome-Statute should be considered a practical guideline for the ICC and (above all) the Prosecutor regarding the type of war crimes they should primarily focus on, given the limited resources of the court[385].

In order for the war crimes provisions of Art. 8 Rome-Statute to apply, an armed conflict must exist in the specific case[386]. The ICTY Appeals Chamber has defined the term "armed conflict" as a situation, in which "there is a resort to armed force between States or protracted armed violence between governmental authorities and organized armed groups or between such groups within a State"[387] – a definition endorsed by the ICC in its early decisions[388]. The existence of an armed conflict shall not be influenced in any way by (i) the reasons invoked by the parties to such a conflict to legitimate their use of force, or (ii) how the parties qualify the armed conflict[389].

War crimes norms have a different structure compared to that of genocide and crimes against humanity, which are established as independent crimes under international law. War crimes are based on violations of International Humanitarian Law, which are criminalized under international law[390]. The core[391] International Humanitarian Law rules subject to criminal sanctions – i.e. war crimes – are listed in Art. 8(2) Rome-Statute.

C.H.Beck (2008), Art. 8, para. 9; The International Centre for Criminal Law Reform and Criminal Justice Policy, *supra* note 338, p. 77.

384 Cottier, *supra* note 383, Art. 8, para. 9; Schabas, *A Commentary on the Rome Statute*, *supra* note 360, Art. 8, pp. 201-202.

385 ICC, *The Prosecutor v. Jean-Pierre Bemba Gombo*, *supra* note 363, para. 211; Cottier, *supra* note 383, Art. 8, para. 9; Boot, *supra* note 316, para. 527.

386 Boot, *supra* note 316, para. 528; Werle, *supra* note 347, para. 978.

387 ICTY, *The Prosecutor v. Dusko Tadic* (2 October 1995), *supra* note 321, para. 70.

388 Werle, *supra* note 347, para. 978; ICC, *The Prosecutor v. Germain Katanga and Mathieu Ngudjolo Chui*, *supra* note 364, para. 239.

389 Cottier, *supra* note 383, Art. 8, para. 5.

390 Werle, *supra* note 347, para. 960; Cottier, *supra* note 383, Art. 8, para. 1.

391 Art. 8(2) Rome-Statute is not exhaustive, so that other war crimes can exist under customary international law or other treaty law.

2.1.3.1. War crimes categories under the Rome Statute

Art. 8(2) Rome-Statute categorizes criminal acts mainly according to the type of conflict in which the respective war crime is applicable – namely international and non-international armed conflicts[392] – and, to some degree, according to their International Humanitarian Law source – broadly or even universally ratified treaties[393]. Based on this categorization method, Art. 8(2) Rome-Statute defines four categories of war crimes, over which the ICC has subject-matter jurisdiction.

2.1.3.1.1. Grave breaches of the Geneva Conventions of 12 August 1949

The first category of war crimes is defined in Art. 8(2)(a) Rome-Statute as "[g]rave breaches of the Geneva Conventions of 12 August 1949, namely, any of the [listed criminal] acts against persons or property protected under the provisions of the relevant Geneva Convention". In this provision, the Rome Statute essentially repeats the criminal acts defined as "grave breaches" in the four Geneva Conventions of 12 August 1949 – Art. 50 First Geneva Convention[394], Art. 51 Second Geneva Convention[395], Art. 130 Third Geneva Convention[396] and Art. 147 Fourth Geneva Convention, which as of December 2011, have been ratified (in whole or with reservations) by 194 countries and are generally considered to reflect current customary international law[397].

The material scope of application of the Geneva Conventions – and, thus, the context in which war crimes under Art. 8(2)(a) Rome-Statute must be committed[398] – is indicated in Common Art. 2 of the Geneva Conventions ("Common Art. 2"). According to this provision, the Conventions shall apply to all cases (i) of declared war or of any other armed conflict, which may arise between two or more of the High Contracting Parties – even if the state of war is not recognized by one of them, (ii) of partial or total occupation of the territory

392 Boot, *supra* note 316, para. 521.

393 Cottier, *supra* note 383, Art. 8, para. 8.

394 First Geneva Convention for the Amelioration of the Condition of the Wounded and Sick in Armed Forces in the Field (12 August 1949).

395 Second Geneva Convention for the Amelioration of the Condition of Wounded, Sick and Shipwrecked Members of Armed Forces at Sea (12 August 1949).

396 Third Geneva Convention relative to the Treatment of Prisoners of War (12 August 1949).

397 Dörmann, Knut, in: Triffterer, Otto (ed.), *Commentary on the Rome Statute of the International Criminal Court – Observers' Notes, Article by Article* , 2nd edition, Munich: C.H.Beck (2008), Art. 8, para. 10.

398 *Ibid.*

of a High Contracting Party[399], even if said occupation meets with no armed resistance, and (iii) in which a party to the Conventions is in a conflict with a power which is not – provided that such power accepts and applies the provisions of the Conventions. It makes no difference how long the conflict lasts, or how much slaughter takes place, as the respect due to human personality is not measured by the number of victims[400]. Based on this material scope, grave breaches of the Geneva Conventions are (still considered to be) limited to international armed conflicts[401].

The war crime definition under Art. 8(2)(a) Rome-Statute further requires that the listed criminal acts be committed "against persons or property protected under the provisions of the relevant Geneva Convention". Each of the Geneva Conventions contains one or more provisions listing protected persons – Art. 13, 24-27 First Geneva Convention; Art. 12, 13, 36, 37 Second Geneva Convention; Art. 4, 33 Third Geneva Convention; Art. 4, 13, 20 Fourth Geneva Convention. Protected property is not defined in the Conventions. Instead, the Conventions contain a description of property that cannot be attacked, destroyed or appropriated – Art. 19, 33-35 First Geneva Convention; Art. 22, 24, 25, 27 Second Geneva Convention; Art. 18, 19, 21, 22, 33, 53, 57 Fourth Geneva Convention[402].

2.1.3.1.2. Other serious violations of the laws and customs applicable in international armed conflicts

Art. 8(2)(b) Rome-Statute defines the second category of war crimes as other criminal acts, which constitute "serious violations of the laws and customs applicable in international armed conflict, within the established framework of international law". This definition makes it clear that all war crimes under Art. 8(2)(b) Rome-Statute apply only in international armed conflict situations and that they may be derived from customary and/or treaty International Humanitarian Law[403]. From the 26 offenses listed in this provision, ten are based on the 1907 Hague Regulations[404], four on grave breaches provisions of Additional Protocol I, six on various other provisions of Additional Protocol I or the Geneva

---

399 Elements of Crimes, footnote 34.

400 Cottier, *supra* note 383, Art. 8, para. 5.

401 *The Prosecutor v. Dusko Tadic*, ICTY Appeals Chamber (15 July 1999), para. 80; Dörmann, *supra* note 397, Art. 8, para. 10; Boot, *supra* note 316, para. 539; Elements of Crimes, next-to-last element of each criminal act under Art. 8(2)(a).

402 Dörmann, *supra* note 397, Art. 8, para. 12.

403 *Ibid.*, Art. 8, para. 30.

404 The Hague Convention of 18 October 1907, Section IV, Regulations concerning the Laws and Customs of War on Land.

Conventions, three on other international instruments and another three derive their wording from more than one international instrument[405].

In most respects, the Rome Statute's definitions of war crimes in this category are consistent with pre-existing international law. There are, however, some enhancements. For example: (i) The war crime of launching an attack against a military objective, knowing that it will result in widespread, long-term and severe damage to the natural environment that is clearly excessive in relation to the overall military advantage anticipated[406], is not found in the Geneva Conventions and exceeds the protection of the natural environment found in Additional Protocol I, and (ii) the definitions in the Rome Statute concerning the war crimes of intentionally directing attacks against civilian objects, intentionally launching an attack in the knowledge that the attack will cause incidental civilian losses and attacking or bombarding towns, etc.[407], do not explicitly require "death, serious injury to body or health" in connection with these crimes – as do the corresponding provisions of Additional Protocol I. On the other hand, the fact that the Rome Statute's provisions relating to the use of certain weapons are not as extensive as those found in other treaties shows that not all serious violations of International Humanitarian Law applicable to international armed conflict have been included in this part of the Rome Statute[408].

2.1.3.1.3. Serious violations of Common Art. 3 in non-international armed conflicts

The third category of war crimes – defined in Art. 8(2)(c) Rome-Statute – applies to armed conflicts not of an international character and pertains to "serious violations of article 3 common to the four Geneva Conventions" through the commission of any of the listed criminal acts "against persons taking no active part in the hostilities[409], including members of armed forces who have laid down

---

405 The International Centre for Criminal Law Reform and Criminal Justice Policy, *supra* note 338, p. 78; Dörmann, *supra* note 397, Art. 8, para. 30.

406 Art. 8(2)(b)(iv) Rome-Statute.

407 Art. 8(2)(b)(ii), (iv) and (v) Rome-Statute, respectively.

408 von Hebel, Herman, in: Lee, Roy S. (ed.), *The International Criminal Court – Elements of Crimes and Rules of Procedure and Evidence*, Ardsley: Transnational Publishers, Inc. (2001), p. 110; The International Centre for Criminal Law Reform and Criminal Justice Policy, *supra* note 338, p. 80.

409 "Persons taking no active part in hostilities" refers to civilians and such persons, who possessed combatant status and subsequently ceased to directly take part in the hostilities.

their arms and those placed *hors de combat*[410] by sickness, wounds, detention or any other cause".

A non-international armed conflict typically involves armed confrontations (i) within the boundaries of one single state, and (ii) not only of a sporadic nature, between the authorities of that state and dissident armed forces / non-governmental (organized) armed groups or among such armed groups[411]. Common Art. 3 does not explicitly require the existence of "organized armed groups", however, state practice and *opinio juris* seem to suggest a requirement that the groups confronting each other are armed and possess a minimum degree of organization in order to make humanitarian law applicable[412]. Furthermore, the very term "armed conflict" in itself presupposes the existence of hostilities between armed forces organized to a greater or lesser extent[413]. The term "armed conflict not of an international character" is further defined by Art. 8(2)(d) Rome-Statute[414], which provides that Art. 8(2)(c) Rome-Statute shall not apply to "situations of internal disturbances and tensions, such as riots, isolated and sporadic acts of violence or other acts of a similar nature"[415].

2.1.3.1.4. Other serious violations of the laws and customs applicable in non-international armed conflicts

Art. 8(2)(e) Rome-Statute defines the fourth category of war crimes as other criminal acts, which constitute "serious violations of the laws and customs applicable in armed conflicts not of an international character, within the established framework of international law". This category of war crimes – the recognition of which in the Rome Statute is considered a significant advance in the development of International Humanitarian Law applicable in non-international armed conflicts – was derived from various sources, including Ad-

---

410 In addition to the definition taken from Common Art. 3, Art. 41(2) Additional Protocol I provides that a person is *hors de combat* if he/she (i) is in the power of an adverse party, (ii) clearly expresses an intention to surrender, or (iii) has been rendered unconscious or is otherwise incapacitated by wounds or sickness and therefore is incapable of defending him/herself – provided that in any of these cases he/she abstains from any hostile act and does not attempt to escape.

411 Cottier, *supra* note 383, Art. 8, para. 5.

412 International Committee of the Red Cross ("ICRC"), *Commentary on the Geneva Conventions and the Additional Protocols*, Common Art. 3; Cottier, *supra* note 383, Art. 8, para. 5.

413 *The Prosecutor v. Jean-Paul Akayesu*, ICTR Chamber I (2 September 1998), para. 620; ICTY, *The Prosecutor v. Dusko Tadic* (2 October 1995), *supra* note 321, para. 70.

414 The Elements of Crimes under Art. 8(2)(c) are also subject to the limitations addressed in Art. (8)(2)(d) Rome-Statute (Elements of Crimes, war crimes, Introduction, para. 1).

415 Taken from Art. 1(2) Additional Protocol II – see *infra* note 416.

ditional Protocol II[416], various treaties on the laws of warfare and customary international law[417].

The criminal acts listed under Art. 8(2)(e) Rome-Statute are largely identical in their formulation to many of the crimes listed in Art. 8(2)(b) Rome-Statute – whereby approximately half of the criminal acts under Art. 8(2)(b) Rome-Statute, which were not taken over by Art. 8(2)(e) Rome-Statute[418], are (for the most part) by their very nature not applicable to internal warfare situations[419].

Art. 8(2)(f) Rome-Statute[420] further provides that Art. 8(2)(e) Rome-Statute shall not apply "to situations of internal disturbances and tensions, such as riots, isolated and sporadic acts of violence or other acts of a similar nature". It shall apply to "armed conflicts that take place in the territory of a State when there is protracted armed conflict between governmental authorities and organized armed groups or between such groups"[421].

Finally, Art. 8(3) Rome-Statute provides that nothing in Art. 8(2)(c) and (e) shall affect "the responsibility of a Government to maintain or re-establish law and order in the State or to defend the unity and territorial integrity of the State, by all legitimate means". The words "legitimate means" in this provision – which appears to have been inspired by Art. 3(1) Additional Protocol II – refer to the criminal acts listed in Art. 8(2)(c) and (e) Rome-Statute, so that even (necessary) state-security related government action shall be legitimate only as long as it does not include the commission of any of the war crimes listed in these provisions[422].

---

416 Additional Protocol II to the Geneva Conventions of 12 August 1949, relating to the Protection of Victims of Non-International Armed Conflicts (8 June 1977).

417 The International Centre for Criminal Law Reform and Criminal Justice Policy, *supra* note 338, pp. 81-82.

418 Art. 8(2)(b)(ii), (iv), (v), (vi), (vii), (xiv), (xv-xxi), (xxiii), (xxiv) and (xxv) Rome-Statute.

419 Zimmermann, *supra* note 335, Art. 8, para. 239; Boot, *supra* note 316, para. 590.

420 The Elements of Crimes under Art. 8(2)(e) are also subject to the limitations addressed in Art. (8)(2)(f) Rome-Statute (Elements of Crimes, war crimes, Introduction, para. 1).

421 This general scope is significantly larger than that defined in Art. 1(1) Additional Protocol II, as Art. 8(2)(f) Rome-Statute does not require that organized armed groups be under responsible command or in control of territory.

422 Zimmermann, *supra* note 335, Art. 8, para. 358; Schabas, *A Commentary on the Rome Statute*, *supra* note 360, Art. 8, p. 256.

2.1.3.2. *Additional requirements regarding the applicability of Art. 8 Rome-Statute*

As in the case of genocide and crimes against humanity, in order to distinguish an ordinary crime from a war crime, there must be a nexus (functional link) between the criminal act and the armed conflict[423]. This requirement is formulated in the Elements of Crimes, in which the next-to-last element of each war crime requires that "the conduct took place in the context of and was associated with an international armed conflict / armed conflict not of an international character". According to Pre-Trial Chamber I of the ICC, this means that the criminal act is required "to have been closely related to the hostilities occurring in any part of the territories controlled by the parties to the conflict" – a requirement fulfilled if the armed conflict played "a substantial role in the perpetrator's decision [and] ability to commit the crime or in the manner in which [it] was ultimately committed"[424]. Sufficient nexus would be given in all cases, in which the criminal act was committed in the course / as part of the hostilities between the adversary parties to the armed conflict[425].

In addition to the mental element requirements under Art. 30(1) Rome-Statute, the last element of each war crime listed in the Elements of Crimes requires that the "perpetrator was aware of factual circumstances that established the existence of an armed conflict". This requirement is further clarified by the Elements of Crimes, which provide that:

> There is no requirement for a legal evaluation by the perpetrator as to the existence of an armed conflict or its character as international or non-international; [. . .] there is no requirement for awareness by the perpetrator of the facts that established the character of the conflict as international or non-international; There is only a requirement for the awareness of the factual circumstances that established the existence of an armed conflict that is implicit in the terms "took place in the context of and was associated with"[426].

These additional clarifications make it clear that the perpetrator is not required to understand the whole complexity of facts determining the existence of an armed conflict or to know whether his/her crime was committed in the context of an international or non-international armed conflict. Sufficient would be

---

423 Boot, *supra* note 316, para. 530; Werle, *supra* note 347, para. 1001; Cottier, *supra* note 383, Art. 8, para. 6.

424 *The Prosecutor v. Thomas Lubanga Dyilo*, ICC Pre-Trial Chamber I (29 January 2007), para. 287.

425 *The Prosecutor v. Zdravko Mucic, et al.*, ICTY Trial chamber (16 November 1998), para. 193; Cottier, *supra* note 383, Art. 8, para. 6.

426 Elements of Crimes, war crimes, Introduction, para. 2.

awareness of the existence of some kind of armed conflict, based on the knowledge and understanding of a number of basic related facts[427].

2.1.4. Implementation in the case at hand

Following a number of investigations – conducted by international and non-governmental organizations – of the Gaza armed conflict and its devastating results (mostly) on the Palestinian side, Israel has been the target of severe international criticism and allegations concerning the violation of international law by its armed forces during the conflict. The following analysis will (i) categorize the main allegations[428] made against Israel, and (ii) address the question whether such allegations / crimes fall within the subject-matter jurisdiction of the ICC[429].

2.1.4.1. The crime of genocide

Apart from one exception, none of the main reports published around the world following the investigation of events during the Gaza armed conflict (even) mentioned the possibility of the crime of genocide being committed by the Israeli military during the Gaza conflict. The one report that did mention such possibility argued that while there might be room for discussion concerning the possible fulfillment of the substantive requirements of the crime of genocide by the Israeli military forces, there can be no doubt that said forces did not act with the intent to destroy – in whole or in part – the Palestinian people, as such[430].

The possibility of individual Israeli soldiers acting with such specific intent[431] (i) has been clearly rejected by the vast majority of the international

---

427 Dörmann, Knut, Eve La Haye and Herman von Hebel, in: Lee, Roy S. (ed.), *The International Criminal Court – Elements of Crimes and Rules of Procedure and Evidence*, Ardsley: Transnational Publishers, Inc. (2001), pp. 122-123.

428 Main allegations are those included in all / most of the reports published by international and non-governmental organizations following the investigation of the Gaza armed conflict. Such reports include: (i) The Goldstone Report of the UN Fact-Finding Mission on the Gaza Conflict, (ii) "Operation 'Cast Lead': 22 Days of Death and Destruction", Amnesty International, (iii) "No Safe Place", Fact Finding Committee to the League of Arab States, (iv) "Guidelines for Israel's Investigation into Operation Cast Lead", B'Tselem, (v) "Targeted Civilians", Palestinian Center for Human rights.

429 The substantive question of whether the allegations made against Israel and its military forces are founded – and if yes, to what degree – shall not be discussed or implied in this analysis in any way.

430 The Independent Fact Finding Committee on Gaza to the League of Arab States, *supra* note 7, Executive Summary, paras. 29, 30.

431 *Ibid.*, para. 30.

community[432], and (ii) could under no circumstances be attributed to Israel's senior government officials and military commanders during the Gaza conflict.

In conclusion, as no (serious) genocide allegations have been made against the Israeli military forces following the Gaza armed conflict, ICC subject-matter jurisdiction over the conduct of such forces, in accordance with Art. 5(1)(a), 6 Rome-Statute, must be rejected.

2.1.4.2. Crimes against humanity

Following the Gaza armed conflict, the Israeli military was accused of committing a number of crimes, which could constitute crimes against humanity under Art. 5(1)(b), 7 Rome-Statute. The main allegations pertain to the crimes of torture and persecution.

2.1.4.2.1. Allegations concerning the crime of torture

The crime of torture – Art. 7(1)(f) Rome-Statute, requires that:

1. The perpetrator inflicted severe physical or mental pain or suffering upon one or more persons.
2. Such person or persons were in the custody or under the control of the perpetrator.
3. Such pain or suffering did not arise only from, and was not inherent in or incidental to, lawful sanctions[433].

Although no catalog of torture practices can be considered exhaustive, the following conducts are, as a rule, classified as torture: Pulling out teeth, fingernails or toenails; electric shocks to sensitive parts of the body; blows to the ears that cause the eardrums to burst; breaking bones; burning parts of the body; spraying eyes or other sensitive parts of the body with acid; hanging from a pole; submersion in water until symptoms of drowning occur; plugging nose and mouth to cause asphyxiation; causing hypothermia with strong fans; withholding food, water or sleep; rape[434].

Following the investigations of the Gaza armed conflict, the Israeli military has been accused of committing torture against the civilian population of the Gaza Strip, by (i) subjecting civilians, including women and children, to cruel, inhuman and degrading treatment, in order to terrorize, intimidate and humiliate them, (ii) beating or otherwise physically abusing civilians in order to obtain information, and (iii) depriving civilian detainees of food and water. Furthermore, according to these accusations, such incidents were not isolated, but rather

432 See *supra* note 151.

433 Elements of Crimes, Art. 7(1)(f), elements 1-3.

434 Werle, *supra* note 347, paras. 865, 866.

reflected a (systematic) pattern of behavior on the part of the Israeli military[435]. Consequently, the torture allegations made against the Israeli military fulfill the substantive requirements of Art. 7(1)(f) Rome-Statute and would fall within the subject-matter jurisdiction of the ICC.

2.1.4.2.2. Allegations concerning the crime of persecution

The elements of the crime of persecution – Art. 7(1)(h) Rome-Statute, require that:

1. The perpetrator severely deprived, contrary to international law, one or more persons of fundamental rights.
2. The perpetrator targeted such person or persons by reason of the identity of a group or collectivity or targeted the group or collectivity as such.
3. Such targeting was based on political, racial, national, ethnic, cultural, religious, gender [. . .] or other grounds that are universally recognized as impermissible under international law.
4. The conduct was committed in connection with any act referred to in article 7, paragraph 1 [Rome-Statute] or any crime within the jurisdiction of the Court[436].

According to the ICTY, the crime of persecution "encompasses a variety of acts, including, *inter alia*, those of a physical, economic or judicial nature, that violate an individual's right to the equal enjoyment of his basic rights"[437].

Following the investigations of the Gaza armed conflict by a number of international and non-governmental organizations, Israel has been accused of (i) depriving the Palestinians in the Gaza Strip of their means of subsistence, employment, housing and water, (ii) denying the Gaza-Palestinians freedom of movement and the right to leave and enter their own "country", and (iii) limiting the Gaza-Palestinians' rights to access a court of law and an effective remedy[438]. Furthermore, the Israeli military has been accused of intentionally depriving Palestinian civilians of these fundamental rights in a widespread and systematic

---

435 Goldstone Report, *supra* note 28, paras. 1164, 1175, 1927; Palestinian Centre for Human Rights, *Targeted Civilians – A PCHR Report on the Israeli Military Offensive against the Gaza Strip, 27 December 2008 - 18 January 2009* (2009), p. 120; Hussein, Adam, *Israel and the International Criminal Court: The United Nations Fact-Finding Mission on the Gaza Conflict and its Role in the Arab-Israeli Conflict* (2010), p. 15.

436 Elements of Crimes, Art. 7(1)(h), elements 1-4.

437 ICTY, *The Prosecutor v. Dusko Tadic* (7 May 1997), *supra* note 363, para. 710.

438 Goldstone Report, *supra* note 28, para. 1936; Palestinian Centre for Human Rights, *supra* note 435, pp. 124, 179, 182; The Independent Fact Finding Committee on Gaza to the League of Arab States, *supra* note 7, paras. 522-526; Amnesty International, *supra* note 5, p. 51.

manner[439], and in connection with other crimes within the jurisdiction of the ICC[440]. Therefore, the persecution allegations made against the Israeli military fulfill the substantive and mental requirements of Art. 7(1)(h) Rome-Statute and would, therefore, fall within the subject-matter jurisdiction of the ICC.

2.1.4.3. War crimes

The majority of allegations made against the conduct of the IDF following the Gaza armed conflict pertain to criminal acts, which could constitute war crimes under Art. 5(1)(c), 8 Rome-Statute. In order to categorize such allegations within Art. 8(2) Rome-Statute, one must first address the question concerning the character of the Gaza armed conflict.

2.1.4.3.1. International / non-international armed conflict

The international debate regarding the question how to qualify military confrontations, which (i) take place between the military forces of a state and a non-state entity, and (ii) are characterized by the fact that they do not occur within the territory of the respective state (cross-border), has yet to be decided[441]. The difficulty to reach a decision in this debate is based on the fact that, on the one hand, such "transnational armed conflicts" possess a clear international character, given that military force is being used on the territory of another state / outside the territory of the respective state. On the other hand, such conflicts lack a genuine inter-state element, given that the military action is not directed against another state, as such, but rather against a non-state entity[442]. In the *Hamdan* case, the United States ("US") Supreme Court held that "transnational armed conflicts" cannot be international armed conflicts within the meaning of Common Art. 2, as non-state armed entities cannot be High Contracting Parties to the Geneva Conventions. According to the US Supreme Court, the phrase "not of an international character" should be interpreted literally and include every kind of armed conflict that is not carried out between sovereign states[443].

---

439 Goldstone Report, *supra* note 28, paras. 1502, 1929.

440 The Independent Fact Finding Committee on Gaza to the League of Arab States, *supra* note 7, para. 524.

441 Zimmermann, *supra* note 335, Art. 8, para. 262; The State of Israel, *The Operation in Gaza: Factual and Legal Aspects*, *supra* note 1, para. 29.

442 Zimmermann, *supra* note 335, Art. 8, para. 263.

443 *Salim Ahmed Hamdan v. Donald Rumsfeld, et al.*, Supreme Court of the United States (29 June 2006), p. 67; Zimmermann, *supra* note 335, Art. 8, paras. 267, 269; Horovitz, Sigall, *Accountability of the Hamas under International Humanitarian Law*, Jerusalem Center for Public Affairs (2009).

In the *Targeted Killings* case, Israel's Supreme Court, sitting as the High Court of Justice, reached a different conclusion, stating that the Law of (international) Armed Conflict should apply to any armed conflict that crosses the border of the respective state – thus equating the term "international" with "trans-border"[444]. This conclusion – in addition to the context of the belligerent occupation – led Israel's Supreme Court in December 2005 to consider the confrontation between Israeli armed forces and militant Palestinian (terrorist) organizations, active in the (occupied) Palestinian territories, as an international armed conflict[445].

In conclusion, based on the above and the fact that (i) since January 2008, Israel considered the Gaza strip neither a sovereign state nor a territory occupied / controlled by Israel[446] and, therefore, as a matter of policy, applied to its military operations during the Gaza conflict both the rules of international and non-international armed conflict, and (ii) the classification of the Gaza armed conflict as international or non-international in the current context is largely only of theoretical concern, as many similar norms and principles govern both types of conflict[447], the Gaza armed conflict shall be considered an international armed conflict in the following analysis.

2.1.4.3.2. Main allegations of grave breaches of the Geneva Conventions – Art. 8(2)(a) Rome-Statute

2.1.4.3.2.1. Willful Killing

The crime of willful killing – Art. 8(2)(a)(i) Rome-Statute, requires that:

1. The perpetrator killed one or more persons.
2. Such person or persons were protected under one or more of the Geneva Conventions of 1949.
3. The perpetrator was aware of the factual circumstances that established that protected status[448].

With regard to the mental element of the crime, the ICTY has stated that the term "willful" requires that the perpetrator acted either intentionally or reckless-

444 *The Public Committee against Torture in Israel v. The Government of Israel*, Israel Supreme Court, sitting as the High Court of Justice (13 December 2006), para. 18.

445 Horovitz, *supra* note 443; Goldstone Report, *supra* note 28, para. 282.

446 *Jaber Al-Bassiouni Ahmed and others v. The Prime Minister of Israel*, Israel Supreme Court, sitting as the High Court of Justice (30 January 2008), para. 12.

447 The State of Israel, *The Operation in Gaza: Factual and Legal Aspects*, *supra* note 1, para. 30.

448 Elements of Crimes, Art. 8(2)(a)(i), elements 1-3.

ly, by intending to cause serious bodily harm and being reasonably aware that death would be a likely consequence of his/her actions[449].

In all reports published following the Gaza armed conflict, the IDF has been accused of killing civilians in the Gaza Strip, by (i) conducting direct and intentional strikes against the civilian population, and (ii) bombing and shelling densely populated areas[450]. Such alleged conduct could, according to these reports, constitute willful (or reckless) killing of civilians and, thus, a grave breach of the Fourth Geneva Convention[451]. In addition to the substantive and mental elements of the crime of willful killing, there can be no doubt that the Gaza armed conflict was sufficiently intense and long, in order to constitute an armed conflict under International Humanitarian Law[452, 453]. Furthermore, as the alleged crimes were committed in the course of hostilities between the Israeli military and Hamas, the required nexus between the crime and the armed conflict is given as well[454].

Since the existence of a plan, policy or large scale commission of the alleged crimes is not a substantive element of war crimes under Art. 8(2) Rome-Statute[455], one must conclude that the willful killing allegations made against the IDF fulfill the requirements of Art. 8(2)(a)(i) Rome-Statute and would fall within the subject-matter jurisdiction of the ICC.

2.1.4.3.2.2. Willfully causing great suffering or serious injury to body or health

The crime of willfully causing great suffering or serious injury to body or health – Art. 8(2)(a)(iii) Rome-Statute, requires that:

1. The perpetrator caused great physical or mental pain or suffering to, or serious injury to body or health of, one or more persons.
2. Such person or persons were protected under one or more of the Geneva Conventions of 1949.

---

449 *The Prosecutor v. Miroslav Kvocka, et al.*, ICTY Appeals Chamber (28 February 2005), para. 261; ICTY, *The Prosecutor v. Dario Kordic and Mario Cerkez, supra* note 364, para. 36; Dörmann, *supra* note 397, Art. 8, para. 17; Werle, *supra* note 347, para. 1033.

450 Goldstone Report, *supra* note 28, paras. 883, 884, 1921; The Independent Fact Finding Committee on Gaza to the League of Arab States, *supra* note 7, para. 485; Amnesty International, *supra* note 5, p. 24; B'Tselem – The Israeli Information Center for Human Rights in the Occupied Territories, *Guidelines for Israel's Investigation into Operation Cast Lead, 27 December 2008 - 18 January 2009* (2009), pp. 9-10.

451 Goldstone Report, *supra* note 28, para. 1935.

452 Horovitz, *supra* note 443.

453 This shall apply to all alleged war crimes discussed in this analysis.

454 *Ibid.*

455 See *supra* notes 383, 384.

3. The perpetrator was aware of the factual circumstances that established that protected status[456].

According to the ICTY, the term "willfully" in this context requires that the act or omission be intentional – i.e. when judged objectively, a deliberate and non-accidental act[457].

Most accusations against the Israeli military with regard to this crime have been made in connection with those cases, in which the alleged conduct of the IDF – described under "willful killing" – has not killed the attacked civilians, but caused them serious injuries and great physical / mental suffering[458]. As in the case above, the alleged conduct of the Israeli military could constitute a serious criminal act against protected persons and, thus, a grave breach of the Fourth Geneva Convention. Therefore, the allegations made against the IDF concerning the willful causing of great suffering / serious injury to Palestinian civilians fulfill the substantive requirements of Art. 8(2)(a)(iii) Rome-Statute and would fall within the subject-matter jurisdiction of the ICC.

2.1.4.3.2.3. Extensive destruction of property, not justified by military necessity and carried out unlawfully and wantonly

The war crime of unjustified and unlawful destruction – Art. 8(2)(a)(iv) Rome-Statute, requires that:

1. The perpetrator destroyed or appropriated certain property.
2. The destruction or appropriation was not justified by military necessity.
3. The destruction or appropriation was extensive and carried out wantonly.
4. Such property was protected under one or more of the Geneva Conventions of 1949.
5. The perpetrator was aware of the factual circumstances that established that protected status[459].

The severe destruction in the Gaza Strip discovered by the international community following the Gaza armed conflict was one of the main reason for the severe criticism and allegations targeted at Israel since the end of the conflict. In their concluding reports, all international and non-governmental committees, which investigated the events and aftermath of the Gaza conflict, accused Israel of destroying: Buildings used by the civil and administrative gov-

---

456 Elements of Crimes, Art. 8(2)(a)(iii), elements 1-3.

457 *The Prosecutor v. Radislav Krstic*, ICTY Trial Chamber (2 August 2001), para. 511.

458 Goldstone Report, *supra* note 28, paras. 815, 842, 885; B'Tselem, *Guidelines for Israel's Investigation into Operation Cast Lead*, *supra* note 450, pp. 9-10; The Independent Fact Finding Committee on Gaza to the League of Arab States, *supra* note 7, para. 485.

459 Elements of Crimes, Art. 8(2)(a)(iv), elements 1-5.

ernment in Gaza, a large amount of residential housing, industrial facilities and infrastructure, water and sewage installations, agricultural facilities / land and greenhouses. According to these reports, this extensive destruction was – for the most part – (i) unlawful and wanton, and (ii) not justified by military necessity, but rather was part of Israel's deliberate and systematic policy of deterrence and punishment through disproportionate destruction[460].

Since all forms of civilian (private and public) property mentioned above are protected under Art. 33 and 53 Fourth Geneva Convention, the alleged conduct of the Israeli military could constitute a grave breach of the Fourth Geneva Convention. Therefore, the allegations made against Israel and the IDF concerning the extensive and unlawful destruction of protected property fulfill the requirements of Art. 8(2)(a)(iv) Rome-Statute and would fall within the subject-matter jurisdiction of the ICC.

2.1.4.3.3. Main allegations concerning serious violations of the laws and customs applicable in international armed conflicts – Art. 8(2)(b) Rome-Statute

2.1.4.3.3.1. Using civilians as human shields[461]

According to Art. 8(2)(b)(xxiii) Rome-Statute, the act of utilizing the presence of a civilian or other protected person, in order to render certain points, areas or military forces immune from military operations, constitutes a war crime. The crime requires that:

> The perpetrator moved or otherwise took advantage of the location of one or more civilians or other persons protected under the international law of armed conflict [and] intended to shield a military objective from attack or shield, favour or impede military operations[462].

Following the Gaza armed conflict, the Israeli military was accused of (repeatedly) using Palestinian civilians as human shields during the fighting with Hamas, by forcing them to (i) walk in front of advancing military forces, (ii) en-

---

460 Goldstone Report, *supra* note 28, paras. 32, 50, 51, 53, 54, 1215, 1304, 1891, 1929; Amnesty International, *supra* note 5, pp. 54 *et seq.*; Palestinian Centre for Human Rights, *supra* note 435, pp. 124-135; The Independent Fact Finding Committee on Gaza to the League of Arab States, *supra* note 7, paras. 500-504.

461 The use of Palestinian civilians as human shields during the fighting was (also) one of the main allegations made against Hamas concerning its conduct during the Gaza conflict – see The State of Israel, *The Operation in Gaza: Factual and Legal Aspects*, *supra* note 1, para. 186; The Independent Fact Finding Committee on Gaza to the League of Arab States, *supra* note 7, para. 124.

462 Elements of Crimes, Art. 8(2)(b)(xxiii), elements 1-2.

ter buildings, in which Hamas fighters or booby-traps were suspected, (iii) inspect suspicious objects for explosives, and (iv) remain in homes, from which military operations were being conducted[463].

Furthermore, (at least most of) the Palestinians allegedly forced to take part in such conducts did not belong to any of the categories listed in Art. 4(A)(1) - (3) and (6) Third Geneva Convention or Art. 43 Additional Protocol I and, thus, were protected as civilians under Art. 50(1) Additional Protocol I. Consequently, since the alleged conduct of the IDF could constitute a serious violation of Art. 51(7) Additional Protocol I and Art. 28 Fourth Geneva Convention, the human shield allegations against the Israeli military fulfill the requirements of Art. 8(2)(b)(xxiii) Rome-Statute and would fall within the subject-matter jurisdiction of the ICC.

2.1.4.3.3.2. Employment of weapons and methods of warfare which cause superfluous injury or unnecessary suffering, or which are inherently indiscriminate

According to Art. 8(2)(b)(xx) Rome-Statute, the employment of weapons, projectiles or methods of warfare, which are (i) of a nature to cause superfluous injury or unnecessary suffering, or (ii) inherently indiscriminate in violation of the international Law of Armed Conflict, (iii) the subject of a comprehensive prohibition, and (iv) included in an annex to the Rome Statute[464], constitutes the commission of a war crime.

During and following the Gaza armed conflict, the Israeli military has been severely criticized by international and non-governmental organizations for its use of munitions containing white phosphorus and flechettes in densely populated civilian areas[465]. According to these organizations, the nature of the weapons – which cannot be directed at a specific military objective – in combination with the area, in which they were used, (i) constituted an indiscriminate attack, prohibited under Art. 51(4)(b) Additional Protocol I, and (ii) caused superfluous

---

463 Goldstone Report, *supra* note 28, paras. 1095, 1104, 1105; Amnesty International, *supra* note 5, pp. 48-50; B'Tselem, *Guidelines for Israel's Investigation into Operation Cast Lead*, *supra* note 450, p. 11; Palestinian Centre for Human Rights, *supra* note 435, pp. 75-77.

464 By an amendment in accordance with the relevant provisions set forth in Art. 121, 123 Rome-Statute.

465 See *supra* notes 44, 49; The State of Israel, *The Operation in Gaza: Factual and Legal Aspects*, *supra* note 1, para. 405.

injuries and unnecessary suffering to the civilian victims of such attacks, prohibited under Art. 35(2) Additional Protocol I[466].

With regard to the third requirement of Art. 8(2)(b)(xx) Rome-Statute, a "comprehensive prohibition" may exist under customary international law as evidenced by the *opinio juris* and practice of states, or under conventional international law – in particular where a treaty prohibiting the employment of a specific weapon has been widely ratified[467]. Despite the controversy surrounding the use of munitions containing white phosphorus and flechettes[468], such use was not prohibited under the Law of Armed Conflict or by any specific international treaty prior to or during the Gaza armed conflict[469]. Therefore, despite Israel's alleged conduct possibly constituting a serious violation of the Laws of Armed Conflict, the allegations against the IDF concerning the use of prohibited weapons under Art. 8(2)(b)(xx) Rome-Statute do not fulfill the substantive requirements thereof and would not fall within the subject-matter jurisdiction of the ICC.

2.1.4.3.3.3. Additional possible allegations under Art. 8(2)(b) Rome-Statute

In addition to possibly constituting grave breaches of the Geneva Conventions and, thus, war crimes under Art. 8(2)(a) Rome-Statute (as discussed above), the main accusations concerning the alleged conduct of the IDF during the Gaza armed conflict – namely, (i) conducting direct and intentional strikes against the civilian population of the Gaza Strip, (ii) deliberately bombing and shelling densely populated civilian areas, and (iii) unlawfully and wantonly destroying, without military necessity, protected property in the Gaza Strip on a large scale – could fulfill the requirements of a number of war crimes under Art. 8(2)(b) Rome-Statute and, thus, fall within the subject-matter jurisdiction of the ICC.

Such war crimes include: Intentionally directing attacks against the civilian population as such or against individual civilians not taking direct part in hostilities – Art. 8(2)(b)(i) Rome-Statute; intentionally directing attacks against civilian objects, that is, objects which are not military objectives – Art. 8(2)(b)(ii) Rome-Statute; intentionally launching an attack in the knowledge that such at-

---

466 The Independent Fact Finding Committee on Gaza to the League of Arab States, *supra* note 7, paras. 472, 487; Amnesty International, *supra* note 5, p. 40; Palestinian Centre for Human Rights, *supra* note 435, p. 70; Goldstone Report, *supra* note 28, paras. 894, 895, 901, 903.

467 Cottier, *supra* note 383, Art. 8, para. 187.

468 See *supra* notes 47, 48.

469 The State of Israel, *The Operation in Gaza: Factual and Legal Aspects*, *supra* note 1, paras. 411, 431; Goldstone Report, *supra* note 28, paras. 880, 901; Palestinian Centre for Human Rights, *supra* note 435, p. 70.

tack will cause incidental loss of life or injury to civilians or damage to civilian objects or widespread, long-term and severe damage to the natural environment which would be clearly excessive in relation to the concrete and direct overall military advantage anticipated[470] – Art. 8(2)(b)(iv) Rome-Statute; attacking or bombarding, by whatever means, towns, villages, dwellings or buildings which are undefended and which are not military objectives – Art. 8(2)(b)(v) Rome-Statute; intentionally directing attacks against buildings dedicated to religion, education, art, science or charitable purposes, historic monuments, hospitals and places where the sick and wounded are collected, provided they are not military objectives – Art. 8(2)(b)(ix) Rome-Statute.

2.1.5. Conclusion

A number of allegations made against the conduct of the IDF during the Gaza armed conflict fulfill the substantive requirements of crimes against humanity and war crimes defined in the Rome Statute, and, thus, would fall within the subject-matter jurisdiction of the ICC. The focus of all post-conflict investigative reports, in which such allegations were published, was on the following ICC-relevant crimes:

(i) Willful killing – Art. 8(2)(a)(i) Rome-Statute;

(ii) Extensive destruction of property, not justified by military necessity and carried out unlawfully and wantonly – Art. 8(2)(a)(iv) Rome-Statute;

(iii) Using civilians as human shields – Art. 8(2)(b)(xxiii) Rome-Statute.

---

470 The principle of proportionality – reflected in Art. 51(5)(b) and 57(2)(a)(iii) Additional Protocol I – is one of the main requirements (in addition to the principle of distinction) employed in customary international law, in order to protect civilians not taking part in the hostilities and civilian objects. The proportionality test determines that attack upon innocent civilians is not permitted if the collateral damage caused to them is not proportionate to the military advantage (in protecting combatants and civilians). In other words, attack is proportionate if the benefit stemming from the attainment of the proper military objective is proportionate to the damage caused to innocent civilians harmed by it (Israel Supreme Court, *The Public Committee against Torture in Israel v. The Government of Israel*, *supra* note 444, para. 45). Following the Gaza armed conflict, the Israeli military was accused by all the international and non-governmental organizations, which investigated the events of the conflict, of failing to respect the principle of proportionality in a number of cases during the conflict.

2.2. ICC personal jurisdiction (*ratione personae*)

2.2.1. Jurisdiction over natural persons over the age of eighteen

The Nuremberg Tribunal stated in 1946 that "crimes against international law are committed by men, not by abstract entities, and only by punishing individuals who commit such crimes can the provisions of international law be enforced"[471]. The fact that the ICC follows the same philosophy is confirmed in a number of Rome Statute provisions. According to Art. 1 Rome-Statute, the ICC shall be a permanent institution and shall "have the power to exercise its jurisdiction over persons"[472] for the most serious crimes of international concern. Art. 25(1) Rome-Statute provides that the ICC shall "have jurisdiction over natural persons pursuant to [its] Statute". Finally, the fact that according to Art. 26 Rome-Statute, the ICC shall "have no jurisdiction over any person who was under the age of 18 at the time of the alleged commission of a crime", emphasizes the fact that the ICC deals only with natural persons[473].

The decision whether to include "legal" or "juridical" persons within the jurisdiction of the ICC was controversial, but seriously considered at the Rome Conference[474]. The states which supported ICC jurisdiction over juridical persons (in particular France), considered it to be important in terms of restitution and compensation orders for victims[475]. Eventually, it was agreed to exclude this possibility, as broadening ICC personal jurisdiction beyond natural persons

---

471 *France et al. v. Goering et al.*, 22 International Military Tribunal (Nuremberg), 1 October 1946, p. 203; Schabas, *An Introduction to the International Criminal Court*, 3rd edition, *supra* note 336, pp. 210-211.

472 There is no explicit reason for omitting the word "natural" before the word "persons" in Art. 1 Rome-Statute.

473 Frulli, Micaela, "Jurisdiction *Ratione Personae*", in: Cassese, Antonio, Paola Gaeta and John R.W.D. Jones (eds.), *The Rome Statute of the International Criminal Court: A Commentary*, Volumes 1, Oxford: Oxford University Press (2002), p. 532.

474 Schabas, *An Introduction to the International Criminal Court*, 3rd edition, *supra* note 336, p. 211.

475 Ambos, Kai, in: Triffterer, Otto (ed.), *Commentary on the Rome Statute of the International Criminal Court – Observers' Notes, Article by Article* , 2nd edition, Munich: C.H.Beck (2008), Art. 25, para. 4; Gallant, Kenneth S., "Jurisdiction to Adjudicate and Jurisdiction to Prescribe in International Criminal Courts", *Villanova Law Review* 48 (2003), p. 800.

would lead to serious – possibly overwhelming – problems[476], which could significantly reduce the court's ability to function[477].

Art. 26 Rome-Statute, which bars prosecution of persons under the age of 18 – at the time of the alleged commission of the crime – constitutes the first time an age limit was introduced in the statute of an international tribunal[478]. After debating the proposed age limit tediously[479], the States Parties came to the conclusion that it would be preferable to leave persons below the age of 18 to the national courts, for they are much better equipped to take care of the specific situation[480], in which children have been committing crimes under international law[481]. In addition, States Parties wanted to avoid the (controversial) discussion regarding the age when criminal responsibility should start and how the period of growing maturity should be dealt with – which could have negatively impacted the standing and, thus, the functionality of the court[482].

With regard to state responsibility, Art. 25(4) Rome-Statute provides that no provision in the Statute relating to individual criminal responsibility shall affect the responsibility of states under (other[483]) international law or treaties. The meaning of this is that the punishment of an individual, who has committed a crime within the jurisdiction of the ICC as an agent / on behalf / in the name of

---

476 Such as: (i) The fact that there are not yet universally recognized common standards regarding the criminal liability of juridical persons (the concept is not even recognized in some major criminal law systems), could render the principle of complementarity unworkable, and (ii) collective liability is very difficult to prove, even in the case of crimes committed on a massive scale, and the ICC could be confronted with a very serious (possibly overwhelming) problem of evidence.

477 Frulli, *supra* note 473, pp. 532-533.

478 *Ibid.*, p. 533.

479 Due to the fact that Art. 26 Rome-Statute is purely jurisdictional in nature, as despite the exclusion of ICC jurisdiction over perpetrators under the age of 18 at the time of the alleged commission of the crime, persons over the age of 15 are considered (criminally responsible) lawful combatants under international law and the Rome-Statute.

480 The execution of sentences on perpetrators, who were under the age of 18 when committing the crimes, would require very specific care, in order to take into consideration their whole behavior and their former situations, their growing maturity since then as well as the social surrounding to which they will return.

481 Frulli, *supra* note 473, p. 534.

482 Clark, Roger S. and Otto Triffterer, in: Triffterer, Otto (ed.), *Commentary on the Rome Statute of the International Criminal Court – Observers' Notes, Article by Article* , 2nd edition, Munich: C.H.Beck (2008), Art. 26, para. 11.

483 Eser, Albin, "Individual Criminal Responsibility", in: Cassese, Antonio, Paola Gaeta and John R.W.D. Jones (eds.), *The Rome Statute of the International Criminal Court: A Commentary*, Volumes 1, Oxford: Oxford University Press (2002), p. 779.

the state, does not exhaust the prosecution of the international responsibility incumbent upon the state for acts attributed to it by the conduct of its organs[484].

2.2.2. Implementation in the case at hand and conclusion

All members of the Israeli military and Government, who took part in the Gaza armed conflict, are natural persons, who were above the age of 18 at the time of the alleged commission of the crimes – Art. 25(1), 26 Rome-Statute. Therefore, the ICC would have personal jurisdiction over all Israeli military personnel and government officials, on which the court is expected to focus its investigative / prosecutorial efforts[485].

2.3. ICC temporal jurisdiction (*ratione temporis*)

2.3.1. Temporal jurisdiction based on the entry into force of the Rome Statute

According to Art. 11(1) Rome-Statute, the ICC shall have jurisdiction "only with respect to crimes committed after the entry into force of [the Rome] Statute" – i.e. 1 July 2002. The fact that (retroactive) ICC jurisdiction is ruled out in cases involving crimes, which (i) are listed in Art. 5(1) Rome-Statute, (ii) were criminal under international law at the time of their commission, but (iii) were committed before 1 July 2002, is a generally recognized principle of international law codified in the 1969 Vienna Convention on the Law of Treaties[486].

Art. 24(1) Rome-Statute, which provides that "[n]o person shall be criminally responsible under [the Rome] Statute for conduct prior to the entry into force of the Statute", essentially restates the norm expressed in Art. 11(1) Rome-Statute, although from the standpoint of individual criminal responsibility, rather than jurisdiction *ratione temporis*[487].

---

484 Schabas, *A Commentary on the Rome Statute*, *supra* note 360, Art. 25, pp. 440-441; Case Concerning Application of the Convention on the Prevention and Punishment of the Crime of Genocide (*Bosnia and Herzegovina v. Serbia and Montenegro*), ICJ (26 February 2007), para. 173.

485 Official capacity and immunity, as a possible limitation to ICC personal jurisdiction, shall be discussed below, see Chapter Two – 3.1.

486 Art. 28 of the 1969 Vienna Convention on the Law of Treaties (non-retroactivity of treaties).

487 Schabas, *A Commentary on the Rome Statute*, *supra* note 360, Art. 11, p. 275.

2.3.2. Temporal jurisdiction based on state ratification after entry into force of the Rome Statute

Art. 11(2) Rome-Statute provides that if a state becomes a State Party after the entry into force of the Rome Statute, "the [ICC] may exercise its jurisdiction only with respect to crimes committed after the entry into force of [the] Statute for that State[488, 489], unless that State has made a declaration under article 12, paragraph 3" – which allows it to accept the jurisdiction of the ICC over crimes committed prior to the state's ratification of the Rome Statute[490].

Despite this notable exception to the principle of non-retroactivity, in no case shall the ICC exercise jurisdiction over crimes committed prior to the coming into force of the Rome Statute on 1 July 2002[491]. When read in conjunction with Art. 11(2) Rome-Statute, Art. 24(1) Rome-Statute shall be supplemented by "for the state of nationality of such person" – due to the "individual" start date of ICC jurisdiction in the case of the former[492].

2.3.3. *Nullum crimen sine lege*

Art. 22(1) Rome-Statute provides that "[a] person shall not be criminally responsible under [the Rome] Statute unless the conduct in question constitutes, at the time it takes place, a crime within the [subject-matter] jurisdiction of the [ICC]. This provision is based on *nullum crimen sine lege*, a fundamental prin-

---

488 In accordance with Art. 126(2) Rome-Statute.

489 Similar reasoning applies to Article 121(5) Rome-Statute, which ensures that until a State Party has accepted an amendment that modifies an existing ICC crime or adds a new crime to the court's subject-matter jurisdiction, the ICC shall have no jurisdiction over such State Party's territory / nationals with respect to the new or newly modified crime. The temporal jurisdiction with respect to such new or newly modified crime commences for that State Party's territory / nationals only one year following ratification of the amendment by such State Party and, thus, would have only prospective application.

490 Bourgon, Stephane, "Jurisdiction *Ratione Temporis*", in: Cassese, Antonio, Paola Gaeta and John R.W.D. Jones (eds.), *The Rome Statute of the International Criminal Court: A Commentary*, Volumes 1, Oxford: Oxford University Press (2002), p. 551.

491 Elagab, Omer Y., "The Darfur Situation and the ICC: An Appraisal", *Journal of Politics and Law* 1.3 (2008), p. 47; Scheffer, David J., "How to Turn the Tide Using the Rome Statute's Temporal Jurisdiction", *Journal of International Criminal Justice* 2 (2004), p. 32.

492 Scheffer, "How to Turn the Tide Using the Rome Statute's Temporal Jurisdiction", *supra* note 491, p. 30.

ciple of any criminal justice system aspiring to act in conformity with the rule of law[493] and recognized in all major human rights treaties[494].

The principle contributes to a legal system's legitimacy by limiting the interventions of the criminal justice process to those which have been clearly prescribed by law in advance. It assumes a rational, autonomous legal subject and a known or knowable law. It posits that the deterrent effect of the law – which is its power to influence the decision-making of individuals in a socially constructive way – arises from its rational and knowable character. Where legal subjects make choices relying on the apparent sense of the law and, nonetheless, find themselves tried and convicted, the law has effectively been applied *ex post facto* to them and the administration of justice is accordingly brought into disrepute[495].

Finally, due to the fact that (i) the wording of Art. 22(1) Rome-Statute bears a close resemblance to that of Art. 24(1) Rome-Statute, and (ii) the sense of both is, to some degree, coextensive with that of Art. 11(1) Rome-Statute, the overlap between these three provisions makes them a favorable candidate for eventual harmonization in future Review Conferences[496].

2.3.4. Limits to ICC temporal jurisdiction

Art. 16 Rome-Statute provides that:

> No investigation or prosecution may be commenced or proceeded with under [the Rome] Statute for a period of 12 months after the Security Council, in a resolution adopted under Chapter VII of the Charter of the [UN], has requested the [ICC] to that effect; that request may be renewed by the [Security] Council under the same conditions.

According to Art. 39 UN Charter, a resolution adopted by the Security Council under Chapter VII must include a determination of the existence of a threat to the peace, breach of the peace or act of aggression. Thus, the request for deferral under Art. 16 Rome-Statute amounts to a Security Council measure not involving the use of armed force, pursuant to Art. 41 UN Charter[497].

---

493 Broomhall, Bruce, in: Triffterer, Otto (ed.), *Commentary on the Rome Statute of the International Criminal Court – Observers' Notes, Article by Article* , 2nd edition, Munich: C.H.Beck (2008), Art. 22, para. 1.

494 Art. 11(2) of the 1948 Universal Declaration of Human Rights; Art. 15(1) of the 1966 International Covenant on Civil and Political Rights.

495 Broomhall, *supra* note 493, Art. 22, para. 9.

496 *Ibid.*, paras. 53, 54.

497 Bourgon, *supra* note 490, p. 554.

Although Art. 16 Rome-Statute seems to give the UN Security Council a veto power over the work of the ICC[498], the rationale behind the provision was to prevent the ICC from becoming involved in matters, in which delicate peace was underway or in the process of being undertaken. It was not intended to be a "blanket deferral", but a measure to be employed by the UN Security Council only (i) when a threat to international peace and security exists, and (ii) on a case-by-case basis[499].

According to Art. 124 Rome-Statute – the second limitation of ICC temporal jurisdiction – on becoming a State Party, a state may:

> [D]eclare that, for a period of seven years after the entry into force of [the] Statute for the State concerned, it does not accept the jurisdiction of the Court with respect to the category of crimes referred to in article 8 when a crime is alleged to have been committed by its nationals or on its territory.

Declarations made according to Art. 124 Rome-Statute – known as the "transitional provision" – can be (i) made only once, and (ii) withdrawn at any time[500].

2.3.5. Implementation in the case at hand and conclusion

In the case at hand, all alleged crimes the Israeli military has been accused of committing have taken place during the Gaza armed conflict – i.e. between 27 December 2008 and 18 January 2009. Accordingly, the first and most basic requirement of ICC temporal jurisdiction – that the alleged crimes were committed after 1 July 2002 – would be fulfilled[501].

ICC temporal jurisdiction further requires that the alleged crimes took place after ICC jurisdiction over the respective situation has been established. This would be the case if either one (or both) of the parties involved in the Gaza armed conflict – the state on the territory of which the conduct in question occurred or the state of which the person accused of the crime is a national[502] – would have ratified or acceded to the Rome Statute prior to the conflict.

---

498 Art. 16 Rome-Statute contains no limitation on the number of times a request for deferral may be renewed – which implies that it could be indefinite.

499 Williams, Sharon A., in: Triffterer, Otto (ed.), *Commentary on the Rome Statute of the International Criminal Court – Observers' Notes, Article by Article* , 2nd edition, Munich: C.H.Beck (2008), Art. 11, para. 4.

500 Bourgon, *supra* note 490, p. 555.

501 In addition to Art. 11(1) Rome-Statute, this fact would fulfill the requirements of Art. 22(1) and 24(1) Rome-Statute as well.

502 Art. 12(2)(a) and (b) Rome-Statute.

The State of Israel signed[503] the Rome Statute on 31 December 2000. On 28 August 2002, Israel effectively withdrew its signature when it stated in a letter to the UN[504] that it does not intend to become a party to the Rome Statute. Due to the fact that signing of the Statute is not tantamount to ratification or accession thereto, Israel was never a State Party to the Rome Statute[505, 506]. On the Palestinian side – without going into the highly controversial question regarding Palestinian statehood and the (legal) ability of its representatives to do so – the Palestinian Authority has never attempted to become a State Party either prior, during or after the Gaza armed conflict.

Based on the first part of Art. 11(2) Rome-Statute[507] – according to which the ICC may exercise its jurisdiction only with respect to crimes committed after the entry into force of the Rome Statute for the respective state – these facts would lead to the clear rejection of ICC temporal jurisdiction in the case at hand. This conclusion is not changed by the second part of Art. 11(2) Rome-Statute, which provides an exception to the rule in the first part of the provision for those cases, in which the respective state has made a declaration under Art. 11(2) in conjunction with Art. 12(3) Rome-Statute, as such declaration must be made by a State Party[508].

The final theoretical option to establish ICC temporal jurisdiction in the case at hand would require that one (or both) of the non-States Parties involved in the Gaza armed conflict declared its *ad hoc* acceptance of ICC jurisdiction over crimes allegedly committed during the conflict, in accordance with Art. 12(3) Rome-Statute.

On 21 January 2009, the Palestinian Authority lodged such a declaration "for the purpose of identifying, prosecuting and judging the authors and accomplices of acts committed on the territory of Palestine since 1 July 2002"[509]. Although the Palestinian declaration made no mention of the Gaza armed conflict, the fact that the declaration was made within days after the end of said conflict,

503 "Simple signature" – subject to ratification.

504 Art. 127(1) Rome-Statute.

505 Benoliel, Daniel and Ronen Perry, "Israel, Palestine, and the ICC", *Michigan Journal of International Law* 32 (2010), p. 74; Blumenthal, Daniel A., "The Politics of Justice: Why Israel Signed the International Criminal Court Statute and what the Signature Means", *Georgia Journal of International and Comparative Law* 30 (2002), p. 596.

506 Israel's complex relationship with the ICC is discussed below in further detail.

507 In combination with Art. 24(1) Rome-Statute.

508 See *infra* notes 643, 645.

509 Palestinian National Authority – Ministry of Justice, *Declaration Recognizing the Jurisdiction of the International Criminal Court* (21 January 2009).

established a clear connection to the latter[510]. In addition, as the Palestinian declaration did not provide an exact definition of the "territory of Palestine", such territory would presumably include (at least) the Gaza Strip and the West Bank of the Jordan River[511].

The declaration of the Palestinian Authority of 21 January 2009 would suffice to establish ICC temporal jurisdiction in the case at hand (only) if it fulfilled the formal requirements of Art. 12(3) Rome-Statute at the time it was lodged with the Registrar – the main requirement being that the declaration was issued by a state[512]. As the highly controversial and legally complex question of Palestinian statehood will be the main focus of the analysis concerning the Palestinian Authority's *ad hoc* acceptance of ICC territorial jurisdiction over the events of the Gaza armed conflict, said question will be left unanswered at this point and the conclusion of the *ad hoc* jurisdiction acceptance analysis will determine the final outcome of this section – concerning ICC temporal jurisdiction – as well.

2.4. State consent as a precondition to the exercise of ICC jurisdiction

Art. 12 Rome-Statute regulates one of the most controversial issues in the Rome Statute[513], namely, state consent as a precondition to the exercise of ICC jurisdiction in all cases not referred to the Prosecutor by the UN Security Council acting under Chapter VII of the UN Charter[514]. In this regard, Art. 12(2) Rome-Statute provides that in cases, in which a situation is referred to the Prosecutor by a State Party[515] or where the Prosecutor has initiated an investigation *proprio motu*[516], acceptance of ICC jurisdiction by the territorial state or the state of the nationality of the accused is necessary.

---

510 Gold, Dore and Diane Morrison, *Discussion on Whether the Declaration Lodged by the Palestinian Authority Meets Statutory Requirements: Historical and Diplomatic Considerations* (2010), pp. 1-2.

511 Quigley, John, *The Palestine Declaration to the International Criminal Court: The Statehood Issue*, Rutgers Law Record (2009), p. 2.

512 Ronen, Yaël, "ICC Jurisdiction over Acts Committed in the Gaza Strip – Article 12(3) of the ICC Statute and Non-state Entities", *Journal of International Criminal Justice* 8 (2010), p. 11.

513 Williams and Schabas, *supra* note 331, Art. 12, para. 1.

514 Art. 13(b) Rome-Statute; The International Centre for Criminal Law Reform and Criminal Justice Policy, *supra* note 338, p. 69; See *infra* note 872.

515 Art. 13(a), 14 Rome-Statute.

516 Art. 13(c), 15 Rome-Statute.

Art. 12(1) Rome-Statute provides the fundamental rule that a state, which becomes a State Party, automatically[517] accepts / consents to the jurisdiction of the ICC with respect to the crimes referred to in Art. 5 Rome-Statute.

2.4.1. ICC nationality based jurisdiction (active personality jurisdiction)

Art. 12(2)(b) Rome-Statute provides that the ICC may exercise its jurisdiction if the state, of which the person accused of the crime is a national, is a State Party or has accepted ICC jurisdiction in accordance with Art. 12(3) Rome-Statute. In such cases, the ICC shall have jurisdiction, regardless of (i) where the acts were perpetrated, and (ii) the state, in which the accused person is present or in custody[518].

Nationality based jurisdiction – which was the least controversial form of jurisdiction and the absolute minimum proposed by some states at the Rome Conference[519] – is well entrenched in the domestic law of the majority of states. By virtue of such state practice and *opinio juris*, it is a permissive rule derived from international custom that establishes extraterritorial jurisdiction. Civil law jurisdictions provide for its use extensively and relate it to domestic common crimes as well as to crimes against the common interests of states. It is a corollary to their rules concerning the non-extradition of nationals. Common law states, on the other hand, use it for the most part only with regard to crimes prescribed by international law, as envisaged in Art. 5 Rome-Statute and international treaty crimes. In this context it is universally accepted[520].

---

517 Kaul, Hans-Peter, "Preconditions to the Exercise of Jurisdiction", in: Cassese, Antonio, Paola Gaeta and John R.W.D. Jones (eds.), *The Rome Statute of the International Criminal Court: A Commentary*, Volumes 1, Oxford: Oxford University Press (2002), p. 606; Schabas, *A Commentary on the Rome Statute*, *supra* note 360, Art. 12, p. 284; Gerding, Marc, "Völkerstrafrecht vor internationalen Strafgerichten", in: Kühne, Hans-Heiner, Robert Esser and Marc Gerding (eds.), *Völkerstrafrecht*, Osnabrück: Julius Jonscher Verlag (2007), pp. 278-279.

518 Schabas, *An Introduction to the International Criminal Court*, 3rd edition, *supra* note 336, p. 71; Kaul, *supra* note 517, p. 610.

519 Schabas, *A Commentary on the Rome Statute*, *supra* note 360, Art. 12, p. 286; Schabas, *An Introduction to the International Criminal Court*, 3rd edition, *supra* note 336, p. 71.

520 Williams and Schabas, *supra* note 331, Art. 12, para. 16.

2.4.1.1. *Israel and the ICC*

2.4.1.1.1. *Israel's unique interest in the creation of the ICC*

The idea of the ICC was originally proposed as far back as the early 1950s in the wake of the Nazi atrocities during World War II[521]. The State of Israel – home of the Jewish People, who had borne the brunt of the Holocaust, the greatest and most heinous crime to have been committed in the history of mankind[522] – was one of the first countries to call for the establishment of an international criminal court, as a vital means of ensuring that criminals who commit such heinous and terrible crimes will be duly brought to justice[523], and is considered one of the architects and founding fathers of the concept and idea of the ICC[524].

The State of Israel considered that it had a moral responsibility to accompany the development of the future ICC and to actively assist in the molding of its personality and character[525]. Thus, from the very beginning of the process, leading Israeli (and non-Israeli Jewish) lawyers, scholars and statesmen have figured in all development stages of the concept of the future ICC[526]. At a later stage, an active Israeli delegation enthusiastically and responsibly participated in all stages of preparation of the Rome Statute, which to this day contains many provisions Israeli experts helped draft[527]. In addition, Israel's deeply rooted interest in punishing human rights violations and its determination that – as the Rome Statute proclaims – accountability trump impunity, was highlighted in the Eichmann Trial[528] of 1961, which took place in Jerusalem and played a major role in the evolution of international criminal law[529].

---

521 Office of the Legal Adviser to the Israeli Ministry of Foreign Affairs, *Israel and the International Criminal Court* (2002).

522 Baker, Alan, "The International Criminal Court: Israel's Unique Dilemma", *Justice Magazine* 18 (1998), p. 20.

523 Israel Ministry of Foreign Affairs, *Statement by Judge Eli Nathan – Head of the Delegation of Israel to the Rome Conference* (1998).

524 *Ibid.*; Baker, "The International Criminal Court: Israel's Unique Dilemma", *supra* note 522, p. 25.

525 Baker, "The International Criminal Court: Israel's Unique Dilemma", *supra* note 522, p. 20.

526 *Ibid.*, p. 21.

527 *Ibid.*; Judge Eli Nathan, *supra* note 523; Baker, Alan, *Reasons not to Join the International Criminal Court in The Hague*, Jerusalem Center for Public Affairs (2010).

528 *The Attorney General v. Adolf Eichmann*, District Court of Jerusalem (December 1961).

529 Blumenthal, *supra* note 505, p. 603; Scheinert, Josh, *A Just Dilemma – Does the International Criminal Court Have Anything to Offer Israel?*, The Jerusalem Post (2008).

2.4.1.1.2. Israel's objections and concerns regarding the Rome Statute

Despite the fact that the State of Israel has always been one of the most fervent supporters of the creation of an international criminal court, several factors have led the former (i) to doubt whether the original goals and aspirations of the ICC can be effectively achieved under the present Rome Statute[530], and eventually (ii) to the decision not to ratify said Statute[531]. Israel's main objections to the Rome Statute include the following.

2.4.1.1.2.1. Abuse of the Rome Statute as a political tool in the Arab-Israeli conflict

The main reason for Israel's opposition to the Rome Statute in its present form is its objection to Art. 8(2)(b)(viii) Rome-Statute, which (i) provides that:

> The transfer, directly or indirectly, by the Occupying Power of parts of its own civilian population into the territory it occupies, or the deportation or transfer of all or parts of the population of the occupied territory within or outside this territory

constitutes a prosecutable war crime within the subject-matter jurisdiction of the ICC, and (ii) clearly shows how the Rome Statute has been abused and utilized as a political tool specifically directed against Israel's settlement activity in the West Bank, Gaza Strip and the Golan Heights[532] – as, according to the Israeli view, the offence under Art. 8(2)(b)(viii) Rome-Statute neither represents a grave breach of the Fourth Geneva Convention nor does it reflect customary international law[533].

---

530 Office of the Legal Adviser to the Israeli Ministry of Foreign Affairs, *supra* note 521.

531 See *supra* note 505.

532 Judge Eli Nathan, *supra* note 523; Levy, Ayelet, "Israel Rejects its own Offspring: The International Criminal Court", *Loyola of Los Angeles International & Comparative Law Review* 22 (1999), p. 209; Baker, "The International Criminal Court: Israel's Unique Dilemma", *supra* note 522, p. 24; Bothe, Michael, "War Crimes", in: Cassese, Antonio, Paola Gaeta and John R.W.D. Jones (eds.), *The Rome Statute of the International Criminal Court: A Commentary*, Volumes 1, Oxford: Oxford University Press (2002), p. 413; Lenk, Arthur, "International Justice – Political Misuses of International Law: The Development of the 'Crime' of Population Transfer in International Criminal Court", *Eyes on the ICC* 1.1 (2004), p. 82.

533 Office of the Legal Adviser to the Israeli Ministry of Foreign Affairs, *supra* note 521; Baker, "The International Criminal Court: Israel's Unique Dilemma", *supra* note 522, p. 24.

2.4.1.1.2.1.1. The Fourth Geneva Convention

The first international law provision to directly prohibit settlements in occupied territories was Art. 49(6) Fourth Geneva Convention[534], which provides that "[t]he Occupying Power shall not deport or transfer parts of its own civilian population into the territory it occupies".

With regard to the question whether the Geneva Conventions represent customary international law, the prevailing opinion within the legal community is that the majority of provisions of said Conventions indeed do represent customary international law and should, therefore, be observed by all states – including Israel with regard to its occupied territories – whether or not they have ratified the Conventions[535]. Some scholars even claim that the Geneva Conventions and many of the humanitarian norms they embody have acquired the status of *jus cogens*[536].

In addition to its refusal to accept the full *de jure* applicability of the Fourth Geneva Convention to the occupied territories[537], Israel insists that based on the purpose and historical context of Art. 49(6) Fourth Geneva Convention, Israel's settlements in the occupied territories are not prohibited by said provision[538]. The drafting of Art. 49 Fourth Geneva Convention was influenced by the fresh memories of the Nazi atrocities in Europe during World War II, forcibly moving hundreds of thousands of civilians in all directions for resettlement and extermination. Paragraph 6 was a response to the mass deportations and forced transfers of Germans eastward – carried out by Nazi Germany, in order to colonize the territories in the east – and was intended to prevent similar criminal acts in the future[539].

---

534 The issue of population transfer was not dealt with (or even mentioned) in the Hague Regulations of 1907.

535 Henckaerts, Jean-Marie and Louise Doswald-Beck, *Customary International Humanitarian Law*, Volume 1, Cambridge: Cambridge University Press (2009), Introduction, p. 50; ICJ, *Legality of the Threat or Use of Nuclear Weapons*, *supra* note 169, para. 79; Levy, *supra* note 532, p. 230.

536 Levy, *supra* note 532, p. 227.

537 Israel Ministry of Foreign Affairs, *Israel's Settlements – Their Conformity with International Law* (1996); Levy, *supra* note 532, p. 229; Israel Supreme Court, *The Public Committee against Torture in Israel v. The Government of Israel*, *supra* note 444, para. 20.

538 Israel Ministry of Foreign Affairs, *Israel's Settlements – Their Conformity with International Law*, *supra* note 537.

539 Lenk, *supra* note 532, pp. 72-73; ICRC Commentary, *supra* note 412, Art. 49(6) Fourth Geneva Convention; Blumenthal, *supra* note 505, p. 598.

Due to the fact that (i) the movement of Israeli citizens to settlements in the occupied territories is completely voluntary[540], and (ii) although many Palestinians in the occupied territories have endured hardship during Israeli occupation, Israel has made no institutionalized attempt to destroy the Palestinian people economically or exterminate them as a race, as was the case in World War II[541], Israel's settlement activity in the occupied territories and the Middle East conflict are completely incomparable with the atrocities Art. 49 Fourth Geneva Convention was designed to prevent[542]. When considering the evil at which this provision was aimed, the diversion of its meaning to justify prohibition of the (voluntary) settlement of Jews in the West Bank carries an irony bordering on the absurd[543, 544].

Art. 147 Fourth Geneva Convention does list the "unlawful deportation or transfer" of protected persons as a grave breach of international law, which could and should be punished by any state[545] – whereby there is no doubt this grave breach is based on Art. 49(1) Fourth Geneva Convention, which provides that:

> Individual or mass forcible transfers, as well as deportations of protected persons from occupied territory to the territory of the Occupying Power or to that of any other country, occupied or not, are prohibited, regardless of their motive.

With regard to Art. 49(6) Fourth Geneva Convention, the meaning of the words "transfer" and "deport" in this provision is different than that used in Art. 49(1) Fourth Geneva Convention, as Art. 49(6) pertains to nationals of the occupying power and not to protected persons[546]. Therefore, the deportation or transfer of

---

540 Israel Ministry of Foreign Affairs, *Israel's Settlements – Their Conformity with International Law*, *supra* note 537.

541 Levy, *supra* note 532, p. 231.

542 *Ibid.*; Israel Ministry of Foreign Affairs, *Israel's Settlements – Their Conformity with International Law*, *supra* note 537; Lenk, *supra* note 532, p. 73.

543 Stone, Julius, *Israel and Palestine: Assault on the Law of Nations*, Baltimore: Johns Hopkins University Press (1981), p. 180.

544 In its advisory opinion concerning the *Wall*, the ICJ came to a different conclusion. The ICJ stated that Art. 49(6) Fourth Geneva Convention not only prohibits deportations or forced transfers of population, such as those carried out during World War II, but also any measures taken by an occupying power in order to organize or encourage transfers of parts of its own population into the occupied territory. The ICJ practically interpreted "deport and transfer" as meaning also "allow or encourage". Based on this interpretation, the ICJ concluded that the Israeli settlements in the occupied Palestinian territory (including East Jerusalem) have been established in breach of international law.

545 Art. 146 Fourth Geneva Convention.

546 ICRC Commentary, *supra* note 412, Art. 49(6) Fourth Geneva Convention.

the occupying power's civilian population into the territory it occupies does not represent a grave breach of international law under Art. 147 Fourth Geneva Convention.

2.4.1.1.2.1.2. Additional Protocol I

Art. 85(4)(a) Additional Protocol I provides that:

> [T]he transfer by the occupying Power of parts of its own civilian population into the territory it occupies, or the deportation or transfer of all or parts of the population of the occupied territory within or outside this territory, in violation of Article 49 of the Fourth [Geneva] Convention

shall be regarded as grave breaches of Additional Protocol I, when committed willfully and in violation of the Geneva Conventions or Additional Protocol I.

Although Art. 85(4)(a) Additional Protocol I makes reference to Art. 49 Fourth Geneva Convention, by clearly shifting the focus from the issue of transfer or deportation of civilians from the occupied territory (1st paragraph of Art. 49) to the issue of transfer of civilians of the occupying power into the occupied territory (6th and final paragraph of Art. 49), Art. 85(4)(a) Additional Protocol I completely alters the emphasis of Art. 49 Fourth Geneva Convention[547]. Since the unlawful deportation or transfer of civilians from the occupied territory was already a grave breach of international law under Art. 147 Fourth Geneva Convention, the key new addition made by Art. 85(4)(a) Additional Protocol I to international law was that the transfer by the occupying power of its own civilians into the occupied territory could now constitute a grave breach of international law as well[548]. According to the Israeli view, the approval of Art. 85(4)(a) Additional Protocol I – and the clear political targeting of Israel's settlement activity in an instrument of International Humanitarian Law – was the result of the diplomatic success of Arab states and their desire to see International Humanitarian Law and universal criminal jurisdiction play a decisive role in Middle East politics[549].

Whether Addition Protocol I reflects customary international law is not entirely clear. While some claim that it is applicable only between parties to a conflict that have ratified it, as it has not yet gained universal adherence[550], others suggest that despite being controversial at the time of its drafting, over time Ad-

---

547 Lenk, *supra* note 532, p. 77.

548 *Ibid.*, pp. 77-78; ICRC Commentary, *supra* note 412, Art. 85(4)(a) Additional Protocol I.

549 Bothe, *supra* note 532, p. 413; Lenk, *supra* note 532, pp. 76-78.

550 Henckaerts and Doswald-Beck, *supra* note 535, Introduction, p. 34; Lenk, *supra* note 532, p. 82.

ditional Protocol I has gained general acceptance[551], so that (at least most of) its provision can be regarded as reflecting customary international law[552].

Israel, for a range a reasons, never ratified Additional Protocol I and, in fact, did not even sign the Final Act reached in Geneva on 10 June 1977[553]. Despite not being a party to Additional Protocol I, Israel does accept that customary international law principles are accurately reflected in certain provisions of the Protocol – in particular Art. 75, which embodies the minimum standard of humane treatment, and the provisions addressing the principles of distinction and proportionality – which makes them a part of Israeli law[554].

2.4.1.1.2.1.3. Art. 8(2)(b)(viii) Rome-Statute

Israel's objection to this provision is based on two basic claims, namely that (i) Art. 8(2)(b)(viii) Rome-Statute fails to accurately reflect preexisting international law, and (ii) the inclusion of this provision in the Rome Statute was politically motivated, as the issue / crime of transfer of civilians by the occupying power into the occupied territory is not of sufficient weight to be considered a war crime[555].

Despite the fact that Art. 49(6) Fourth Geneva Convention is the only fully accepted international law that directly prohibits settlements, the text of Art. 8(2)(b)(viii) Rome-Statute is nearly identical to that of Art. 85(4)(a) Additional Protocol I, whereby the two main differences between these provisions – the addition of the phrase "directly or indirectly" and the removal of the reference to Art. 49 Fourth Geneva Convention – buttress the war crime in the Rome Statute and clearly break from the traditional version of Art. 49(6) Fourth Geneva Convention[556].

---

551 As of December 2011, 171 states have ratified Additional Protocol I.

552 Oxford Public Interest Lawyers, *Legal Consequences of Israel's Construction of a Separation Barrier in the Occupied Territories*, University of Oxford (2004), para. 76; Kattan, Victor, "Operation Cast Lead: Use of Force Discourse and *jus ad bellum* Controversies", *Palestine Yearbook of International Law* 15 (2009), footnote 67; Kreß, Claus, "Reflections on the *Iudicare* Limb of the Grave Breaches Regime", *Journal of International Criminal Justice* 7 (2009), p. 793.

553 Lenk, *supra* note 532, p. 77.

554 The State of Israel, *The Operation in Gaza: Factual and Legal Aspects*, *supra* note 1, footnote 67; Israel Supreme Court, *The Public Committee against Torture in Israel v. The Government of Israel*, *supra* note 444, para. 20; Oxford Public Interest Lawyers, *supra* note 552, para. 76.

555 Levy, *supra* note 532, p. 238; Lenk, *supra* note 532, p. 79.

556 Lenk, *supra* note 532, p. 80.

In Israel's view, these two differences cause Art. 8(2)(b)(viii) Rome-Statute to inappropriately expand and depart from preexisting international law. The phrase "directly or indirectly" indicates that the population of the occupying power need not necessarily be physically forced or otherwise compelled to transfer into the occupied territory[557], so that the voluntary movement of civilians into the occupied territory could constitute a war crime[558]. The phrase has been inserted in order to "custom tailor" Art. 8(2)(b)(viii) Rome-Statute to the case of Israeli settlements[559], as under the provision in its current form, Israel's settlement activity (undoubtedly) constitutes a war crime within the subject-matter jurisdiction of the ICC[560]. The removal of the reference to Art. 49 Fourth Geneva Convention from Art. 8(2)(b)(viii) Rome-Statute was an additional step in the attempt to break from preexisting international law with regard to the transfer of the occupying power's civilian population into the occupied territory, as it created a clear separation between Israeli settlements and the "old argument" regarding the purpose and historical context of Art. 49 Fourth Geneva Convention[561]. Such a separation would prevent Israel and its supporters from arguing that a provision based on Art. 49 Fourth Geneva Convention must be about "Nazi style" forced transfers and deportations and not the politics of the Middle East[562].

With regard to its second claim concerning the political motivation behind the inclusion of Art. 8(2)(b)(viii) in the Rome Statute, Israel has always maintained that even if its settlements in the Palestinian occupied territories do constitute a violation of the Fourth Geneva Convention (which Israel clearly does

557 ICRC, *Working Paper to Assist the Preparatory Commission in its Work to Establish the Elements of Crimes for the International Criminal Court* (1999).

558 Levy, *supra* note 532, p. 241.

559 Baker, *Reasons not to Join the International Criminal Court in The Hague*, *supra* note 527; Blumenthal, *supra* note 505, p. 511.

560 While the second (the conduct took place in the context of and was associated with an international armed conflict) and third (the perpetrator was aware of factual circumstances that established the existence of an armed conflict) Elements of Crimes under Art. 8(2)(b)(viii) are clearly given in the case of Israeli settlements in the occupied territories, Element 1(a), which requires that the perpetrator transferred, directly or indirectly, parts of its population into the territory it occupies, cannot be definitively analyzed, as according to footnote 44 in the Elements of Crimes, the term "transfer" needs to be interpreted in accordance with the relevant provisions of International Humanitarian Law. Nevertheless, the "directly or indirectly" addition suggests that any possible definition of the term "transfer" must include Israeli settlement activity.

561 See *supra* note 539.

562 Lenk, *supra* note 532, p. 81.

not accept[563]), such a violation cannot be ranked among war crimes described as "unimaginable atrocities that deeply shock the conscience of humanity"[564] and "the most serious crimes of concern to the international community as a whole"[565, 566]. Furthermore, since a breach of international law does not necessarily / automatically constitute a war crime or a crime against humanity[567], Israel is convinced that the elevation of Israeli settlements to the level of a war crime, one of the most serious international offenses, is clear proof for the cynical abuse of the ICC as a political tool[568] and the fact that the Rome Statute was deliberately and openly drafted to meet the political agenda of certain states – resulting in Art. 8(2)(b)(viii) Rome-Statute, a direct political attack against Israel[569].

2.4.1.1.2.2. The scope of ICC jurisdiction

Israel's first objection to the scope of ICC jurisdiction is based on the claim that the court's subject-matter jurisdiction is both too narrow and too broad[570]. Israel considers the ICC's subject-matter jurisdiction to be too narrow, as it excludes some very serious crimes – far more heinous than the transfer of civilians into an occupied territory[571] – such as terrorism, biological / chemical warfare and drug trafficking. Such crimes are not included in the Rome Statute because of political disputes over their definition and scope[572], resulting in the paradoxical situation that a state fighting terrorism may find itself under the scrutiny of the ICC for the way it exercises its right of self-defense, while the terrorists themselves are outside the court's jurisdiction[573]. On the other hand, in certain cases, the Rome Statute expands the scope of preexisting international law to include specific acts as war crimes that have not before been recognized as such – Art.

---

563 Judge Eli Nathan, *supra* note 523.
564 Preamble para. 2 Rome-Statute.
565 Preamble para. 4 Rome-Statute.
566 Judge Eli Nathan, *supra* note 523; Levy, *supra* note 532, pp. 209-210; Lenk, *supra* note 532, p. 81.
567 Levy, *supra* note 532, p. 240.
568 *Ibid.*, p. 246; Office of the Legal Adviser to the Israeli Ministry of Foreign Affairs, *supra* note 521; Baker, *Reasons not to Join the International Criminal Court in The Hague*, *supra* note 527.
569 Lenk, *supra* note 532, p. 82; Levy, *supra* note 532, p. 246.
570 Levy, *supra* note 532, p. 209.
571 Blumenthal, *supra* note 505, p. 601.
572 See *supra* note 343.
573 Office of the Legal Adviser to the Israeli Ministry of Foreign Affairs, *supra* note 521.

8(2)(b)(viii) Rome-Statute being the best example from Israel's point of view – which makes its subject-matter jurisdiction too broad[574].

Israel's second objection to the scope of ICC jurisdiction is based on the fact that the Rome Statute provides the ICC with jurisdiction over the nationals of non-States Parties[575]. This practice (i) is contrary to the fundamental principle of international treaty law, whereby only a state party to a treaty can be bound by its terms[576], (ii) undermines the international law principles of sovereignty and the "persistent objector", and (iii) infringes on states' right to negotiate bilaterally and, thus, discourages them from negotiating tailored agreements, as regardless of any previously negotiated agreement, the ICC could prosecute nationals of such states[577].

2.4.1.1.2.3. The appointment of ICC judges

A further cause for concern for Israel is the selection process of ICC judges. According to Art. 36(8)(a)(ii) Rome-Statute, States Parties shall, in the selection of judges, take into account the need, within the membership of the ICC, for "[e]quitable geographical representation". This formula reflects the standard mode for elections in UN organs based on the UN regional grouping system[578]. As Israel is the only UN member state, which is not accepted as a full member of any of the regional groups in the system[579], it seems that no Israeli candidate –

---

574 Levy, *supra* note 532, p. 209; Baker, "The International Criminal Court: Israel's Unique Dilemma", *supra* note 522, p. 24.

575 Discussed below in further detail.

576 Art. 34-38 of the 1969 Vienna Convention on the Law of Treaties.

577 Levy, *supra* note 532, pp. 210, 249.

578 The member states of the UN are unofficially divided into five geopolitical regional groupings. As of December 2011, the 193 UN member states are divided as following: The African Group (54 member states); the Asia-Pacific Group (53 member states); the Eastern European Group (23 member states); the Latin American and Caribbean Group (33 member states); the Western European and Others Group (28 member states plus 1 observer).

579 Prior to May 2000, Israel was the only UN member state excluded from a UN regional grouping – a result of the rejection by Arab states of Israel's membership in the Asian Group, Israel's natural geographic regional group. Consequently, Israel could not sit on any UN body where membership in a regional group was required (such as the Security Council or the Economic and Social Council), nor could it be elected to leadership positions on the vast majority of bodies in the UN system, where voting is based on membership in a regional group. As a result of intense efforts to end Israel's isolation in the regional grouping system, in May 2000, Israel became a full member – on a temporary basis – of the Western European and Others Group ("WEOG") in New York (only). In May 2004, Israel obtained a permanent renewal to its WEOG membership, effective on-

however competent professionally – could be elected as ICC judge as long as Israel's position in the system remains unchanged[580].

2.4.1.1.2.4. Additional Israeli concerns

According to Art. 15(1) Rome-Statute, "[t]he Prosecutor may initiate investigations *proprio motu* on the basis of information on crimes within the jurisdiction of the [ICC]". Despite the fact that this far reaching capacity is restrained by the Pre-Trial Chamber of the ICC, which must authorize an investigation[581], Israel expressed reservations against this power of the Prosecutor, as it believes such a power (i) is inconsistent with checks and balances necessary in any legal system[582], and (ii) could prejudice the independent, impartial and professional functioning of the Prosecutor, and expose the Office of the Prosecutor to endless political pressure[583].

Furthermore, Israel is concerned by the fact that the Rome Statute does not provide States Parties with the right to withhold from the ICC information and documents, which could prejudice national security interests[584]. Although according to Art. 93(4) Rome-Statute, a State Party may deny, in whole or in part, a request for assistance from the ICC[585], if such request "concerns the production of any documents or disclosure of evidence which relates to its national security", Art. 72(7)(a)(ii) Rome-Statute provides that if the ICC (i) determines that the evidence is relevant and necessary for the establishment of the guilt or innocence of the accused, and (ii) concludes that by invoking the ground for refusal under Art. 93(4) Rome-Statute, the requested State Party is not acting in accordance with its obligations under the Statute, the ICC may refer the matter to the

---

ly in New York, so that Israel (i) cannot participate in WEOG meetings and consultations outside New York, and (ii) remains excluded / an observer at the UN offices in Geneva, Nairobi, Rome and Vienna. Israel continues to work towards its full inclusion in the regional grouping system on an equal basis with all other states.

580 Office of the Legal Adviser to the Israeli Ministry of Foreign Affairs, *supra* note 521; Baker, "The International Criminal Court: Israel's Unique Dilemma", *supra* note 522, p. 24; ; Baker, *Reasons not to Join the International Criminal Court in The Hague, supra* note 527.

581 Art. 15(3) Rome-Statute.

582 Office of the Legal Adviser to the Israeli Ministry of Foreign Affairs, *supra* note 521.

583 Baker, "The International Criminal Court: Israel's Unique Dilemma", *supra* note 522, p. 23.

584 Blumenthal, *supra* note 505, p. 596.

585 Art. 86, 93(1)(i) Rome-Statute.

ASP or the UN Security Council (in cases, in which the latter referred the case to the ICC)[586].

Israel insists that it cannot agree to a system, which puts the decision regarding the disclosure of highly sensitive, national security relevant information and documents in hands other than its own[587].

2.4.1.1.3. The result of Israel's dilemma

The combination between Israel's unique and genuine interest in the creation of the ICC, on the one hand, and its objections and concerns regarding certain provisions of the Rome Statute, on the other, created a very serious political and moral dilemma for Israel's delegation to the Rome Conference[588]. Once it became clear that Israel would have to accept or reject the Rome Statute in its entirety – as the Statute does not permit reservations[589] – the fact that Art. 8(2)(b)(viii) Rome-Statute would put Israeli settlers and government officials within the scope of ICC prosecution[590], left Israel with no other choice but to vote against the adoption of the Rome Statute[591, 592].

Israel's position regarding the ICC and the Rome Statute has not changed over the years and to this day the country has not ratified the Rome Statute to become a State Party. Israel's signing of the Rome Statute on 31 December 2000 – a signature withdrawn on 28 August 2002 – does not change this fact, as signing of the Rome Statute is not tantamount to ratification or accession thereto[593].

2.4.1.2. Implementation in the case at hand and conclusion

Based on the fact that (i) Israel is not a State Party to the Rome Statute and is not likely to become one in the foreseeable future[594], and (ii) a scenario, in which Israel accepts *ad hoc* the jurisdiction of the ICC, in accordance with Art. 12(3) Rome-Statute, is extremely unlikely, ICC nationality based jurisdiction over the events of the Gaza armed conflict, in accordance with Art. 12(2)(b) Rome-Statute, must be ruled out.

---

586 Art. 87(7) Rome-Statute.

587 Baker, "The International Criminal Court: Israel's Unique Dilemma", *supra* note 522, p. 24.

588 Office of the Legal Adviser to the Israeli Ministry of Foreign Affairs, *supra* note 521.

589 Art. 120 Rome-Statute.

590 Blumenthal, *supra* note 505, p. 599; Levy, *supra* note 532, p. 209.

591 From 148 nations in attendance, 120 voted in favor and 7 against (including Israel, the US and China) the adoption of the Rome Statute.

592 Judge Eli Nathan, *supra* note 523; Levy, *supra* note 532, p. 209.

593 See *supra* note 505.

594 Schabas, *An Introduction to the International Criminal Court*, 3rd edition, *supra* note 336, p. 77.

2.4.2. ICC territorial jurisdiction (*ratione loci*)

Art. 12(2)(alt. 1)(a) Rome-Statute provides that the ICC may exercise its jurisdiction if the state, on the territory of which the conduct in question occurred, is a State Party to the Rome Statute. Therefore, if a core crime is committed by an individual on the territory of a State Party, the ICC will have jurisdiction regardless of (i) whether the alleged perpetrator is a national of the respective State Party or an alien national of another State Party / a non-State Party, and (ii) the state, in which the accused person is present or in custody[595].

ICC territorial jurisdiction is not limited to the territory of the respective State Party, over which the latter actually exercises effective control[596]. Furthermore, it is estimated that approximately 50% of international boundaries and borders are disputed. Due to the fact that the regions where these disputes are most acute are those, in which the ICC is expected to be called upon the most, part of the ICC's decision process concerning territorial jurisdiction will most likely include determining where international borders are placed and making pronouncements about title to specific territory[597]. A precedent for the idea that an international criminal tribunal could have jurisdiction over crimes committed on the territory of a state party, can be found in Art. 6 of the 1948 Convention on the Prevention and Punishment of the Crime of Genocide[598].

2.4.2.1. The lawfulness of the ICC's jurisdiction over nationals of non-States Parties

The objection to the ICC's jurisdiction over nationals of non-States Parties, as a result of its territorial jurisdiction under Art. 12(2)(a) Rome-Statute, was led by the US, which claimed that such jurisdiction would conflict irreconcilably with the fundamental principle of international treaty law, whereby only states parties to a treaty (and their respective nationals) can be bound by its terms[599, 600].

This claim has been rejected by the majority of international legal experts[601], based on the following argumentation: First, the principle of territorial jurisdic-

---

595 Kaul, *supra* note 517, pp. 607-608.

596 For example, the ratification by Cyprus of the Rome Statute gives the ICC jurisdiction over northern Cyprus, although it has been occupied by Turkey since 1974; Schabas, *A Commentary on the Rome Statute*, *supra* note 360, Art. 12, p. 285.

597 Schabas, *An Introduction to the International Criminal Court*, 3rd edition, *supra* note 336, pp. 76-77.

598 Schabas, *A Commentary on the Rome Statute*, *supra* note 360, Art. 12, p. 285.

599 See *supra* note 576.

600 Scheffer, David J., "The United States and the International Criminal Court", *American Journal of International Law* 93.1 (1999), p. 18; See *supra* note 329.

601 Kaul, *supra* note 517, p. 608.

tion is firmly anchored both in international law and in the domestic law of most states. Based on the latter, states ascribe to themselves the right to exercise criminal jurisdiction over crimes committed by an alien on their territory, regardless of whether the crime in question is a domestic ordinary crime or a crime under international criminal law. In such a case, the territorial state has the right under international law to either initiate criminal proceedings against the alien perpetrator or use its sovereign discretion to make dispositions with regard to this right in international agreements – i.e. voluntarily delegate its sovereign authority to prosecute to other states or international criminal tribunals; in both cases without having to seek the consent of the state of nationality of the individual in question[602].

While there has never been doubt with regard to the right of states to delegate their criminal jurisdiction to other states, some have questioned whether delegation of criminal jurisdiction to an international criminal tribunal, such as the ICC, is lawful when it concerns nationals of a non-State Party, which has not consented thereto[603]. Such a differentiation could be based on the fundamentally different consequences of the exercise of jurisdiction when carried out by an international criminal tribunal as opposed to a national court. While decisions of foreign national criminal courts can be dismissed by the perpetrator's state of nationality as a disagreement between equals, a decision by an international criminal court would carry more weight and have much greater political impact[604].

The prevailing opinion, however, does not accept this differentiation and considers the delegation of national criminal jurisdiction to international criminal tribunals, in particular the ICC, lawful. This view is based on the fact that the majority of ICC crimes are such crimes, over which states have universal jurisdiction when the accused is present on their territory. International law permits (and even requires in certain cases) all states to exercise criminal jurisdiction in respect of specific crimes, which are deemed to be prejudicial to the interests of the international community as a whole – as effective deterrence and punishment depends on there being as broad a basis for prosecution as possible. Accordingly, the state exercising universal jurisdiction is in effect acting on behalf

---

602 *Ibid.*, pp. 607, 609; Williams and Schabas, *supra* note 331, Art. 12, para. 15; Schabas, *A Commentary on the Rome Statute*, *supra* note 360, Art. 12, p. 286.

603 Scheffer, "The United States and the International Criminal Court", *supra* note 600, p. 18.

604 Akande, Dapo, "The Jurisdiction of the International Criminal Court over Nationals of Non-Parties: Legal Basis and Limits", *Journal of International Criminal Justice* 1 (2003), p. 625.

of the international community as a whole. Based on this, it would be extraordinary and incoherent if the rule permitting prosecution of international crimes by individual states – acting as agents of the community – simultaneously prevented those states from acting collectively in the prosecution of such crimes. Therefore, states permitted to individually prosecute criminals for international crimes, on the basis of universal jurisdiction and without the consent of the criminal's state of nationality, should be able to act collectively to achieve the same end – for example, by setting up an international criminal tribunal[605].

Second, the highly important issue of jurisdiction over international core crimes cannot be reduced to a set of bilateral, inter-state legal relationships – while ignoring the position of the individual in the realm of international criminal law[606]. The individual criminal must, for the very specific and limited purpose of international criminal law, be seen as an independent subject of international law, rather than as an extension of his/her national or territorial state[607].

The claim based on the ICJ's judgment in the *Monetary Gold* case[608] of 1954 – whereby ICC jurisdiction over nationals of non-States Parties would be unlawful in cases, in which the accused has acted pursuant to the officially approved policy of the state, as in such cases, in addition to exercising its jurisdiction over individuals, the ICC would be making a ruling on the legality of the acts of a non-State Party, which has not consented thereto[609] – has been rejected based on the prevailing opinion that the *Monetary Gold* doctrine does not prevent adjudication of a case simply because it implicates the interests of a non-consenting third party or because a decision may cast doubt on the legality of actions / imply the legal responsibility of such a non-consenting party. The *Monetary Gold* doctrine is only applicable in cases, in which pronouncement by the court on the rights and responsibilities of the non-consenting party is a necessary prerequisite for the determination of the case[610].

Although there can be no doubt that state responsibility will often flow from the fact that an official of the state has been found to have committed an international crime, the ICC will not be engaged in making determinations about the

---

605 *Ibid.*, pp. 625-626; Kaul, *supra* note 517, pp. 608-609.

606 Kaul, *supra* note 517, p. 609.

607 *Ibid.*

608 Case of the Monetary Gold Removed from Rome in 1943 – Preliminary Question (*Italy v. France, United Kingdom of Great Britain and Northern Ireland and United States of America*), ICJ (15 June 1954).

609 Akande, "The Jurisdiction of the International Criminal Court over Nationals of Non-Parties: Legal Basis and Limits", *supra* note 604, p. 634.

610 *Ibid.*, p. 635.

legal responsibility of the state, nor will it need to do so in order to convict the individual. In fact, the very purpose of international criminal law is to separate the responsibility of individuals from that of the state and to focus on the personal responsibility of those who order, direct, or commit international crimes[611]. In conclusion, ICC jurisdiction over nationals of non-States Parties is lawful, as it does not impose obligations on / infringe upon the rights of non-States Parties, but rather responds to the individual perpetrator's breach of his/her obligation *erga omnes*[612].

2.4.2.2. Implementation in the case at hand

In order for the ICC to have territorial jurisdiction over the events of the Gaza armed conflict, in accordance with Art. 12(2)(alt. 1)(a) Rome-Statute, the Gaza Strip must have been under the sovereignty of a state, which has become a State Party to the Rome Statute either before or during the Gaza armed conflict (27 December 2008 – 18 January 2009)[613].

2.4.2.2.1. Historical background

The territory of the Gaza Strip was under the rule of the Ottoman Empire between 1517 and 1799, when the Middle East was temporarily conquered by Napoleon's invading armies. After the turn of the century, Mohammed Ali – known as the founder of modern Egypt – expanded his power to territories beyond Egypt, including Sudan and Syria. The territory was later recaptured by the Ottoman Empire, which permanently lost control over it to the British during World War I (the 1917 Third Battle of Gaza)[614].

At the end of World War I, a "Class A" Mandate for Palestine (Israel, Jordan, the West Bank and the Gaza Strip) was entrusted to Great Britain by the League of Nations, pursuant to Art. 22(4) Covenant of the League of Nations. The territorial boundaries of the Mandate for Palestine were laid down by various instruments, in particular on the eastern border by a British memorandum of 16 September 1922 and an Anglo-Transjordanian Treaty of 20 February 1928[615]. In 1947, Great Britain announced plans to evacuate the mandated territory by 1 August 1948. Meanwhile, the UN adopted Resolution 181 (II) on the Palestinian

---

611 *Ibid.*, p. 636.

612 *Ibid.*, p. 620; Kaul, *supra* note 517, p. 609.

613 The territoriality principle must work in harmony with the temporal jurisdiction of the ICC.

614 Samson, Elizabeth, "Is Gaza Occupied?: Redefining the Status of Gaza Under International Law", *American University International Law Review* 25 (2010), p. 920.

615 ICJ, *Legal Consequences of the Construction of a Wall in the Occupied Palestinian Territories*, *supra* note 166, para. 70.

question[616], recommending a "plan of partition with economic union" by creating two separate, independent Jewish and Arab states in Palestine, which shall come into existence two months after the evacuation of the armed forces of the mandatory power. The Jewish Authorities in Palestine accepted the UN plan, while Arab representatives in Palestine, as well as the Arab states, rejected it.

In May 1948, Great Britain withdrew its armed forces from Palestine and Israel declared its independence[617]. Following Israel's declaration, the Egyptian army invaded the area from the south – thus commencing Israel's War of Independence – and occupied the territory of the Gaza Strip. Egypt's move was followed by invasions by Israel's other neighbors, namely Jordan, Syria and Lebanon[618]. The territory of the Gaza Strip as it is now known was the product of the subsequent 1949 Armistice Agreement between Egypt and Israel[619]. Egypt imposed a military government on Gaza in the 1950s and 1960s, but never purported to annex it[620].

Israel seized control of the Gaza Strip in the 1967 Six-Day War and immediately established a military government there. Israel maintained that, because it had not displaced a recognized sovereign state in taking control of the Gaza Strip (and the West Bank), the territory was "administered" by Israel, but not "occupied" within the meaning of international law[621]. Israel's position was rejected by most authorities and, over time, its status as an occupying power was confirmed by the ICJ, the Israeli Supreme Court, the UN General Assembly and Security Council, and the US State Department[622].

On 13 September 1993, Israel and the PLO signed the Declaration of Principles on Interim Self-Government Arrangements[623] ("Declaration of Principles")

---

616 UN General Assembly Resolution 181 (II), 29 November 1947.

617 Power, Susan, "War, Invasion, Occupation? A Problem of Status on the Gaza Strip", *Trinity College Law Review* 12 (2009), p. 26.

618 Samson, *supra* note 614, p. 921.

619 ICJ, *Legal Consequences of the Construction of a Wall in the Occupied Palestinian Territories*, *supra* note 166, para. 72.

620 Shany, Yuval, "Farawy, so Close: The Legal Status of Gaza After Israel's Disengagement", *Yearbook of International Humanitarian Law* 8 (2005), p. 371; Samson, *supra* note 614, p. 922; Ronen, "ICC Jurisdiction over Acts Committed in the Gaza Strip – Article 12(3) of the ICC Statute and Non-state Entities", *supra* note 512, Footnote 37.

621 Shany, "Farawy, so Close: The Legal Status of Gaza After Israel's Disengagement", *supra* note 620, p. 371; See *supra* note 537.

622 Bisharat, *et al.*, *supra* note 273, pp. 47-48.

623 International Legal Materials, Volume XXXII, No. 1 (1993), pp. 1525-1544.

– also known as the Oslo Accords[624] – according to which Israel withdrew its military forces from the Gaza Strip (and the Jericho area) and transferred authority regarding matters such as public order, energy, economic development, education and culture, health, social welfare, direct taxation, and tourism to a newly established Palestinian Authority. According to the Declaration, Israel retained full control over matters including external security, Israeli civilians / settlements in the Gaza Strip and foreign relations[625].

Although some have argued that Israel's withdrawal from the Gaza Strip, in combination with the transfer of a large portion of governmental powers and responsibilities to the Palestinian Authority, constituted Israel's loss of effective control over the Gaza Strip and, thus, the end of its occupation of the territory[626], the majority of legal experts maintain that the 1993 Declaration of Principles did not change the legal status of the Gaza Strip as an occupied territory under Israeli military government[627].

In February 2005, the Israeli Government voted to unilaterally disengage from the Gaza Strip[628]. The Disengagement Plan stipulated that all Israeli settlements in the Gaza Strip and the Israeli-Palestinian Erez Industrial Zone be dismantled, military bases be removed and all 9,000 Israeli settlers be relocated from the Gaza Strip[629]. On 12 September 2005, the last group of IDF soldiers left the Gaza Strip. On the same day, the IDF Chief Commander for the Southern Command issued an official decree proclaiming the end of military rule in the

---

624 Reference to the term "Oslo Accords" shall pertain to the 1993 Declaration of Principles and subsequent agreements between Israel and the PLO, including: The Gaza-Jericho Agreement of 1994, the Interim Agreement (Oslo II) of 1995, the Hebron Protocol of 1997, the Wye River Memorandum of 1998 and the Sharm el-Sheik Memorandum of 1999.

625 Samson, *supra* note 614, p. 922; Mari, Mustafa, "The Israeli Disengagement from the Gaza Strip: An End of the Occupation?", *Yearbook of International Humanitarian Law* 8 (2005), p. 364.

626 Benvenisti, Eyal, "The Israeli-Palestinian Declaration of Principles: A Framework for Future Settlement", *European Journal of International Law* 4 (1993), pp. 550-551.

627 Power, *supra* note 617, pp. 27-28; Mari, *supra* note 625, pp. 364, 367; Weiner, Justus R., "Hard Facts Meet Soft Law – The Israel-PLO Declaration of Principles and the Prospects for Peace: A Response to Katherine W. Meighan", *Virginia Journal of International Law* 35 (1995), pp. 940-941; Malanczuk, Peter, "Some Basic Aspects of the Agreements Between Israel and the PLO from the Perspective of International Law", *European Journal of International Law* 7.4 (1996), pp. 495-497.

628 The Disengagement Plan was approved by Israel's cabinet on 6 June 2004 and by the Knesset on 25 October 2004 – see *supra* note 7.

629 Samson, *supra* note 614, pp. 922-923.

Gaza Strip and formally nullifying the decree issued on 6 June 1967, which instituted Israel's military rule over the Gaza Strip[630]. Whether Israel's occupation of the Gaza Strip ended with its 2005 disengagement, remains an unanswered, highly controversial question to this day[631].

Following Hamas' victory in the 2006 elections for the Palestinian Legislative Council – the legislature of the Palestinian Authority – and the formation of a national unity government headed by Ismail Haniyeh of Hamas in March 2007, a violent power struggle between Hamas and Fatah erupted, resulting in Hamas violently seizing control over the Gaza Strip in June 2007 (the Battle of Gaza)[632].

2.4.2.2.2. Analysis and conclusion

Based on the history of the Gaza Strip, the first conclusion one must reach is that naming a possible territorial state for the purpose of Art. 12(2)(alt. 1)(a) Rome-Statute is in the case at hand, by no means, straight forward. The Gaza Strip has never been under the sovereignty of a state, which still exists today, and since World War I has been under the occupational control of states – Great Britain, Egypt and Israel – which have not tried to make / considered the Gaza Strip part of their sovereign territory[633].

Due to the unique circumstances of the Gaza Strip and the injustice of its population – approximately 1.5 million people[634] – having no international representation in this context, one could consider the (exceptional) option of basing the territorial link required by Art. 12(2)(alt. 1)(a) Rome-Statute on the occupying state rather than the (sovereign) state, on the territory of which the conduct in question occurred[635]. Regardless of whether one considers Israel the most recent or the current occupant of the Gaza Strip[636], the former does not create the

---

630 Shany, Yuval, "Binary Law Meets Complex Reality: The Occupation of Gaza Debate", *Israel Law Review* 41 (2008), p. 70.

631 Israel Supreme Court, *Jaber Al-Bassiouni Ahmed and others v. The Prime Minister of Israel*, *supra* note 446, para. 12; Samson, *supra* note 614, p. 966; Benvenisti, Eyal, *The Law on the Unilateral Termination of Occupation*, Tel Aviv University Law School (2008); Bisharat, *et al.*, *supra* note 273, p. 48; Mari, *supra* note 625, p. 367; See *supra* note 8.

632 See *supra* notes 9, 12.

633 Power, *supra* note 617, p. 27; Malanczuk, *supra* note 627, p. 494; See *supra* notes 620, 630.

634 See *supra* note 3.

635 Ronen, "ICC Jurisdiction over Acts Committed in the Gaza Strip – Article 12(3) of the ICC Statute and Non-state Entities", *supra* note 512, Footnote 37.

636 See *supra* note 631.

required territorial link to ICC jurisdiction, as Israel has never ratified the Rome Statute to become a State Party thereto. Furthermore, any (theoretical) possibility of ICC territorial jurisdiction over the Gaza Strip based on the Palestinian Authority (or even the Gaza-based Hamas Government) being a party to the Rome Statute must – without going into the highly controversial question of Palestinian statehood and the (legal) ability of such an interim self-government body to become a party to the Rome Statute – be rejected, as the Palestinian Authority has never attempted to become a party to the Rome Statute either before or during the period between 27 December 2008 and 18 January 2009[637].

In conclusion, ICC territorial jurisdiction over the events of the Gaza armed conflict, in accordance with Art. 12(2)(alt. 1)(a) Rome-Statute, must be ruled out. Despite this fact, the ICC could still have territorial jurisdiction in the case at hand, as Art. 12(2)(alt. 2)(a) Rome-Statute provides that the ICC may exercise its jurisdiction if the state, on the territory of which the conduct in question occurred, has accepted ICC jurisdiction in accordance with Art. 12(3) Rome-Statute. As the Palestinian Authority made a declaration to that effect on 21 January 2009[638], the following analysis will address the highly controversial and significant question of whether said declaration fulfilled the formal requirements of Art. 12(3) Rome-Statute.

2.5. *Ad hoc* acceptance of ICC territorial jurisdiction

Art. 12(2)(alt. 2)(a) Rome-Statute provides that the ICC may exercise its jurisdiction if the state, on the territory of which the conduct in question occurred, has accepted the jurisdiction of the court *ad hoc*, in accordance with Art. 12(3) Rome-Statute.

2.5.1. The nature of declarations under Art. 12(3) Rome-Statute

Art. 12(3) Rome-Statute provides that in cases, in which the consent of a non-State Party is required as a precondition to the exercise of ICC jurisdiction, such a state may:

637 See *supra* note 613.

638 See *supra* note 509.

> [B]y declaration lodged with the Registrar, accept the exercise of jurisdiction[639] by the [ICC] with respect to the crime in question. The accepting state shall cooperate with the court without any delay or exception in accordance with Part 9.

In general terms, a declaration under Art. 12(3) Rome-Statute allows for an extension of the jurisdiction of the ICC and the application of the Statute in circumstances where a non-State Party has a nexus to the alleged crime(s). The underlying premise of the declaration is to enable a non-State Party to accept the jurisdiction of the ICC on an *ad hoc* basis, without becoming a State Party to the Rome Statute[640] – a highly important option, as it significantly contributes to a wider prosecution of international crimes[641].

Declarations under Art. 12(3) Rome-Statute are based on a general idea of reciprocity. In return for gaining access to the ICC, the accepting non-State Party must (i) act within the general system of the Rome Statute and the ICC Rules of Procedure and Evidence, and (ii) cooperate with the court in the course of subsequent investigations and proceedings, in accordance with Part 9 of the Rome Statute – obligations it would otherwise not be under as a non-State Party[642].

The Rome Statute distinguishes two types of declarations under Art. 12(3). In addition to the typical situation, in which the declaration is made by a non-State Party, a declaration can also be made by a State Party under Art. 11(2) in conjunction with Art. 12(3) Rome-Statute[643]. The former extends the personal, temporal and territorial jurisdiction of the ICC to criminal conduct, over which the ICC would otherwise lack jurisdiction under Art. 12(2) Rome-Statute[644]. The

---

639 This includes both territorial and nationality based jurisdiction, as, in addition to the territorial state, Art. 12(2)(alt. 2)(b) Rome-Statute provides that the state of nationality of the accused can accept ICC jurisdiction over crimes allegedly committed by its nationals, in accordance with Art. 12(3) Rome-Statute. The following analysis will focus on the *ad hoc* acceptance of territorial jurisdiction, as Israeli *ad hoc* acceptance of nationality based jurisdiction in the case at hand is practically impossible.

640 Freeland, Steven, "How Open Should the Door Be? – Declarations by non-States Parties under Article 12(3) of the Rome Statute of the International Criminal Court", *Nordic Journal of International Law* 75 (2006), pp. 217-218.

641 Stahn, Carsten, Mohamed M. El Zeidy and Héctor Olásolo, "The International Criminal Court's Ad Hoc Jurisdiction Revisited", *American Journal of International Law* 99.2 (2005), p. 422.

642 *Ibid.*; Freeland, *supra* note 640, p. 230.

643 Stahn, Carsten, "Why Some Doors may be Closed Already: Second Thoughts on a 'Case-by-Case' Treatment of Article 12(3) Declarations", *Nordic Journal of International Law* 75 (2006), p. 244.

644 *Ibid.*

latter is lodged as a "supplement" to a State Party's referral – under Art. 14 Rome-Statute – and is intended to extend the temporal jurisdiction of the ICC to crimes committed on the territory of such State Party before its accession to the Rome Statute – as envisaged by Art 11(2) Rome-Statute[645].

The Rome Statute does not expressly clarify which procedural regime applies when a non-State Party accepts the jurisdiction of the ICC via the lodging of an Article 12(3) Rome-Statute declaration – i.e. should such a declaration be treated as (i) analogous to a State Party referral under Art. 14 Rome-Statute, or (ii) a jurisdictional mechanism that enables the Prosecutor to consider whether or not to initiate an investigation under his/her *proprio motu* powers, in accordance with Art. 15 Rome-Statute[646].

The logic behind treating – genuine, not politically motivated – Art. 12(3) Rome-Statute declarations as analogous to State Party referrals under Art. 14 Rome-Statute is (i) the risk of the Prosecutor deciding – alone and possibly on arbitrary grounds – not to proceed with / initiate an investigation regarding a genuine "cry for help" declaration, and (ii) the need to prevent such a situation by ensuring that genuine declarations be the subject of adequate judicial scrutiny and attention before they can be rejected by the Prosecutor. Such an approach would, in addition, be fully consistent with the overall object and purpose of the Rome Statute, namely that the most serious crimes of concern to the international community as a whole not go unpunished[647].

Despite the positive purpose and logic of this claim, the prevailing opinion among legal experts is that Art. 12(3) Rome-Statute declarations only broaden the potential scope of ICC jurisdiction and do not, by themselves, constitute (analogous) State Party referrals, in accordance with Art. 14 Rome-Statute, or (automatically) trigger the investigative activities of the Prosecutor, in accordance with Art. 15 Rome-Statute. Consequently, an Art. 12(3) Rome-Statute declaration must be followed by a State Party referral or by the Prosecutor's initia-

---

645 An example for such a declaration is the case of Uganda, which became a State Party in September 2002. On 16 December 2003, the country referred the "situation concerning the Lord's Resistance Army" to the ICC under Art. 14 Rome-Statute. In conjunction with this referral, Uganda lodged an Art. 12(3) declaration accepting ICC jurisdiction from the entry into force of the Rome Statute, which resulted in the temporal jurisdiction of the ICC in relation to the situation in Uganda extending back to 1 July 2002.

646 Stahn, El Zeidy and Olásolo, *supra* note 641, p. 424.

647 Freeland, *supra* note 640, pp. 228, 229, 231.

tion of an investigation *proprio motu*, in order for the ICC to exercise its jurisdiction in the respective case[648].

Arguments raised in support of this prevalent view include: First, within the overall scheme of the Rome Statute, Art. 12(3) forms part of the "Preconditions to the exercise of jurisdiction", which are distinct from the ICC's formal "trigger mechanisms" embodied in Art. 13. This suggests that a declaration under Art. 12(3) Rome-Statute gives the ICC and the Prosecutor jurisdiction over the relevant situation, but there is no obligation to exercise such jurisdiction until one of the "trigger mechanisms" under Art. 13 Rome-Statute comes into play[649].

Second, to treat a declaration under Art. 12(3) Rome-Statute as analogous to a State Party referral would grant non-States Parties privileges (explicitly) reserved to States Parties under Art. 14 Rome-Statute – titled "[r]eferral of a situation by a State Party". This limitation to States Parties reflects the Rome Statute's basic idea of reciprocity and equality, whereby a state that does not accept the ICC's automatic jurisdiction over crimes committed by its nationals or on its territory, should not be entitled to initiate court proceedings in relation to crimes committed by other states. Otherwise, non-States Parties would benefit from the advantages of the ICC system without sharing the burdens and obligations assumed by States Parties, such as budgetary contributions and duties of cooperation[650].

Third, any possible decision to treat declarations under Art. 12(3) Rome-Statute as analogous to State Party referrals must include only genuine, not politically motivated declarations ("cry for help"). Since it would be extremely difficult to define the acceptance criteria and circumstances of "genuine declarations", the ICC may be required to assess the motives and background of certain declarations. Such a role is neither provided for in the Rome Statute nor is it desirable from a legal perspective, as it might oblige the court to second guess state intentions or engage in political "motive analysis" before being able to make a judicial determination regarding the appropriate procedure in such cases[651].

The most controversial aspect of Art. 12(3) Rome-Statute was the actual object of declarations made in accordance with the provision, as the wording of the

648 Ronen, "ICC Jurisdiction over Acts Committed in the Gaza Strip – Article 12(3) of the ICC Statute and Non-state Entities", *supra* note 512, p. 10; Stahn, El Zeidy and Olásolo, *supra* note 641, p. 423; Stahn, *supra* note 643, p. 244.

649 Freeland, *supra* note 640, p. 226; Stahn, El Zeidy and Olásolo, *supra* note 641, pp. 423-424.

650 Stahn, El Zeidy and Olásolo, *supra* note 641, pp. 424-425.

651 Stahn, *supra* note 643, p. 247.

latter – the non-State Party may accept ICC jurisdiction "with respect to the crime in question" – is ambiguous in this regard[652]. As a result, it was unclear whether this wording meant (i) one (or more) specific criminal act within the subject-matter jurisdiction of the ICC, or (ii) a specific incident or situation[653]. The controversy was based on the risk of the first interpretation leading to asymmetric liability[654] – i.e. a situation, in which a non-State Party declares its acceptance of ICC jurisdiction with respect to a specific crime, while other crimes, including those perpetrated by its own nationals, are not included in the declaration and, therefore, do not fall within the jurisdiction of the ICC[655].

Although some commentators have taken the view that Art. 12(3) Rome-Statute is flexible enough to allow non-States Parties interested in effectively prosecuting a given crime to accede in relation to that crime only[656], there seems to have been some kind of general agreement, shared by most participants in the deliberations of the Preparatory Committee[657] and most signatory states, that such interpretation of the wording of Art. 12(3) Rome-Statute was not intended and that it could, potentially, distort the meaning and practical relevance of the provision. Furthermore, there was broad agreement within the Preparatory Commission[658] that clarification of this controversial matter should be provided

---

652 Stahn, El Zeidy and Olásolo, *supra* note 641, p. 427.

653 Williams and Schabas, *supra* note 331, Art. 12, para. 17.

654 The US, in particular, objected to what they considered to be the perverse consequences of the first interpretation of the wording of Art. 12(3) Rome-Statute, as they claimed that such interpretation would permit Iraq, as a non-State Party, to invoke the jurisdiction of the ICC over US soldiers and pilots, without requiring the court to scrutinize the conduct of Iraq's regime and military forces (concerning atrocities committed against the people of Iraq) as well.

655 Holmes, John T., "Jurisdiction and Admissibility", in: Lee, Roy S. (ed.), *The International Criminal Court – Elements of Crimes and Rules of Procedure and Evidence*, Ardsley: Transnational Publishers, Inc. (2001), p. 326; Kaul, *supra* note 517, p. 611.

656 Stahn, El Zeidy and Olásolo, *supra* note 641, p. 427.

657 On 11 December 1995, the UN General Assembly decided to establish a Preparatory Committee on the Establishment of an International Criminal Court, which shall (i) discuss the major substantive and administrative issues arising out of the draft statute prepared by the International Law Commission in 1994, and (ii) draft texts with a view to preparing a widely acceptable consolidated text of a convention for an international criminal court as a next step towards consideration by a conference of plenipotentiaries.

658 The Preparatory Commission for the Establishment of an International Criminal Court was established by Resolution F of the Final Act of the United Nations Diplomatic Conference of Plenipotentiaries on the Establishment of an International Criminal Court, which adopted the Rome Statute of the International Criminal Court on 17 July 1998.

in the ICC Rules of Procedure and Evidence, in order to minimize the risk of politically motivated investigations and prosecutions[659].

On 20 June 2000, the Preparatory Commission adopted Rule 44 of the ICC Rules of Procedure and Evidence, which provides (in sub-rule 2) that when a state lodges a declaration pursuant to Art. 12(3) Rome-Statute, the Registrar shall inform the state concerned that such a declaration "has as a consequence the acceptance of jurisdiction with respect to the crimes referred to in article 5 of relevance to the situation". The use of this wording makes it clear that the ICC can consider all crimes within its subject-matter jurisdiction, which arise from a situation referred to it under Art. 12(3) Rome-Statute, without being bound in any way by possible attempts of the accepting state to limit the court's jurisdiction to a certain crime[660].

2.5.2. Implementation in the case at hand

On 21 January 2009, the Palestinian Authority lodged a declaration under Art. 12(3) Rome-Statute with the Registrar of the ICC, in which it accepted the exercise of jurisdiction by the court "for the purpose of identifying, prosecuting and judging the authors and accomplices of acts committed on the territory of Palestine since 1 July 2002". On 23 January 2009, the Registrar acknowledged receipt of the declaration sent by the Palestinian Authority and informed the latter – without prejudice to a judicial determination on the application of Art. 12(3) Rome-Statute to the declaration – of the application of Rule 44, sub-rule 2 of the ICC Rules of Procedure and Evidence, so that the Palestinian declaration shall have the effect of acceptance of jurisdiction with respect to the crimes referred to in Art. 5 Rome-Statute of relevance to the situation[661]. Accordingly, should the Gaza armed conflict reach The Hague, the jurisdiction of the ICC will in no way be limited only to crimes allegedly committed by the Israeli side.

Due to the fact that declarations under Art. 12(3) Rome-Statute do not (automatically) trigger an investigation, but rather only relate to the scope of the ICC's jurisdiction[662], the Prosecutor responded to the Palestinian declaration by announcing that in order to determine whether or not to open an investigation, the Office of the Prosecutor will carefully examine (i) whether the alleged

---

659 Kaul, *supra* note 517, p. 611; Stahn, El Zeidy and Olásolo, *supra* note 641, p. 427; Schabas, *A Commentary on the Rome Statute*, *supra* note 360, Art. 12, p. 289.

660 Holmes, *supra* note 655, p. 327.

661 ICC Registrar, *Acknowledgment of Receipt of the Palestinian Authority's Correspondence of 21 January 2009* (2009).

662 See *supra* note 648.

crimes fall within the category of crimes defined in the Statute, (ii) whether there are national proceedings in relation to those crimes, and most importantly (iii) all relevant issues related to the jurisdiction of the ICC, including whether the declaration by the Palestinian Authority, accepting the exercise of jurisdiction by the ICC, meets statutory requirements[663]. The latter – in combination with the reservation in the Registrar's acknowledgement of receipt – illustrates the uncertainty within the international community as to the existence or non-existence of a State of Palestine[664] and leads to the question of what effect this highly controversial and complex matter could have on the Palestinian declaration – in light of the fact that under Art. 12(3) Rome-Statute only "States" can declare acceptance of ICC jurisdiction on an *ad hoc* basis. The following analysis shall address this question.

2.5.2.1. The Palestinian Authority's declaration as that of a full-fledged state

According to those who support a literal interpretation of Art. 12(3) Rome-Statute, the term "State" therein must be interpreted in accordance with Art. 31(4) of the 1969 Vienna Convention on the Law of Treaties, which provides that "[a] special meaning[665] shall be given to a term [only] if it is established that the parties [to the treaty] so intended". Examples of such cases can be found in Additional Protocol I, where express provision was made for the possibility of a non-state entity lodging a declaration with the depository[666], and the 1982 United Nations Convention on the Law of the Sea, which provides that the Convention shall be open for signature and accession by all states and all territories, which (i) enjoy full internal self-government, recognized as such by the UN, (ii) have not attained full independence in accordance with UN General Assembly Resolution 1514, and (iii) have competence over the matters governed by the Convention – including the competence to enter into treaties concerning such matters[667]. Clearly, when negotiators of international agreements intend for the possibility of acceptance by non-state entities, they provide for it in expressed and unambiguous language[668].

---

663 ICC Office of the Prosecutor, *Visit of the Palestinian National Authority Minister of Foreign Affairs, Mr. Riad al-Malki, and Minister of Justice, Mr. Ali Khashan, to the Prosecutor of the ICC* (2009).

664 ICC, *Declarations Art. 12(3).*

665 Different than the ordinary meaning of the term under international law.

666 Art. 96(3) in conjunction with Art. 1(4) Additional Protocol I.

667 Art. 305(1)(a) and (e), 307 of the 1982 United Nations Convention on the Law of the Sea.

668 Shaw, Malcolm N., *In the Matter of the Jurisdiction of the International Criminal Court with regard to the Declaration of the Palestinian Authority* (2010), para. 7.

Since the Rome Statute gives no special meaning to the term "State" and there is no express provision to support or infer an interpretation that includes entities that do not qualify as such under the general rules of international law, a literal interpretation of Art. 12(3) Rome-Statute would require the existence of a generally recognized State of Palestine as a prerequisite for the application of the provision. In order to conclude whether this requirement was fulfilled on 21 January 2009, the main arguments for and against the existence of a State of Palestine shall be presented, discussed and analyzed.

2.5.2.1.1. Pre-existing Palestinian statehood from the time of the British Mandate

The first argument in favor of the existence of a State of Palestine is based on the claim that Palestine became an international entity upon the demise of the Ottoman Empire in the wake of World War I – as the Ottoman Empire lost sovereignty, a Palestine emerged[669, 670].

Following World War I, the League of Nations established the mandate system, as those colonies and territories, which as a consequence of the war have ceased to be under the sovereignty of the states which formally governed them, were inhabited by peoples not yet able to stand by themselves under the strenuous conditions of the modern world[671]. The first group of mandates – "Class A" mandates – were territories formally controlled by the Ottoman Empire that were deemed to have reached a stage of development where their existence as independent nations can be provisionally recognized, subject to the rendering of administrative advice and assistance by a Mandatory until such time as they are able to stand alone[672]. The British Mandate of Palestine belonged to this class of mandates.

The mandate system was predicated upon the fact that the people of the respective territory were the ultimate holder of sovereignty and that the role of the mandatory power – which did not hold sovereignty – was to promote self-governing institutions, after which it would cease its administration[673]. This claim was supported by the ICJ in its *South West Africa* opinion, in which the

669 Quigley, *The Palestine Declaration to the International Criminal Court: The Statehood Issue*, *supra* note 511, p. 8.

670 This argument pertains solely to the legal status of the territory of Palestine as a state, not to its ethnic character or to the question of Arab rights versus Jewish rights over the territory.

671 Art. 22(1) Covenant of the League of Nations.

672 Art. 22(4) Covenant of the League of Nations.

673 Quigley, *The Palestine Declaration to the International Criminal Court: The Statehood Issue*, *supra* note 511, p. 8; Shaw, *supra* note 668, para. 11.

Court stated that (i) the ultimate objective of the mandate system was the "self-determination and independence of the people concerned"[674], and (ii) under the mandate system, a mandatory power was forbidden to claim title to the territory, the operative principle being "[no] annexation"[675]. The sovereignty of Palestine, despite the British Mandate, is further supported by the fact that Palestine was party to international treaties, which were published in the League of Nations Treaty Series – similar to treaties of other states[676]. Among these treaties, the most indicative was the Agreement between the Post Office of the United Kingdom of Great Britain and Ireland and the Post Office of Palestine for the Exchange of Money Orders, signed in London and Jerusalem on 10 and 23 January 1922, respectively. The significance of this agreement lies in the fact that had Britain and Palestine constituted a single sovereignty, there would have been no point to a treaty between them[677]. Finally, the sovereignty of Palestine was reflected in the arrangement for citizenship. Upon the fall of the Ottoman Empire, the inhabitants of Palestine lost their Ottoman nationality and gained a new nationality, namely that of Palestine. The latter was recognized by other governments which honored Palestine passports. Even though it was Britain who represented individual Palestinians abroad, such individuals were not British nationals[678].

According to this argument, neither the demise of the League of Nations nor the withdrawal of Britain from Palestine in 1948 changed the international recognized status of Palestine, as Art. 80(1) of the Charter of the newly formed United Nations protected the rights of states or peoples under "existing international instruments to which Members of the United Nations may respectively be parties". Britain, as party to the agreement with the League of Nations for mandate in Palestine, fell under this provision. The 1967 Israeli occupation of the

---

674 ICJ, *Legal Consequences for States of the Continued Presence of South Africa in Namibia (South West Africa) Notwithstanding Security Council Resolution 276 (1970)*, *supra* note 249, para. 53.

675 *Ibid.*, para. 50.

676 Such treaties include: (i) International Agreement for the Establishment of an International Bureau of Intelligence on Locusts, 1926, (ii) agreement with Egypt regarding the reciprocal enforcement of judgments, 1929, (iii) bilateral treaties on the exchange of postal parcels with Switzerland, Italy, Greece and France, 1929-1936.

677 Quigley, *The Palestine Declaration to the International Criminal Court: The Statehood Issue*, *supra* note 511, p. 9.

678 *Ibid.*; Quigley, John, *The ICC Prosecutor has Authority to Investigate, and the ICC has Jurisdiction, because the Prosecutor has in Hand a Consent Declaration from the State on whose Territory the Alleged Crimes were Committed*, UCLA School of Law, Human Rights & International Criminal Law Online Forum.

territory of Palestine, over which Egypt and Jordan assumed administration in 1948, also had no impact on the statehood of Palestine, as despite the fact that the latter was deprived of control in its territory, belligerent occupation effects no change in the statehood of territory[679].

Those who object to the possibility of a Palestinian state emerging under the mandatory system base their claim on formal and historical arguments: The first formal argument is based on Art. 94 of the 1920 Treaty of Sèvres[680], which provides that Syria and Mesopotamia (Iraq) were to be "provisionally recognized as independent States subject to the rendering of administrative advice and assistance by a Mandatory until such time as they are able to stand alone" – whereas no such provisional recognition as an independent state was given to Palestine. This (clear) distinction between Syria (including Lebanon) and Mesopotamia (Iraq), on the one hand, and Palestine, on the other, would continue in the language of the diplomatic instruments creating all three League of Nations Mandates in the years that followed[681]. Reason for this distinction is that despite the fact that all three mandates were categorized as "Class A" mandates, they were not uniform entities in internal, constitutional and administrative law. In fact, it would be best to think of the Mandate for Palestine as *sui generis* among mandated territories[682].

The second formal argument pertains to the question of sovereignty. While it is legally correct to say that Britain was never sovereign over Palestine, it is not legally correct to say that Palestine was a sovereign state as from 1922. In fact, in no situation was a mandated territory regarded as a sovereign state prior to the termination of the mandate over the respective territory[683]. The terms of the Palestine Mandate clearly demonstrate the complete absence of any intention that the inhabitants of that territory constitute a state. The extensive competences

---

679 Quigley, *The ICC Prosecutor has Authority to Investigate, and the ICC has Jurisdiction, supra* note 678.

680 The Treaty of Sèvres (1920) was the peace treaty between the Ottoman Empire and the Allies at the end of World War I, according to which the Ottoman Empire relinquished sovereignty over its Asiatic territories to the south of modern-day Turkey. As a result of an internal national uprising, the Treaty of Sèvres was not ratified by the Ottoman Empire. The succeeding state, the new Republic of Turkey, signed a new agreement, the Treaty of Lausanne, in 1923, reconfirming the surrender of all non-Turkish territories and the renunciation of Turkish rights with respect to them.

681 Gold and Morrison, *supra* note 510, pp. 13-14.

682 *Ibid.*, pp. 14-15.

683 Shaw, *supra* note 668, para. 15; Benoliel and Perry, *supra* note 505, p. 88; Crawford, James, "The Creation of the State of Palestine: Too Much Too Soon?", *European Journal of International Law* 1 (1990), p. 312.

granted to the mandatory power[684], coupled with the fact that the consent of the Council of the League of Nations was required for any modification of the terms of the Mandate[685], leave no doubt that the range of powers available to the inhabitants of the territory were far too limited to amount to anything close to the requirements for statehood[686]. Leading legal experts of the time have confirmed this view by concluding that within the mandatory system, sovereignty lied with the League of Nations and was derived from it[687]. Furthermore, supporters of this view agree there is no doubt that over time the right of self-determination was seen as applicable to non-self-governing territories – including mandated and trust territories[688]. However, at no stage was the fact that a (certain group of) people was accepted as having the right to self-determination automatically equated as such to sovereignty and independence. The right of self-determination in international law is the right of a particular people to decide for itself its own political future, not the right to constitute a state as of that moment[689].

The historical argument against the possibility that a Palestinian state already existed from the time of the British Mandate is based on the claim that the pre-state entity was – and was recognized as – an expression of Jewish national rights and, in fact, the precursor to the modern State of Israel, whose claims to

---

684 According to Art. 1 of the Palestine Mandate of 24 July 1922, The Mandatory shall have full powers of legislation and of administration, save as they may be limited by the terms of the Mandate. Such powers include (i) being entrusted with the control of the foreign relations of Palestine and the right to issue exequaturs to consuls appointed by foreign powers, as well as being entitled to afford diplomatic and consular protection to citizens of Palestine when outside its territorial limits – Art. 12, and (ii) the treaty-making competence, being able to adhere on behalf of the Administration of Palestine to any general international conventions already existing, or which may be concluded hereafter with the approval of the League of Nations – Art. 19.

685 Art. 27 of the Palestine Mandate. One modification to the situation was specifically built into the terms of the Mandate in Art. 25, which gave the Mandatory the power to change the provisions of the Mandate with regard to the territories lying between the Jordan and the eastern boundary of Palestine, subject to the consent of the Council of the League of Nations. This provision led to the removal of the area east of the river Jordan in order to create the new territory of Transjordan.

686 Shaw, *supra* note 668, para. 16.

687 Lauterpacht, Elihu (ed.), *International Law – Being the Collected Papers of Hersch Lauterpacht*, Volume 3, Cambridge: Cambridge University Press (1977), p. 68; Gold and Morrison, *supra* note 510, pp. 18-19.

688 See *supra* note 674.

689 Shaw, *supra* note 668, para. 17.

sovereignty are in part based on it[690]. This was reflected in (i) Art. 95(1) of the Treaty of Sèvres, which provides that:

> The Mandatory [entrusted with the administration of Palestine] will be responsible for putting into effect the [Balfour Declaration of 1917][691] in favor of the establishment in Palestine of a national home for the Jewish people, it being clearly understood that nothing shall be done which may prejudice the civil and religious rights of existing non-Jewish communities in Palestine,

and (ii) the Palestine Mandate, which provides that:

> [R]ecognition has [. . .] been given to the historical connection of the Jewish people with Palestine and to the grounds for reconstituting their national home in that country (Preamble para. 3).
>
> The Mandatory shall be responsible for placing the country under such political, administrative and economic conditions as will secure the establishment of the Jewish national home, as laid down in the preamble, and the development of self-governing institutions, and also for safeguarding the civil and religious rights of all the inhabitants of Palestine, irrespective of race and religion (Art. 2).

The only time the Great Powers, who drafted these documents, sought to territorially limit the Jewish national home was in 1922 when they separated from it the East Bank of the Jordan – which years later became the Hashemite Kingdom of Jordan[692]. The rest of Palestine remained the area designated by both the Balfour Declaration and the League of Nations Mandate for the re-establishment of a Jewish homeland[693]. It was only later on, in November 1947, that the UN General Assembly adopted Resolution 181 (II), recommending partition of Palestine by creating two separate, independent Jewish and Arab states in Palestine. Supporters of this view maintain that not only does the above mentioned clearly show that a State of Palestine did not emerge under the British Mandate, any attempt to reinvent the area as an already existing (Arab) State of Palestine would be (i) tantamount to wiping out the historical and legal roots of the State of Israel and the internationally recognized right of the Jewish people to a homeland in Palestine, and (ii) deeply flawed both legally and historically[694].

---

690 Gold and Morrison, *supra* note 510, p. 20.

691 The Balfour Declaration of 2 November 1917 was a letter from the British Foreign Secretary Arthur James Balfour to Baron Rothschild, a leader of the British Jewish community. In the letter, Balfour declared his support for the establishment of a Jewish homeland in the area known as Palestine. This communication was accepted by the Jewish community as Great Britain's support for a Jewish homeland.

692 See *supra* note 685.

693 Gold and Morrison, *supra* note 510, p. 20.

694 *Ibid.*, p. 21; Shaw, *supra* note 668, para. 18.

Despite the fact that this debate has not yet been conclusively decided, it should be mentioned that the possibility of a full-fledged Palestinian state coming into existence upon the demise of the Ottoman Empire (under the mandatory system) is not considered one of the more controversial questions within the highly complex debate regarding Palestinian statehood, as the arguments in favor of such possibility are supported (only) by a small minority of international law scholars.

2.5.2.1.2. The 1988 Palestinian Declaration of Independence

On 15 November 1988, the Palestinian National Council – the legislative body of the PLO – adopted in Algiers the Palestinian Declaration of Independence, which stated that:

> The Palestine National Council hereby declares, in the Name of God and on behalf of the Palestinian Arab people, the establishment of the State of Palestine in the land of Palestine with its capital at Jerusalem [. . .]. The State of Palestine shall be an Arab State and shall be an integral part of the Arab nation, of its heritage and civilization and of its present endeavour for the achievement of the goals of liberation, development, democracy and unity[695].

The Declaration referred to UN General Assembly Resolution 181 (II) as the legitimate authority for the establishment of the State of Palestine by stating:

> Despite the historical injustice done to the Palestinian Arab people in its displacement and in being deprived of the right to self-determination following the adoption of General Assembly resolution 181 (II) of 1947, which partitioned Palestine into an Arab and a Jewish State, that resolution nevertheless continues to attach conditions to international legitimacy that guarantee the Palestinian Arab people the right to sovereignty and national independence.

The Declaration did not stipulate the territorial boundaries of the State of Palestine.

The question concerning the legal significance of the Palestinian Declaration of Independence – i.e. whether as a result of the latter a Palestinian state came into existence[696] – is controversial.

---

695 International Legal Materials, Volume XXVII, No. 1 (1988), pp. 1668-1671.

696 For those who support the existence of a Palestinian state under the British Mandate, the 1988 Palestinian Declaration of Independence was not a declaration of a new statehood, but rather, of an existing statehood. This view is supported by the fact that the 1988 Palestinian declaration referred expressly to the Covenant of the League of Nations, stating "the international community, in article 22 of the Covenant of the League of Nations of 1919 and in the Lausanne Treaty of 1923, recognized that the Palestinian Arab people

2.5.2.1.2.1. UN General Assembly Resolution 43/177

Following the Palestinian Declaration of Independence, PLO Chairman Yasser Arafat was invited to address the UN General Assembly, which subsequently adopted Resolution 43/177, in which it (i) acknowledged the proclamation of the State of Palestine by the Palestine National Council on 15 November 1988, and (ii) decided that the designation "Palestine" should be used in place of the designation "Palestine Liberation Organization" in the UN system – without prejudice to the observer status and functions of the PLO within the UN system[697]. 104 states voted in favor of Resolution 43/177, 44 states abstained and only two states (Israel and the US) voted against it.

Supporters of the argument that a Palestinian state came into existence following the 1988 Declaration of Independence claim that the fact that the majority of the world's states voted in favor of Resolution 43/177 indicates that Palestine was regarded as a state[698]. Furthermore, when considering the negative reaction of the UN to the 1983 declaration of statehood for a "Turkish Republic of Northern Cyprus"[699], one must conclude that had the international community viewed the 1988 Palestinian Declaration of Independence as invalid, it would have said so loudly and clearly. There can be no doubt it did not[700]. Finally, a draft resolution proposed in 1989 in the UN General Assembly, in order to make it clear that the intent of the Assembly was to have the designation "Palestine" construed as the State of Palestine, was not voted on only because the US threatened to withhold its assessed contribution (approximately 25%) to the budget of the UN should the status of "Palestine" / the PLO be upgraded from an observer organization to that of an observer state[701].

---

was no different from the other Arab peoples detached from the Ottoman State and was a free and independent people".

697 UN General Assembly Resolution 43/177 (15 December 1988).

698 Quigley, *The Palestine Declaration to the International Criminal Court: The Statehood Issue*, *supra* note 511, p. 4; Mendes, Errol, *Statehood and Palestine for the Purpose of Article 12(3) of the ICC Statute* (2010), p. 9.

699 The international community found this declaration invalid on the grounds that Turkey had occupied Cypriot territory militarily and that the putative state was an infringement on Cypriot sovereignty. In Resolution 541 (1983) the UN Security Council considered the attempt to create a "Turkish Republic of Northern Cyprus" legally invalid (and one which will contribute to a worsening of the situation in Cyprus) and called for its withdrawal.

700 Quigley, *The Palestine Declaration to the International Criminal Court: The Statehood Issue*, *supra* note 511, p. 4.

701 *Ibid.*, p. 5; Mendes, *supra* note 698, p. 12.

Those who reject this view, on the other hand, claim that in light of the (i) actual text of Resolution 43/177, and (ii) subsequent UN practice, there can be no doubt that Palestine was not regarded as a state following the 1988 declaration[702]. The fact that the decision to use the designation "Palestine" in place of the designation PLO was followed by a clause stating that the change should be undertaken "without prejudice to the observer status and functions of the Palestine Liberation Organization within the United Nations system", clearly shows that Resolution 43/177 was essentially a symbolic move, as the UN did not act in a manner supportive of the declaration of statehood as such, but simply retitled the Palestinian observer delegation while denying substantive change[703]. The very fact that the Palestinian declaration was not declared invalid, as in the case of the "Turkish Republic of Northern Cyprus", cannot be read *a contrario* to mean that such declaration was accepted. It was merely "acknowledged" in Resolution 43/177, which is a neutral term demonstrating knowledge of the fact of the matter in question without further legal consequence[704]. In practice, in the years that followed Resolution 43/177, the PLO Observer Mission continued to physically sit along with other UN observer missions, including the Arab League and the Islamic Conference, and not with the member states of the UN. According to the *Permanent Missions to the United Nations*, published in 2011 by the Executive Office of the Secretary-General, Protocol and Liaison Service, Palestine appears in a special category termed "[e]ntities having received a standing invitation to participate as observers in the sessions and the work of the General Assembly and maintaining permanent observer missions at Headquarters"[705]. Palestine has a special observer status at the UN, but is clearly not accepted as a state by the organization[706].

2.5.2.1.2.2. Palestinian statehood following the 1988 declaration according to the declarative theory of statehood

According to the declarative theory, statehood is acquired by satisfaction of objective criteria. Consequently, since the act of recognition does not confer status,

702 Shaw, *supra* note 668, para. 19.

703 *Ibid.*; Gold and Morrison, *supra* note 510, p. 23; Ronen, "ICC Jurisdiction over Acts Committed in the Gaza Strip – Article 12(3) of the ICC Statute and Non-state Entities", *supra* note 512, pp. 11-12.

704 Shaw, *supra* note 668, para. 19.

705 Executive Office of the Secretary-General, Protocol and Liaison Service, *Permanent Missions to the United Nations – No. 301* (March 2011).

706 Gold and Morrison, *supra* note 510, p. 24; Shaw, *supra* note 668, para. 20.

the former is merely acknowledgment of existing statehood status[707]. The declarative theory of statehood was most famously expressed in the 1933 Convention on Rights and Duties of States ("Montevideo Convention"[708]), which provides that:

> The state as a person of international law should possess the following qualifications: (a) a permanent population; (b) a defined territory; (c) government; and (d) capacity to enter into relations with the other states (Art. 1).
>
> The political existence of the state is independent of recognition by other states. Even before recognition the state has the right to defend its integrity and independence, to provide for its conservation and prosperity, and consequently to organize itself as it sees fit, to legislate upon its interests, administer its services, and to define the jurisdiction and competence of its courts (Art. 3).
>
> The recognition of a state merely signifies that the state which recognizes it accepts the personality of the other with all the rights and duties determined by international law (Art. 6).

Despite the declarative theory's weaknesses – for example, the fact that in practice states do not acquire rights on the international plane until they are recognized and the difficulty in selecting and applying objective statehood criteria unanimously accepted by states – the majority of contemporary scholars and commentators favor this theory[709], as it attempts to prevent a situation, in which state existence depends on subjectivity and individual state discretion[710].

Based on this background information, the question which immediately arises is whether, following the 1988 Palestinian Declaration of Independence, Palestinian statehood has been acquired as a result of the four statehood requirements of the Montevideo Convention being fulfilled.

2.5.2.1.2.2.1. Permanent population

Both supporters and opponents of the Montevideo Convention requirements being fulfilled following the 1988 Palestinian declaration agree that the criterion of permanent population was satisfied prior to and following said declaration[711], as Palestinians (i) were the original Arab inhabitants of the land designated as the

---

707 Worster, William Thomas, "Law, Politics, and the Conception of the State in State Recognition Theory", *Boston University International Law Journal* 27 (2009), p. 118.

708 Signed in Montevideo, Uruguay, on 26 December 1933.

709 Worster, *supra* note 707, p. 119.

710 *Ibid.*, p. 128.

711 ICC Office of the Prosecutor, *Situation in Palestine – Summary of Submissions on whether the Declaration Lodged by the Palestinian National Authority Meets Statutory Requirements* (2010), para. 40.

West Bank and Gaza, and (ii) are a fixed and distinguishable population with identified ethnicity, culture and traditions[712].

2.5.2.1.2.2.2. Territory

The right to be a state is dependent upon the exercise of governmental powers with respect to some area of territory, whereby there appears to be no rule prescribing the minimum size of such area. Furthermore, there is no rule requiring contiguity of the territory of the state, so that little bits of state can be enclaved within other states. Claims to less than the entire territory of a new state, in particular boundary disputes, do not affect statehood[713]. Uncertainty with regard to a state's boundaries cannot affect its territorial rights, as there is no rule that the land frontiers of a state must be fully delimited and defined[714].

Those in support of the 1988 Palestinian declaration leading to statehood base their claim that the territory requirement in the case at hand is given on the fact that it is quite clear from reading the Palestinian declaration – and the attached Political Communiqué – that the PLO contemplated that the new State of Palestine will consist essentially of what has been called the West Bank and Gaza Strip, with its capital being East Jerusalem[715]. In the *Wall* opinion, the ICJ confirmed that all these territories (does not pertain to the Gaza Strip), which were occupied by Israel in 1967, remain occupied territory and cannot be claimed by Israel, so that Palestine retains sovereignty over these territories despite the fact they are under Israeli belligerent occupation[716]. Furthermore, the fact that the Palestinian territories are indeterminate and fragmented has no effect on those territories fulfilling the Montevideo Convention "territory" requirement – the same way (i) Israel is internationally recognized as a state, despite the fact that its borders with the Palestinian territories are far from fixed or determinate, and (ii) Alaska is recognized as a part of the US despite being separated from the contiguous US[717].

---

712 Mendes, *supra* note 698, p. 15; Prince, James L., "The International Legal Implications of the November 1988 Palestinian Declaration of Statehood", *Stanford Journal of International Law* 25 (1989), p. 691.

713 Crawford, James, *The Creation of States in International Law*, 2nd edition, Oxford: Oxford University Press (2006), pp. 46-49.

714 North Sea Continental Shelf Cases (*Federal Republic of Germany v. Denmark; Federal Republic of Germany v. Netherlands*), ICJ (20 February 1969), para. 46.

715 Boyle, Francis A., "The Creation of the State of Palestine", *European Journal of International Law* 1 (1990), p. 302.

716 ICJ, *Legal Consequences of the Construction of a Wall in the Occupied Palestinian Territories*, *supra* note 166, para. 78; Mendes, *supra* note 698, pp. 15-16.

717 Mendes, *supra* note 698, p. 16; Boyle, *supra* note 715, p. 302.

Opponents of this view maintain that the fragmentation and indeterminacy of the Palestinian territories undermine the requirement of a defined territory, noting that borders were one of the permanent status issues left unresolved by the Oslo Accords[718]. Furthermore, such requirement cannot be fulfilled as long as competing claims on certain portions of the territory in question exist[719]. However, based on the definition above, it seems that these claims cannot justify rejection of the "territory" requirement in the case at hand.

2.5.2.1.2.2.3. Government

The requirement that a putative state have an effective government could be regarded as the most important single criterion of statehood, as it provides the basis for all other statehood criteria; international law defines "territory" not by adopting private law analogies of real property, but by reference to the extent of governmental power exercised, or capable of being exercised, with respect to some territory and population[720].

To be a state, an entity must possess a government or a system of government in general control of its territory, to the exclusion of other entities not claiming through or under it. International law lays down no specific requirements as to the nature and extent of this control, except that it includes some degree of maintenance of law and order, and the establishment of basic institutions[721]. Scholars, such as Professor James Crawford, have argued that the four Montevideo Convention requirements really point to the question whether in the specific case an independent state exists – i.e. an organized community on a particular territory, exclusively or substantially exercising self-governing power, with no exercise of (including the right to exercise) such power by another state over the whole of the same territory (principle of state independence)[722].

2.5.2.1.2.2.3.1. Prior to the 1993 Declaration of Principles

With regard to the need to demonstrate effective government as an internationally accepted criterion of statehood, it is quite clear that the prevailing opinion

---

718 Benoliel and Perry, *supra* note 505, p. 95; Mckinney, Kathryn M., "The Legal Effects of the Israeli-PLO Declaration of Principles: Steps Towards Statehood for Palestine", *Seattle University Law Review* 18 (1994), p. 106; Art. V(3) Declaration of Principles.

719 ICC Office of the Prosecutor, *Summary of Submissions on whether the Declaration Lodged by the Palestinian National Authority Meets Statutory Requirements*, *supra* note 711, para. 42.

720 Crawford, *The Creation of States in International Law*, *supra* note 713, pp. 55-56.

721 *Ibid.*, p. 59.

722 Crawford, "The Creation of the State of Palestine: Too Much Too Soon?", *supra* note 683, p. 309; Benoliel and Perry, *supra* note 505, pp. 91-92.

among legal experts is that until the establishment of the Palestinian Authority in 1993 (at the earliest), the Palestinians did not fulfill the factual requisites of statehood, as they had no control over the territory they claimed. The whole territory of Palestine was occupied by Israel, which functioned as a government there and claimed the right to do so until further agreement. The PLO had never functioned as a government and lacked the means to do so, given strong Israeli opposition. Therefore, without even a minimum foundation of control, recognition of Palestinian statehood in the period between 1988 and 1993 – either under the traditional Montevideo test or the more streamlined approach proposed by Crawford and others[723] – would be legally incorrect[724].

Those who do not agree with the prevailing opinion – and maintain that despite full Israeli control over Gaza and the West Bank between 1988 and 1993, the effective government requirement was fulfilled by Palestine – base their claim on the theory that the normal requirement of effective government control over territory is applied less strictly if the belligerent occupant does not claim sovereignty over the occupied territory[725], as when territory is taken via belligerent occupation, sovereignty is not affected and remains vested where it was before the territory was occupied[726]. In the case at hand, this theory can only be considered if it is perceived as a (direct) continuation of the argument in favor of the emergence of the State of Palestine under the British Mandate – based on the claim that the people of Palestine were the ultimate holders of sovereignty, not the mandatory power[727]. Despite the fact that (i) Israel has never claimed sovereignty over the Gaza Strip and the West Bank[728], and (ii) directly and indirectly, the PLO exercised considerable influence within the occupied territories and commanded the allegiance of a significant part of the population of those territo-

723 Davenport, David, Kenneth Anderson, Samuel Estreicher, Eugene Kontorovich, Julian G. Ku and Abraham D. Sofaer, *The Palestinian Declaration and ICC Jurisdiction* (2009), p. 8.

724 Ronen, "ICC Jurisdiction over Acts Committed in the Gaza Strip – Article 12(3) of the ICC Statute and Non-state Entities", *supra* note 512, p. 12; Shaw, *supra* note 668, para. 21; Crawford, *The Creation of States in International Law*, *supra* note 713, p. 437; Benoliel and Perry, *supra* note 505, pp. 86-87; Crawford, "The Creation of the State of Palestine: Too Much Too Soon?", *supra* note 683, pp. 308-309; Prince, *supra* note 712, pp. 693-694.

725 Quigley, *The Palestine Declaration to the International Criminal Court: The Statehood Issue*, *supra* note 511, p. 5.

726 Crawford, *The Creation of States in International Law*, *supra* note 713, p. 73.

727 See *supra* note 673.

728 See *supra* notes 633, 679.

ries[729], when considering the requirement of effective government under the Montevideo Convention and (especially) Crawford's principle of state independence, this argument seems less convincing than the prevailing opinion discussed above.

2.5.2.1.2.2.3.2. Following the 1993 Declaration of Principles

As a result of the Declaration of Principles, much has changed in the Palestinian territories[730], as the former provided, *inter alia*, for the establishment of the Palestinian Interim Self-Government Authority and Palestinian self-rule, for Israeli withdrawal from the Gaza Strip and Jericho, and for the establishment of Palestinian authorities[731]. Whether these significant changes created a situation, in which the statehood requirement of effective government was fulfilled, is controversial.

Those who answer this question in the negative base their claim on the following arguments: First, the Oslo Accords – and the 1995 Israeli-Palestinian Interim Agreement on the West Bank and the Gaza Strip[732] ("Interim Agreement") flowing from it – gave the Palestinian Authority only temporal and limited powers, as the latter was not created by Palestinians independently, but was specifically formed as a provisional body with clearly delineated limits to its authority until status negotiations were completed[733]. The 1995 Interim Agreement split the West Bank and Gaza into three Areas, designated A, B and C, with different security and administrative arrangements and authorities[734] – Area A: full civil and security control by the Palestinian Authority[735]; Area B: Palestinian civil control and joint Israeli-Palestinian security control[736]; Area C: Full Israeli civil and security control, except over Palestinian civilians[737]. Taken together, Areas A and B constitute approximately 40% of the entire West Bank, whereby Area C – which remains under virtually complete Israeli control – con-

---

729 Crawford, "The Creation of the State of Palestine: Too Much Too Soon?", *supra* note 683, p. 309.

730 Benoliel and Perry, *supra* note 505, p. 87.

731 Mckinney, *supra* note 718, p. 99.

732 International Legal Materials, Volume XXXVI, No. 1 (1997), pp. 551 *et seq.*

733 European Centre for Law and Justice, *Legal Memorandum in Opposition to the Palestinian Authority's January 2009 Attempt to Accede to ICC Jurisdiction over Alleged Acts Committed on Palestinian Territory Since 1 July 2002* (2009), p. 17; Mendes, *supra* note 698, pp. 16-17.

734 Art. XI Interim Agreement.

735 Art. XI(2)(b), XIII(1) Interim Agreement.

736 Art. XI(2)(b), XIII(2)(a) Interim Agreement.

737 Art. XI(2)(c), IV(4) (Annex III) Interim Agreement.

stitutes the remainder[738]. In addition, Art. XII(1) Interim Agreement provides that:

> Israel shall continue to carry the responsibility for defense against external threats, including the responsibility for protecting the Egyptian and Jordanian borders, and for defense against external threats from the sea and from the air, as well as the responsibility for overall security of Israelis and Settlements, for the purpose of safeguarding their internal security and public order, and will have all the powers to take the steps necessary to meet this responsibility.

Finally, Art. XXXI(7) Interim Agreement provides that "[n]either side shall initiate or take any step that will change the status of the West Bank and the Gaza Strip pending the outcome of the permanent status negotiations" – whereby according to Art. XXXI(5) Interim Agreement:

> It is understood that these negotiations shall cover remaining issues, including: Jerusalem, refugees, settlements, security arrangements, borders, relations and cooperation with other neighbors, and other issues of common interest.

In light of these very severe limitations the Palestinian Authority was subjected to, there is no legal base for a claim supporting Palestinian effective government in the West Bank and Gaza following the 1993 Declaration of Principles[739].

Second, any possible argument in support of Palestinian effective government in the Palestinian territories following the 1993 Declaration of Principles has been severely weakened by Hamas – a sponsor of terrorism and listed as a terrorist organization by several countries, including the US, the European Union ("EU") and Canada – violently seizing control over the Gaza Strip in June 2007[740]. The Hamas, which openly rejects the Palestinian Authority and the ideology of the PLO[741], has since seized control over all internal civil administrative

---

738 European Centre for Law and Justice, *supra* note 733, p. 18.

739 Ash, Robert Weston, *Is Palestine a "State"? A Response to Professor John Quigley's Article, "The Palestine Declaration to the International Criminal Court: The Statehood Issue"*, Rutgers Law Record (2009), pp. 192-193; ICC Office of the Prosecutor, *Summary of Submissions on whether the Declaration Lodged by the Palestinian National Authority Meets Statutory Requirements*, *supra* note 711, para. 47.

740 Mendes, *supra* note 698, p. 35; See *supra* note 12.

741 In February 2010 Hamas and Fatah began talks aimed at reconciliation. In April 2011 the two parties announced an agreement, according to which (i) a joint transitional government of technocrats shall be formed as preparation for presidential and legislative elections to be held in 2012, (ii) Hamas shall be permitted to enter into the PLO, and (iii) the Palestinian Authority and Hamas shall continue to handle security in the West Bank and Gaza Strip, respectively, whereby a joint security committee shall be formed

agencies, religious institutions, the education system, judicial organs and religious / militant police forces in the Gaza Strip. The Palestinian Authority and/or the PLO have lost all control and influence over public institutions and services in the Gaza Strip, as those of their sympathizers remaining in the Gaza Strip risked persecution and death at the hands of Hamas[742]. The declared aim of the peace negotiations between the State of Israel and the PLO – the recognized representative of the Palestinian people[743] – was, *inter alia*, to establish a Palestinian Interim Self-Government Authority to enable the Palestinian people in the West Bank and Gaza Strip to govern themselves during a transitional period, leading to a permanent settlement between the parties[744]. The fact that since June 2007 Palestinian Authority governance in the Gaza Strip has been completely nonexistent (i) significantly reduces the portion of Palestinian territory under the effective government of the Palestinian Authority, and (ii) limits the claim in support of Palestinian effective government following the Declaration of Principles, as Art. IV of the latter provides that Israel and the PLO "view the West Bank and the Gaza Strip as a single territorial unit, whose integrity will be preserved during the interim period"[745].

Hamas' complete control of the Gaza Strip since 2007 raises the possibility of Gaza as a sovereign state under the government of Hamas[746]. Despite the fact that under the Montevideo Convention requirements, some would consider this to be more than a theoretical possibility, this option will not be discussed in this analysis, as the declaration under Art. 12(3) Rome-Statute, which is the subject-matter of this section, was lodged with the ICC by the Palestinian Authority, not the Hamas Government[747].

Those who maintain that the changes brought about by the Declaration of Principles and subsequent agreements between Israel and the PLO did create a situation, in which the statehood requirement of effective government was fulfilled, claim the following: First, the statehood requirements of the Montevideo

to decide future security arrangements. It still remains to be seen if and how this agreement will be implemented.

742 Davenport, *et al.*, *supra* note 723, pp. 9-11; Brown, Nathan J., "The Hamas-Fatah Conflict: Shallow but Wide", *Fletcher Forum of World Affairs* 34.2 (2010), pp. 42-44.

743 UN General Assembly Resolutions 3210 (XXIX) of 14 October 1974 and 3236 (XXIX) of 22 November 1974.

744 Art. I, III(1) Declaration of Principles.

745 See also Art. XI(1) Interim Agreement.

746 Ronen, "ICC Jurisdiction over Acts Committed in the Gaza Strip – Article 12(3) of the ICC Statute and Non-state Entities", *supra* note 512, Footnote 18; Benoliel and Perry, *supra* note 505, pp. 101-108.

747 See *supra* note 509.

Convention should not be mechanically applied in all situations in which statehood is strived for, as in certain cases, in which all other requirements are fulfilled, the right to self-determination[748] could be more important than an effective government[749]. In 1974 the UN expressly recognized the Palestinian people's right of self-determination – when the UN General Assembly reaffirmed "the inalienable rights of the Palestinian people in Palestine", including "[t]he right to self-determination without external interference"[750] – and by the time of the 1988 Palestinian Declaration of Independence, said right was fully developed as a principle of international law and a universal human right[751]. In support of this argument, its advocates make reference to the Democratic Republic of the Congo – which was admitted as a member state of the UN in September 1960, despite the fact that Belgium was still in full control of the country and the Congolese authorities were in no sense the effective government thereof[752] – and Guinea-Bissau, which was accepted as a member state of the UN in September 1974, despite being under the active control of Portugal[753].

Those who oppose this argument agree that these states were recognized based on their right to self-determination and before their aspirant governments exercised effective control over their entire territory. However, they maintain that both examples cannot be compared with and, thus, do not apply to the Palestinian situation. In the case of the Democratic Republic of the Congo, the latter was recognized as a state and admitted to the UN because Belgium, which had the right to govern and exercise authority in the country, surrendered that

---

748 Declaration on Principles of International Law concerning Friendly Relations and Co-operation among States in accordance with the Charter of the United Nations: "By virtue of the principle of equal rights and self-determination of peoples enshrined in the Charter of the United Nations, all peoples have the right freely to determine, without external interference, their political status and to pursue their economic, social and cultural development, and every State has the duty to respect this right in accordance with the provisions of the Charter".

749 Mendes, *supra* note 698, p. 11.

750 UN General Assembly Resolution 3236 (XXIX) of 22 November 1974; Quigley, John, "David v. Goliath: Humanitarian and Human Rights Law in Light of the Palestinian Right of Self-Determination and Right to Recapture Territory Taken by Force", *NYU Journal of International Law and Politics* 21 (1989), p. 490.

751 ICJ, *Legal Consequences for States of the Continued Presence of South Africa in Namibia (South West Africa) Notwithstanding Security Council Resolution 276 (1970), supra* note 249, para. 52; ICJ, *Western Sahara, supra* note 176, para. 55.

752 Quigley, *The Palestine Declaration to the International Criminal Court: The Statehood Issue, supra* note 511, p. 6.

753 *Ibid.*, pp. 6-7.

right to the new entity. Since a new state, which is granted full formal independence by a former sovereign, has the international right to govern its territory, such entity will be recognized as a state even before it can actually exercise effective government in said territory. This is not the case in secessionary situations, in which the seceding entity must exercise effective and stable government, in order to obtain statehood[754]. With regard to Guinea-Bissau, recognition of statehood was extended in that case only after (full) effective government control was being exercised over at least part of the claimed territory. This is still not the case in the Palestinian territories following the Declaration of Principles[755].

Second, the statehood requirements of the Montevideo Convention were significantly influenced by the fact that the treaty arose out of a meeting of independent Latin American states, which had emerged out of colonial status and were eager to demonstrate their full personality to the world and counter any last vestige of claims by their former colonial masters[756]. Consequently, the Montevideo Convention requirements are simply not "designed" to provide an objective and reliable "statehood formula" in more modern scenarios – which increasingly involve secessionist movements and belligerent occupation – and, perhaps, are no longer representative of customary international law. In particular, the requirement of effective and independent government cannot be automatically applied in cases of belligerent occupation, as in such cases it is almost certain that the pre-existing government would lack the capacity to function independently in a wide variety of governmental spheres while still under occupation. Instead, it should be examined whether despite the circumstances that limit general government powers over the claimed territory, there are legitimate representatives of the (occupied) people, who are asserting the sovereignty of such people under the right to self-determination. Should this be the case, the focus should be on whether (i) these representatives are rightly exercising their claim to represent the sovereign rights of the people under an asserted international legal personality, and (ii) such legitimate representation will seek an independent and full capacity to govern once the occupation ends[757].

Advocates of this argument name the cases of Bosnia (the Republic of Bosnia and Herzegovina) and Kosovo (the Republic of Kosovo) as examples of states / entities that declared independence despite the fact that their aspirant

754 Crawford, *The Creation of States in International Law*, *supra* note 713, pp. 57-58.

755 See *supra* note 739.

756 Mendes, *supra* note 698, p. 14.

757 *Ibid.*, pp. 17-18; Quigley, *The ICC Prosecutor has Authority to Investigate, and the ICC has Jurisdiction*, *supra* note 678.

governments lacked the capacity to function independently in a wide variety of governmental spheres – as a result of belligerent occupation of their territory. Bosnia was recognized as a state by the US and the European Community on 2 April 1992. At the time of recognition, the capital of the new state was in effect under siege by the Bosnian Serb militias and the Yugoslav army, and the government of Alija Izetbegovic had very limited control over the territory of the state and its borders. Despite these circumstances, Bosnia was admitted as a member state of the UN on 22 May 1992. Kosovo declared independence on 17 February 2008 in the aftermath of the civil war with Serbia and military intervention by NATO. Despite the fact that the territory has been under interim administration of the United Nations Mission in Kosovo since 1999 (and the European Union Rule of Law Mission in Kosovo since 2008), to date, 85 UN member states have recognized the independence of Kosovo – including Germany, Italy, Australia, Poland, Turkey, Croatia, Denmark, Japan, Canada, and three UN Security Council members, the US, the United Kingdom and France – and it has become a member of the IMF and the World Bank.

Advocates of this argument further maintain that applying this more modern approach to the Palestinian situation shows that the Palestinian Authority fulfills the requirements of statehood despite the lack of effective government resulting from belligerent occupation. The PLO, which established the Palestinian Authority, is neither a state nor an international organization. It derives its legal status from being the legitimate representative of the sovereign Palestinian people[758] and it reflects the recognized right of that people to self-determination. Furthermore, there can be no doubt that once Israel's occupation of the Palestinian territories ends, the Palestinian Authority will immediately seek to broaden its authority, in order to create an independent and fully effective government in Palestine.

Those who oppose this argument point out a few significant weakness, which create serious doubt whether this theory can be successfully applied in the case of the Palestinian territories: First, this argument is based on the Palestinians being a sovereign people under occupation[759], so that the Declaration of Principles should be taken as a method of resolving a belligerent occupation under UN Security Council Resolutions 242 and 338, and agreeing on the division of powers and territorial jurisdiction within the occupied territory between two existing states, while the belligerent occupation continues[760]. This conflicts with the widely accepted view discussed above that in no situation was a mandated

758 See *supra* note 743.

759 Mendes, *supra* note 698, p. 26; See *supra* note 673.

760 Mendes, *supra* note 698, p. 24.

territory regarded as a sovereign state prior to the termination of the mandate over the respective territory[761]. Second, the example of Bosnia brought in support of this argument, involves a situation, in which the government of the nascent state is not in effective control of its claimed territory, because it is in a situation of civil war. In this category of cases, the key issue as to the determination of claimed statehood is admission to the UN, which removes all doubt as to the asserted statehood. Since Bosnia was admitted as a member state of the UN, that situation is remarkably different and, thus, inapplicable to the Palestinian situation[762]. Finally, despite the broad support and recognition Kosovo received upon its 2008 declaration of independence, Kosovo statehood is still controversial and opposed by a number of major states. Furthermore, Kosovo has not been admitted as a member state of the UN, so that it cannot serve as precedent in support of Palestinian statehood[763].

2.5.2.1.2.2.4. Capacity to enter into relations with the other states

This requirement – which is closely related to the requirement of effective government[764] – shall be discussed at length below[765].

2.5.2.1.2.3. Palestinian statehood following the 1988 declaration according to the constitutive theory of statehood

According to the constitutive theory of statehood, an entity is a state if, and only if, it is recognized as such by other states[766]. This 19th century theory does not suggest that a state is not in existence as long as it is not recognized, but rather that international law takes no notice of it before its recognition. Through recognition only and exclusively, a state becomes an international person and a subject of international law[767]. Consequently, entities not recognized as states are not bound by international law, nor are recognized existing states so bound in their dealings with them[768]. Many states and scholars assert that the declarative

761 See *supra* note 683.

762 Shaw, *supra* note 668, para. 23.

763 *Ibid.*

764 Crawford, *The Creation of States in International Law*, *supra* note 713, p. 62; See *supra* note 724.

765 See Chapter Two – 2.5.2.2.3.1 and 2.5.2.2.3.4.

766 Crawford, "The Creation of the State of Palestine: Too Much Too Soon?", *supra* note 683, p. 309.

767 Oppenheim, Lassa, *International Law – A Treatise*, 7th edition, Volume 1, London: Longmans, Green and Co. Ltd. (1952), p. 122.

768 Hillier, Tim, *Sourcebook on Public International Law*, London: Cavendish Publishing Limited (1998), p. 201.

theory, not the constitutive theory, predominates in practice. Reason for this is a number of significant weaknesses related to the constitutive theory:

(i) The fact that recognition is not automatic, but rather based on the discretion of other states, (theoretically) permits states to ignore the facts – i.e. the existence of a state, acting as such and acknowledged as such by the nationals and perhaps neighbors thereof;
(ii) There is a need for the law to reflect facts. Any other conclusion would result in the assignment of recognition to the purely (subjective) political process rather than the justiciable, rights-based process[769];
(iii) On an ethical level, it is questionable whether other, existing states should be the gatekeeper to the international plane – a situation, which could lead to larger, more powerful states using recognition as a tool for their continued domination of other states[770];
(iv) Since there is no rule that majority recognition is binding on third states in international law, the extreme subjectivity of the constitutive theory could lead to the unacceptable situation, in which a putative state exists only for states that have – formally or informally – recognized it[771].

Since the 1988 Palestinian Declaration of Independence, a number of developments have taken place, which led advocates of Palestinian statehood to claim that under the constitutive theory of statehood, Palestine has been effectively recognized as a state by the international community. As can be expected, this claim was met with opposition and is far from being accepted as the consensus view.

2.5.2.1.2.3.1. Formal and informal recognition by other states

In support of Palestinian statehood, its advocates maintain that shortly after the 1988 Declaration of Independence, Palestine was (formally) recognized by 89[772] states, which is far more than the handful of states that recognized the State of Israel in the period after its declaration of independence[773]. The fact that many, if not most, of the states that recognized Palestinian statehood were not from the western world cannot invalidate the legal consequences of such recognition. It would be an undermining of any traditional conception of customary interna-

769 Worster, *supra* note 707, p. 120.

770 *Ibid.*, pp. 120-121.

771 *Ibid.*, p. 128; Crawford, "The Creation of the State of Palestine: Too Much Too Soon?", *supra* note 683, p. 309.

772 Over time, the number of states recognizing the State of Palestine grew to 129.

773 Quigley, *The Palestine Declaration to the International Criminal Court: The Statehood Issue*, *supra* note 511, p. 5; Mendes, *supra* note 698, p. 9.

tional law to make any established majority state practice and emerging *opinio juris* to be dependent on the consent of a certain minority group of states. The fact that a majority of states have recognized Palestine should suffice to consider the latter a state, in accordance with the constitutive theory of statehood[774].

Opponents of this view raise two objections thereto: First, a proclamation of independence, even with substantial subsequent recognition as in the case at hand, does not suffice to create a state. While statehood is no longer exclusively a factual matter, it is still primarily dependent on fulfillment of factual requisites, namely, effective governmental control over a population in a specified territory[775]. Second, given that there is no rule that majority recognition is binding on third states in international law[776], the fact that Palestine has not been recognized by crucial local and international actors – such as the US, the EU, the Russian Federation[777] and Israel – supersedes, for the purpose of the constitutive theory of statehood, the recognition it did receive from other states[778].

Proponents of a Palestinian state further maintain that recognition (of statehood) need not be expressed in a formal document. If states treat an entity as a state, then they are considered to recognize it[779]. According to this view, Palestine was recognized in this informal manner by Israel when prior to the signing of the 1993 Declaration of Principles, Israel's Prime Minister, Yitzhak Rabin, demanded that the PLO recognize Israel[780]. Since only sovereign states can rec-

---

774 Mendes, *supra* note 698, pp. 9, 33.

775 Ronen, "ICC Jurisdiction over Acts Committed in the Gaza Strip – Article 12(3) of the ICC Statute and Non-state Entities", *supra* note 512, p. 12.

776 See *supra* note 771.

777 These three crucial actors, together with the UN, make up the Quartet on the Middle East, established in Madrid in 2002, in order to mediate in the Israeli-Palestinian peace process. The fact that members of the Quartet did not recognize Palestinian statehood became obvious in 2002 when the Quartet adopted and endorsed the "Road Map", which called for a future independent Palestinian state living side-by-side with Israel in peace (in his speech of 24 June 2002, President George W. Bush stated "[m]y vision is two states, living side by side in peace and security. There is simply no way to achieve that peace until all parties fight terror. Yet, at this critical moment, if all parties will break with the past and set out on a new path, we can overcome the darkness with the light of hope. Peace requires a new and different Palestinian leadership, so that a Palestinian state can be born").

778 Mendes, *supra* note 698, p. 33.

779 Quigley, *The Palestine Declaration to the International Criminal Court: The Statehood Issue*, *supra* note 511, p. 7.

780 Israel Ministry of Foreign Affairs, *Israel - PLO Recognition: Exchange of Letters between PM Rabin and Chairman Arafat* (1993).

ognize other states[781], if Israel did not regard Palestine as a state, there would have been no point in asking it for recognition. Israel was clearly dealing with Palestine as a state. The same principle could be applied to the international community as well, which encouraged Palestine to recognize Israel, in order to allow the peace process to commence[782].

Those who oppose this argument, base their claim on the Declaration of Principles, which provides that:

> The Government of the State of Israel and the PLO [. . .] agree that it is time to put an end to decades of confrontation and conflict, recognize their mutual legitimate and political rights, and strive to live in peaceful coexistence and mutual dignity and security and achieve a just, lasting and comprehensive peace settlement and historic reconciliation through the agreed political process (Preamble).
>
> The aim of the Israeli-Palestinian negotiations within the current Middle East peace process is, among other things, to establish a Palestinian Interim Self-Government Authority [. . .] for a transitional period not exceeding five years, leading to a permanent settlement based on Security Council Resolutions 242 and 338. It is understood that [. . .] the negotiations on the permanent status will lead to the implementation of Security Council resolutions 242 and 338 (Art. I).

This wording clearly shows that the establishment of a Palestinian state was meant to be the outcome of a (future) mutual agreement between the parties, which, in turn, contradicts the possibility of implicit Israeli recognition of Palestine prior to signing of such agreement[783]. In addition, based on the Oslo Accords, the parties have produced a series of bilateral agreements grounded in UN Security Council Resolutions 242 and 338[784]. All these agreements endorse the principle of Israel relinquishing land in exchange for peace, intentionally avoiding formal adherence to a notion of pre-existing Palestinian statehood[785].

2.5.2.1.2.3.2. Palestine's special status at the UN

Supporters of Palestinian statehood argue that since the 1988 Palestinian Declaration of Independence, the actions and conduct of several UN organs[786] clearly show that Palestine has been assimilated to a state[787].

---

781 Anti-Defamation League, *The United Nations and Palestinian Statehood: Scenarios and Realities* (2011), p. 1.

782 Quigley, *The Palestine Declaration to the International Criminal Court: The Statehood Issue*, *supra* note 511, p. 7.

783 Benoliel and Perry, *supra* note 505, p. 96.

784 See *supra* note 624.

785 Benoliel and Perry, *supra* note 505, p. 83.

786 Whereby the actions and conduct of these UN organs reflect the position and opinions of (at least the majority of) their member states.

The UN General Assembly, which in 1974 invited the PLO to participate in the sessions and the work of the General Assembly in the capacity of observer[788], upgraded the status of the PLO in December 1988, when it decided that the PLO shall be entitled "to have [its] communications relating to the sessions and work of the General Assembly issued and circulated directly, and without intermediary, as official documents of the Assembly"[789]. In 1998, the General Assembly decided to further expand Palestine's "rights and privileges of participation in the sessions and work of the General Assembly", including (i) "[t]he right to participate in the general debate of the General Assembly", (ii) "the right of inscription on the list of speakers under agenda items other than Palestinian and Middle East issues at any meeting of the plenary after the last Member State inscribed on the list of that meeting", (iii) "[t]he right to reply", (iv) "[t]he right to raise points of order related to the proceedings on Palestinian and Middle East issues, provided that [such a] right shall not include the right to challenge the decision of the presiding officer", and (v) "[t]he right to co-sponsor draft resolution and decisions on Palestinian and Middle East issues"[790]. The fact that the PLO / Palestine moved from observer status to enjoying rights and privileges normally reserved for member states, reflects its special status at the UN General Assembly and supports the argument that Palestine has been assimilated to a state[791].

In addition, since 1975 the PLO has been invited routinely by the UN Security Council to participate in discussions concerning the Palestinian issue. These invitations were given under Rule 37 of the Provisional Rules of Procedure of the Security Council, which provides that:

> Any member of the [UN] which is not a member of the Security Council may be invited, as the result of a decision of the Security Council, to participate, without vote, in the discussion of any question brought before the Security Council when the Security Council considers that the interests of that Member are specially affected, or when a Member brings a matter to the attention of the Security Council in accordance with Article 35 (1) of the [UN] Charter.

---

787 Gowlland-Debbas, Vera, *Note on the Legal Effects of Palestine's Declaration under Article 12(3) of the ICC Statute* (2010), para. 4.

788 UN General Assembly Resolution 3237 (XXIX) of 22 November 1974.

789 UN General Assembly Resolution 43/160 A (9 December 1988).

790 UN General Assembly Resolution 52/250 (7 July 1998).

791 Gowlland-Debbas, *supra* note 787, para. 4; Ronen, "ICC Jurisdiction over Acts Committed in the Gaza Strip – Article 12(3) of the ICC Statute and Non-state Entities", *supra* note 512, p. 13.

This, in combination with the fact that under Security Council rules only states are entitled to participate in meetings of the Security Council[792], shows that the UN deals with Palestine as a state[793].

Finally, despite the fact that according to Art. 66(2) ICJ-Statute only states and international organizations can participate in ICJ advisory proceedings, in the *Wall* opinion, the Court decided that "taking into account the fact that the General Assembly had granted Palestine a special status of observer and that the latter was co-sponsor of the draft resolution requesting the advisory opinion", Palestine shall be entitled to submit a written statement on the question and take part in the public hearings, during which oral statements and comments can be presented to the Court "by the United Nations and its Member States"[794]. By doing so, the ICJ assimilated Palestine to a state, in order to allow the Court to effectively address the request for an advisory opinion put to it by the UN General Assembly[795].

Those who oppose this view, claim that while the PLO, in its designation as Palestine, enjoys a status that is higher than that of other non-state observers to the UN, it remains the representative of a non-state entity[796]. In the UN General Assembly, Palestine is not allowed to vote[797] and is not included in the listing of "[n]on-member States having received a standing invitation to participate as observers in the sessions and the work of the General Assembly and maintaining permanent observer missions at Headquarters". Instead, it is listed among "[e]ntities having received a standing invitation to participate as observers in the sessions and the work of the General Assembly and maintaining permanent observer missions at Headquarters"[798] – a fact that clearly contradicts the argument concerning the assimilation of Palestine to a state at the UN[799]. Furthermore, prior to its role as a member of the Quartet[800], the UN was clear on its view that

---

792 Rule 14 of the Provisional Rules of Procedure of the UN Security Council.

793 Quigley, *The Palestine Declaration to the International Criminal Court: The Statehood Issue*, *supra* note 511, p. 5; Mendes, *supra* note 698, p. 12; Gowlland-Debbas, *supra* note 787, para. 4.

794 ICJ, *Legal Consequences of the Construction of a Wall in the Occupied Palestinian Territories*, *supra* note 166, paras. 4, 5.

795 Gowlland-Debbas, *supra* note 787, para. 4.

796 Ronen, "ICC Jurisdiction over Acts Committed in the Gaza Strip – Article 12(3) of the ICC Statute and Non-state Entities", *supra* note 512, p. 13.

797 UN General Assembly Resolution 52/250 (7 July 1998).

798 See *supra* note 705.

799 Davenport, *et al.*, *supra* note 723, p. 5; European Centre for Law and Justice, *supra* note 733, pp. 15-16.

800 See *supra* note 777.

Palestinian statehood had not yet become a reality, through its official policy to support a negotiated final two state solution as of 2000[801].

With regard to the UN Security Council, the opposing view – namely that the Council does not regard Palestine as a state – is based on the explicit wording of its resolutions. For example, in Resolution 1860 of 8 January 2009, the Security Council (i) stressed that the Gaza Strip constitutes an integral part of the territory occupied by Israel in 1967 and "will be a part of the Palestinian state", and (ii) called for renewed efforts by the parties to achieve a comprehensive peace "based on the vision" of a region where two democratic states, Israel and Palestine, live side by side in peace[802]. This is to say that the Gaza Strip will be part of the Palestinian state, which will emerge if and when the peace process between the parties is concluded successfully[803]. Supporters of this view reach the same conclusion with regard to the ICJ and maintain that despite the fact that Palestine was allowed to participate in the proceedings of the *Wall* opinion, it is not a state. Given the advisory opinion context, in which the ICJ may rely upon international organizations as well as states, the fact that the Court allowed a representative of the Palestinian Authority to submit arguments does not set a precedent regarding Palestinian statehood. Indeed, had this been contentious proceedings, where only states may participate[804], the Palestinian Authority would have been excluded[805]. Furthermore, in the very same advisory opinion, in which the ICJ permitted Palestinian participation, the Court confirmed that the Palestinian territories have not achieved statehood[806].

In addition to the above mentioned (main) UN organs, those who oppose the argument that Palestine has been assimilated to a state by the UN, point out that Palestine's efforts to gain membership in several international organizations connected to the UN have not been successful: In 1989, the PLO applied for membership in the WHO. The latter subsequently voted to postpone action on the application and since then never came to a conclusion on the issue of Pales-

801 Reflected in UN General Assembly Resolution 54/42 (1 December 1999), entitled "[p]eaceful settlement of the question of Palestine".

802 Similar wording was used in UN Security Council Resolutions 1397 (12 March 2002) and 1850 (16 December 2008).

803 Davenport, *et al.*, *supra* note 723, p. 6.

804 Art. 34(1) ICJ-Statute; See *supra* note 100.

805 Davenport, *et al.*, *supra* note 723, p. 6.

806 Ash, *supra* note 739, p. 196; ICJ, *Legal Consequences of the Construction of a Wall in the Occupied Palestinian Territories*, *supra* note 166, Separate Opinion of Judge Elaraby, para. 2.3; Gold and Morrison, *supra* note 510, p. 4.

tine membership or statehood[807]. In the same year, a request for the admission of the State of Palestine – as a member state – to the United Nations Educational, Scientific and Cultural Organization ("UNESCO") was submitted. The UNESCO Executive Board deferred consideration of the Palestinian application, while adopting measures to ensure that Palestine had the fullest possible opportunity (short of membership) of participation in the work of the organization[808, 809]. In June 1989, The PLO submitted to the Government of Switzerland – as the depository of the 1949 Geneva Conventions and the 1977 Protocols – ratification documents for the Geneva Conventions. As ratification of the four Conventions is open only to "Powers", the validity of the Palestinian documents depended on the question of Palestinian statehood. In the Note of Information, which Switzerland addressed to states parties, the former reported that it had declined to accept "communication" from the permanent observer of Palestine to the UN office in Geneva, acceding to the Conventions and Protocols, on the grounds that:

> Due to the uncertainty within the international community as to the existence or the non-existence of a State of Palestine and as long as the issue has not been settled in an appropriate framework, the Swiss Government [. . .] is not in a position to decide whether this communication can be considered as an instrument of accession in the sense of the relevant provisions of the Conventions and their additional Protocols[810].

The reluctance of the Swiss Government to take a position on the question of Palestinian statehood, as such position could have had implications for many other members of the international community[811], contradicts the argument that following the 1988 Palestinian Declaration of Independence, Palestine has been

807 The Palestinian WHO effort was "blocked" by the US, which following the PLO's membership application, informed the WHO that its funding – the US provided approximately one quarter of the WHO's funding at the time – would be withheld if Palestine was admitted as a member state. This was described by Yasser Arafat as "blackmail".

808 UNESCO Executive Board, *Report by the Director-General on Appropriate Ways and Means of Giving Effect to Paragraph 8(a) of 131 EX/Decision 9.4* (29 September 1989).

809 On 31 October 2011, Palestine became a full member of UNESCO. The membership was approved by delegates in a vote of 107-14, with 52 abstentions.

810 Crawford, "The Creation of the State of Palestine: Too Much Too Soon?", *supra* note 683, p. 311; Embassy of Switzerland, Note of Information sent to States Parties to the Convention and Protocols (13 September 1989).

811 Quigley, *The Palestine Declaration to the International Criminal Court: The Statehood Issue*, *supra* note 511, p. 4.

assimilated to a state by (a majority of) member states of the UN and other highly significant international treaties and organizations[812].

2.5.2.1.3. Interim conclusion: Full-fledged state

Based on the arguments discussed above, providing one definite and decisive answer to the question of whether a full-fledged State of Palestine existed on 21 January 2009, would be almost impossible, as many of the contradicting arguments brought by both "camps" are historically correct and legally persuasive. That being said, the conclusion of this section will not be left open, as one remaining argument provides the missing and decisive piece required to complete the "puzzle": Statehood is a claim of right and not only of fact, so that effective government over population in the territory and international recognition do not constitute statehood if the respective entity does not claim such status[813]. This provides a very accurate description of the Palestinian Authority, which despite coming very close to fulfilling the factual requirements of statehood following the 1993 Declaration of Principles and the subsequent transfer of autonomous government powers by Israel, chose (and legally undertook) not to claim that a State of Palestine already exists[814]. Therefore, the final conclusion that on 21 January 2009 a full-fledged State of Palestine did not exist, is the direct result of the Palestinians making no claim to that effect – as reflected in the following examples:

---

812 The ICC has always treated (and continues to treat) Palestine as an organization and not as a state. Examples therefor include: (i) Palestine was not credentialed as a "Participating State" at the Rome Conference of 1998, which resulted in the creation of the ICC. Instead, it was placed under the category of "Other Organizations" in the diplomatic roster of the Conference, (ii) in subsequent meetings of the ICC Preparatory Commission (in New York City, April 2002), Palestine was present in the category of "Entities, intergovernmental organizations and other bodies having received a standing invitation to participate as observers in the sessions and the work of the General Assembly" – not as a "State", (iii) at the ICC States Parties meeting in New York City (February 2009), Palestine was grouped with "Entities, intergovernmental organizations, and other entities" – not "Observer States" nor "States invited to be present during the work of the Assembly". The same practice was evident most recently at the Review Conference in Kampala (June 2010).

813 Ronen, "ICC Jurisdiction over Acts Committed in the Gaza Strip – Article 12(3) of the ICC Statute and Non-state Entities", *supra* note 512, p. 13; Crawford, *The Creation of States in International Law*, *supra* note 713, p. 211.

814 Pertains to the Palestinian Authority and the PLO.

2.5.2.1.3.1. Statements and declarations by PLO and Palestinian Authority leaders concerning the future Palestinian state

Over the years, long after the 1988 Palestinian Declaration of Independence, Palestinian leaders made the following statements when referring to a Palestinian state: In 1995, in the heydays of the Oslo peace process, PLO and Palestinian Authority Chairman, Yasser Arafat, proclaimed "[w]e are approaching [the time] to declare an independent Palestinian state and its capital in nobel Jerusalem. I mean it. I mean it"[815].

On 27 March 2002, at the Arab Summit in Beirut, Arafat stated that:

> We are all confident in the inevitability of victory, as well as in the inevitability of achieving our national and Pan-Arab goals [. . .] including the right of return, the right to self-determination and the establishment of the independent state of Palestine, with holy Jerusalem as its capital[816].

On 23 February 2004, during the oral proceedings of the *Wall* opinion, the Palestinians argued before the ICJ that as a matter of law, a State of Palestine does not yet exist, expressly stating (i) "Israel and Palestine are not two States Members of the United Nations"[817], and (ii) "[y]ou are not asked to determine the boundaries of a future Palestinian State"[818].

On 15 January 2005, in his inaugural speech as Palestinian Authority President, Mahmoud Abbas said "[t]he greatest challenge before us, and the fundamental task facing us[,] is national liberation. The task of ending the occupation [and] establishing the Palestinian state"[819].

On 24 November 2008, President Abbas addressed the UN General Assembly in a message delivered by Riad Malki, Minister of Foreign Affairs of the Palestinian Authority:

> We highly appreciate your significant role in supporting our efforts to enable our people to realize their goals. We are certain that your role contributes in [a] clear and effective way in enhancing international solidarity with our just cause and enlarges

---

815 Weiner, Justus R., "Peace and its Discontents: Israeli and Palestinian Intellectuals who Reject the Current Peace Process", *Cornell International Law Journal* 29 (1996), p. 528.

816 Al-bab – An Open Door to the Arab World, *Speech by Yasser Arafat at the Arab Summit in Beirut, 27 - 28 March 2002.*

817 ICJ, *Legal Consequences of the Construction of a Wall in the Occupied Palestinian Territories*, *supra* note 166, Oral Proceedings (23 February 2004), p. 34, para. 22.

818 *Ibid.*, p. 37, para. 33.

819 Ash, *supra* note 739, pp. 188-189.

> the circle of international support for the aspirations of our people for freedom and independence and the establishment of their State[820].

On 4 February 2009, President Abbas spoke before the European Parliament about the then recently concluded Israeli military operation in the Gaza Strip and accused Israel of "preventing [the Palestinian] people from attaining their ultimate goal: an end to occupation, gaining freedom and the right to self-determination and the establishment of an independent Palestinian state on the lands that were occupied in 1967, with Eastern Jerusalem as its capital"[821].

On 22 June 2009, Palestinian Prime Minister Salem Fayyad called for the establishment of a Palestinian state within two years and called on all Palestinians to help create the institutions that will embody the future state[822].

These examples – taken over a period of 14 years – clearly show that even after the 1988 Palestinian Declaration of Independence and the Oslo Accords, Palestinian leaders continued to believe and express the view that a Palestinian state has yet to come into existence[823].

2.5.2.1.3.2. Continued Palestinian threats to unilaterally declare statehood

Despite the 1988 Palestinian Declaration of Independence, the Palestinian leadership continued to threaten Israel and the international community with the possibility of it unilaterally declaring Palestinian independence and statehood.

According to leaders of the Palestinian Authority, which had been created on 4 May 1994, the Palestinian Authority was a five year interim arrangement, at the end of which it was necessary for the Authority to declare statehood. On 4 May 1999, Chairman Arafat was expected to unilaterally declare Palestinian statehood, given the approaching deadline for a permanent settlement without momentous diplomatic progress. Addressing a rally in Nablus on 14 November 1998, Arafat said "[we] will declare our independent state on 4 May 1999, with Jerusalem as its capital." This intention was not fulfilled, as Arafat backed down from his previous statement and instead suggested that he would negotiate for the creation of a state[824].

---

820 Permanent Observer Mission of Palestine to the United Nations, *Statement on the Occasion of the International Day of Solidarity with the Palestinian People* (2008); Ash, *supra* note 739, p. 189.

821 The European Parliament, Press Release: *Mahmoud Abbas at the European Parliament* (2009).

822 Schneider, Howard, *Palestinian Premier Sets Timeline for Establishing State, Asks Constituents to 'Roll Up Their Sleeves'*, The Washington Post (2009).

823 Ash, *supra* note 739, p. 191.

824 Benoliel and Perry, *supra* note 505, pp. 99-100; Gold and Morrison, *supra* note 510, pp. 24-25.

In February 2008, in response to the Albanian majority government in Kosovo seceding from Serbia and declaring it was forming an independent State, the Palestinian leadership threatened to unilaterally declare statehood for the second time. Yasser Abd Rabbo, a senior advisor to Mahmoud Abbas, said in 2009 "[o]ur people have the right to proclaim independence even before Kosovo. And we ask for the backing of the United States and the European Union for our independence"[825]. In a new variation to the unilateral Palestinian declaration, but still invoking the Kosovo example, Chief Palestinian negotiator, Saeb Erekat, said in mid-November 2009 that "it is time [for the Security Council] to recognize a Palestinian state on the borders of 4 June 1967 with Jerusalem as its capital". Simultaneously, Muhammad Dahlan, the former Gaza security chief and senior Fatah leader, provided a more detailed version of this idea. In the Palestinian newspaper al-Ayyam, Dahlan stated that the PA was considering "unilaterally" declaring a state and then approaching the UN Security Council to define the borders of the Palestinian state as the 1967 lines as well as to acknowledge that its capital will be East Jerusalem[826].

In June 2011, following two years of standstill in the Israeli-Palestinian peace process, the PLO officially announced that Palestinians will seek recognition as an independent state at the UN General Assembly in September 2011[827]. Speaking to PLO representatives, President Abbas said "if negotiations have failed[,] we will go to the United Nations for membership. Until now there have been no new incentives to return to negotiations"[828]. Riad Malki, the Palestinian Foreign Minister, explained what the Palestinians hope to achieve through such a move: "Such recognition would create political and legal pressure on Israel to withdraw its forces from the land of another state that is recognized within the 1967 borders by the international organization"[829].

These threats and statements raise the obvious question of why did the Palestinian leadership consider such unilateral acts necessary / possible if the State of Palestine already exists? Apparently, Palestinian leaders did not feel that a

---

825 Diker, Dan, *The Palestinians' Unilateral "Kosovo Strategy": Implications for the PA and Israel*, Jerusalem Center for Public Affairs (2010).

826 Gold and Morrison, *supra* note 510, pp. 25-26.

827 On 23 September 2011, Palestinian Authority President, Mahmoud Abbas, formally submitted to the UN Security Council an application to accept Palestine as a (full) UN member state.

828 The Telegraph, *Mahmoud Abbas Signals Intent to Bid for UN Recognition for Palestinian Statehood* (2012).

829 Gradstein, Linda, *Palestinians to Push for UN Recognition as Independent State*, AOL News (2011).

Palestinian state has come into existence over the years – and the many developments – since 1988[830].

2.5.2.1.3.3. Legal obligations undertaken by the Palestinian leadership

The wording of the 1993 Declaration of Principles leaves no doubt that the Palestinian Authority was specifically formed as a provisional body with clearly delineated limits to its authority, intended to enable the Palestinian people in the West Bank and Gaza Strip to govern themselves during a transitional period, until a permanent settlement can be reached by the parties[831].

When signing the Interim Agreement, the PLO committed itself not to "initiate or take any step that will change the status of the West Bank and the Gaza Strip pending the outcome of the permanent status negotiations"[832]. This significant legal obligation, undertaken by the Palestinians in 1995 – a period, in which the Palestinians were closer than ever to fulfilling the factual / formal requirements of statehood – further reflects the systematic Palestinian determination not to claim or establish Palestinian statehood as long as the peace talks with Israel have not been concluded. Although this seems to fully contradict the goals of the decade-long Palestinian struggle, in light of the complexity of the Israeli-Palestinian conflict, it is not surprising. Palestinian assertion of statehood could be interpreted internationally as acquiescence in the existing state of things vis-à-vis Israel, in particular with regard to the breadth of territory claimed by Palestine and the right of Palestinian refugees to return to homes within Israeli territory. Furthermore, it may also weaken the Palestinian demands by making them a matter of post-conflict resolution between formally equal sovereign states, rather than a condition for the resolution of the conflict on the basis of a legal entitlement to the exercise of self-determination[833].

2.5.2.2. The Palestinian Authority's declaration as that of a quasi-state for the purpose of the Rome Statute only

According to the teleological / functional approach, Art. 12(3) Rome-Statute should be interpreted in accordance with Art. 31(1) of the 1969 Vienna Convention on the Law of Treaties, which provides that:

---

830 Gold and Morrison, *supra* note 510, p. 27; Gold, Dore, *Countdown to September: Israel, the Palestinians, and the UN General Assembly*, Jerusalem Center for Public Affairs (2011).

831 See *supra* notes 733, 744.

832 Art. XXXI(7) Interim Agreement.

833 Ronen, "ICC Jurisdiction over Acts Committed in the Gaza Strip – Article 12(3) of the ICC Statute and Non-state Entities", *supra* note 512, p. 15.

A treaty shall be interpreted in good faith in accordance with the ordinary meaning to be given to the terms of the treaty in their context and in light of its object and purpose.

Based on this approach, in order to support and ensure the fulfillment of the object and purpose of the Rome Statute, namely, that "the most serious crimes of concern to the international community as a whole [. . .] not go unpunished"[834, 835], the term "State" in Art. 12(3) Rome-Statute should be interpreted more widely – according to criteria different from what is (traditionally) used for other purposes in international law – so as to encompass quasi-states, i.e. political entities with strong state-like features, which fall short of full-fledged statehood[836].

The following section shall provide an analysis of (i) the arguments in favor and against the teleological / functional interpretation of Art. 12(3) Rome-Statute, (ii) which criteria should be applied, in order to define a quasi-state for the purpose of the Rome Statute only, and (iii) whether the Palestinian Authority fulfilled such criteria on 21 January 2009.

2.5.2.2.1. The main arguments for and against the teleological / functional interpretation of the term "State" in Art. 12(3) Rome-Statute

Supporters of the teleological / functional approach base their view on three main arguments: First, modern international law conceives the term "State" under the form of a "variable geometry" shape, whose outline depends on the subject at issue, and it relegates it to the rank of general notion, whose interpretation depends on the economy and the aims of the provisions within which it finds itself. In other words, the term "State" is understood differently depending on

834 Preamble para. 4 Rome-Statute.

835 Generally, preambles in international treaties do not carry the same weight as the actual provisions of the treaty and are often regarded as "soft law". However, preambles are of some significance in determining the rationale and objectives of the member states and the history of the negotiations leading to the establishment of the treaty. Therefore, where there is ambiguity about the provisions of a treaty or its objectives and history, the preamble can take on interpretive significance to fill any gaps. Art. 31(2) of the 1969 Vienna Convention on the Law of Treaties confirms that a preamble forms part of the context, in which a treaty has been adopted, and is therefore an important tool for its interpretation.

836 Ronen, "ICC Jurisdiction over Acts Committed in the Gaza Strip – Article 12(3) of the ICC Statute and Non-state Entities", *supra* note 512, p. 17; Shany, Yuval, "In Defence of Functional Interpretation of Article 12(3) of the Rome Statute – A Response to Yaël Ronen", *Journal of International Criminal Justice* 8 (2010), p. 334.

the object and purpose of the norm being applied[837]. As the term "State" is subject to variable defining characteristics under public international law and, therefore, lacks an unambiguous or "ordinary" meaning, it must be interpreted in light of the "object and purpose" of the Rome Statute – as required by Art. 31(1) of the 1969 Vienna Convention on the Law of Treaties[838].

Generally, the teleological / functional approach is extremely frequent in international law[839] – as seen in numerous conventions that define the concepts they refer to "for the purpose of this convention" or "of the present treaty"[840]. Specifically with regard to the interpretation of the term "State", a number of conventions expressly include the functional approach in their respective definitions of the term. Such is the case, for instance, in Art. XXII(1) of the 1972 Convention on International Liability for Damage Caused by Space Objects, which provides that:

> In this Convention, with the exception of articles XXIV to XXVII, references to States shall be deemed to apply to any international intergovernmental organization which conducts space activities if the organization declares its acceptance of the rights and obligations provided for in this Convention.

An additional example is Art. 44 of the 2006 Convention on the Rights of Persons with Disabilities, which provides that (i) the term "[r]egional integration organization" shall mean "an organization constituted by sovereign States of a given region, to which its member States have transferred competence in respect of matters governed by the present Convention", and (ii) references to the term "States Parties" in the Convention "shall apply to such organizations within the limits of their competence".

Finally, Sir Francis Geoffrey Jacobs, Advocate General of the European Court of Justice, reinforced this approach in the *Stardust* case by stating that:

---

837 Pellet, Alain, "The Palestinian Declaration and the Jurisdiction of the International Criminal Court", *Journal of International Criminal Justice* 8 (2010), pp. 987-988.

838 ICC Office of the Prosecutor, *Summary of Submissions on whether the Declaration Lodged by the Palestinian National Authority Meets Statutory Requirements*, *supra* note 711, para. 3; Gowlland-Debbas, *supra* note 787, para. 7.

839 Pellet, *supra* note 837, p. 984.

840 Some of the many examples include: Art. 1 of the 1961 Vienna Convention on Diplomatic Relations; Art. 1(1) of the 1963 Vienna Convention on Consular Relations; Art. 2(1) of the 1969 Vienna Convention on the Law of Treaties; Art. 1(1) of the 1984 Convention against Torture and Other Cruel, Inhuman or Degrading Treatment or Punishment; Art. 1(1) of the 1982 United Nations Convention on the Law of the Sea; Art. 1 of the 1992 United Nations Framework Convention on Climate Change.

> The concept of the State has to be understood in the sense most appropriate to the provisions in question and to their objectives; the Court rightly follows a functional approach, basing its interpretation on the scheme and objective of the provisions within which the concept features[841].

Second, only by embracing a teleological / functional approach, can the Prosecutor assume jurisdiction over the events of the Gaza armed conflict – and thus fulfill the object and purpose of the Rome Statute and the ICC[842] – without taking a position on the highly controversial question of Palestinian statehood[843]. The latter cannot be decided upon by any ICC organ, as only states can determine questions of statehood[844]. The wider interpretation of the term "State" under the teleological / functional approach would allow the Prosecutor to focus only on whether the Palestinian Authority's declaration of 21 January 2009 can be effective as that of a quasi-state solely for the purpose of the Rome Statute – and not as that of a full-fledged state for all purposes[845].

The ICJ was faced with a similar situation in 2008 when it was requested by the UN General Assembly to provide an advisory opinion regarding Kosovo's declaration of independence from Serbia of 17 February 2008. In its request, the UN General Assembly was careful not to ask the ICJ about the state status of Kosovo in general, but only whether "the unilateral declaration of independence by the Provisional Institutions of Self-Government of Kosovo [is] in accordance with international law"[846]. Both cases are similar in the sense that the ICC Prosecutor and the ICJ were requested to determine whether a specific declaration fulfilled certain requirements, without addressing the state status of the entities behind said declarations. This would be possible in the case at hand only under the teleological / functional approach, as a literal interpretation of Art. 12(3) Rome-Statute would require the Prosecutor to decide whether Palestine is a "State"[847] before any further action regarding the Gaza armed conflict could be taken.

---

841 *France v. Commission of the European Communities*, European Court of Justice, Opinion of Advocate General Jacobs (13 December 2001), para. 56.

842 See *supra* note 834.

843 Shany, "In Defence of Functional Interpretation of Article 12(3) of the Rome Statute", *supra* note 836, p. 338.

844 See *supra* note 781; Gowlland-Debbas, *supra* note 787, para. 2; Pellet, *supra* note 837, p. 983.

845 Pellet, *supra* note 837, pp. 983-984; Dugard, John, *Take the Case*, The New York Times (2009); Gowlland-Debbas, *supra* note 787, para. 2.

846 UN General Assembly Resolution 63/3 (8 October 2008).

847 See *supra* notes 664, 844.

Third, declining to interpret Art. 12(3) Rome-Statute in accordance with the teleological / functional approach would be tantamount to creating an impunity zone in the Palestinian territories of the West Bank and the Gaza Strip – contrary to the object and purpose of the Rome Statute and the intentions of its authors[848]. Reason for this is the uniqueness of the Palestinian territories, which are neither claimed by any existing state nor recognized as belonging to one[849], so that there is no territorial state, which could grant the ICC the right to exercise its jurisdiction in the case at hand[850].

One could rightly claim that this fact alone cannot lead to the creation of an impunity zone, as the ICC could still acquire jurisdiction in accordance with Art. 12(2)(b) or 13(b) Rome-Statute. However, the possibility of impunity for grave crimes must be looked at in the context of the real world factual probabilities and not in the abstract world of theoretical possibilities[851]. Although a UN Security Council referral of the situation to the Prosecutor is more likely than Israel accepting ICC jurisdiction in accordance with Art. 12(2)(alt. 2)(b) and (3) Rome-Statute, both options are considered highly unlikely, so that in terms of factual probabilities, the lack of a territorial state would make the Palestinian territories an area, in which the Rome Statute is *de facto* ineffective[852].

To exclude from the scope of ICC jurisdiction a geographical zone, in which war crimes and crimes against humanity have (allegedly) been perpetrated, on the sole premise that it is not generally recognized as a state or part of one, could hardly have been the objective of the signatory states and the thousands of civil society groups and individuals, which labored so hard for so many decades to have the first permanent international criminal tribunal to combat impunity and ensure that the most serious crimes do not go unpunished[853]. Therefore, only by

---

848 ICC Office of the Prosecutor, *Summary of Submissions on whether the Declaration Lodged by the Palestinian National Authority Meets Statutory Requirements*, *supra* note 711, para. 25; Pellet, *supra* note 837, p. 995; Mendes, *supra* note 698, p. 39; Gowlland-Debbas, *supra* note 787, para. 7.

849 This pertains to most of the West Bank and the entire Gaza Strip – see *supra* note 633.

850 Ronen, "ICC Jurisdiction over Acts Committed in the Gaza Strip – Article 12(3) of the ICC Statute and Non-state Entities", *supra* note 512, p. 17; ICC Office of the Prosecutor, *Summary of Submissions on whether the Declaration Lodged by the Palestinian National Authority Meets Statutory Requirements*, *supra* note 711, para. 25; Pellet, *supra* note 837, p. 995.

851 Mendes, *supra* note 698, p. 40.

852 Pellet, *supra* note 837, p. 996.

853 Al-Haq, *Position Paper on Issues Arising from the Palestinian Authority's Submission of a Declaration to the Prosecutor of the International Criminal Court under Article 12(3) of the Rome Statute* (2009), para. 20; Mendes, *supra* note 698, p. 47.

interpreting the term "State" in accordance with the teleological / functional approach, in a manner divorced from the political considerations which otherwise tend to guide state recognition[854], can the Prosecutor prevent the creation of a "criminal accountability vacuum" in the Palestinian territories – thus promoting the principles and purposes of the UN, whereby no-one is excluded from the writ of international justice nor from the protection of international law[855].

This approach was confirmed by the International Law Commission, which observed in the commentary on its final draft articles on the law of treaties that:

> When a treaty is open to two interpretations one of which does and the other does not enable the treaty to have appropriate effects, good faith and the objects and purposes of the treaty demand that the former interpretation [. . .] be adopted[856].

Finally, to emphasize the significant negative impact of letting the Palestinian territories become an impunity zone, proponents of the teleological / functional approach quote Dr. Martin Luther King Jr., who wrote in 1963 that "[i]njustice anywhere is a threat to justice everywhere".

Those who object to the interpretation of Art. 12(3) Rome-Statute in accordance with the teleological / functional approach respond to the arguments brought above as follows: First, the term "State" in international law is very clear. A mix of law and facts ensures that statehood – which is not a flexible concept with gradations of meaning – must involve adherence to the Montevideo criteria coupled with international recognition[857]. Therefore, there is no reason or need to deviate from the wording of Art. 31(1) of the 1969 Vienna Convention on the Law of Treaties, which commences with – and thus prioritizes – the requirement to interpret treaties in accordance with "the ordinary meaning to be given to [their] terms"[858].

Furthermore, The Rome Statute clearly sets out the basis for the jurisdiction of the ICC, requiring (i) that the alleged crime took place within the territory or by a national of a "State" party to the Statute, or (ii) in the case of "a State which is not a Party", that such state accept the jurisdiction of the court, pursuant to Art. 12(3) Rome-Statute. There is nothing within the text of Art. 12 or any other provision of the Rome Statute to suggest that the term "State" was intended to

---

854 Al-Haq, *supra* note 853, para. 20.

855 *Ibid.*, para. 42; Ronen, "ICC Jurisdiction over Acts Committed in the Gaza Strip – Article 12(3) of the ICC Statute and Non-state Entities", *supra* note 512, p. 17.

856 United Nations, *Yearbook of the International Law Commission 1966*, Volume 2 (1967), p. 219.

857 Shaw, *supra* note 668, para. 33.

858 *Ibid.*, paras. 37, 71(iv).

include non-state entities or be attributed with a special / flexible meaning[859]. Nor is there any indication that the "State" requirement in Art. 12(3) Rome-Statute is merely guidance or a non-exclusive example of the sort of entity that could provide the ICC with jurisdiction[860]. Any doubt regarding this matter has been removed when Mahmoud Cherif Bassiouni stated that "[a]s chairman of the Diplomatic Conference's Drafting Committee, I can attest to the fact that referrals under Article 12(3) were intended to be by States only"[861].

Despite the fact that reference to the "object and purpose" of the respective treaty is a secondary or ancillary process in the application of the general rule on interpretation[862], it is, of course, necessary that the treaty be interpreted in a way that fulfills its objectives[863]. Nevertheless, the "object and purpose" of a treaty can never be used to alter the clear meaning of terms used therein[864]. In the case at hand, the "object and purpose" of the Rome Statute is not only to promote the fight against impunity, but to do so within the jurisdictional framework of the Statute, so that said "object and purpose" may not be simplistically asserted as implying a lack of jurisdictional limitation for the ICC[865].

It is a well-known fact that the jurisdictional provisions of the Rome Statute have been the most important, politically most difficult and, therefore, most controversial[866] question of the negotiations leading up to the signing of the Rome Statute – as summarized by ICC Judge Hans-Peter Kaul "the question of questions of the entire project"[867]. As a result, the jurisdictional provisions of the Rome Statute form a carefully negotiated balance of interests[868], which would be completely undermined by the extravagant reading of any jurisdiction related

---

859 Davenport, *et al.*, *supra* note 723, p. 2.

860 Shaw, *supra* note 668, para. 28.

861 Bassiouni, M. Cherif, *Comment on the Gaza Question: "Does the Prosecutor of the ICC have the Authority to Open an Investigation into Alleged Crimes Committed in the 2008-2009 Gaza Conflict?*", UCLA School of Law, Human Rights & International Criminal Law Online Forum (2010).

862 Sinclair, Ian, *The Vienna Convention on the Law of Treaties*, 2nd edition, Manchester: Manchester University Press (1984), p. 130.

863 Shaw, *supra* note 668, para. 34.

864 Gardiner, Richard K., *Treaty Interpretation*, Oxford: Oxford University Press (2008), p. 198.

865 Shaw, *supra* note 668, para. 36.

866 See *supra* notes 513, 514.

867 Kaul, *supra* note 517, p. 584.

868 Schiff, Benjamin N., *Building the International Criminal Court*, Cambridge: Cambridge University Press (2008), pp. 69, 71-72.

term[869]. With regard to the highly significant Art. 12 Rome-Statute, the main challenge facing the drafters was to find an acceptable balance between pure consent-based jurisdiction and cause-based jurisdiction – which required a delicate balance between the desire to prevent impunity for the most serious violations of international law, the authority of the Prosecutor and the protection of state sovereignty[870]. Such a balance has been achieved through the insertion of Art. 13(b) Rome-Statute, which – in conjunction with Art. 12(2) Rome-Statute[871] – provides that only the UN Security Council shall have the competence to place before the ICC allegations of international crimes, which would otherwise be barred by the requirements of Art. 12 Rome-Statute[872]. Vesting only the UN Security Council – and not the Prosecutor or any other ICC or UN organ – with the ability to extend the jurisdiction of the ICC beyond the consent limitations established by Art. 12 Rome-Statute, clearly reflects the fact that States Parties considered such limitations to be as important as preventing impunity for the most serious violations of international law – the declared purpose of the ICC[873].

Finally, the argument in favor of the teleological / functional interpretation of the term "State" based on Art. XXII(1) and 44 of the 1972 Convention on International Liability for Damage Caused by Space Objects and the 2006 Convention on the Rights of Persons with Disabilities, respectively, actually provides a strong argument against such interpretation. The fact that a convention specifically declares in a provision that a particular meaning is to be given to a certain term, means that such a provision is necessary, in order to achieve the desired (unusual) interpretation. Therefore, in the absence of such a provision, the terms provided in the convention can only bear their normal meaning, as otherwise there would be no need for provisions such as those referred to above[874].

---

869 Davenport, *et al.*, *supra* note 723, p. 3.

870 European Centre for Law and Justice, *supra* note 733, p. 21.

871 Art. 12(2) Rome-Statute provides that in the case of Art. 13(a) and (c) Rome-Statute, the ICC may exercise its jurisdiction only if (i) territorial / nationality based jurisdiction is given, or (ii) a non-State Party has made a declaration under Art. 12(3) Rome-Statute. This does not apply to Art. 13(b) Rome-Statute (UN Security Council referral), so that in such cases the ICC may exercise its jurisdiction regardless of the mentioned limitations in Art. 12(2) Rome-Statute.

872 The possibility of the UN Security Council referring a situation related to the Gaza armed conflict to the ICC under Art. 13(b) Rome-Statute has not been analyzed in this research due to its unlikelihood – see *supra* note 266.

873 European Centre for Law and Justice, *supra* note 733, pp. 21-22.

874 Shaw, *supra* note 668, para. 42; See *supra* note 668.

Second, any pursuit of the Palestinian declaration under Art. 12(3) Rome-Statute – whether as a full-fledged state or as a quasi-state for the purpose of the Rome Statute only – would constitute *de facto* recognition of Palestinian statehood[875]. The notion that such a decision by the Prosecutor or the ICC can be isolated and restricted to the specific context of ICC territorial jurisdiction is largely illusory[876].

Statehood is for the most part a package deal. Where non-states have been granted rights and obligations, which ordinarily attach only to states, this was usually not through *ad hoc* recognition or limited statehood, but through express extensions of those rights and obligations to non-state entities or the gradual expansion of international law to non-state entities. There are few and remote precedents of an entity being regarded under international law as a state for some purposes but not for others. Thus, it would be naive to expect that the determination that a State of Palestine exists – either generally or solely for the purpose of the Rome Statute – by a legal organ of an international organization, which brings together over half of the world's states, would have no repercussions outside the immediate context in which such determination was made[877].

Should the Prosecutor decide to take such a step and interpret the term "State" in accordance with the teleological / functional approach, the ICC would be assuming an almost unprecedented competence, which incurs onto the political sphere – traditionally the prerogative of states[878]. This could lead to a general perception of politicization of the court, which in turn, could have very negative implications for its reputation[879]. Therefore, a decision by the Prosecutor to grant status under the Rome Statute to a non-state entity such as the Palestinian Authority would be an irregular event in the practice of international organizations, the merit of which would be seriously outweighed by negative costs to both the

---

875 European Centre for Law and Justice, *supra* note 733, p. 2.

876 Brubacher, Matthew R., "Prosecutorial Discretion within the International Criminal Court", *Journal of International Criminal Justice* 2.1 (2004), p. 83.

877 Ronen, "ICC Jurisdiction over Acts Committed in the Gaza Strip – Article 12(3) of the ICC Statute and Non-state Entities", *supra* note 512, pp. 21, 24.

878 *Ibid.*, p. 22.

879 Fletcher, George P., N*o Jurisdictional Basis for an Investigation Pursuant to the Palestinian Declaration*, UCLA School of Law, Human Rights & International Criminal Law Online Forum; Gold and Morrison, *supra* note 510, p. 36; ICC Office of the Prosecutor, *Summary of Submissions on whether the Declaration Lodged by the Palestinian National Authority Meets Statutory Requirements*, *supra* note 711, para. 29.

ICC as an institution and to the discipline of international criminal justice more broadly[880].

Third, the alternative to recognizing Palestine as a quasi-state for the purpose of Art. 12(3) Rome-Statute is not a legal vacuum or alleged impunity as some have claimed[881]. In addition to the possibility of the UN Security Council referring the situation to the ICC, any war crimes allegedly committed by Israelis[882] are undeniably susceptible to the exercise of Israeli jurisdiction – including both its criminal jurisdiction and the administrative jurisdiction of its Supreme Court, sitting as the High Court of Justice[883]. It is internationally accepted that Israel's legal system is independent, credible and effective[884] – as has been explicitly recognized by the Supreme Court of Canada[885], the House of Lords of the United Kingdom[886] and the European Court of Justice[887].

With regard to the option of a UN Security Council referral, the argument that such a referral is currently very unlikely cannot be used to claim that the Rome Statute is ineffective in the Palestinian territories, as the refusal of the Security Council to exercise its power is based on internal political constraints, which the drafters of the Rome Statute were fully aware of and have agreed to tolerate[888]. The fact that in a specific situation, at a specific moment in time, none of the three bases for ICC jurisdiction – i.e. territory, nationality or UN Security Council referral – has successfully led to acquisition of jurisdiction, does not mean that the rules on jurisdiction are inadequate – and must, therefore, be

---

880 Ronen, "ICC Jurisdiction over Acts Committed in the Gaza Strip – Article 12(3) of the ICC Statute and Non-state Entities", *supra* note 512, p. 26.

881 *Ibid.*, p. 17; Shaw, *supra* note 668, para. 38.

882 The Palestinian Authority's power to prosecute Palestinians, subject to its jurisdictional powers established by the Oslo Accords, shall be discussed below.

883 Shaw, *supra* note 668, para. 38.

884 *Ibid.*; Gold and Morrison, *supra* note 510, p. 11.

885 *Application under s. 83.28 of the Criminal Code*, Supreme Court of Canada (23 June 2004), p. 17, para. 7.

886 *A and others v. Secretary of State for the Home Department*, UK House of Lords (8 December 2005), p. 80, para. 150.

887 *Yassin Abdullah Kadi v. Council of the European Union and Commission of the European Communities*, European Court of Justice, Opinion of Advocate General Poiares Maduro (16 January 2008), para. 45.

888 Bergsmo, Morten and Jelena Pejic, in: Triffterer, Otto (ed.), *Commentary on the Rome Statute of the International Criminal Court – Observers' Notes, Article by Article* , 2nd edition, Munich: C.H.Beck (2008), Art. 16, paras. 7, 8.

innovatively interpreted – but merely demonstrates that the ICC is not omnipotent[889].

Finally, it is worth noting that the status of the Palestinian territories as non-sovereign territory under control of a non-state entity never arose during the drafting of the Rome Statute. Arguably, given the prominence of the territories in other aspects of the negotiations, the absence of territorial nexus can hardly be considered an oversight; rather, it seems that the drafters were content to accept the consequences of the limits of that nexus – including dependency on the UN Security Council to provide the ICC with jurisdiction over the Palestinian territories[890].

2.5.2.2.2. Interim conclusion: The application of the teleological / functional approach in the case at hand

The arguments of both sides of the discussion concerning the teleological / functional interpretation of the term "State" in Art. 12(3) Rome-Statute make it very clear that there is no single – significant and undisputed – argument, which can be considered the decisive "weight" in the very balanced discussion presented above. Both sides make convincing and legally acceptable arguments concerning (i) the "ordinary meaning" of the term "State" in international law and the corresponding application of Art. 31(1) of the 1969 Vienna Convention on the Law of Treaties, (ii) the connection between acceptance of the Palestinian Authority's declaration under the teleological / functional interpretation of the term "State" and the *de facto* recognition of Palestinian statehood, and (iii) the Palestinian territories as an impunity zone resulting from the lack of a territorial state.

Due to the fact that this discussion is currently still open – and could have a negative impact on the ICC's functionality – leading legal experts argue that the solution to this disagreement lies in the connection between two basic facts, namely (i) the state delegation mechanism – according to which international criminal courts exercise jurisdiction that was delegated to them by states that had an internationally recognized right to prosecute the crimes in question before their own domestic courts – while representing an important limit on the ICC's jurisdiction, should ultimately be regarded as a means to an end – not an end in itself[891], and (ii) the ultimate goal, for which the ICC was established, is ensuring that the most serious violations of international law not go unpunished.

889 Ronen, "ICC Jurisdiction over Acts Committed in the Gaza Strip – Article 12(3) of the ICC Statute and Non-state Entities", *supra* note 512, p. 17.

890 *Ibid.*, p. 18.

891 Shany, "In Defence of Functional Interpretation of Article 12(3) of the Rome Statute", *supra* note 836, p. 336.

It cannot be denied that the ultimate object and purpose of the Rome Statute and ICC would be well-served by a teleological / functional approach regarding the state delegation mechanism[892]. Therefore, cases, in which the differences between "ordinary" states and quasi-states do not appear to be particularly relevant for the purpose of applying criminal jurisdiction under the Rome Statute, should be dealt with through the exercise of a case-by-case discretion by the Prosecutor as to whether to initiate proceedings[893] – based on the nature and function of the legal arrangement in question[894].

In the case at hand, most legal experts agree that the Palestinian Authority is a quasi-state with strong state-like features – to the point that all that separates it from full-fledged statehood may be a formal declaration to that effect[895]. In addition, the Palestinian Authority has criminal jurisdiction (to a certain degree[896]) over a territory, to which it – or the PLO, the overarching political entity – has an internationally recognized sovereignty claim, and which – at least in the case of the Gaza Strip – no other state is contesting. Therefore, the Palestinian Authority's lack of formal statehood appears insignificant for the purpose of invoking the ICC's delegation-based jurisdiction[897].

This conclusion is reinforced by the uniqueness of the case at hand, in which there is no territorial state, which could delegate jurisdiction over the Palestinian territories to the ICC. The actual reach of the court depends on the combined effect of its delegation-based and universalistic[898] jurisdictional powers. Cutting one of these "jurisdiction branches" would leave the ICC with truncated capabilities to fulfill its mandate[899]. Interpreting Art. 12(3) Rome-Statute literally would be doing exactly that, as it would result in the ICC's *de facto* dependency on a UN Security Council referral, in order to acquire jurisdiction over the events of

---

892 *Ibid.*, pp. 336-337.

893 Such Prosecutor discretion shall be monitored by the ICC in accordance with Art. 19 and 53 Rome-Statute.

894 Shany, "In Defence of Functional Interpretation of Article 12(3) of the Rome Statute", *supra* note 836, pp. 336, 338, 342-343.

895 Ronen, "ICC Jurisdiction over Acts Committed in the Gaza Strip – Article 12(3) of the ICC Statute and Non-state Entities", *supra* note 512, p. 26.

896 Discussed below in further detail.

897 Shany, "In Defence of Functional Interpretation of Article 12(3) of the Rome Statute", *supra* note 836, p. 343.

898 Reflected in the ICC's ability to exercise its jurisdiction over cases, which do not fall within its territorial or nationality based jurisdiction – as long as such cases are referred to the court by the UN Security Council, in accordance with Art. 13(b) Rome-Statute.

899 Shany, "In Defence of Functional Interpretation of Article 12(3) of the Rome Statute", *supra* note 836, p. 337.

the Gaza armed conflict. The need to ensure that the ICC maintains the capability to fulfill the object and purpose for which it was established, despite the unique circumstances of the Palestinian territories, strongly militates in favor of introducing some degree of interpretive flexibility to the term "State" in Art. 12(3) Rome-Statute[900].

Following the conclusion that the teleological / functional approach is preferable in the case at hand, the question which immediately arises is whether the Palestinian Authority fulfilled the requirements of a quasi-state for the purpose of the Rome Statute only on 21 January 2009 – i.e. a quasi-state able to make a declaration under Art. 12(3) Rome-Statute. The following analysis shall address this question.

2.5.2.2.3. The Palestinian Authority as a quasi-state for the purpose of the Rome Statute only

The crucial and most basic characteristic of a quasi-state for the purpose of the Rome Statute only is the possession of adequate "government capacity" to delegate the relevant criminal jurisdiction to the ICC[901]. Whether the Palestinian Authority fulfilled this requirement on 21 January 2009 shall be based on the outcome of the following three questions: (i) Did the Palestinian Authority have the capacity to enter into international agreements?, (ii) did the Palestinian Authority have the capacity to try Palestinians on criminal charges?, and (iii) did the Palestinian Authority have the capacity to try Israeli citizens on criminal charges[902]?

2.5.2.2.3.1. The Palestinian Authority's capacity to enter into international agreements

The capacity to enter into the full range of international relations is a useful criterion, as it is independent of its recognition by other states and of its exercise by

900 *Ibid.*, p. 343.

901 Kearney, Michael, *It is Imperative that in Considering the Issue at Hand, the Correct Question be Asked, and that Palestinian Jurisdiction over Crimes set out in the Rome Statute be Acknowledged as Giving the ICC the Ability to Accept the PA Declaration*, UCLA School of Law, Human Rights & International Criminal Law Online Forum; ICC Office of the Prosecutor, *Summary of Submissions on whether the Declaration Lodged by the Palestinian National Authority Meets Statutory Requirements*, *supra* note 711, paras. 5, 30; Ronen, "ICC Jurisdiction over Acts Committed in the Gaza Strip – Article 12(3) of the ICC Statute and Non-state Entities", *supra* note 512, p. 18.

902 Al-Haq, *supra* note 853, para. 22; Kearney, *supra* note 901; Shany, "In Defence of Functional Interpretation of Article 12(3) of the Rome Statute", *supra* note 836, pp. 331-333; For opposing view see Shaw, *supra* note 668, paras. 48-50.

the entity concerned[903]. Furthermore, such capacity provides an important indicator for (a certain level of) government ability and independence, as it is based partly on the power of internal government of a territory, without which international obligations may not be carried into effect, and partly on the entity concerned being separate for the purpose of international relations, so that no other entity both carries out and accepts responsibility for them[904].

Those who claim that the Palestinian Authority has the capacity to enter into international agreements base their view, first of all, on the Palestinian international legal personality – i.e. the status as a subject of international law, which provides the respective entity with the capacity to possess rights / duties in international law and to operate upon the international plane[905]. In this regard, the ICJ stated in the *Wall* opinion that "both Israel and Palestine are under an obligation scrupulously to observe the rules of international humanitarian law, one of the paramount purposes of which is to protect civilian life"[906]. By referring to Israel and Palestine as equal international actors (with obvious different capacities) in terms of their obligations under international law, the ICJ clearly confirmed the Palestinian international legal personality. The capacity to enter into international agreements is, without a doubt, one of the main rights guaranteed by such international legal personality[907].

However, due to the political and legal complexity of the conflict and agreements between Israel and the Palestinians, the key to the question of whether the Palestinian Authority had the capacity to enter into international agreements is the nature of its relationship with the PLO[908]. The Oslo Accords reflect the existence of two Palestinian entities, which are very different in terms of the power to engage in foreign relations. With regard to the PLO, there is no doubt regarding the organization's ability, in its internationally recognized capacity as the legitimate representative of the Palestinian people[909], to enter into international agreements[910]. In addition to agreements with the Arab League and

903 Crawford, *The Creation of States in International Law*, *supra* note 713, p. 61.
904 *Ibid.*, p. 62.
905 Greig, D. W., *International Law*, 2nd edition, London: Butterworths (1976), p. 92.
906 ICJ, *Legal Consequences of the Construction of a Wall in the Occupied Palestinian Territories*, *supra* note 166, para. 162.
907 Mendes, *supra* note 698, pp. 43, 45.
908 Al-Haq, *supra* note 853, para. 25.
909 See *supra* note 743.
910 Al-Haq, *supra* note 853, para. 25.

Arab states, the PLO entered into international agreements with the US[911] and Israel – considering the fact that the Oslo Accords themselves constitute binding international agreements[912]. Furthermore, according to the 1995 Interim Agreement, only in cases concerning economic agreements, agreements with donor countries, and cultural / scientific / educational agreements "[may] the PLO conduct negotiations and sign agreements with states or international organizations for the benefit of the [Palestinian Authority]"[913]. The phrase "for the benefit" was chosen (i) to avoid the possibility of the PLO being perceived merely as the agent or foreign-policy branch of the Palestinian Authority, and thereby (ii) to emphasize the fact that the Palestinian Authority:

> [W]ill not have powers and responsibilities in the sphere of foreign relations, which [. . .] includes the establishment abroad of embassies, consulates or other types of foreign missions and posts or permitting their establishment in the West Bank or the Gaza Strip, the appointment of or admission of diplomatic and consular staff, and the exercise of diplomatic functions[914].

Despite the clear formal "division of labor" between the PLO and the Palestinian Authority – whereby one has the power to engage in foreign relations, but not to control territory (PLO), and the other has the power to control and govern territory, but not to engage in foreign relations (Palestinian Authority)[915] – the overlap between the two entities led to a situation, in which the distinction between the two has been exponentially blurred in practice[916]. This development has been reflected in various international agreements over the years: (i) On 20 April 2005, the European Union Coordinating Office for Palestinian Police Support (EU COPPS) was formally established by an exchange of letters between the Palestinian Prime Minister, Ahmed Qurei, and the EU Special Representa-

---

911 Agreement on the Encouragement of Investment Between the United States of America and the Palestine Liberation Organization for the Benefit of the Palestinian Authority Pursuant to the Agreement on the Gaza Strip and the Jericho Area (1994); Watson, Geoffrey R., *The Oslo Accords – International Law and the Israeli-Palestinian Peace Agreements*, Oxford: Oxford University Press (2000), pp. 98-99.

912 See *supra* notes 623, 624; Watson, *supra* note 911, pp. 91-102; Quigley, John, "The Israel-PLO Interim Agreements: Are they Treaties?", *Cornell International Law Journal* 30 (1997), p. 740.

913 Art. IX(5)(b)(1-4) Interim Agreement.

914 Art. IX(5)(a) Interim Agreement.

915 Watson, *supra* note 911, p. 245.

916 *Ibid.*; Al-Haq, *supra* note 853, para. 26; Kearney, *supra* note 901.

tive to the Middle East Peace Process, Marc Otte[917]. Furthermore, following the explicit written invitation of the Palestinian Authority, in November 2005 the Council of the EU established the EU Police Mission in the Palestinian Territories (EUPOL COPPS) under the European Security and Defence Policy[918], (ii) the Palestinian Authority joined Airports Council International and is recognized as a regular member thereof[919], (iii) the PLO signed a protocol on security cooperation with Russia in the name of the Palestinian Authority – clearly breaching the provisions of the 1995 Interim Agreement, which does not list security cooperation matters as one of the cases, in which the PLO is permitted to conclude agreements for the benefit of the Palestinian Authority[920].

These examples clearly show that the international community no longer considers the "Oslo limitations" imposed on the Palestinian Authority with regard to its power to enter into international agreements to be legitimate, as such limitations conflict with the inalienable right of the Palestinian people to self-determination, which includes the right to engage in relations with other states and international organizations[921]. Therefore, the question whether the Palestinian Authority had the ability to enter into international agreements on 21 January 2009 can only be answered positively[922].

Those who maintain that the Palestinian Authority does not have the capacity to enter into international agreements (i) claim that the PLO and the Palestinian Authority are clearly separate and distinct entities, and (ii) reject the notion that since the signing of the 1995 Interim Agreement the clear division between the entities, in terms of the capacity and ability to engage in foreign relations, has been the subject of increasingly broader interpretation in practice – eventually allowing the Palestinian Authority to (directly) enter into international agreements[923].

In addition to the above mentioned provisions of the Interim Agreement[924] – a valid, binding and unchanged legal agreement between Israel and the Palestin-

---

917 European Union Coordinating Office for Palestinian Police Support and the Palestinian National Authority – Ministry of Interior, *Factsheet.*

918 Council of the European Union, *Council Joint Action 2005/797/CFSP on the European Union Police Mission for the Palestinian Territories* (2005).

919 Airports Council International – Asia-Pacific Region, *Dateline – the Official Newsletter of the Asia-Pacific Region of Airports Council International*, Volume 14, Number 1 (2006).

920 Al-Haq, *supra* note 853, para. 26; See *supra* note 913.

921 Watson, *supra* note 911, p. 245.

922 Al-Haq, *supra* note 853, para. 28.

923 Shaw, *supra* note 668, para. 54.

924 See *supra* notes 913, 914.

ian side[925] – which leave no doubt regarding the clear intention to exclude the sphere of foreign relations – including the power to conclude international agreements – from the phased transfer of defined powers from the Israeli military government to the newly created Palestinian Authority[926], the following provisions further illustrate the focus put on guaranteeing said exclusion: According to Art. I(1) Interim Agreement, "Israel shall transfer powers and responsibilities as specified in [the] Agreement [. . .] [and] shall continue to exercise powers and responsibilities not so transferred". Art. XVII(1)(a) of the same agreement further provides that:

> In accordance with the [Declaration of Principles], the jurisdiction of the [Palestinian Authority] will cover West Bank and Gaza Strip territory as a single territorial unit, except for: issues that will be negotiated in the permanent status negotiations: Jerusalem, settlements [. . .] foreign relations and Israelis.

Professor James Crawford has explained the relationship between the PLO and the Palestinian Authority as follows: The PLO, which has been recognized to possess an independent international personality as representative of the Palestinian people, has been delegated the power to act on behalf of the Palestinian Authority in the international arena with regard to specific substantive areas. Nevertheless, the Palestinian Authority's constituent organs form a local government with largely municipal functions and – with regard thereto – these organs are independent of the PLO. Moreover, the powers withheld from the PLO by the 1993 Declaration of Principles – i.e. the authority to conclude international agreements (with parties other than Israel) that affect the status or security of the Palestinian territories – are held by Israel, not the Palestinian Authority. Therefore, the Palestinian Authority is in a position of subordination to both the PLO and Israel[927].

In his leading work on the Oslo Accords, Geoffrey Watson concluded that:

> Once there is a Palestinian State, it will of course enjoy the full right to conduct its own foreign policy. In the meantime, the Accords implicitly recognize that the Pal-

925 Shany, "In Defence of Functional Interpretation of Article 12(3) of the Rome Statute", *supra* note 836, pp. 341-342; Shaw, *supra* note 668, para. 69.

926 Shaw, *supra* note 668, para. 52.

927 Crawford, *The Creation of States in International Law*, *supra* note 713, pp. 444-445; Dajani, Omar M., "Stalled Between Seasons: The International Legal Status of Palestine During the Interim Period", *Denver Journal of International Law and Policy* 26.1 (1997), pp. 90-91.

estinians have a right to do so – but only through the PLO, and only on certain matters[928].

With regard to the examples provided in support of the Palestinian Authority's ability to enter into international agreements, those who object thereto claim the following: (i) The EU Police Mission in the Palestinian territories (EUPOL COPPS) was indeed established following the explicit written invitation of the Palestinian Authority. However, this fact cannot be used as evidence for the Palestinian Authority's power to (independently) engage in foreign relations, as the entire process concerning the establishment of EUPOL COPPS was closely coordinated and specifically agreed with Israel[929], (ii) the Palestinian Authority joining Airport Council International does not reflect the capacity to enter into international agreements, as the latter is not an intergovernmental organization, but rather an association created by airport operators around the world, in order to represent their common interests and foster cooperation with partners throughout the air transport industry[930], (iii) although the security cooperation agreement signed between Russia and the PLO – in the name of the Palestinian Authority – constitutes a clear breach of Art. IX(5)(b) Interim Agreement, it actually reinforces the argument against the Palestinian Authority's capacity to enter into international agreements, as the Palestinian Authority was not able to sign the agreement itself, but required a separate entity – the PLO – to do so in its name.

It cannot be denied that during the 18 years since the signing of the Oslo Accords, there have been isolated breaches of their provisions concerning foreign relations by the PLO and the Palestinian Authority. However, a comparison with the hundreds of international agreements entered into by states and intergovernmental organizations around the world over this period clearly shows that the international community's approach towards the Oslo Accords and the original intents behind them has not changed[931]. In conclusion, based on the wording of the 1995 Interim Agreement and the subsequent conduct of the PLO, the Palestinian Authority and the international community, one must conclude that on 21 January 2009, the Palestinian Authority did not have the capacity to enter into international agreements or otherwise conduct foreign relations[932].

---

928 Watson, *supra* note 911, p. 246.

929 Shaw, *supra* note 668, para. 56.

930 *Ibid.*

931 *Ibid.*, para. 58.

932 *Ibid.*; Davenport, *et al.*, *supra* note 723, p. 10.

2.5.2.2.3.2. The Palestinian Authority's criminal jurisdiction over Palestinians

Unlike the question regarding its capacity to enter into international agreements, the Palestinian Authority's criminal jurisdiction over Palestinians is not considered highly controversial. This was not always the case. In the pre-Oslo era, the Israeli authorities seriously undermined the independence of the West Bank judicial system, guaranteed under Jordanian law. The Israeli military courts established in the West Bank gradually expanded their jurisdiction at the expense of the local courts – eventually reaching a situation, in which the Israeli military courts tried everything from traffic and drug offences to murder and other serious crimes committed by Palestinians against fellow Palestinians[933].

The Oslo Accords restored – to a certain extent – Palestinian civil and criminal jurisdiction over Palestinians in the West Bank and Gaza Strip[934]. The subject of Palestinian criminal jurisdiction is regulated in Annex IV to the 1995 Interim Agreement: In Area A[935] of the West Bank and in the Gaza Strip, the Palestinian Authority exercises criminal jurisdiction over all offences committed by Palestinians and/or non-Israelis[936] – subject to Israel's retained right to exercise concurrent criminal jurisdiction in respect of offences committed against Israel or an Israeli[937]. In Area B[938] of the West Bank, the criminal jurisdiction of the Palestinian Authority covers offences committed by Palestinians and/or non-Israelis – including those which relate to the Palestinian Authority's responsibility for public order for Palestinians, but not in relation to offences within the remit of Israel's overriding responsibility for security for the purposes of protecting Israelis and confronting the threat of terrorism[939]. Furthermore, Palestinian criminal jurisdiction is subject to Israel's concurrent criminal jurisdiction in respect of offences committed against Israel or an Israeli[940]. In Area C[941] of the West Bank, jurisdiction with respect to criminal offences is exercised by the Palestinian Authority with regard to Palestinians and their visitors, who have

933 Shehadeh, Raja, *Occupier's Law: Israel and the West Bank*, Washington: Institute for Palestine Studies (1985), pp. 77, 85; Brown, Nathan J., *The Palestinian Reform Agenda*, United States Institute of Peace, Peaceworks No. 48 (2002), p. 30; Khalil, Asem, *Which Constitution for the Palestinian Legal System*?, Roma: Pontificia Università Lateranense (2003), pp. 28-29.

934 Al-Haq, *supra* note 853, para. 30.

935 See *supra* note 735.

936 Art. I(1)(a) Annex IV to the Interim Agreement.

937 Art. I(7)(a) Annex IV to the Interim Agreement.

938 See *supra* note 736.

939 Art. I(1)(a) and (c) Annex IV to the Interim Agreement.

940 See *supra* note 937.

941 See *supra* note 737.

committed offences against Palestinians or their visitors in the West Bank and Gaza Strip – provided that the offences are not related to Israel's security interests[942].

Beyond these security-related limitations, there can be no doubt regarding the intent of the Oslo Accords to make the Palestinian Authority responsible for trying Palestinians on criminal charges at the national level – whereby the question of if / how the Palestinian Authority's (formal) criminal jurisdiction over Palestinians has been negatively affected by Hamas seizing complete (including judicial) control over the Gaza Strip in 2007[943], remains controversial[944].

2.5.2.2.3.3. The Palestinian Authority's criminal jurisdiction over Israeli citizens

The basis of the discussion concerning possible Palestinian Authority criminal jurisdiction over Israeli citizens should be the undisputed fact that under the Oslo Accords, the approximately 500,000 Israeli citizens residing in the Palestinian territories are excluded from the criminal jurisdiction of the Palestinian Authority. In addition to the above mentioned Art. XVII(1)(a) Interim Agreement – which provides that the jurisdiction of the Palestinian Authority will not cover "issues that will be negotiated in the permanent status negotiations: Jerusalem, settlements [. . .] foreign relations and Israelis" – Art. XVII(2)(c) Interim Agreement reads "[t]he territorial and functional jurisdiction of the [Palestinian Authority] will apply to all persons, except for Israelis, unless otherwise provided in this Agreement". Art. I(2)(b) Annex IV to the Interim Agreement provides that "Israel has sole criminal jurisdiction over [. . .] offenses committed in the Territory[945] by Israelis"; and with regard to Area C, Art. I(2)(a) Annex IV to the Interim Agreement provides that "Israel has sole criminal jurisdiction over [. . .] offenses committed outside the Territory" – except in the case of crimes committed by Palestinians against Palestinians[946].

The difference of opinion in this matter pertains to the possibility of the Palestinian Authority having criminal jurisdiction over Israeli citizens despite the above mentioned provisions – given the unique circumstances of the case at hand.

---

942 Art. I(1)(b) Annex IV to the Interim Agreement.

943 See *supra* notes 12, 742.

944 Davenport, *et al.*, *supra* note 723, p. 11; Al-Haq, *supra* note 853, para. 36.

945 "Territory" is defined in Art. I(1)(a) Annex IV to the Interim Agreement as West Bank territory, except for Area C – which except for the settlements and the military locations, will be gradually transferred to the Palestinian side – and Gaza Strip territory, except for the settlements and the military installation area.

946 See *supra* note 942.

The first argument in favor of such possibility is based on the claim that in concluding the Interim Agreement with Israel, to temporarily exclude Israelis from the scope of their criminal jurisdiction in the West Bank and Gaza Strip, the Palestinians waived an inherent right, which, as bearers of the right to self-determination and to an independent state in the West Bank and Gaza Strip, they continues to hold. Such a waiver was conceived of along with many other compromises – such as the continued presence of Israeli settlements in the Palestinian territories – not as acceptance of any Israeli claims to such effect, but as part of a *bona fide* effort to secure an end to the ongoing Israeli-Palestinian conflict[947]. The fact that the Palestinians would automatically regain their inherent right to exercise criminal jurisdiction over Israeli citizens in the West Bank and Gaza Strip, should they decide to unilaterally withdraw from the Oslo Accords[948], reflects the importance of both the Palestinian right and the Accords. However, given the unique circumstances of the case at hand, the unlimited criminal jurisdiction of the Palestinian Authority in the West Bank and Gaza Strip should not be denied based on a bilateral instrument, which has limited effect as against third parties and can be unilaterally withdrawn from at any time[949].

The second argument in favor of Palestinian Authority criminal jurisdiction over Israeli citizens is based on the customary nature of the grave breaches regime of International Humanitarian Law[950]. Crimes within the jurisdiction of the ICC, including grave breaches of the Geneva Conventions[951], crimes against humanity and genocide, are crimes under customary international law[952] and many are widely recognized as being subject to universal jurisdiction[953]. The Palestinians – whose ratification documents for the Geneva Conventions were declined by the Government of Switzerland[954] – are not officially bound by the principle of *aut dedere aut iudicare* in respect of the grave breaches of the Geneva Conventions, which obliges all High Contracting Parties to enact legislation necessary to provide effective penal sanctions for those committing grave

947 Al-Haq, *supra* note 853, para. 32.

948 *Ibid.*

949 Ronen, "ICC Jurisdiction over Acts Committed in the Gaza Strip – Article 12(3) of the ICC Statute and Non-state Entities", *supra* note 512, p. 19.

950 Al-Haq, *supra* note 853, para. 33.

951 War crimes – Art. 8(2)(a) Rome-Statute.

952 ICJ, *Legality of the Threat or Use of Nuclear Weapons*, *supra* note 169, para. 79.

953 Macedo, Stephen, *et al.*, *The Princeton Principles on Universal Jurisdiction*, Princeton University, Program in Law and Public Affairs (2001), Principles 1(2) and 2(1).

954 See *supra* note 810.

breaches and to search for and prosecute offenders, regardless of nationality[955]. Nevertheless, following the publication of the Goldstone Report – which documented alleged Israeli grave breaches of the Geneva Conventions, which could constitute war crimes and, possibly, crimes against humanity[956] – the UN General Assembly endorsed the Report and urged the "Palestinian side" to:

> [Undertake] investigations that are independent, credible and in conformity with international standards into the serious violations of international humanitarian and international human rights law reported by the Fact-Finding Mission, towards ensuring accountability and justice[957].

This represents an acknowledgement by the international community that, irrespective of the question of formal Palestinian statehood, the "Palestinian side" not only has the ability to investigate and prosecute international crimes, it has the duty to do so – whereby, in order to conform to international standards, such investigations must be directed against all those responsible for the alleged crimes and not discriminate on grounds of nationality[958]. Therefore, while accepting the fact that Israeli citizens are excluded from (ordinary) Palestinian Authority criminal jurisdiction under the Oslo Accords, such exclusion cannot legitimately be considered as extending to international crimes, such as war crimes and crimes against humanity, as to do so would be incompatible with international law and standards[959].

Based on this argument – namely that the Palestinians have the duty to investigate and prosecute alleged international crimes committed on their territory, including grave breaches of the Geneva Conventions – some claim that despite not being a High Contracting Party, the Palestinians are bound by Art. 146 Fourth Geneva Convention. This, in turn, would cast doubt on the legality and effectiveness of (at least part of) the Interim Agreement, in which the Palestinians – protected persons under the occupation of a power of which they are not nationals[960] – explicitly exclude Israeli citizens from Palestinian criminal jurisdiction and, thus, surrender their rights and duties under Art. 146 Fourth Geneva

---

955 Art. 49 First Geneva Convention, Art. 50 Second Geneva Convention, Art. 129 Third Geneva Convention, Art. 146 Fourth Geneva Convention.

956 See *supra* notes 435, 450, 451, 458, 460.

957 UN General Assembly Resolution 64/10 (5 November 2009).

958 Al-Haq, *supra* note 853, para. 34; Kearney, *supra* note 901.

959 Al-Haq, *supra* note 853, para. 36; ICC Office of the Prosecutor, *Summary of Submissions on whether the Declaration Lodged by the Palestinian National Authority Meets Statutory Requirements*, *supra* note 711, para. 32; Gowlland-Debbas, *supra* note 787, para. 29.

960 Art. 4(1) Fourth Geneva Convention.

Convention. The drafters of the Convention, conscious of the experience during World War II when national governments struck agreements with occupying powers, which in many cases involved very serious drawbacks for the occupied people, addressed this problem in Art. 8 Fourth Geneva Convention, which provides that "[p]rotected persons may in no circumstances renounce in part or in entirety the rights secured to them by the present Convention". This is reinforced by Art. 47 Fourth Geneva Convention which reads:

> Protected persons who are in occupied territory shall not be deprived, in any case or in any manner whatsoever, of the benefits of the present Convention by any change introduced [. . .] into the institutions or government of the said territory, nor by any agreement concluded between the authorities of the occupied territories and the Occupying Power.

In conclusion, despite the Oslo Accords, on 21 January 2009, the Palestinian Authority had criminal jurisdiction over Israeli citizens alleged to have committed international crimes. Those who consider the Palestinian right / duty to investigate and prosecute alleged grave breaches of the Geneva Conventions as an indication of the Palestinian Authority being bound by Art. 146 Fourth Geneva Convention, go further and doubt the legal effect of (at least part of) the Interim Agreement – in which the protected persons renounce their rights under said provision – based on Art. 8 and 47 Fourth Geneva Convention.

Those who object to the possibility of the Palestinian Authority having criminal jurisdiction over Israeli citizens respond to the arguments brought above as follows: First, the claim that the Palestinian Authority would automatically regain its inherent right to exercise criminal jurisdiction over Israeli citizens, should it decide to unilaterally withdraw from the Oslo Accords, is based on the incorrect view that the possession of the right to self-determination (and independence), as such, grants inherent rights to exercise comprehensive criminal jurisdiction. There is no practice to this effect. On the contrary, the practice that does exist in similar cases clearly demonstrates that before full independence has been achieved, the administrating power continued to exercise criminal jurisdiction and no inherent or latent jurisdiction as such was recognized as belonging to the people possessing the right to self-determination[961]. It is important to note that this rule applies to the entire criminal jurisdiction in a certain territory – i.e. both over locals and foreigners. The only reason the Palestinian Authority has basic criminal jurisdiction over Palestinians despite said rule, is the fact that such jurisdiction was part of the Oslo Accords signed by Israel and the

961 Shaw, *supra* note 668, para. 62.

PLO[962]. Therefore, based on the above, it is very difficult to understand the logic behind the claim that the Palestinian Authority's criminal jurisdiction over Israeli citizens should be approved based on the Authority's possibility to withdraw from the Oslo Accords – the legal instrument, which created and defined its (limited) jurisdictional powers[963].

Second, the argument that the exclusion of Israeli citizens from Palestinian Authority criminal jurisdiction under the Interim Agreement does not extend to international crimes, cannot be based on the international community calling upon the Palestinians to investigate the commission of alleged war crimes during the Gaza armed conflict, as both Israel and the Palestinians were called upon to investigate (only) alleged crimes committed by their own side. Thus, it would be a mistake to interpret the Palestinian Authority's capacity and responsibility to investigate and prosecute alleged international crimes committed by its people as the capacity and responsibility to do the same with respect to Israeli citizens[964]. Furthermore, any attempt to establish a connection between possible Palestinian Authority criminal jurisdiction over Israeli citizens, on the one hand, and the fact that the grave breaches of the Geneva Conventions constitute crimes under customary international law, subject to universal jurisdiction, on the other, is incorrect. The Palestinian Authority is not a state[965] and as a non-High Contracting Party to the Geneva Conventions it is not affected by Art. 146 Fourth Geneva Convention. In addition, the fact that the grave breaches constitute violations of customary international law means that once incorporated into the relevant domestic legal system of a state, they would constitute domestic criminal offences – provided that the necessary jurisdictional provisions were in place. In the case at hand, there is no evidence that the Palestinian Authority has either incorporated the Geneva Conventions into its domestic law or, more significantly, provided its local courts with jurisdiction to hear relevant cases[966].

With regard to the view that doubts the legal effect of (at least part of) the Interim Agreement based on Art. 8 and 47 Fourth Geneva Convention – whereby protected persons may under no circumstances renounce rights and benefits secured to them by the Convention; assuming, for the sake of argument, that the Palestinians are bound by Art. 146 Fourth Geneva Convention, the connection between the obligation to investigate and prosecute international crimes under

---

962 See *supra* notes 933, 934.

963 Shaw, *supra* note 668, para. 62; Shany, "In Defence of Functional Interpretation of Article 12(3) of the Rome Statute", *supra* note 836, p. 339.

964 Shaw, *supra* note 668, para. 65.

965 See *supra* notes 813, 814; Macedo, *et al.*, *supra* note 953, Principle 1(2).

966 Shaw, *supra* note 668, paras. 64, 65.

said provision, on the one hand, and the rights and benefits protected by Art. 8 and 47 Fourth Geneva Convention, on the other, appears to amount to a *non sequitur*[967]. The legality of the Palestinians not fulfilling their "obligation" under Art. 146 Fourth Geneva Convention is further reinforced by Art. 98(2) Rome-Statute, which provides that the ICC "may not proceed with a request for surrender which would require the requested State to act inconsistently with its obligations under international agreements". Since no state should be placed in a situation, in which it is required to act inconsistently with its obligations under international agreements, it would be very difficult to explain why a non-state entity, such as the Palestinian Authority, would be expected to act in such a manner in the case at hand[968].

In conclusion, since its signing in 1995, the status of the Interim Agreement as a valid and binding legal agreement between Israel and the PLO has not changed[969]. This is especially true with regard to the provisions excluding Israeli citizens from Palestinian Authority criminal jurisdiction, so that on 21 January 2009, the Palestinian Authority did not have the capacity to exercise criminal jurisdiction over Israeli citizens.

2.5.2.2.3.4. Interim conclusion: The Palestinian Authority as a quasi-state for the purpose of the Rome Statute only

Prior to reaching a conclusion concerning the different views presented above with regard to the three main requirements of a quasi-state for the purpose of the Rome Statute only, one fundamental and undisputed fact concerning the Palestinian Authority, the entity which lodged the declaration under Art. 12(3) Rome-Statute on 21 January 2009, must be emphasized: The Palestinian Authority was created by the Oslo Accords and its legal and jurisdictional powers were explicitly defined therein by both signatories – the State of Israel and the PLO, the recognized representative of the Palestinian people[970].

The pivotal importance of this fact is fully reflected in the widely accepted[971] criminal jurisdiction of the Palestinian Authority over Palestinians. Prior to the commencement of the Oslo peace process between Israel and the Palestinians,

967 *Ibid.*, para. 66.

968 *Ibid.*, paras. 66, 67.

969 See *supra* note 925.

970 Brown, *The Palestinian Reform Agenda*, *supra* note 933, p. 12; See *supra* notes 743, 963.

971 Commission of the European Communities, *Commission Staff Working Paper, European Neighbourhood Policy – Country Report: Palestinian Authority of the West Bank and Gaza Strip* (2004), pp. 8-9; Brown, *The Palestinian Reform Agenda*, *supra* note 933, pp. 29-31; Shaw, *supra* note 668, para. 59; Al-Haq, *supra* note 853, para. 29.

the courts of the latter were gradually repressed and replaced by the Israeli military courts, eventually reaching a situation, in which even traffic and drug offences committed by Palestinians were no longer tried by the local Palestinian courts[972]. However, following the agreements reached in the course of the peace process, the pre-Oslo situation changed dramatically as a result of Israel transferring criminal jurisdiction over Palestinians – in all Palestinian territories – to the Palestinian Authority, while retaining the right to exercise concurrent criminal jurisdiction only in cases (i) of criminal offences committed against Israel or Israelis[973], and (ii) concerning Israel's security and its fight against terrorism[974].

With regard to the question concerning the possible (legal) effect of Hamas seizing complete control over the Gaza Strip on the Palestinian Authority's criminal jurisdiction over Palestinians, the prevailing opinion is that the Palestinian Authority's loss of effective control over the Gaza Strip is immaterial, as it has no effect on the Palestinian Authority's capacity to delegate its criminal jurisdiction over Palestinians to the ICC[975]. The Palestinian Authority remains the only internationally recognized government in the Palestinian territories and the sole political entity that can exercise jurisdiction over such territories in accordance with international law (excluding the above mentioned right of Israel to exercise concurrent criminal jurisdiction). The right to delegate jurisdiction is reflective of an internationally recognized legal authority, not of the material ability to exercise it[976]. In fact, situations, in which a state (or quasi-state) loses control over parts of its territory, represent a paradigmatic case for self-referral of situations to the ICC, as in such cases the respective state is "unable to carry out [the] proceedings"[977].

In conclusion, on 21 January 2009, the requirement of Palestinian Authority criminal jurisdiction over Palestinians was fulfilled. This conclusion is, without a doubt, fully based on the Oslo Accords; in order to ensure an equal and consistent decision process, the Oslo Accords shall play a central role in the decisions concerning the additional two requirements as well.

With regard to the question concerning the capacity of the Palestinian Authority to enter into international agreements, both proponents and opponents of such capacity agree that, formally, the Oslo Accords provide for a clear "divi-

---

972 See *supra* note 933.

973 See *supra* note 937.

974 See *supra* notes 939, 942.

975 Shany, "In Defence of Functional Interpretation of Article 12(3) of the Rome Statute", *supra* note 836, p. 338.

976 *Ibid.*, p. 339.

977 Art. 17(3) Rome-Statute.

sion of labor" between the Palestinian Authority and the PLO, whereby the former has the power to control and govern territory, but no power to engage in foreign relations[978], and the latter has no power to control territory, but full ability to engage in foreign relations – including negotiating and signing agreements with states or international organizations for the benefit of the Palestinian Authority in certain, clearly defined, cases[979].

The disagreement between the two views pertains to the current relevance of the mentioned "division of labor" and whether the international community still considers the limitations imposed on the Palestinian Authority in terms of foreign relations legitimate and valid. The arguments brought by both sides in this regard are relevant and correct, as there have been cases, in which the Palestinian Authority – either directly or through the PLO – has entered into international agreements in defiance of the Oslo Accords. However, considering the number of such cases and the respective time frame, such cases must be considered isolated. Accordingly, one could argue that such isolated cases reflect (i) a slow trend within the international community towards accepting the Palestinian Authority's right to freely enter into international agreements, or (ii) the exact opposite, as the very limited number of cases since 1993 clearly show that the approach of the overwhelming majority within the international community towards the validity, legal effect, intents and goals of the Oslo Accords has not changed since their conclusion.

That being said, one must keep in mind that the subject of the discussion at hand is not whether the Palestinian Authority was able to enter into international agreements in the past or if certain members of the international community consider the Palestinian Authority free to enter into such agreements, but only whether on 21 January 2009 the Palestinian Authority had the legal capacity to engage in foreign relations and enter into international agreements. Once again, the answer to this question is based on the Oslo Accords, according to which the Palestinian Authority was created and on which its legal powers depend. Although questions have often been raised concerning the continued validity of the Oslo Accords[980], none of the parties to the agreements have renounced them and they are regarded by Israel, the Palestinian Authority and the international community to be the principal benchmark for assessing the legal rights and powers

978 See *supra* note 914.

979 See *supra* note 913.

980 Shany, "Farawy, so Close: The Legal Status of Gaza After Israel's Disengagement", *supra* note 620, p. 381; Orkand, *supra* note 112, pp. 426-429.

attendant to the Palestinian Authority[981]. This fact, in combination with the clear wording of the Interim Agreement, which provides that "the [Palestinian Authority] will not have powers and responsibilities in the sphere of foreign relations"[982], leads to the conclusion that on 21 January 2009, the Palestinian Authority did not have the legal capacity to enter into international agreements. In this context it should be mentioned once again that the ability of the PLO to engage in foreign relations, enter into international agreements and represent the Palestinian self-determination unit on the international plane, was in no way limited by the Oslo Accords' "division of labor". Therefore, the conclusion reached here may have been very different, had the Art. 12(3) Rome-Statute declaration of 21 January 2009 been issued by the PLO and not the Palestinian Authority[983].

With regard to the requirement of Palestinian Authority criminal jurisdiction over Israeli citizens, both advocates and opponents of such jurisdiction agree that under the Oslo Accords all Israeli citizens residing in the Palestinian territories are excluded from the criminal jurisdiction of the Palestinian Authority[984]. The (main) disagreement between the two sides is based on the possibility that said exclusion pertains only to ordinary crimes, so that in the case of international crimes – such as war crimes and crimes against humanity – the Palestinian Authority would have criminal jurisdiction over Israeli citizens.

The analysis of arguments brought by both sides to this debate leads to the conclusion that the arguments of those opposing the possibility of Palestinian Authority criminal jurisdiction over Israeli citizens accused of committing international crimes are more convincing. First, the Palestinian Authority is not a state or a High Contracting Party to the Geneva Conventions and, therefore, cannot claim to be bound by universal jurisdiction[985] or Art. 146 Fourth Geneva Convention. Second, the Palestinian Authority was indeed called upon by the international community to investigate the alleged commission of international crimes during the Gaza armed conflict, however, such calls pertained only to the investigation of international crimes possibly committed by Palestinians, not Israelis. Therefore, the fact that the international community recognized the capacity of the Palestinian Authority to investigate and prosecute international

---

981 Shany, "In Defence of Functional Interpretation of Article 12(3) of the Rome Statute", *supra* note 836, pp. 341-342; See *supra* note 925.

982 See *supra* note 914.

983 Shany, "In Defence of Functional Interpretation of Article 12(3) of the Rome Statute", *supra* note 836, p. 341.

984 Art. XVII(1)(a) and (2)(c) Interim Agreement; Art. I(2)(a) and (b) Annex IV to the Interim Agreement.

985 Macedo, *et al.*, *supra* note 953, Principle 1(2).

crimes in its own territory, should not be understood as the capacity to do the same with respect to Israeli citizens[986]. Consequently, on 21 January 2009, the Palestinian Authority did not have criminal jurisdiction over Israeli citizens, as the exclusion of such jurisdiction by the Oslo Accords covers both ordinary and international crimes.

In conclusion, on 21 January 2009, the Palestinian Authority did not constitute a quasi-state for the purpose of the Rome Statute only, as it possessed only one of the three characteristics of adequate "government capacity" to delegate criminal jurisdiction to the ICC.

2.5.3. Conclusion

In light of the fact that Art. 12(3) Rome-Statute specifically uses the term "State", the first step in analyzing whether the Palestinian Authority's declaration under said provision met statutory requirements[987] was to examine whether the Palestinian Authority constituted a full-fledged state on 21 January 2009 – in accordance with a literal interpretation of the term "State". This possibility was analyzed extensively and was finally rejected due to the Palestinians' decision not to claim that a State of Palestine already exists – despite coming very close to fulfilling the factual requirements of statehood.

The rejection of full-fledged Palestinian statehood led to the alternative possibility of considering the Palestinian declaration as that of a quasi-state for the purpose of the Rome Statute only – in accordance with a teleological / functional interpretation of the term "State". The result of the debate regarding the possible advantages / disadvantages of applying such an interpretation was that – under the circumstances of the case at hand – the ultimate object and purpose of the Rome Statute would be well-served by applying the teleological / functional approach. This was followed by a discussion regarding the requirements of the term "quasi-state for the purpose of the Rome-Statute only" and whether the Palestinian Authority fulfilled such requirements on 21 January 2009. The latter was answered in the negative, as although the Palestinian Authority had obvious quasi-state features, the Oslo Accords (i) deprived it from exercising jurisdiction over Israelis, (ii) seriously restricted its ability to conduct foreign relations, and, thus, (iii) significantly limited its ability to delegate criminal jurisdiction to the ICC. Acceptance of ICC jurisdiction by way of delegation must respect such limitations, both conceptually (an entity cannot delegate more rights than it pos-

---

986 See *supra* note 964.

987 See *supra* note 663.

sesses) and in practice, in order to minimize the disruptive effects of the exercise of ICC jurisdiction on the international legal system[988].

In conclusion, according to both a literal and teleological / functional interpretation of the term "State", the Palestinian Authority's declaration of 21 January 2009, in which it accepted the exercise of ICC jurisdiction with respect to the events of the Gaza armed conflict, did not fulfill the requirements of Art. 12(3) Rome-Statute[989]. Accordingly, ICC territorial jurisdiction, in accordance with Art. 12(2)(alt. 2)(a) Rome-Statute, must be ruled out.

3. The ICC and individual participants in the Gaza armed conflict

Once the jurisdiction of the ICC over the events of a certain situation has been determined, the focus shifts from the standard (more general) requirements to the individuals involved in the specific situation. On this level, there are two main factors, which directly affect both if and how the ICC deals with specific individuals, namely (i) official capacity and immunity, and (ii) individual criminal responsibility. The effect these factors have on the actions taken by the ICC shall be analyzed in the following section.

3.1. Official capacity and immunity

One of the main declared goals of the ICC is to put an end to impunity for perpetrators responsible for crimes so grave that they threaten the peace, security and well-being of the world[990]. The importance of this goal was emphasized by UN Secretary-General Kofi Annan, who stated that the ICC shall "ensure that no ruler, no State, no junta, and no army anywhere can abuse human rights with impunity"[991]. In light of this ambitious goal and due to the fact that impunity and immunity are closely related, the way the ICC deals with the latter is of great significance.

---

988 Shany, "In Defence of Functional Interpretation of Article 12(3) of the Rome Statute", *supra* note 836, p. 343.

989 This final conclusion also pertains to the open question left in Chapter Two – 2.3.5, leading to the negation of ICC temporal jurisdiction over the events of the Gaza armed conflict.

990 Preamble paras. 3 and 5 Rome-Statute.

991 Statement to the International Bar Association in New York (11 June 1997).

3.1.1. Immunity *ratione materiae*[992]

According to its Art. 27(1), the Rome Statute shall:

> [A]pply equally to all persons without any distinction based on official capacity. In particular, official capacity as a Head of State or Government, a member of a Government or parliament, an elected representative or a government official shall in no case exempt a person from criminal responsibility under [the] Statute, nor shall it, in and of itself, constitute a ground for reduction of sentence.

The purpose of this provision[993] is to ensure that senior leaders do not evade criminal responsibility by arguing that they were acting in an official capacity and are, therefore, entitled to functional immunity[994].

Functional immunity, a well-established rule of customary international law[995], covers activities performed by every state official in the exercise of his/her function, regardless of where they are discharged. Such immunity does not come to an end when the relevant state organ relinquishes his/her official position and it has an *erga omnes* effect, so that it is opposable to any foreign state[996]. The rationale behind functional immunity is that crimes are committed by the state through the state official – acting as a mere vehicle for government policies, not as an individual criminal – so that such crimes should be attributed to the state, on behalf of which the official has acted[997].

Art. 27(1) Rome-Statute excludes the possibility of defense under functional immunity provided for both in international and national law[998]. The fairly detailed – yet not exhaustive[999] – list of state officials provided in Art. 27(1) Rome-

---

992 Also referred to as "functional immunity".

993 This provision is recognized under customary international law: Art. 7 of the Charter of the International Military Tribunal, Art. 4 of the 1948 Convention on the Prevention and Punishment of the Crime of Genocide, Art. 7(2) ICTY-Statute, Art. 6(2) ICTR-Statute.

994 Gaeta, Paola, "Official Capacity and Immunities", in: Cassese, Antonio, Paola Gaeta and John R.W.D. Jones (eds.), *The Rome Statute of the International Criminal Court: A Commentary*, Volumes 1, Oxford: Oxford University Press (2002), p. 990; Schabas, *A Commentary on the Rome Statute*, *supra* note 360, Art. 27, p. 449; Tunks, Michael A., "Diplomats or Defendants? Defining the Future of Head-of-State Immunity", *Duke Law Journal* 52 (2002), pp. 660-661.

995 *The Prosecutor v. Tihomir Blaskic*, ICTY Appeals Chamber (29 October 1997), para. 38.

996 Gaeta, *supra* note 994, pp. 975-976.

997 *Ibid.*, p. 976; Schabas, *A Commentary on the Rome Statute*, *supra* note 360, Art. 27, pp. 447-448; Akande, Dapo, "International Law Immunities and the International Criminal Court", *American Journal of International Law* 98 (2004), p. 413.

998 Gaeta, *supra* note 994, p. 978.

999 Werle, *supra* note 347, para. 653.

Statute emphasizes the principle that all officials – from the head of state to the last government official – are covered by Art. 27(1) Rome-Statute and, thus, can be prosecuted and tried[1000].

3.1.2. Immunity *ratione personae*[1001]

Art. 27(2) Rome-Statute provides that:

> Immunities or special procedural rules which may attach to the official capacity of a person, whether under national[1002] or international law[1003], shall not bar the [ICC] from exercising its jurisdiction over such a person.

Personal immunity, which is only granted to some specific classes of individuals performing state functions abroad, pertains to the particular status of the holder and is meant to enable him/her to carry out his/her official duties within the territory of a foreign state[1004]. This immunity covers all acts performed by the state official – both during / prior to assumption of the official function and within / outside the territory of the relevant foreign state[1005]. Personal immunity provides inviolability from arrest and exemption from criminal, civil and administrative jurisdiction only vis-à-vis the legal system of the state where the individual is discharging his/her official function, and may be withdrawn upon request from the state to which the individual organ belongs[1006]. Unlike functional immunity, personal immunity lasts only as long as the specific individual's tenure in office[1007].

3.1.2.1. Art. 27(2) Rome-Statute and officials of non-States Parties

Art. 27(2) Rome-Statute is very clear with regard to the fact that any type of personal immunity enjoyed by officials of States Parties shall have no effect on the ICC's ability to exercise its personal jurisdiction over such individuals. The matter becomes more difficult when officials of non-States Parties are involved.

1000 Gaeta, *supra* note 994, p. 990; Ambos, Kai, "General Principles of Criminal Law in the Rome Statute", *Criminal Law Forum* 10 (1999), pp. 23-24.

1001 Also referred to as "Head of State immunity" or "personal immunity".

1002 Including national law ranked as constitutional law.

1003 The 1961 Vienna Convention on Diplomatic Relations; The 1969 Convention on Special Missions; Case Concerning the Arrest Warrant of 11 April 2000 (*Democratic Republic of the Congo v. Belgium*), ICJ (14 February 2002), paras. 54, 55.

1004 Akande, "International Law Immunities and the International Criminal Court", *supra* note 997, pp. 409-410.

1005 Gaeta, *supra* note 994, p. 976.

1006 *Ibid.*, pp. 976-977.

1007 Werle, *supra* note 347, paras. 655, 656.

According to one opinion, by ratifying or acceding to the Rome Statute, States Parties in effect renounce their right to immunity, which exists by virtue of customary international law. States Parties can make such a decision in their own name, but there is no doubt they cannot (i) make such a decision on behalf of non-States Parties, or (ii) decide – by treaty – to deprive non-States Parties from their right to immunity under international law[1008]. This conclusion is further confirmed by Art. 34 of the 1969 Vienna Convention on the Law of Treaties, which states that "[a] treaty does not create either obligations or rights for a third State without its consent".

On the other hand, in the *Al Bashir* case, Pre-Trial Chamber I of the ICC stated that "the current position of Omar Al Bashir as Head of a state which is not a party to the Statute, has no effect on the Court's jurisdiction over the present case"[1009]. Two of the main reasons provided by the Pre-Trial Chamber[1010] in favor of the application of Art. 27(2) Rome-Statute to officials of non-States Parties were: First, According to Art. 21 Rome-Statute, the other sources of law provided for in Art. 21(1)(b) and (c) Rome-Statute can only be resorted to when there is a *lacuna* in the written law contained in the Rome Statute, the Elements of Crimes and the ICC Rules of Procedure and Evidence[1011]. This means that even if general public international law provides for head of state immunity, it is not formally contemplated by Art. 27(2) Rome-Statute and, therefore, cannot be invoked in proceedings before the ICC. In other words, Art. 27(2) Rome-Statute applies to officials of non-States Parties because the provision does not state the contrary[1012].

Second, by referring the Darfur situation to the ICC, the UN Security Council[1013] has accepted that the investigation into the situation and the possible prosecution arising therefrom will take place in accordance with the statutory framework provided in the Rome Statute, the Elements of Crimes and the ICC Rules of Procedure and Evidence[1014]. This, in combination with the fact that one

---

1008 Schabas, *An Introduction to the International Criminal Court*, 3rd edition, *supra* note 336, p. 74.

1009 ICC, *The Prosecutor v. Omar Hassan Ahmad Al Bashir*, *supra* note 365, para. 41.

1010 In total, Pre-Trial Chamber I provided four reasons for its conclusion – see *ibid.*, para. 42.

1011 ICC, *The Prosecutor v. Omar Hassan Ahmad Al Bashir*, *supra* note 365, para. 44.

1012 Schabas, *A Commentary on the Rome Statute*, *supra* note 360, Art. 27, p. 451.

1013 The argument that UN Security Council referrals automatically imply the removal of immunity must be rejected, as this would lead to the unacceptable consequence of a different legal regime for Security Council referrals, on the one hand, and State Party referrals and *proprio motu* triggering by the Prosecutor, on the other.

1014 ICC, *The Prosecutor v. Omar Hassan Ahmad Al Bashir*, *supra* note 365, para. 45.

must assume that the UN Security Council knew of (i) Art. 34 of the 1969 Vienna Convention on the Law of Treaties, and (ii) the framework of customary international law concerning immunities of state officials, provides a (more) convincing argument for the application of Art. 27(2) Rome-Statute to officials of non-States Parties[1015].

3.1.2.2. Art. 27(2) in relation to Art. 98(1) Rome-Statute

Despite the very clear message – regarding the ineffectiveness of any kind of official capacity and immunity before the ICC – conveyed by Art. 27 Rome-Statute, the issue of immunity in connection with international crimes and the ICC is still much misunderstood, due to the fact that two provisions in different parts of the Rome-Statute – namely Art. 27 and 98 – play a decisive role therein[1016].

Art. 98(1) Rome-Statute provides that:

> The [ICC] may not proceed with a request for surrender or assistance which would require the requested State to act inconsistently with its obligations under international law[1017] with respect to the State or diplomatic immunity of a person or property of a third State, unless the [ICC] can first obtain the cooperation of that third State for the waiver of the immunity.

The immediate question arising from this provision concerns the alleged conflict between Art. 27(2) Rome-Statute, which provides that immunities or special procedural rules shall not bar the ICC from exercising its jurisdiction, and Art. 98(1) Rome-Statute, which provides that the ICC may not exercise its jurisdiction without obtaining a waiver of immunity from the third state[1018]. At first glance, Art. 98(1) Rome-Statute seems to significantly narrow the scope of Art. 27(2) Rome-Statute, as the ICC may find a considerable impediment to the exercise of its jurisdiction over individuals who, as a result of their official function, enjoy personal immunity in foreign states by virtue of international law. The ICC's dependency on a waiver of immunity from the sending state of such individuals, in combination with the fact that (i) the ICC cannot execute arrest

---

1015 Schabas, *A Commentary on the Rome Statute*, *supra* note 360, Art. 27, p. 451.

1016 Schabas, *An Introduction to the International Criminal Court*, 3rd edition, *supra* note 336, p. 72.

1017 Resulting either from treaty or customary law.

1018 Triffterer, Otto, in: Triffterer, Otto (ed.), *Commentary on the Rome Statute of the International Criminal Court – Observers' Notes, Article by Article* , 2nd edition, Munich: C.H.Beck (2008), Art. 27, para. 31.

warrants by itself and is, therefore, dependent on international cooperation[1019], and (ii) the Rome Statute does not allow trial in *absentia*[1020], could lead to the conclusion that, contrary to the wording of Art. 27(2) Rome-Statute, personal immunity can bar the ICC from exercising its jurisdiction[1021].

A more in-depth analysis of the two provisions and their position in the Rome Statute shows that there is no incompatibility or inconsistency between the two, as Art. 27 Rome-Statute governs the exercise of jurisdiction over an accused before the ICC and Art. 98 Rome-Statute, on the other hand, applies solely to obligations of cooperation[1022]. In addition, Art. 98(1) Rome-Statute, which in no way deals with or (directly) limits the ability of the ICC to exercise its jurisdiction, has an indirect influence on ICC jurisdiction[1023] only in the case, in which the sending (third) state is a non-State Party[1024]. Therefore, if both the requested and the sending states are States Parties, the ICC may request the arrest and surrender of an individual without obtaining a waiver of immunity from the sending state, and the requested state would be obliged to comply with such requests[1025].

3.1.3. Implementation in the case at hand and conclusion

Should the events of the Gaza armed conflict reach The Hague – as a result of (i) the Prosecutor reaching a different conclusion than the one presented above, thus, deciding that the crimes allegedly committed during the Gaza conflict fall within the jurisdiction of the ICC, or (ii) a UN Security Council referral pursuant to Art. 13(b) Rome-Statute[1026] – the court's personal jurisdiction shall in no way be (directly) affected or limited by any type of immunity possibly enjoyed by Israeli officials: Art. 27(1) Rome-Statute, which provides that the Statute shall apply equally to all persons without distinction based on official capacity, excludes any possibility of functional immunity based on the argument that crimes

---

1019 Akande, "International Law Immunities and the International Criminal Court", *supra* note 997, p. 420.

1020 Art. 63(1) Rome-Statute.

1021 Gaeta, *supra* note 994, pp. 992-993.

1022 Schabas, *A Commentary on the Rome Statute*, *supra* note 360, Art. 27, p. 452.

1023 Gadirov, Javid, *Mapping International Justice: Immunity of State Officials and Individual Criminal Responsibility*, Budapest: CEU, Budapest College (2008), p. 202.

1024 So that "third State" in Art. 98(1) Rome-Statute means non-State Party.

1025 Gaeta, *supra* note 994, p. 994; Akande, "International Law Immunities and the International Criminal Court", *supra* note 997, p. 425; Gallant, "Jurisdiction to Adjudicate and Jurisdiction to Prescribe in International Criminal Courts", *supra* note 475, p. 805.

1026 See *supra* note 872.

are committed by the state involved in the armed conflict, not by its senior government officials[1027], who merely execute state policies. Art. 27(2) Rome-Statute further provides that any kind of personal immunity (still[1028]) enjoyed by Israel's senior government officials shall in no way limit the ICC from executing its personal jurisdiction over such officials[1029].

The fact that the ICC's personal jurisdiction over senior Israeli government officials would in no way be affected by functional or personal immunity enjoyed by the latter, leads to the very important question concerning the ICC's actual ability to bring about the arrest and surrender of such officials if necessary[1030]. Since Israel and other non-States Parties are not expected to assist the ICC with any such request[1031], this question applies only to States Parties, on the territory of which said Israeli government officials may be found. This case is addressed in Art. 98(1) Rome-Statute, which states that despite its undisputed personal jurisdiction over such government officials, the ICC would be barred from proceeding with the request for their arrest and surrender, if such request would require States Parties to violate internationally recognized personal immunity enjoyed by senior Israeli government officials while representing their state abroad – a state which did not renounce the right of its representatives to immunity by becoming a State Party to the Rome Statute and (most likely) will not waive such right under Art. 98(1) Rome-Statute.

Therefore, in the case at hand one must make a distinction between the effect of immunity on the court's personal jurisdiction *per se* and the court's ability to exercise such jurisdiction. With regard to the former, the provisions of the Rome Statute clearly state that ICC personal jurisdiction over Israeli government officials, who took part in the Gaza armed conflict and are expected to be the focus of the court's efforts, shall in no way be affected or limited by functional or personal immunity enjoyed by such officials. However, personal immunity – established and recognized under customary international law – shall have an

---

1027 Senior military commanders do not enjoy any kind of immunity dealt with in Art. 27 Rome-Statute.

1028 Since personal immunity lasts only as long as the specific individual's tenure in office, such immunity could be immediately ruled out if the specific individual no longer holds an official position.

1029 The fact that Israel is a non-State Party has no effect on the applicability of Art. 27(2) Rome-Statute – see *supra* note 1009.

1030 The answer to this question could significantly influence Israel's position in the international community and its ability to maintain its ties with some of the most influential nations in the world.

1031 Scheffer, David J., "Article 98(2) of the Rome Statute: America's Original Intent", *Journal of International Criminal Justice* 3 (2005), pp. 336, 338.

effect on the court's ability to exercise its personal jurisdiction, as it would prevent the automatic arrest and surrender to the ICC of Israeli government officials by States Parties.

3.2. Individual criminal responsibility

According to Art. 25(2) Rome-Statute, a person who commits a crime[1032] within ICC jurisdiction shall be individually responsible and liable for punishment in accordance with the Statute. Since commission of a crime by a person is not limited to direct perpetration[1033] and, therefore, can have different modes of participation and expansion of attribution, Art. 25(3) Rome-Statute regulates in detail the modalities of individual criminal responsibility and distinguishes four modes of criminal participation: Committing a crime as a perpetrator – Art. 25(3)(a) Rome-Statute; ordering, soliciting or inducing a crime – Art. 25(3)(b) Rome-Statute; aiding and abetting – Art. 25(3)(c) Rome-Statute; and contributing in any other way to the commission of a crime by a group – Art. 25(3)(d) Rome-Statute[1034].

The practical effect of this differentiation in terminology and placement into separate categories is based on the fact that the particular mode of participation may serve as an indicator of the degree of criminal responsibility that must be taken into account at the sentencing stage[1035].

3.2.1. Commission of a crime

Art. 25(3)(a) distinguishes between three forms of commission: Immediate perpetration ("as an individual"), co-perpetration ("jointly with another"), and perpetration by means ("through another person")[1036]. When large scale atrocities of the kind likely to attract the interest of international criminal tribunals take

---

1032 The term "crime" shall include the plural thereof and vice versa – as applicable.

1033 The ICC, like its earlier models at Nuremberg, The Hague and Arusha, targets the major criminals responsible for large-scale atrocities. Most of its "clientele" will not be the actual perpetrators of the crimes, soiling their hands with flesh and blood. Rather, they will be those who organize, plan and incite genocide, crimes against humanity and war crimes.

1034 Art. 25(3)(e) and (f) Rome-Statute do not concern modes of participation, but criminalize certain preparatory actions, namely incitement to commit genocide and attempt.

1035 Werle, *supra* note 347, para. 448.

1036 These three forms of commission under Art. 25(3)(a) Rome-Statute are described as "principal liability" or "perpetration", while modes of participation under Art. 25(3)(b) - (d) Rome-Statute are described as "accessory / accomplice liability".

place, those who bear the greatest responsibility are often several layers removed from the physical perpetrators who actually carry out the killings, rapes and other acts – and are, therefore, considered under some approaches to be only accessories or accomplices to the crimes. This so-called objective theory of liability – based on the personal performance of the substantive elements of a crime – has been discarded by the ICC and replaced by a theory emphasizing the control a person has over the commission of the crime[1037]. This criterion of control, common to all three forms of commission[1038], is the criterion which warrants the higher degree of responsibility that distinguishes commission from other forms of participation[1039].

3.2.1.1. Immediate perpetration

In accordance with customary international law, a person commits a crime as an individual under the first alternative of Art. 25(3)(a) Rome-Statute if he/she physically[1040], either completely alone or with an accomplice[1041], fulfills all substantive elements of the crime and, in addition, meets the required *mens rea* in his/her own person. Furthermore, a perpetrator can commit a crime under this alternative by omission[1042].

3.2.1.2. Co-perpetration

Co-perpetration under the second alternative of Art. 25(3)(a) Rome-Statute, is characterized by a functional division of the criminal tasks between the different (at least two) co-perpetrators, who are normally interrelated by a common plan or agreement. Each co-perpetrator fulfills a certain task, which contributes[1043] to the commission of the crime and without which the commission of such crime would not be possible[1044]. Because each co-perpetrator could frustrate the commission of the crime by not carrying out his/her task, the co-perpetrators depend

---

1037 Schabas, *A Commentary on the Rome Statute*, *supra* note 360, Art. 25, p. 424.

1038 ICC, *The Prosecutor v. Thomas Lubanga Dyilo* (29 January 2007), *supra* note 424, paras. 330 *et seq*.

1039 Werle, *supra* note 347, para. 452.

1040 Ambos, *supra* note 475, Art. 25, para. 7.

1041 Eser, *supra* note 483, p. 789.

1042 Werle, *supra* note 347, para. 453.

1043 Such a contribution is not restricted to the direct execution of the crime. Contributions removed from the actual crime, such as planning and organization, can be essential and can indicate a particularly high degree of responsibility.

1044 Responsibility for co-perpetration can only be attributed to someone who renders an essential contribution to the commission of the crime. Acts of lesser weight fall short of this standard, but may qualify as "assistance" or "contribution to the commission of a crime by a group" under Art. 25(3)(c) and (d) respectively.

on one another and, thus, share control over the commission of the crime[1045]. The common plan or agreement forms the basis of a reciprocal or mutual attribution of the different contributions, holding each co-perpetrator responsible for the entire crime[1046]. The requirement of a common plan is not fulfilled if a certain consequence of the commission of the crime, that is not in itself a part of the common plan, is merely foreseeable for a participant. Rather, it is necessary that the co-perpetrator knew of the risk concerning the certain consequence and accepted its occurrence as a possible result of the execution of the original common plan[1047]. With regard to the mental element, each co-perpetrator must fulfill all elements of the crime's *mens rea* in his/her own person[1048], as attribution of subjective elements is not possible[1049].

3.2.1.3. Perpetration by means

The Rome Statute is probably the first international instrument, in which the mode of perpetration by means – i.e. by using another person as a tool – is explicitly regulated[1050]. Perpetration by means is characterized by the predominance of an indirect perpetrator, who as the mastermind or the "man in the background" uses the direct perpetrator as an instrument or tool to commit the crime[1051]. The underlying rationale for this mode of perpetration is that the indirect perpetrator exercises control over the will of the direct perpetrator[1052], so that typically the "human tool" will be an innocent agent, not responsible for the criminal act – in particular because he/she acted erroneously, is not culpable because of a mental defect, is of minor age or otherwise excused[1053].

The wording "regardless of whether that other person is criminally responsible" in Art. 25(3)(a) Rome-Statute confirms, however, that perpetration by means is also possible when the direct perpetrator is (fully) criminally responsible. In this context, the notion of "(indirect) perpetrator behind the (direct) perpetrator" – which is especially characteristic for military organizations and other

1045 Schabas, *A Commentary on the Rome Statute*, *supra* note 360, Art. 25, pp. 428-429.

1046 Ambos, *supra* note 475, Art. 25, para. 8.

1047 Werle, *supra* note 347, para. 469.

1048 ICC, *The Prosecutor v. Thomas Lubanga Dyilo* (29 January 2007), *supra* note 424, para. 349; ICC, *The Prosecutor v. Germain Katanga and Mathieu Ngudjolo Chui*, *supra* note 364, para. 527.

1049 Werle, *supra* note 347, para. 471.

1050 Eser, *supra* note 483, p. 793.

1051 *Ibid.*; Ambos, *supra* note 475, Art. 25, para. 10.

1052 Werle, *supra* note 347, para. 473.

1053 Ambos, *supra* note 475, Art. 25, para. 10; Eser, *supra* note 483, p. 793.

hierarchically organized power structures[1054] – is of particular relevance. In such cases, attribution of the crime committed by the direct perpetrator to the indirect perpetrator is only possible if the latter has such organizational control that he/she dominates the conduct of the former[1055]. Due to the fact that a fully responsible direct perpetrator can, at any time, decide to abandon the criminal plan, his/her conduct is never fully dominated by the indirect perpetrator. Therefore, perpetration by means is only then given, when the lack of conduct domination on the part of the indirect perpetrator is compensated by control over the organization (or parts of it), which provides him/her with a high degree of flexibility regarding the personnel necessary to commit the crime[1056].

According to Pre-Trial Chamber I of the ICC, indirect co-perpetration (joint perpetration by means) is also possible. If several persons who control differing hierarchies agree to commit a crime, the crime committed under the agreement by the direct perpetrators they employ as "tools" are subject to reciprocal attribution[1057]. As a result, indirect perpetration in this situation extends even to acts by direct perpetrators who are not subordinate to the persons to whom their acts are attributed[1058].

With regard to the mental element, perpetration by means requires that the accused personally fulfill all subjective elements of the envisaged crime – including any required specific intent[1059]. In addition he/she must be aware of the factual circumstances enabling him/her to control the commission of the crime through another person[1060].

3.2.2. Encouragement of a crime

According to Art. 25(3)(b) Rome-Statute, a person shall be criminally responsible and liable for punishment for a crime within the jurisdiction of the ICC, if that person orders, solicits or induces the commission of such a crime. All these

1054 Eser, *supra* note 483, p. 795.

1055 This concept has been recognized and applied by the Jerusalem District Court in the Eichmann Trial, where the court invoked – for the specific macro crimes in question – a type of organizational responsibility or domination of the act by the man at the desk.

1056 Ambos, *supra* note 475, Art. 25, para. 11.

1057 ICC, *The Prosecutor v. Germain Katanga and Mathieu Ngudjolo Chui*, *supra* note 364, paras. 520 *et seq.*; ICC, *The Prosecutor v. Omar Hassan Ahmad Al Bashir*, *supra* note 365, para. 213.

1058 Werle, *supra* note 347, para. 479.

1059 ICC, *The Prosecutor v. Germain Katanga and Mathieu Ngudjolo Chui*, *supra* note 364, para. 527.

1060 *Ibid.*, para. 538.

modes of instigation[1061] – which are listed as secondary or accessory liability[1062] – have in common that the participant does not execute the crime him/herself, but instigates another person to do so, whereby such instigation leads to criminal responsibility only if the crime is executed in fact or has at least been attempted[1063].

3.2.2.1. Ordering the commission of a crime

The criminal responsibility and liability of a person who ordered the commission of a crime within the jurisdiction of the ICC – as stated in Art. 25(3)(b)(alt. 1) Rome-Statute – reflects customary international law[1064]. The term "ordering" assumes the existence of a relationship, typically military in nature, of subordination between the person giving and the person receiving the order[1065] – whereby the person giving the order uses his/her position in the relationship[1066] to convince or coerce the other to commit a crime[1067].

Despite the fact that ordering the commission of a crime is clearly considered the strongest form of instigation – as in addition to violating his/her duty to hinder his/her subordinates from wrongdoing, the person in the superior position actively abuses his/her powers in ordering the commission of the crime[1068] – some question whether it would have been more appropriate to deal with a matter such as "ordering" in other provisions[1069]. Some legal experts argue that a person ordering the commission of a crime is not a mere accomplice, but rather a perpetrator by means[1070]. According to this opinion, while the case of commanders not preventing the commission of crimes by subordinates is covered as an offence of omission by Art. 28 Rome-Statute[1071], the active ordering of a subordinate to commit a crime constitutes the intentional exploitation of the hierarchical power structure, in order to commit a crime through others, and must, therefore, be dealt with under Art. 25(3)(a) Rome-Statute[1072]. Pre-Trial Chamber

---

1061 Eser, *supra* note 483, p. 795.

1062 Schabas, *A Commentary on the Rome Statute*, *supra* note 360, Art. 25, p. 431.

1063 Werle, *supra* note 347, para. 481.

1064 See Art. 7(1) ICTY-Statute, Art. 6(1) ICTR-Statute, Art. 129(1) Third Geneva Convention, Art. 146(1) Fourth Geneva Convention.

1065 Werle, *supra* note 347, para. 486.

1066 Either *de jure* or *de facto* authority to order.

1067 Schabas, *A Commentary on the Rome Statute*, *supra* note 360, Art. 25, p. 432.

1068 Eser, *supra* note 483, pp. 796-797.

1069 *Ibid.*, p. 797.

1070 Ambos, *supra* note 475, Art. 25, para. 14.

1071 Discussed below in further detail.

1072 Eser, *supra* note 483, p. 797; Ambos, *supra* note 475, Art. 25, para. 14.

I of the ICC, on the other hand, has noted that Art. 25(3)(b)(alt. 1) Rome-Statute presents a different kind of "ordering" than that of the leader in command of an organization, who commits crimes through others and thereby incurs liability as a principle perpetrator under Art. 25(3)(a) Rome-Statute[1073]. "The highest authority does not merely order the commission of a crime, but through his control over the organisation, essentially decides whether and how the crime would be committed"[1074].

This question could, perhaps, be answered by the mental element of "ordering", which requires that the person giving the order intend that a crime be committed in the execution of that order or, at least, be aware of the substantial likelihood that a crime will be committed[1075]. The intent of the person giving the order must be directed at causing the principal to commit the specific crime – in the specific state of mind required by the Rome Statute[1076]. It is not, however, necessary for the person giving the order to possess the specific intent required by the crime. This lesser standard of *mens rea* adequately reflects the fact that ordering the commission of a crime warrants a higher level of responsibility within accessory liability – resulting from the authority within the hierarchical structure – but does not constitute perpetration by means[1077].

3.2.2.2. Soliciting or inducing the commission of a crime

"Soliciting" (a crime) means, *inter alia*, urging, advising, commanding, authorizing, or otherwise inciting another person to commit a crime[1078]. "Inducing" means to affect, cause, influence an act or course of conduct, led by persuasion or reasoning[1079]. Since a comparison between the two definitions does not provide clear demarcations between them, it seems advisable to use the term "inducing" as an umbrella term – covering "soliciting" as a stronger, more specific method of instigating another person to commit a crime[1080].

1073 ICC, *The Prosecutor v. Germain Katanga and Mathieu Ngudjolo Chui*, *supra* note 364, para. 517.

1074 *Ibid.*, para. 518.

1075 Werle, *supra* note 347, para. 487.

1076 Eser, *supra* note 483, p. 797.

1077 Werle, *supra* note 347, para. 488.

1078 Kim, Young Sok, *The Law of the International Criminal Court*, Buffalo: William S. Hein & Co., Inc. (2007), p. 159.

1079 Eser, *supra* note 483, p. 796.

1080 *Ibid.*; Kim, *supra* note 1078, p. 159.

Criminal responsibility under Art. 25(3)(b)(alt. 2 and 3) Rome-Statute requires a causal link[1081] between the "inducing" and the execution of the crime by the perpetrator. Such a causal link is given when the "inducing" substantially contributed[1082] to the conduct of the perpetrator[1083] – whereby it is not necessary to show that the crime would not have occurred had it not been for the involvement of the instigator[1084]. In contrast to "ordering", a superior-subordinate relationship in not required in the case of "inducing"[1085].

Subjectively, "inducing" requires that the instigator wished to provoke or induce the commission of the crime, or that he/she was aware of the substantial likelihood that the commission of the crime would result from his/her conduct. Sharing the intent required by the specific crime is not required[1086]. The instigator cannot be held liable for crimes which go beyond his/her intent[1087], so that an excess[1088] by the principal shall not be attributed to the instigator[1089].

3.2.3. Assisting the commission of a crime

Art. 25(3)(c) Rome-Statute, which codifies any other assistance not covered by Art. 25(3)(b) Rome-Statute[1090], states that a person shall be criminally responsible if he/she, for the purpose of facilitating the commission of a crime, aids, abets or otherwise assists in its commission or its attempted[1091] commission – including providing the means for its commission. The term "aiding" can be defined as giving assistance to someone, while the term "abetting" would involve

---

1081 Such a causal link / influence is normally of psychological nature, but may also take the form of physical pressure within the meaning of *vis compulsiva*. It may also occur in a chain – i.e. a person induces another to induce a third person to commit a crime.

1082 "Inducing" can take the form of an omission as well as an act. Mere presence when an atrocity is being committed may amount to "inducing" if the accused is a figure of authority who does nothing to discourage or halt the attack.

1083 Werle, *supra* note 347, para. 483.

1084 Schabas, *A Commentary on the Rome Statute*, *supra* note 360, Art. 25, p. 433.

1085 Ambos, *supra* note 475, Art. 25, para. 15.

1086 Werle, *supra* note 347, paras. 484, 485.

1087 Eser, *supra* note 483, p. 798.

1088 This is clearly the case when (i) the principal commits another crime than he was instigated to, or (ii) the principal does more than he was instigated to. When the deviation of the actual from the proposed crime is inessential, the excess is irrelevant.

1089 This applies to "ordering" (alt. 1) as well.

1090 Kim, *supra* note 1078, p. 160.

1091 Preparatory contributions, though determined to enable the commission of a crime, remain unpunishable if the intended principal crime is not carried out, or at least reaches the stage of an attempt.

facilitating the commission of an act by being sympathetic thereto[1092]. Due to the fact that "aiding" is practically identical with assisting, and "abetting" comes very close to instigation, it appears to be preferable to resort to the umbrella term of "assistance" when referring to a contribution facilitating the commission of a crime under Art. 25(3)(c) Rome-Statute[1093].

Assisting the commission of a crime, as the weakest form of complicity, could cover any act which contributes to the commission (or attempted commission) of a crime[1094]. The main challenge is to define minimum requirements, which distinguish between "assistance" – punishable under Art. 25(3)(c) Rome-Statute – and any remote involvement in / connection with the planning or performing of the crime[1095]. The prevailing opinion requires that the "assistance" contribute to the commission of the crime in a direct and substantial way[1096] – whereby "substantial" means that the contribution has an effect on / causal relationship with the commission of the crime[1097]. The "assistance" need not be rendered at the location or at the time the crime is committed, as it can be given before, during or even after the execution of the crime[1098].

Art. 25(3)(c) Rome-Statute requires two different forms of *mens rea*: (i) With regard to facilitating the commission of the crime, the accused must act with "purpose" – i.e. more than the mere knowledge thereof, the accused must know and wish that his/her assistance shall facilitate the commission of the crime[1099], (ii) with regard to other mental elements, the person giving assistance must have intent concerning (both) the intentional commission of the crime by the principal and the requisite elements of his/her assistance[1100].

3.2.4. Any other contribution to the commission of a crime

According to Art. 25(3)(d) Rome-Statute, a person shall be criminally responsible and liable for punishment if that person intentionally[1101] contributes – in any

---

1092 ICTR, *The Prosecutor v. Jean-Paul Akayesu*, *supra* note 413, para. 484.
1093 Eser, *supra* note 483, p. 799.
1094 Ambos, *supra* note 475, Art. 25, para. 17.
1095 Eser, *supra* note 483, p. 799.
1096 ICTY, *The Prosecutor v. Dusko Tadic* (7 May 1997), *supra* note 363, paras. 674, 688-692.
1097 *Ibid.*, para. 688.
1098 Werle, *supra* note 347, para. 491; Ambos, *supra* note 475, Art. 25, para. 17.
1099 Ambos, *supra* note 475, Art. 25, para. 23; Eser, *supra* note 483, p. 801.
1100 Eser, *supra* note 483, p. 801.
1101 Art. 25(3)(d) Rome-Statute: The contribution shall be made (i) "with the aim of furthering the criminal activity or criminal purpose of the group, where such activity or pur-

other way[1102] – to the commission (or attempted commission) of a crime within ICC jurisdiction by a group[1103] of persons acting with a common purpose.

The text of Art. 25(3)(d) Rome-Statute was derived from the 1997 International Convention for the Suppression of Terrorist Bombings, which, in turn, was borrowed from Art. 3(4) of the 1996 Convention Relating to Extradition between the Member States of the European Union[1104]. Due to the wording of its ancestor in the Preparatory Committee Draft Statute[1105], this "catch-all" rule[1106] has been described as encompassing the notion of conspiracy. However, the provision was replaced entirely at the Rome Conference and language evoking the concept of conspiracy disappeared[1107]. Since the threshold of "assistance" under Art. 25(3)(c) Rome-Statute is already so low, it is difficult to imagine many cases, in which a special provision such as Art. 25(3)(d) Rome-Statute would be needed[1108].

3.2.5. Superior responsibility

Art. 28(a) Rome-Statute provides that – in addition to other grounds of criminal responsibility under the Rome Statute – a military commander[1109] shall be criminally responsible for crimes within the jurisdiction of the ICC committed (or at least attempted[1110]) by forces under his/her effective command and control, as a result of his/her failure to exercise proper control over such forces. Art. 28(b)

---

pose involves the commission of a crime within the jurisdiction of the [ICC]", or (ii) "in the knowledge of the intention of the group to commit the crime".

1102 Meaning any contribution not covered by another form of participation – especially "assistance".

1103 Any association of at least three persons.

1104 Schabas, *A Commentary on the Rome Statute, supra* note 360, Art. 25, p. 436.

1105 Which reads "agrees with another person or persons that such a crime be committed and an overt act in furtherance of the agreement is committed by any of these persons that manifests their intent".

1106 Werle, *supra* note 347, para. 494.

1107 Schabas, *A Commentary on the Rome Statute, supra* note 360, Art. 25, pp. 436-437.

1108 Eser, *supra* note 483, p. 803.

1109 Art. 28(a) Rome-Statute applies also to persons "effectively acting as a military commander", which refers to those who are not elected by law to carry out a military commander's role, yet they perform it *de facto* by exercising effective control over a group of persons through a chain of command. Such "military-like commanders" include superiors who have authority and control over regular government forces, such as armed police units, or irregular (non-government) forces, such as rebel groups and paramilitary units.

1110 Triffterer, *supra* note 1018, Art. 28, para. 81.

Rome-Statute regulates the criminal responsibility of superiors – not covered by Art. 28(a) Rome-Statute – whose failure to properly control their subordinates, led to the commission of crimes within the jurisdiction of the ICC by such subordinates.

The concept of superior responsibility – which is an original creation of international criminal law, for which there are no paradigms in national legal systems[1111] – expresses one of the main differences between criminal law, which focuses primarily on the physical perpetrator of the crime, and international criminal law, which puts a much greater focus on those who are not direct perpetrators in this sense, but lead, order or permit the commission of the crime from a higher (superior) position[1112].

The wording "in addition to other grounds of criminal responsibility" refers to the modes of liability described in Art. 25 Rome-Statute (especially paras. 2 and 3). Although framed in the Rome Statute as a form, by which crimes within the jurisdiction of the ICC are perpetrated, superior responsibility under Art. 28 Rome-Statute – which has been described as a subsidiary mode of participation *sui generis*[1113] – stands alone as a distinct crime whose gravamen is the failure to supervise or punish, not a specific crime of omission[1114]. Accordingly, if the superior's conduct also qualifies as participation in the crime of the subordinate, Art. 25 Rome-Statute shall take precedence over superior responsibility under Art. 28 Rome-Statute[1115].

Art. 28 Rome-Statute distinguishes between military and non-military (civilian) superior responsibility.

3.2.5.1. Superior responsibility of military commanders

In order for the military commander[1116] of a perpetrator, who committed a crime within the jurisdiction of the ICC, to be found criminally responsible under Art.

1111 Werle, *supra* note 347, para. 497.

1112 Cryer, Robert, "Prosecuting the Leaders: Promises, Politics and Practicalities", *Göttingen Journal of International Law* 1.1 (2009), p. 56.

1113 Werle, *supra* note 347, para. 503.

1114 Schabas, *A Commentary on the Rome Statute, supra* note 360, Art. 28, p. 457.

1115 Werle, *supra* note 347, para. 503.

1116 The term "military commander" refers to persons who are formally or legally appointed to carry out a military command function – i.e. *de jure* commanders. The concept applies regardless of the actual rank or level in the military hierarchy, so that the commander could be the person at the highest level in the chain of command or a mere leader with few soldiers under his/her command. The term "military commander" also applies to those situations, in which the superior does not exclusively perform a military

28(a) Rome-Statute, four requirements must be fulfilled: (i) A superior-subordinate relationship between the military commander and the perpetrator exists, (ii) the superior knew or had reason to know that the subordinate was about to commit such a crime or had done so, (iii) the superior failed to take the necessary and reasonable measures to prevent such a crime or punish the perpetrator, and (iv) a causal link between the superior's dereliction of duty and the commission of the crime exists[1117].

3.2.5.1.1. Superior-subordinate relationship

The existence of a superior-subordinate relationship – which aims at the disciplined execution of orders by the subordinates and the facilitated control thereof by the superior – is implied by the existence of a hierarchical (military) structure with a strictly defined chain of command[1118]. The core element of a superior-subordinate relationship is a position of effective control[1119] on the part of the superior vis-à-vis the subordinates. Evidence of such effective control is the superior's material ability to prevent and punish commission of the offences[1120]. Several additional indications of a superior position of authority and effective control are the official position of the individual within the military structure, the power to issue or give orders, the capacity to ensure compliance with orders, the capacity to order forces to engage in hostilities, and the power to promote, replace, remove, or discipline[1121].

An analogy can be made between the superior-subordinate relationship and the concept of "guarantor position", known to civil law systems. Such guarantor position is attached to persons who (i) have the legal obligation to protect a specific person / object, which is set under their supervision, from external dangers, or (ii) have originated a source of danger to the external world and are, thus, under the obligation to prevent third parties from being affected thereby. The in-

---

function. This is the situation in some countries where a head of state is the commander in chief of the armed forces.

1117 Ronen, Yaël, "Superior Responsibility of Civilians for International Crimes Committed in Civilian Settings", *Vanderbilt Journal of Transnational Law* 43 (2010), p. 316.

1118 Arnold, Roberta, in: Triffterer, Otto (ed.), *Commentary on the Rome Statute of the International Criminal Court – Observers' Notes, Article by Article* , 2nd edition, Munich: C.H.Beck (2008), Art. 28, para. 86.

1119 Not every factual possibility of controlling the conduct of another person is sufficient. Rather, the capability to exercise control must be embedded within a hierarchical structure with a certain degree of stability and organization that is independent of the concrete situation.

1120 Werle, *supra* note 347, para. 506.

1121 Schabas, *A Commentary on the Rome Statute*, *supra* note 360, Art. 28, p. 461.

trinsic meaning of the superior-subordinate relationship requirement is that a superior shall, first of all, be responsible towards his/her own men/women by protecting them from external dangers and, secondly, be responsible towards the "outside world" by supervising them as a potential source of danger[1122].

Given the differences in the organization of military chains of command, a distinction is sometimes made between tactical, operative and regional command. In all cases, the decisive factor regarding effective control is the military commander's actual capability to effectively influence the conduct of the people / organization subordinate to him/her[1123]. Since it may occur that, notwithstanding "on paper" superior status, a person holding a higher rank does not exercise *de facto* effective control over "on paper" subordinates, it is always important to assess in each single case what the real responsibilities of a higher ranking officer were before assessing responsibility under international law. This holds true, in particular, for very senior military commanders, upon whom there is a tendency to attach responsibility for any crimes committed by lower-ranking members of the military[1124].

3.2.5.1.2. Superior knew / had reason to know of the crime

Art. 28(a)(i) Rome-Statute requires that the military commander either knew or, owing to the circumstances at the time, should have known that the forces under his/her command were committing or about to commit crimes within the jurisdiction of the ICC.

Actual knowledge of the crime being / about to be committed cannot be presumed and must be established through direct or circumstantial evidence[1125]. The "should have known" standard requires negligent failure – i.e. active duty[1126] – on the part of the military commander to acquire information and knowledge concerning the (illegal) conduct of his/her subordinates[1127]. There is no doubt that a military commander (especially higher ranking officers) cannot keep track of all events taking place on the ground during a military operation[1128]. Never-

1122 Arnold, *supra* note 1118, Art. 28, para. 87.
1123 Werle, *supra* note 347, para. 509.
1124 Arnold, *supra* note 1118, Art. 28, para. 88.
1125 ICC, *The Prosecutor v. Jean-Pierre Bemba Gombo*, *supra* note 363, para. 430.
1126 *Ibid.*, para, 433; Werle, *supra* note 347, para. 516.
1127 Schabas, *A Commentary on the Rome Statute*, *supra* note 360, Art. 28, p. 462.
1128 If there is more than one officer responsible for the acts of certain military forces in the same chain of command – be this horizontally or vertically – all officers may be held responsible under Art. 28(a) Rome-Statute. Accordingly, a general could be held responsible for the conduct of private soldiers – even though there were other responsible

theless, lack of knowledge concerning the commission of ICC-relevant crimes by subordinates of the commander cannot be claimed when it is the result of negligence to obtain all possible information[1129]. In addition to criminal dereliction, resulting from the failure to exercise the means available to him/her to gain knowledge of the crime, "should have known" may also be presumed when the commission of the crime was so widespread that no reasonable observer would deny the conclusion that the military commander in charge should / must have known of it[1130].

Art. 30(1) Rome-Statute (mental element) states that "[u]nless otherwise provided, a person shall be criminally responsible and liable for punishment for a crime within the jurisdiction of the [ICC] only if the material elements are committed with intent and knowledge". Superior responsibility under Art. 28(a) Rome-Statute, however, does not require that the military commander share the intent of the perpetrator(s) regarding the specific crime. This follows from (i) the nature of superior responsibility as a subsidiary mode of criminal liability for omission, and (ii) the *mens rea* requirement under Art. 28(a) Rome-Statute, whereby the superior need not even know of the commission of the crime itself, so that he/she cannot, *a fortiori*, be required to share the perpetrator's specific intent[1131]. As Art. 28(a) Rome-Statute provides for criminal responsibility based only on knowledge or the negligent lack thereof, one must conclude that said provision applies as *lex specialis* in relation to Art. 30(1) Rome-Statute[1132] and is one of the cases sheltered by its wording "unless otherwise provided"[1133].

3.2.5.1.3. Superior's failure to take necessary measures

Art. 28(a)(ii) Rome-Statute requires that the military commander failed to take all necessary and reasonable measures within his/her power to prevent or repress the commission of the crime, or to submit the matter to the competent authorities for investigation and prosecution – whereby each of these three duties can constitute a distinct violation of Art. 28(a) Rome-Statute and therefore be the basis for a separate criminal charge[1134].

---

officers in between, who failed to control the forces and take the necessary measures to prevent / repress the crime.

1129 Arnold, *supra* note 1118, Art. 28, para. 95.

1130 *Ibid.*

1131 Werle, *supra* note 347, para. 518.

1132 Arnold, *supra* note 1118, Art. 28, para. 114.

1133 Schabas, *A Commentary on the Rome Statute*, *supra* note 360, Art. 28, p. 463; Ambos, "General Principles of Criminal Law in the Rome Statute", *supra* note 1000, pp. 20-21.

1134 Schabas, *A Commentary on the Rome Statute*, *supra* note 360, Art. 28, p. 464.

On the military operational level, measures to prevent the commission of crimes within the jurisdiction of the ICC could include: (i) Ensuring the forces are adequately trained in International Humanitarian Law, (ii) ensuring that due regard is paid to International Humanitarian Law in operational decision making, (iii) ensuring that an effective reporting system is established, so that the military commander is informed of incidents, which could lead to violations of International Humanitarian Law, and (iv) taking corrective actions when the military commander becomes aware that violations of International Humanitarian Law are about to occur[1135].

The commander's duty to repress the commission of crimes involves stopping ongoing crimes, highlighting the illegality of the conduct, in order to prevent similar events in the future, and initiating the necessary investigations into the alleged crimes[1136]. Due to their severity, crimes within the jurisdiction of the ICC cannot be punished by "regular" military commanders and must, therefore, be submitted to the competent authorities – which shall delegate the case to the military justice[1137]. The retroactive initiation of investigative or punitive measures does not free the military commander from liability for derelict failure to take preventive measures[1138].

"Necessary and reasonable" – with regard to the measures to be taken by the commander – shall be determined on the basis of the commander's *de jure* power as well as his/her *de facto* ability to take such measures at the time he/she was required to do so[1139].

3.2.5.1.4. Causal link

The words "as a result of" in Art. 28(a) Rome-Statute reflect the need for a causal link between the commission of the crime and the commander's failure to properly exercise control over his/her forces[1140]. Despite the fact that failure of the commander to report or punish a crime can increase the risk of (similar) crimes being committed in the future, the element of causality required by Art. 28(a) Rome-Statute relates only to the commander's duty to prevent the commission of crimes not yet committed[1141].

1135 Arnold, *supra* note 1118, Art. 28, para. 104.

1136 *Ibid.*, para. 120; Schabas, *A Commentary on the Rome Statute*, *supra* note 360, Art. 28, p. 464; Werle, *supra* note 347, para. 521; ICC, *The Prosecutor v. Jean-Pierre Bemba Gombo*, *supra* note 363, para. 439.

1137 Arnold, *supra* note 1118, Art. 28, para. 120.

1138 Werle, *supra* note 347, para. 522.

1139 ICC, *The Prosecutor v. Jean-Pierre Bemba Gombo*, *supra* note 363, para. 443.

1140 *Ibid.*, para. 423.

1141 *Ibid.*, para. 424.

With regard to the level of causality required by Art. 28(a) Rome-Statute, Pre-Trial Chamber II of the ICC suggested the use of the "but for test" – i.e. to examine if but for the commander's failure to fulfill his/her duty to take reasonable and necessary measures to prevent a crime, such a crime would not have been committed by his/her forces[1142]. Since, however, it would not be practical (or possible) to exactly predict what would have happened had the commander fulfilled his/her obligations to prevent the crime, no direct causality is required. Rather, it would be sufficient to show that the commander's breach of duty increased the risk of the crime being committed by his/her forces[1143].

3.2.5.2. Superior responsibility of civilians

Art. 28(b) Rome-Statute – which also regulates the criminal responsibility of superiors, whose subordinates committed crimes within the jurisdiction of the ICC, resulting from the superiors' failure to exercise proper control over such subordinates – pertains to civilian superiors, who are not *de facto* enrolled in / part of the military, but have the power to exercise a similar kind of authority and control over military forces[1144] – in particular non-military members of government[1145].

Many of the requirements regarding the criminal responsibility of a civilian superior, whose subordinates committed crimes within the jurisdiction of the ICC, are identical / similar to the requirements regarding the criminal responsibility of military commanders regulated in Art. 28(a) Rome-statute[1146]: The "effective authority and control" a civilian superior is required to have over the military forces, which committed the crimes, are comparable to a superior-subordinate relationship in terms of intensity, degree of hierarchical integration and stability[1147]. This view is further supported by Pre-Trial Chamber II of the ICC, which stated that the term "effective command and control", which pertains to military commanders, and the term "effective authority and control", which pertains to military-like commanders and civilian superiors, are applicable alternatives[1148].

Furthermore, the wording of Art. 28(b)(iii) Rome-Statute – regarding the failure of the civilian superior to take all necessary and reasonable measures within his/her power to prevent or repress the commission of the crimes, or

1142 *Ibid.*, para. 425.

1143 *Ibid.*

1144 Arnold, *supra* note 1118, Art. 28, para. 124.

1145 Werle, *supra* note 347, para. 511.

1146 Art. 28(b) Rome-Statute is a subsidiary provision of Art. 28(a) Rome-Statute.

1147 Werle, *supra* note 347, para. 511.

1148 ICC, *The Prosecutor v. Jean-Pierre Bemba Gombo*, *supra* note 363, para. 412.

submit the matter to the competent authorities for investigation and prosecution – is identical to the wording of Art. 28(a)(ii) Rome-Statute, which regulates the failure of the military commander to do the same.

Finally, the words "as a result of" in Art. 28(b) Rome-Statute indicate that the required causal link between the failure of the civilian superior to properly exercise control over his/her subordinates and the commission of the crimes by those subordinates, is identical to the causal link required in Art. 28(a) Rome-Statute.

In addition to the many similarities between the criminal responsibility of military commanders and civilian superiors, there are two significant differences between the two[1149]:

3.2.5.2.1. The mental element

While Art. 28(a)(i) Rome-Statute requires that the military commander knew or, owing to the circumstances at the time, should have known that his/her forces were committing / about to commit the crimes, Art. 28(b)(i) Rome-Statute requires that the civilian superior knew or consciously disregarded information, which clearly indicated that his/her subordinates were committing / about to commit crimes within the jurisdiction of the ICC. The concept of "consciously disregarded information" amounts to a form of recklessness and is clearly much more demanding than the standard applicable to military commanders, which can be convicted on the basis of negligence[1150]. Although Art. 28(b)(i) Rome-Statute might still be an exception to the general requirements of Art. 30(1) Rome-Statute, it is certainly much closer to the latter than Art. 28(a)(i) Rome-statute[1151]. "Consciously disregarded information" is given when (i) information clearly indicating a significant risk that subordinates were committing / about to commit crimes existed, (ii) such information was available to the civilian superior, and (iii) the civilian superior, while aware that such a category of information existed, declined to refer to it[1152].

The different *mens rea* requirements applicable to military commanders and civilian superiors can be explained / justified as follows: (i) Military commanders are in charge of an inherently lethal force with a direct effect on life and death, and the corollary to this enormous power is more responsibility; when

1149 Ronen, "Superior Responsibility of Civilians for International Crimes Committed in Civilian Settings", *supra* note 1117, p. 319.

1150 Ambos, "General Principles of Criminal Law in the Rome Statute", *supra* note 1000, pp. 17-18.

1151 Schabas, *A Commentary on the Rome Statute*, *supra* note 360, Art. 28, p. 463.

1152 Arnold, *supra* note 1118, Art. 28, para. 128.

soldiers abuse their power, it is the commander's failure no less than that of his/her soldiers[1153], (ii) unlike civilian superiors, military commanders have a severe disciplinary apparatus at their disposal and, therefore, the means to ensure the compliance of their subordinates with international law[1154], and (iii) involvement in international crimes in the context of organizational conduct is more likely in military settings than in civilian ones; therefore, military commanders must be more alert to the possibility of international crimes being committed by their subordinates and should be held to a higher level of responsibility to acquire knowledge of and prevent the commission of crimes[1155].

3.2.5.2.2. Art. 28(b)(ii) Rome-Statute

This provision further limits the criminal responsibility of civilian superiors for crimes committed by their subordinates[1156], by stating that such crimes must concern "activities that were within the effective responsibility and control of the [civilian] superior". While military commanders are held responsible for controlling their subordinates at all times[1157], the control authority of civilian superiors is limited in place and time to their official function, so that there is no civilian superior criminal responsibility under Art. 28(b) Rome-Statute for crimes committed outside the scope of the subordinates' duties[1158].

3.2.6. Implementation in the case at hand

The following analysis – of the possible individual criminal responsibility of Israeli participants in the Gaza armed conflict[1159] – shall focus on Israeli military and civilian leaders, rather than lower-level military commanders and soldiers. Reason for this distinction is the fact that the former will be the focus of ICC

1153 Ronen, "Superior Responsibility of Civilians for International Crimes Committed in Civilian Settings", *supra* note 1117, p. 352.

1154 *Ibid.*; Arnold, *supra* note 1118, Art. 28, para. 131.

1155 Ronen, "Superior Responsibility of Civilians for International Crimes Committed in Civilian Settings", *supra* note 1117, pp. 353-354.

1156 Werle, *supra* note 347, para. 512.

1157 Ronen, "Superior Responsibility of Civilians for International Crimes Committed in Civilian Settings", *supra* note 1117, p. 350.

1158 Werle, *supra* note 347, para. 512; Arnold, *supra* note 1118, Art. 28, para. 129.

1159 Until the grave allegations against the conduct of the Israeli military during the Gaza armed conflict are officially examined and confirmed in accordance with international law, the individual criminal responsibility analyzed in this section pertains only to the *alleged* commission of crimes within the jurisdiction of the ICC.

investigation / prosecution, should the events of the Gaza armed conflict ever reach The Hague[1160].

The policy of "going for leaders"[1161] is not based on a binding provision in the Rome Statute, but when considering the actions / statements of both the Prosecutor[1162] and the ICC, such policy cannot be doubted. A quick analysis of the cases currently before the ICC shows that all accused persons are either civilian or military senior leaders charged with different forms of participation in crimes within the jurisdiction of the ICC[1163]. In addition, according to Art. 17(1)(d) Rome-Statute, cases that are not of sufficient gravity to justify further action by the ICC, shall be determined inadmissible by the court. In the *Lubanga Dyilo* case, Pre-Trial Chamber I of the ICC stated that the required gravity threshold – in addition to the basic fact that the crimes before the ICC are the most serious crimes of concern to the international community as a whole[1164] – is a key tool provided to the ICC, in order to maximize its deterrent effect[1165] by ensuring that "the Court initiates cases only against the most senior leaders sus-

---

1160 See *supra* note 1026.

1161 Cryer, *supra* note 1112, p. 51.

1162 In its 2003 "Paper on some Policy Issues before the Office of the Prosecutor", the ICC OTC stated that because the ICC is an institution with limited resources, the OTC will function with a two-tiered approach to combat impunity. On the one hand it will initiate prosecutions of the leaders who bear most responsibility for the crimes. On the other hand it will encourage national prosecutions, where possible, for the lower-ranking perpetrators, or work with the international community to ensure that the offenders are brought to justice by some other means. In addition, the Prosecutor has himself said that his focus is on those that bear greatest responsibility for international crimes and that he will not be concerning himself with lower-level offenders, unless perhaps they have committed particularly egregious crimes.

1163 A few examples include: (i) Jean-Pierre Bemba Gombo – alleged President and Commander-in-Chief of the Mouvement de libération du Congo, (ii) Thomas Lubanga Dyilo – alleged founder of Union des Patriotes Congolais (UPC) and the Forces patriotiques pour la libération du Congo (FPLC) / alleged former Commander-in-Chief of the FPLC / alleged president of the UPC, (iii) Germain Katanga – alleged commander of the Force de résistance patriotique en Ituri (FRPI), (iv) Mathieu Ngudjolo Chui – alleged former leader of the Front des nationalistes et intégrationnistes (FNI), (v) Omar Hassan Ahmad Al Bashir – President of the Republic of Sudan since 16 October 1993, and (vi) Ahmad Muhammad Harun – former Minister of State for the Interior of the Government of Sudan / Minister of State for Humanitarian Affairs of Sudan.

1164 Preamble para. 4 Rome-Statute.

1165 *The Prosecutor v. Thomas Lubanga Dyilo*, ICC Pre-Trial Chamber I (24 February 2006), para. 48.

pected of being the most responsible for the crimes [. . .] under investigation"[1166]. Pre-Trial Chamber I further explained that by concentrating on such individuals the deterrent effects of the ICC can be maximized, as "other senior leaders in similar circumstances will know that [only] by doing what they can to prevent the [. . .] commission of crimes within the jurisdiction of the [ICC], can they be sure that they will not be prosecuted by the Court"[1167].

Despite severe criticism from the ICC Appeals Chamber against the Pre-Trial Chamber's interpretation of Art. 17(1)(d) Rome-Statute[1168] and the logic and importance of bringing (also) lower-level perpetrators to justice[1169], the limited resources of the ICC[1170] and the relevant arguments in favor of focusing those resources on prosecuting the most senior leaders[1171], will not allow the ICC to change its current policy – without negatively impacting its ability to prosecute and prevent international crimes.

1166 *Ibid.*, para. 50.

1167 *Ibid.*, para. 54.

1168 In its Judgment on the Prosecutor's appeal against the decision of Pre-Trial Chamber I entitled "Decision on the Prosecutor's Application for Warrants of Arrest, Article 58" of 13 July 2006 (paras. 73, 75, 79), the Appeals Chamber stated that it may indeed have a deterrent effect if (only) high-ranking leaders who are suspected of being responsible for having committed crimes within ICC jurisdiction are brought before the court. However, it seems more likely that a higher deterrent rate can be achieved if no category of perpetrator is *per se* excluded from potentially being brought before the court. The predictable exclusion of all lower-level perpetrators on the grounds proposed by Pre-Trial Chamber I could severely hamper the preventive or deterrent role of the court – which is a cornerstone of the creation of the ICC. The Chamber further argued that the Preamble to the Rome Statute mentions "most serious crimes", not "most serious perpetrators". The reference in para. 5 of the Preamble to "perpetrators" is not prefixed by the delineation "most senior" or "most responsible". Had the drafters of the Rome Statute intended to limit its application only to the most senior / responsible leaders, they could have done so expressly.

1169 Cryer, *supra* note 1112, p. 53.

1170 Schabas, *An Introduction to the International Criminal Court*, 3rd edition, *supra* note 336, pp. 86, 90.

1171 Such arguments include: (i) Prosecuting the most senior leaders sends a very strong signal that no one is above the law – not even the most powerful and influential, (ii) removal of the senior leaders – who are usually the driving force behind the conflict – from the conflict area would help prevent future conflicts, (iii) when prosecuting the horrendous crimes within the jurisdiction of the ICC, public closure and the feeling that justice has been served, can only then be achieved when the people responsible for such crimes have been brought to justice.

3.2.6.1. The individual criminal responsibility of senior military commanders

The individual criminal responsibility of Israel's (most) senior military commanders during the Gaza armed conflict[1172] would be given if such senior officers are found to (i) have participated in the alleged commission of crimes within the jurisdiction of the ICC, or (ii) be responsible for such alleged crimes. When analyzing these possibilities, one must differentiate between the following possible scenarios: Scenario 1 – the alleged crimes were ordered / approved by the senior commanders and properly executed by their forces; scenario 2 – the alleged crimes resulted from operational errors and mistakes[1173] during the execution of orders issued / approved by the senior commanders; scenario 3 – the alleged crimes were ordered and committed by lower-level members of the military.

3.2.6.1.1. Commission of crimes

Individual criminal responsibility of Israel's senior military commanders would be given if such commanders committed crimes within the jurisdiction of the ICC during the Gaza armed conflict, in accordance with Art. 25(3)(a) Rome-Statute.

The senior Israeli military commanders led and had ultimate military command over IDF forces during the Gaza armed conflict, but did not take an active part in the military operations themselves. Therefore, immediate commission of the alleged crimes under Art. 25(3)(a)(alt. 1 and 2) Rome-Statute can be ruled out.

Perpetration by means in the military context – Art. 25(3)(a)(alt. 3) Rome-Statute, could be considered if the alleged crimes of the (direct) perpetrators could be attributed to the senior military commanders (as indirect perpetrators). Such attribution would require that (i) the senior commanders had such organizational control (similar to the "superior-subordinate relationship"[1174]) that they were able to dominate the conduct of their forces on the ground, and (ii) the senior commanders personally fulfilled all subjective elements of the crimes allegedly committed by forces under their command.

1172 According to Israeli and foreign publications, should the events of the Gaza armed conflict reach the ICC, the court / Prosecutor will focus on a few of the most senior Israeli military commanders, which took part in the conflict. These include: The Chief of General Staff, the Deputy Chief of General Staff, the Commander of the Israeli Air-force, the Commander of the Israeli Navy, the Chief Commander for the Southern Command, the Gaza Division Commander and the Head of the Operations Directorate.

1173 The State of Israel, *The Operation in Gaza: Factual and Legal Aspects*, *supra* note 1, paras. 211, 386, 387.

1174 Eser, *supra* note 483, p. 795.

The required organizational control and domination of conduct are given when due to the nature and size of the hierarchical organization, senior military commanders can be sure that their orders will be carried out (almost) automatically – whereby the identity of the subordinate to carry out such orders is of lesser significance[1175]. When dealing with the most senior commanders of a highly-modern, western military, there is no doubt such senior commanders had sufficient organizational control in order to dominate – i.e. monitor, supervise and determine – the conduct of their forces on the ground.

With regard to the subjective element of Art. 25(3)(a)(alt. 3) Rome-Statute, Art. 30(1) Rome-Statute requires that the senior military commanders had both intent and knowledge regarding the material elements of the crimes allegedly committed by forces under their commend. In scenario 1, intent and knowledge would undoubtedly be given, as the orders to commit the alleged crimes came directly from the senior commanders. In such cases the crimes allegedly committed by the forces under their command would be attributed to the senior military commanders under Art. 25(3)(a)(alt. 3) Rome-Statute.

In scenario 2 – in which the commanders had no intent to order the commission of the alleged crimes and, in addition, accurate and proper execution of the commanders' orders would not have led to commission of the alleged crimes – the subjective element of Art. 25(3)(a)(alt. 3) Rome-Statute depends on the amount of risk involved in the orders issued by the senior commanders, i.e. the chance that imperfect execution of such orders would lead to the commission of the alleged crimes. According to Pre-Trial Chamber I of the ICC, the requirement of intent and knowledge is also fulfilled in cases, in which the commanders were aware of the high risk and accepted / made peace with the possible outcome (*dolus eventualis*)[1176]. According to the Chamber, *dolus eventuals* is also given in connection with low risk orders, if the commanders clearly or expressly accepted the idea that the imperfect execution of orders could lead to the commission of the alleged crimes[1177]. Accordingly, in cases, in which the orders issued by IDF senior commanders involved substantial risk, crimes allegedly committed during execution of such orders could be attributed to the senior military commanders under Art. 25(3)(a)(alt. 3) Rome-Statute. Such attribution of alleged crimes would not be possible in cases involving low risk orders – unless it can be proven that the senior commanders clearly expressed acceptance of the involved risk and possible outcome.

1175 Werle, *supra* note 347, para. 478.

1176 ICC, *The Prosecutor v. Thomas Lubanga Dyilo* (29 January 2007), *supra* note 424, para. 352.

1177 *Ibid.*, para. 354.

In scenario 3, one must differentiate between two possible cases: If the senior commanders had no knowledge of the alleged crimes ordered and committed by lower-level members of the military, the required intent and knowledge – and thus attribution of the alleged crimes to the senior military commanders under Art. 25(3)(a)(alt. 3) Rome-Statute – would be rejected. If, on the other hand, the senior commanders did not order the alleged commission of the crimes, but had knowledge of them being ordered and committed by lower-level members of the military (i.e. did nothing to prevent / stop their commission), the subjective element of Art. 25(3)(a)(alt. 3) Rome-Statute would be fulfilled, as despite not having the concrete intent (*dolus directus* of the first degree) to bring about the commission of the alleged crimes, the senior commanders were aware that such alleged crimes will be the necessary outcome of the actions taken by their subordinates (*dolus directus* of the second degree)[1178]. In such cases, the crimes allegedly committed by the forces under their command would be attributed to the senior Israeli military commanders under Art. 25(3)(a)(alt. 3) Rome-Statute.

3.2.6.1.2. Encouragement of crimes

The possible individual criminal responsibility of the IDF's most senior commanders, who participated in the Gaza armed conflict, could also be based on such military commanders ordering their subordinates to commit (alleged) crimes within the jurisdiction of the ICC – Art. 25(3)(b)(alt. 1) Rome-Statute[1179].

Due to the military context in the case at hand, participation in the form of "ordering" – which pertains only to scenario 1, in which the alleged crimes were the direct result of the execution[1180] of orders received from the senior commanders – would clearly be given, as there can be no doubt concerning (i) the existence of the required subordination relationship between the senior commanders giving the orders and the military forces receiving them, and (ii) the former using their position in the relationship to convince or coerce the latter to commit the alleged crimes. Therefore, with regard to those crimes allegedly committed by IDF forces in execution of orders issued by the military's senior commanders, participation of the latter in such alleged crimes would be given in the form of "ordering" under Art. 25(3)(b)(Alt. 1) Rome-Statue.

1178 *Ibid.*, para. 352.

1179 Due to the commander-subordinate relationship resulting from the military context, "ordering" is the only relevant form of encouragement / instigation relevant in the case at hand.

1180 Applies only to the proper / accurate execution of orders issued by the senior military commanders.

The immediate question arising from this conclusion pertains to the distinction between "ordering" and perpetration by means (scenario 1) discussed above. While some believe that "ordering" is actually a form of perpetration by means that belongs in Art. 25(3)(a) Rome-Statute[1181], Pre-Trial Chamber I of the ICC distinguishes between the two based on the position of the person giving the orders in the organization. According to the Chamber, the commanders with the highest authority within the organization do not merely order the commission of a crime, but through their control over the organization and its members, essentially decide whether and how the crime will be committed. This (organizational) control is the basis for the senior commanders' principal – rather than accessorial – liability[1182], so that "ordering", which constitutes a form of accessory liability that entails a lower degree of responsibility, pertains to intermediate-level commanders, who both receive and issue orders[1183].

In the case at hand, the subject-matter of the analysis is a limited group of the most senior IDF commanders, who possessed full organizational control over the forces they headed during the Gaza conflict. Therefore, it must be concluded that orders from said group of senior commanders – which led to the alleged commission of crimes within the jurisdiction of the ICC – would constitute perpetration by means under Art. 25(3)(a)(alt. 3) Rome-Statute, rather than "ordering" under Art. 25(3)(b)(alt. 1) Rome-Statute.

3.2.6.1.3. Superior responsibility

In addition to the grounds of criminal responsibility regulated in Art. 25(3) Rome-Statute, the individual criminal responsibility of Israel's most senior military commanders during the Gaza armed conflict could be based on those commanders' superior responsibility for crimes allegedly committed by forces under their effective command and control – Art. 28(a) Rome-Statute.

The first requirement of Art. 28(a) Rome-Statute, a superior-subordinate relationship between the senior military commanders and the forces, which allegedly committed the crimes, is undoubtedly given in the case at hand[1184] (see above).

1181 Ambos, *supra* note 475, Art. 25, para. 14.

1182 ICC, *The Prosecutor v. Germain Katanga and Mathieu Ngudjolo Chui*, *supra* note 364, para. 518.

1183 Werle, *supra* note 347, para. 488.

1184 All members of the group of senior Israeli military commanders expected to be the focus of possible ICC investigation / prosecution fulfilled a role as tactical commanders in charge of certain military operations during the armed conflict in Gaza and were not mere "on paper" senior commanders with little or no *de facto* control over the military forces on the ground.

With regard to the second requirement of Art. 28(a) Rome-Statute, whereby the senior military commanders knew / should have known that the forces under their command were committing / about to commit alleged crimes within the jurisdiction of the ICC, one must differentiate between the possible scenarios. In scenario 1, there can be no doubt that the senior military commanders, who issued the orders leading to the alleged crimes, had full knowledge thereof. In scenario 2, the second requirement of Art. 28(a) Rome-Statute would be fulfilled in cases, in which (i) the orders issued by the senior commanders involved substantial risk of the alleged crimes being committed during execution of such orders, or (ii) the issued orders involved low risk of the alleged crimes being committed during execution thereof – provided that the senior commanders, who issued the orders, clearly or expressly accepted said risk[1185]. In scenario 3, the focus must be on those cases, in which the senior commanders did not know of the alleged crimes[1186], but due to their position of control in the military organization and owing to the circumstances at the time, should have known. The "should have known" standard would be given in two cases: (i) The military commanders did not fulfill their duty to acquire information and knowledge concerning possible illegal conduct of the forces under their command, or (ii) the alleged commission of the crimes was so widespread among the military forces that no reasonable observer would deny the conclusion that the most senior commanders (ultimately) in charge of such forces should have known of them. With regard to the first possibility, one must keep in mind that after a certain point in the military hierarchy, the commanders in charge cannot keep track of all events on the ground, in which the forces under their command are involved. Since this analysis deals with a small group of the most senior commanders of quite a large military force during a short period of very intensive fighting, one must conclude that (sufficient) negligent failure under these circumstances would be very difficult to prove. With regard to the second possibility, should there have been alleged crimes, not known to the senior commanders, but sufficiently widespread that there can be no doubt the senior commanders should (or even must) have known of them being committed by the forces under their command, the second requirement of Art. 28(a) Rome-Statute would be fulfilled in such cases.

1185 See *supra* notes 1176, 1177.

1186 As the second requirement of Art. 28(a) Rome-Statute is clearly fulfilled in cases, in which the senior commanders knew of the alleged crimes being / about to be committed.

Art. 28(a) Rome-Statute further requires that the senior military commanders failed to take all necessary and reasonable measures within their powers to prevent or repress the commission of the alleged crimes. The failure to prevent the commission of alleged crimes would be undoubtedly given in scenario 1, in which the senior commanders directly ordered the commission of the alleged crimes. In scenario 2, the failure to prevent the alleged commission of crimes would be given in high risk cases, in which the senior commanders did not take sufficient preventive measures[1187] to minimize the substantial risk of their orders. Due to the fact that any type of military operation – especially in densely populated areas – will involve a certain (minimal) amount of risk, the third requirement of Art. 28(a) Rome-Statute would be more difficult to prove in low-risk cases, and must be assessed on a case-by-case basis. In cases, in which it has been determined that preventive measures would have been possible, the retroactive initiation of investigative or punitive measures by senior military commanders would not free the latter from their liability for the failure to take the necessary preventive measures when still possible.

The failure to repress ongoing alleged crimes would be relevant (and given) in scenario 3 – in those cases, in which alleged crimes were being committed by lower-level members of the military and after gaining knowledge thereof, the senior military commanders failed to take the necessary measures[1188] to immediately repress the commission of such alleged crimes. In cases, in which the senior commanders had no knowledge of alleged crimes being ordered and committed by lower levels of the military hierarchy, but should have known thereof, both failure to prevent and failure to repress such alleged crimes would be given.

Finally, Art. 28(a) Rome-Statute requires a causal link between the commission of the alleged crimes and the senior commanders' failure to exercise proper control over their forces. Such a causal link would be given if the senior commanders' breach of duty and failure to take necessary and reasonable preventive measures increased the risk of the alleged crimes being committed by their forces. When dealing with the most senior commanders of a well-organized, well-equipped western military, there is no doubt such commanders had the necessary *de jure* power as well as the *de facto* ability to prevent the crimes allegedly committed by forces under their command. Based on this fact, one must con-

---

1187 Such efforts could include ensuring (i) the forces are adequately trained in International Humanitarian Law, (ii) that due regard is paid to International Humanitarian Law during combat, (iii) that an effective reporting system is established, so that any violations of International Humanitarian Law are immediately reported.

1188 Such as immediately stopping the commission of the alleged crimes and initiating the necessary investigations.

clude that in all scenarios discussed above, in which the senior military commanders failed to prevent the alleged commission of crimes by their forces, despite the fact they knew / should have known of their forces' intent to commit such crimes[1189], the former significantly increased the risk of such alleged crimes being committed.

In conclusion, in all scenarios and cases, in which all four requirements of military commander superior responsibility are fulfilled, the individual criminal responsibility of senior IDF officers would be given under Art. 28(a) Rome-Statute. Following this conclusion, the question concerning the "ranking" of individual criminal responsibility under Art. 28(a) Rome-Statute – compared to Art. 25 Rome-Statute – must be addressed. As Art. 28 Rome-Statute is not a specific crime of omission, but concentrates solely on the failure to supervise or punish, it is considered a subsidiary mode of participation *sui generis* and thus "lower-ranked" in comparison with Art. 25 Rome-Statute. Accordingly, individual criminal responsibility under Art. 28(a) Rome-Statute would apply only to those senior IDF commanders, whose specific conduct during the Gaza armed conflict does not qualify as participation in the alleged crimes under Art. 25(3)(a) and (b) Rome-Statute.

3.2.6.2. The individual criminal responsibility of non-military (civilian) leaders

Israel's Basic Law concerning The Military states that "[t]he Army is subject to the authority of the Government" and "[t]he Minister in charge of the Army on behalf of the Government is the Minister of Defence". In addition, the Chief of General Staff – the supreme command level in the Army – "is subject to the authority of the Government and subordinate to the Minister of Defence"[1190]. Based on the position of the government in its relationship with the military, individual criminal responsibility of Israel's senior government officials during the Gaza armed conflict[1191] could be given if such officials are found to (i) have participated in crimes allegedly committed by Israeli military forces during the Gaza armed conflict, or (ii) be (ultimately) responsible for such alleged crimes.

1189 This includes the cases, in which senior military commanders knew of the substantial risk involved in planned operations.

1190 Art. 2(a) and (b), 3(a) and (b) Basic Law of Israel: The Military.

1191 According to Israeli and foreign publications, should the events of the Gaza armed conflict reach the ICC, the court / Prosecutor will focus on the "troika" of top government decision-makers, who charted the course of the Gaza conflict: the Israeli Prime Minister, the Defense Minister and the Foreign Minister.

3.2.6.2.1. Commission or ordering of crimes

As civilians, Israel's senior government officials did not take any active part in the military operations during the Gaza armed conflict, so that the only forms of participation, which could apply in this case, are perpetration by means – Art. 25(3)(a)(alt. 3) Rome-Statute, and "ordering" – Art. 25(3)(b)(alt. 1) Rome-Statute.

The first requirement of both forms of participation is that – based on a relationship of subordination between the government and the military – the senior government officials were able to control the conduct of the military forces on the ground. The role of Israeli senior government officials in times of crisis and war is to consider the "big picture" (i.e. diplomatic, political and economic aspects – in addition to military considerations) and make key strategic decisions, which are then implemented and carried out by the military. Based on their specific role and the fact that senior government officials are not *de facto* members of the military, who lack "day-to-day" operational control over the conduct of the forces, one must conclude that the required control over the forces during the alleged commission of ICC-relevant crimes would only be given in those cases, in which the orders concerning the alleged crimes were directly issued / approved by the senior government officials. In all other cases, in which the alleged crimes were the result of orders issued / approved by military commanders in implementation of strategic guidelines provided by the government, the required control over the forces would be rejected.

The mental element required by Art. 25(3)(a)(alt. 3) Rome-Statute, whereby the senior government officials must have had intent and knowledge regarding the material elements of the crimes allegedly committed by forces under their (ultimate) command[1192], would be given (only) in those cases, in which the alleged crimes were the result of the (proper[1193]) execution of orders directly received from / approved by the government. In such cases, the conduct of the forces on the ground could be attributed to the senior government officials, in accordance with Art. 25(3)(a)(alt. 3) Rome-Statute. Should there be cases of proper execution of orders directly received from / approved by senior government officials, in which the mental element of intent (regarding the material aspects of the alleged crimes) is uncertain, the individual criminal responsibility of

1192 Art. 30(1) Rome-Statute.

1193 The mental element of Art. 25(3)(a)(alt. 3) Rome-Statute could also be given in scenario 2 cases (the alleged crimes were the result of an operational error during the execution of an order received from senior government officials) – provided that the *dolus eventualis* requirements are given and can be proved.

senior government officials could be given in the form of "ordering" – Art. 25(3)(b)(alt. 1) Rome-Statute, which has a lesser *mens rea* standard.

3.2.6.2.2. Superior responsibility

The individual criminal responsibility of Israel's senior government officials could, in addition, be based on such officials' superior responsibility over their subordinates, who allegedly committed crimes within the jurisdiction of the ICC during the Gaza armed conflict – Art. 28(b) Rome-Statute.

The first requirement of Art. 28(b) Rome-Statute, according to which the senior government officials must have had effective authority and control over the forces that allegedly committed the crimes, would be given (only) in cases, in which – based on the hierarchical relationship between the government and the military – senior government officials issued specific orders and thereby exercised effective control over the conduct of the forces on the ground.

Art. 28(b) Rome-Statute further requires that the senior government officials failed to take all necessary and reasonable measures within their power to prevent or repress the alleged commission of crimes. This requirement would be fulfilled in cases, in which the senior government officials ordered / approved / knew of the alleged crimes being planned / committed and did nothing to prevent or repress them. This leads to the question concerning the possibility of individual criminal responsibility of senior government officials in cases, in which such officials did not order / approve / know of the alleged crimes being planned / committed by their subordinates. This matter is addressed in Art. 28(b)(i) Rome-Statute, which provides that individual criminal responsibility would be possible in such cases – provided that the senior government officials consciously (and recklessly) disregarded information, which clearly indicated that the subordinates were committing or about to commit the alleged crimes. "Conscious disregard" would only then be given should there be sufficient proof showing that the senior government officials declined to refer to information (i) available to them, and (ii) to which they were aware.

Finally, Art. 28(b)(ii) Rome-Statute requires that the alleged crimes concerned activities that were within the effective responsibility and control of the senior government officials. Since all crimes allegedly committed by the IDF took place in connection with military activities during the Gaza armed conflict, which were within the effective superior responsibility of Israel's senior government officials, Art. 28(b)(ii) Rome-Statute would be fulfilled in the case at hand.

In conclusion, individual criminal responsibility of senior Israeli government officials under Art. 28(b) Rome-Statute would be given in those cases, in which such officials (i) ordered / approved / knew of the alleged crimes, or (ii) did not know thereof, but consciously disregarded available information which would have provided them with the opportunity to exercise effective control over the involved forces and prevent the alleged crimes[1194]. As mentioned above, individual criminal responsibility under Art. 28(b) Rome-Statute is "lower-ranked" compared to such responsibility based on participation under Art. 25(3) Rome-Statute, so that the former would be the basis of individual criminal responsibility only for those senior government officials, whose conduct during the Gaza armed conflict does not fulfill the requirements of perpetration by means or "ordering".

3.2.6.3. The individual criminal responsibility of lower-level military commanders and soldiers

Although any ICC investigation / prosecution following the Gaza armed conflict will most likely – for the reasons discussed above – focus on those who ordered and approved the alleged crimes, rather than on those whose role was to execute such orders on the ground, lower-level military commanders and soldiers could – in specific cases – be the subject of such ICC investigation / prosecution as well.

The individual criminal responsibility of lower-level Israeli military commanders could – in addition to the grounds of individual criminal responsibility of the most senior military commanders[1195], which could apply to lower-level commanders as well – be based on:

(i) Immediate perpetration of a crime – Art. 25(3)(a)(alt. 1) Rome-Statute, in those cases, in which the lower-level commander (intentionally) committed the alleged crime while physically taking part in the military operations;
(ii) Co-perpetration of a crime – Art. 25(3)(a)(alt. 2) Rome-Statute, in cases, in which the lower-level commander committed the alleged crime together with another (at least one) lower-level commander or soldier, who shared control over the common plan or agreement to commit the alleged crime;
(iii) Assisting the commission of a crime – Art. 25(3)(c) Rome-Statute, in cases, in which the lower-level commander (substantially) contributed to the crime allegedly committed by others – for example by providing the means for its commission[1196].

1194 In both cases the causality requirement of Art. 28(b) Rome-Statute would be also fulfilled, as the conduct of the senior government officials clearly increased the risk of the alleged crimes being committed by their subordinates.

1195 Perpetration by means – Art. 25(3)(a)(alt. 3) Rome-Statute, "ordering" – Art. 25(3)(b)(alt. 1) Rome-Statute, superior responsibility – Art. 28(a) Rome-Statute.

1196 The State of Israel, *Gaza Operation Investigations: Second Update* (2010), para. 74.

The individual criminal responsibility of Israeli soldiers[1197] could – due to their position in the military hierarchy – be based only on immediate perpetration[1198] / co-perpetration[1199] of the alleged crime – Art. 25(3)(a)(alt. 1 and 2) Rome-Statute, or "assistance" under Art. 25(3)(c) Rome-Statute.

3.2.7. Conclusion

Based on the above, the individual criminal responsibility of those individuals, on which any possible ICC investigation / prosecution is expected to focus – i.e. the most senior IDF commanders and Israeli government officials involved in the Gaza conflict – could be given in the following three forms:

(i) Commission of a crime through another person (perpetration by means) – Art. 25(3)(a)(alt. 3) Rome-Statute;
(ii) Ordering the commission of a crime – Art. 25(3)(b)(alt. 1) Rome-Statute;
(iii) Superior responsibility for a crime committed by subordinates – Art. 28(a) and (b) Rome-Statute.

As these three possibilities "rank" very differently in terms of criminal responsibility, the decision which category to apply shall be based solely on the specific circumstances of each case (scenarios 1-3 in the case of military commanders).

1197 Some of the names on the lists of alleged Israeli perpetrators published following the Gaza armed conflict were of low-level soldiers.

1198 The State of Israel, *Gaza Operation Investigations: An Update* (2010), paras. 134, 135; The State of Israel, *Gaza Operation Investigations: Second Update*, *supra* note 1196, paras. 99, 109.

1199 The State of Israel, *Gaza Operation Investigations: Second Update*, *supra* note 1196, para. 41.

Chapter Three
POSSIBLE ADMISSIBILITY OF CASES RELATED TO THE GAZA ARMED CONFLICT BEFORE THE INTERNATIONAL CRIMINAL COURT

As is the case with other international judicial institutions – such as the ICJ and human rights courts – the issues of admissibility and jurisdiction in the sense of competence in the pending case have to be distinguished. Even though both concepts are closely related, the situation may arise, in which the ICC has jurisdiction, but cannot exercise it due to the case being inadmissible. Consequently, the inadmissibility of a case does not affect the existence of ICC jurisdiction as such, but regulates when this jurisdiction may be exercised by the court[1200]. The admissibility of cases before the ICC is based on the concept of complementarity, whereby ICC jurisdiction "shall be complementary to national criminal jurisdiction"[1201]. Accordingly, if a national judicial system is functioning properly in a certain case, the ICC shall determine that the case is inadmissible, as there is no reason for it to assume jurisdiction[1202].

1. The rationale behind the principle of complementarity

Despite the fact that the term "complementarity" is not explicitly used or defined in the Rome Statute, it has been adopted by many negotiators of the Statute and later on by commentators thereof to refer to the entirety of norms governing the

---

1200 Pichon, Jakob, "The Principle of Complementarity in the Cases of the Sudanese Nationals Ahmad Harun and Ali Kushayb before the International Criminal Court", *International Criminal Law Review* 8 (2008), p. 188; Benzing, Markus, "The Complementarity Regime of the International Criminal Court: International Criminal Justice between State Sovereignty and the Fight against Impunity", *Max Planck Yearbook of United Nations Law* 7 (2003), p. 594; This is reflected in Rule 58, sub-rule 4 of the ICC Rules of Procedure and Evidence, which provides that "[t]he Court shall rule on any challenge or question of jurisdiction first and then on any challenge or question of admissibility".

1201 See *supra* note 286.

1202 Gioia, Federica, "State Sovereignty, Jurisdiction, and 'Modern' International Law: The Principle of Complementarity in the International Criminal Court", *Leiden Journal of International Law* 19 (2006), p. 1101.

complementary relationship between the ICC and national jurisdiction[1203]. Unlike the two *ad hoc* tribunals – the ICTY and ICTR – which have primary jurisdiction over national jurisdictions, the ICC plays a subsidiary role and (only) supplements the domestic investigation and prosecution of the most serious crimes of international concern[1204]. The rationale behind this complementary role of the ICC can be explained as follows:

First, the most apparent interest that the complementarity regime is designed to protect and serve is state sovereignty, under which "it is the duty of every State to exercise its criminal jurisdiction over those responsible for international crimes"[1205]. It is common knowledge that every state traditionally conceives the jurisdictional function (the function of *jus dicere*), either civil or criminal, as one of the expressions of its sovereignty – the exercise of which is to be protected from external interference[1206]. The legitimacy of such protection is sanctioned by the UN Charter – which (i) identifies "the sovereign equality of all its Members"[1207] as the principle, on which the organization is based, and (ii) prohibits the UN from intervening "in matters which are essentially within the domestic jurisdiction of any state"[1208] – and the Rome Statute – which reaffirms "the Purposes and Principles of the Charter of the United Nations, and in particular that all States shall refrain from the threat or use of force against the territorial integrity or political independence of any State"[1209]. Therefore, the principle of complementarity can be considered a compromise[1210] / balance[1211] between the interest of the international community to see the ICC establish itself as a strong, independent and impartial international organization, with the power to determine its own competence and capable of effectively investigating and prosecuting the horrendous crimes set forth in the Rome Statute, on the one hand, and the desire to protect state sovereignty and the right of states under general international law to exercise jurisdiction over criminal acts committed within their jurisdiction, on the other.

1203 Benzing, *supra* note 1200, p. 592.
1204 Pichon, *supra* note 1200, p. 187; Gerding, *supra* note 517, p. 284.
1205 Preamble para. 6 Rome-Statute.
1206 Gioia, *supra* note 1202, p. 1096.
1207 Art. 2(1) UN Charter.
1208 Art. 2(7) UN Charter.
1209 Preamble para. 7 Rome-Statute.
1210 Gioia, *supra* note 1202, p. 1097.
1211 Benzing, *supra* note 1200, p. 597.

Second, a more practical explanation of the complementarity regime is based on the limited resources of the ICC, which cannot investigate and prosecute all international crimes committed around the world. Therefore, in order to fulfill the object and purpose of the ICC[1212] in the most effective way, the Rome Statute envisages a network of courts on the national and international level (possibly including hybrid tribunals, similar to those established in Sierra Leone, Kosovo or East Timor), in which the ICC shall serve only as court of last resort for those cases, in which justice cannot be achieved on a national level[1213]. Furthermore, the complementarity principle pays tribute to the realization that national authorities are closer to evidence and witnesses, and that the crimes under ICC jurisdiction are usually best prosecuted in the state where they have been committed[1214]. The principle is, therefore, not just a reluctant concession to *realpolitik*, but a substantive and sound operating rule which recognizes that trials closer to the scene of events at issue have inherent practical as well as expressive value[1215]. Finally, the nature of the complementarity regime automatically supports such an international network of courts, as it encourages States Parties to implement the provisions of the Rome Statute in national legislation and strengthen national jurisdiction over international crimes, in order to ensure that their state sovereignty remains unaffected by ICC intervention[1216].

The Rome Statute does not limit itself to enunciating the principle of complementarity; it also specifies the requirements triggering the complementary role of the ICC. The following section shall provide an analysis of these requirements.

1212 See *supra* note 834.

1213 Yang, Lijun, "On the Principle of Complementarity in the Rome Statute of the International Criminal Court", *Chinese Journal of International Law* 4.1 (2005), p. 125; Benzing, *supra* note 1200, p. 599.

1214 Benvenuti, Paolo, "Complementarity of the International Criminal Court", in: Ellis, Mark S. and Richard J. Goldstone (eds.), *The International Criminal Court: Challenges to Achieving Justice and Accountability in the 21st Century*, New York: International Debate Education Association (2008), p. 59; Gioia, *supra* note 1202, p. 1101; Yang, *supra* note 1213, p. 125.

1215 Alvarez, Jose E., "The New Dispute Settlers: (Half) Truths and Consequences", *Texas International Law Journal* 38 (2003), p. 437.

1216 Yang, *supra* note 1213, p. 123; Gerding, *supra* note 517, p. 285.

2. The criteria for admissibility of cases before the ICC

According to Art. 17 Rome-Statute, which sets out the substantive criteria for a determination of the admissibility of cases before the ICC, a case shall be inadmissible if one of the following four scenarios – listed in Art. 17(1) Rome-Statute – is given:

(a) The case is being investigated or prosecuted by a state – not necessarily a State Party – which has jurisdiction over it, unless the state is unwilling or unable genuinely[1217] to carry out the investigation or prosecution;

(b) The case has been investigated by a state which has jurisdiction over it and the state has decided not to prosecute the person concerned, unless the decision resulted from the unwillingness or inability of the state genuinely to prosecute;

(c) The person concerned has already been tried for conduct which is the subject of the complaint, and a trial by the ICC is not permitted under Art. 20(3) Rome-Statute (*ne bis in idem)*;

(d) The case is not of sufficient gravity to justify further action by the ICC.

2.1. Unwillingness – Art. 17(1)(a) and (b) Rome-Statute

In order to give the ICC criteria to determine when a state is unwilling to genuinely carry out an investigation or prosecution, Art. 17(2) Rome-Statute provides that the ICC shall:

> [C]onsider, having regard to the principles of due process recognized by international law, whether one or more of the following exist, as applicable:
>
> (a) The proceedings were or are being undertaken or the national decision was made for the purpose of shielding the person concerned from criminal responsibility for crimes within the jurisdiction of the Court [. . .];
>
> (b) There has been an unjustified delay in the proceedings which in the circumstances is inconsistent with an intent to bring the person concerned to justice;
>
> (c) The proceedings were not or are not being conducted independently or impartially [. . .], [but] in a manner which, in the circumstances, is inconsistent with an intent to bring the person concerned to justice.

1217 The term "genuinely" mainly serves to stress the need for effective prosecution referred to in the Preamble (para. 4), as it underlines that only those national criminal proceedings undertaken with the serious intent of eventually bringing the offender to justice shall bar the exercise of jurisdiction by the ICC.

Although Art. 17(2) Rome-Statute does not indicate whether this criteria list is exhaustive, the prevailing opinion among legal experts is that, in light of the consideration that "unwillingness" is meant to be an exception to the general rule that a case is inadmissible if the state investigates or prosecutes, the factors specifying the term should be construed narrowly and the list deemed exhaustive[1218].

With regard to the chapeau of Art. 17(2), which requires the ICC to have regard to "the principles of due process recognized by international law" in its assessment of the three factors circumscribing "unwillingness", the majority of international criminal law scholars agrees that the objective of said requirement cannot be to protect the individual (accused or victims) in that a state may be deemed unwilling where it breaches their rights, but may be interpreted to give the ICC some criteria at hand in order to interpret the terms used by Art. 17(2) Rome-Statute. For example, in order to establish what amounts to an "unjustified delay" in accordance with Art. 17(2)(b) Rome-Statute, the court may look at jurisprudence defining such delay under the relevant human rights instruments[1219]. Consequently, violations of fair trial rights – other than those pertaining to the independence or impartiality of the judiciary, Art. 17(2)(c) Rome-Statute – cannot lead to the admissibility of a case before the ICC[1220].

The "purpose of shielding the person concerned from criminal responsibility", in accordance with Art. 17(2)(a) Rome-Statute, may be assessed in light of such indicators as, *inter alia*, the scope of the investigation and, in particular, whether the focus is on the most responsible of the most serious crimes or marginal perpetrators or minor offences; manifestly insufficient steps in the investigation or prosecution; deviations from established practices and procedures; ignoring evidence or giving it insufficient weight; intimidation of victims, witnesses or judicial personnel; and irreconcilability of findings with evidence tendered[1221]. The simple initiation of national proceedings, merely to prevent the ICC from acting, does not fall under Art. 17(2)(a) Rome-Statute, as this is clearly allowed and even desired under the principle of complementarity[1222]. Finally, the requirement of a national decision made for the "purpose of shielding" the alleged perpetrator could, under certain circumstances, be fulfilled by the deci-

---

1218 Benzing, *supra* note 1200, p. 606.

1219 *Ibid.*, p. 609.

1220 Pichon, *supra* note 1200, p. 193.

1221 ICC Office of the Prosecutor, *Draft Policy Paper on Preliminary Examinations* (2010), para. 61.

1222 Pichon, *supra* note 1200, p. 195.

sion of the competent state organ not to investigate or prosecute due to immunity given to the person concerned[1223].

An "unjustified delay" in the proceedings, in accordance with Art. 17(2)(b) Rome-Statute, is given when (i) the proceedings have taken longer than other similar proceedings in the states concerned, and (ii) the delay was avoidable but not prevented by state agents with the obligatory due diligence. Furthermore, such "unjustified delay" must be "inconsistent with an intent to bring the person concerned to justice". Unlike in Art. 17(2)(a) Rome-Statute, where it is necessary to positively prove that there was an intent to shield the alleged perpetrator, here the establishment of a mere "inconsistency" with a *bona fide* investigation or prosecution is sufficient, so that the Prosecutor – having regard to the peculiarities of the specific case – must only demonstrate that a genuine state interest in holding the person concerned accountable under due process of law is no longer plausible[1224].

According to the European Court of Human Rights, in order to establish whether a tribunal is independent, in accordance with Art. 17(2)(c) Rome-Statute,

> regard must be had, *inter alia*, to the manner of appointment of its members and their term of office, the existence of guarantees against outside pressures and the question whether the body presents an appearance of independence[1225].

As to impartiality, the tribunal must be subjectively free of personal prejudice or bias and it must be impartial from an objective point of view – i.e. it must offer sufficient guarantees to exclude any legitimate doubt in this respect[1226]. In this context, it is important to note that a lack of independence or impartiality of the proceedings can only lead to the admissibility of a case where it works / worked in favor of the accused[1227].

2.2. Inability – Art. 17(1)(a) and (b) Rome-Statute

The notion of "inability" was inserted to cover situations, in which a state lacks a central government due to a breakdown of state institutions ("failed state"), or suffers from chaos due to civil war, natural disasters or any other event leading

---

1223 *Ibid.*, pp. 194-195.

1224 *Ibid.*, pp. 195-196.

1225 *Morris v. The United Kingdom*, European Court of Human Rights (26 February 2002), para. 58.

1226 Benzing, *supra* note 1200, pp. 612-613.

1227 Pichon, *supra* note 1200, pp. 194, 196.

to public disorder[1228]. "Inability" is defined in Art. 17(3) Rome-Statute as a situation, in which:

> [D]ue to a total or substantial collapse or unavailability of its national judicial system, the State is unable to obtain the accused or the necessary evidence and testimony or otherwise unable to carry out its proceedings.

A "total collapse" of the national judicial system can be defined as a complete breakdown of the national administration of justice, either due to the state's loss of control over the territory or due to the national decision to efface the national administration of justice. A "substantial collapse" comprises a situation, in which the state authorities are not necessarily completely dysfunctional, but neither generally capable of ensuring the investigation of the case[1229].

"Unavailability" is given where the authorities for the administration of justice do exist and are generally functional, but cannot deal with a specific case for legal or factual reasons[1230]. With regard to the question whether "unavailability" is given when international crimes can be punished under domestic law only as "ordinary crimes", the majority of law scholars agrees that the question should be answered in the affirmative only if (i) the respective state does not penalize a conduct proscribed under the Rome Statute at all, or (ii) the legislative path chosen by the respective state does not enable courts to impose an adequate sentence and would lead to a gross understatement of the actual gravity of the crime[1231].

2.3. Gravity of the offence – Art. 17(1)(d) Rome-Statute

Art. 17(1)(d) Rome-Statute is distinct from the other admissibility criteria in Art. 17(1) Rome-Statute, as it applies to all cases brought before the ICC – not just those with respect to which national authorities have already taken action[1232]. The practical intention behind the rule was to prevent the ICC from being flooded with "ordinary" cases, so that it has sufficient resources to deal with the most serious cases of truly international concern[1233]. The term "sufficient gravity" is

1228 Benzing, *supra* note 1200, p. 613.
1229 Pichon, *supra* note 1200, p. 196.
1230 Benzing, *supra* note 1200, p. 614.
1231 *Ibid.*, p. 617.
1232 *Ibid.*, p. 619.
1233 Sacouto, Susana and Katherine Cleary, "The Gravity Threshold of the International Criminal Court", *American University International Law Review* 23 (2008), pp. 818, 822.

not defined in the Rome Statute and will have to be developed by the ICC over time. As relevant factors for "sufficient gravity", the ICC may take into account the degree and magnitude of the wrongdoing, including the extent to which they were planned or part of a general policy, and the detrimental effect the crimes had or still have on the social and cultural fabric of the region or state where they occurred[1234].

According to the Office of the Prosecutor, the concept of gravity should not be exclusively attached to the act that constituted the crime, but also to the degree of participation in its commission[1235]. Although this statement does not constitute an official limitation of Prosecutor efforts to high-level perpetrators[1236], in most cases the Office of the Prosecutor will focus its investigative and prosecutorial efforts and resources on those who bear the greatest responsibility, such as the leaders of the state or organization allegedly responsible for the crimes in question[1237]. This, in turn, leaves no doubt regarding the significance of rank and overall responsibility in the determination of "sufficient gravity" under Art. 17(1)(d) Rome-Statute.

3. Implementation in the case at hand

Should the Prosecutor decide – in derogation from the conclusion reached above[1238] – that the information available to him/her provides a reasonable basis to believe that a crime within the jurisdiction of the ICC has been committed[1239, 1240], prior to initiating an investigation the Prosecutor must consider whether (i) the case would be admissible under Art. 17 Rome-Statute[1241] , and (ii) there are substantial reasons to believe that an investigation would not serve the interests of justice – taking into account the gravity of the crime and the interests of victims[1242].

1234 *Ibid.*, pp. 824-825; Benzing, *supra* note 1200, pp. 619-620.

1235 ICC Office of the Prosecutor, *Paper on some Policy Issues before the Office of the Prosecutor* (2003), p. 6.

1236 Benzing, *supra* note 1200, p. 620.

1237 ICC Office of the Prosecutor, *Paper on some Policy Issues before the Office of the Prosecutor*, *supra* note 1235, p. 7.

1238 See Chapter Two – 2.5.3.

1239 Art. 53(1)(a) Rome-Statute.

1240 See *supra* note 1026.

1241 Art. 53(1)(b) Rome-Statute.

1242 Art. 53(1)(c) Rome-Statute.

The following analysis will provide the main factors to be considered by the Prosecutor in the case at hand and whether, based on said factors, the Prosecutor is expected to conclude that cases related to the alleged conduct of the IDF during the Gaza armed conflict are admissible under Art. 17 Rome-Statute[1243].

3.1. Investigations conducted by Israel following the Gaza armed conflict

Israel has always been very clear regarding its commitment to fully investigate alleged violations of its legal obligations – including the Law of Armed Conflict – and to take appropriate and effective action, including penalizing IDF commanders or soldiers found to have committed offences[1244]. Prior to discussing the actual steps taken by Israel to investigate the allegations made against the conduct of its military forces during the Gaza conflict, the legal system within which such steps were taken should be understood.

3.1.1. Israel's system for investigating misconduct allegations

To ensure compliance with the rule of law, including international law and the Law of Armed Conflict, the IDF has established a system to investigate and pursue allegations of misconduct. This system, like its counterparts in many western states, includes multiple components and layers of review: (i) An internal military disciplinary procedure, (ii) a network of military police, prosecutors and courts, and (iii) a process for oversight by civilian authorities and the judiciary[1245].

1243 Should the Prosecutor decide to answer this question in the affirmative and to submit to the Pre-Trial Chamber a request for authorization of an investigation – in accordance with Art. 15(3) Rome-Statute – the factors and arguments presented in this analysis shall also apply to the scenario, in which the Pre-Trial Chamber is requested to authorize the investigation despite an Israeli request under Art. 18(2) Rome-Statute.

1244 The State of Israel, *The Operation in Gaza: Factual and Legal Aspects*, *supra* note 1, para. 283.

1245 The State of Israel, *Gaza Operation Investigations: An Update*, *supra* note 1198, para. 11.

3.1.1.1. The military justice system

Israel's military justice system is part of the state's military forces, but is professionally independent[1246]. Israel's Military Justice Law of 1955 established the Court Martial system and governs the investigation, indictment and prosecution of those accused of misconduct. The military justice system deals with all allegations of offences or violations of law committed by IDF personnel – including allegations of improper conduct on the battlefield. Israel's military justice system includes three main components: The Military Advocate General's Corps ("MAG"), the Military Police Criminal Investigation Division ("MPCID") and the Military Courts[1247].

The MAG is responsible for enforcing the rule of law throughout the IDF. It also provides advice on military, domestic and international law to the Chief of General Staff and all divisions of the IDF. Although he/she serves on the General Staff of the IDF, the Military Advocate General is legally independent. IDF Supreme Command Orders state that in executing his/her powers and authority, the Military Advocate General is "subject to no authority but the law"[1248]. Thus, the Chief of General Staff has no authority over the Military Advocate General regarding legal matters and the latter is subject to no direct orders of any superior officer – excluding the Chief of General Staff in non-legal matters. The independence of the Military Advocate General extends to every officer within the MAG. Each is subordinate only to the Military Advocate General and is not subject to direct orders by commanders outside the Corps. The Military Advocate General's dual enforcement and advisory responsibilities parallel those of chief military lawyers in other countries; i.e. the units within the MAG that issue legal guidance to the IDF and the units that examine and prosecute alleged crimes by IDF forces (military prosecution – comprised of the Chief Military Prosecutor, Military Advocates and military prosecutors) are separate from one another. In 2007, the Military Advocate General established a specialized unit within the military prosecution, the Office of the Military Advocate for Operational Affairs, to oversee all investigations and to conduct all prosecutions of alleged operational misconduct – in particular alleged misconduct by IDF soldiers against Palestinian civilians during military operations. The mandate of the Office in-

---

1246 The State of Israel, *The Operation in Gaza: Factual and Legal Aspects*, *supra* note 1, para. 285.

1247 The State of Israel, *Gaza Operation Investigations: An Update*, *supra* note 1198, paras. 12, 13.

1248 IDF Supreme Command Order 2.0613(9)(A).

cludes investigation and prosecution of alleged violations of the Law of Armed Conflict[1249].

The MPCID is the primary entity within the IDF for investigating alleged crimes committed by soldiers. The scope of the MPCID's activities is substantial. In the last five years, the unit opened almost 3,300 investigations on average each year and collected more than 11,000 testimonies. The MPCID investigates an average of 5,500 suspects and arrests an average of 1,400 people a year. In 2009, 7% of these investigations involved Palestinian complaints – whereby MPCID investigators who handle complaints by Palestinians undergo specialized training, including in international law. At the conclusion of an investigation, the MPCID reports to the military prosecution and transfers the file for review by a prosecutor. In many cases, the military prosecution returns the file to the MPCID with concrete instructions to conduct a supplemental investigation. If no supplement is needed, a Military Advocate or the Chief Military Prosecutor decides whether to initiate criminal or disciplinary proceedings, based on the evidence available and the nature of the alleged misconduct. In cases of heightened complexity or sensitivity, this decision is made in consultation with the Military Advocate General[1250].

The Military Courts adjudicate charges against IDF soldiers for military and other criminal offences through a Court Martial. The Courts, which include the Military Court of Appeals and several regional courts, are composed of both professional military judges and regular officers. Every Court Martial must include at least one professional military judge and professionals must comprise a majority of any appellate panel. The Military Justice Law provides that "[i]n judicial matters, a military judge is not subject to any authority save that of the law, and is not subject in any way to the authority of his commanders"[1251]. Military commanders do not appoint professional military judges. Rather, an independent commission – comprised of the Minister of Defense, the Minister of Justice, members of the Israeli Supreme Court and the Military Court of Appeals, and a representative of the Israeli Bar Association – make the appointments. Professional military judges serve in a separate military courts unit, headed by the President of the Military Court of Appeals. The cadre of professional military judges includes many civilian judges, who may preside over military proceedings as part of their military reservist duties. Professional military judges can be removed only for gross misconduct, in accordance with a special

1249 The State of Israel, *Gaza Operation Investigations: An Update*, *supra* note 1198, paras. 14-20.

1250 *Ibid.*, paras. 21-25.

1251 § 184 Israel Military Justice Law.

procedure. Even though Military Courts are located within military bases, their proceedings are generally open to the public. The news media can, and does, cover Military Court proceedings and many judgments of the Military Courts are published on the official website of the Israeli judiciary, as well as on various public online databases. In general, the rules of evidence in the Military Courts are practically identical to the rules applicable in civilian criminal proceedings[1252].

3.1.1.2. Civilian supervision over the military justice system

A MAG decision whether or not to open a criminal investigation / file an indictment may be subject to further review by the Attorney General of the State of Israel – an independent figure of high authority. Such review by the Attorney General can be triggered by any complainant or non-governmental organization by submitting a written request to such effect[1253].

In addition, civilian judicial review of the military justice system is possible in two ways: First, the Supreme Court of Israel has discretion to hear direct appeals of judgments of the Military Court of Appeals "concerning an important, difficult or innovative legal question"[1254]. Second, the Supreme Court, sitting as the High Court of Justice, can review and reverse a decision of the Military Advocate General, the military prosecution and the Attorney General whether to investigate or file a criminal indictment concerning alleged misconduct by soldiers. Any interested party (including non-governmental organizations) or any person (including non-citizens and non-residents) affected or potentially affected by a government action can petition the Supreme Court, sitting as the High Court of Justice, on a claim that the action is *ultra vires*, unlawful or substantially unreasonable. When warranted, the Supreme Court can enjoin the government or grant other relief. Under Israel's legal system, a ruling of the Supreme Court against the IDF or another government agency is final and binding.

Israel's Supreme Court has earned international respect for its jurisprudence and independence in enforcing international law. Its rulings, able to balance security and individual rights, are highly regarded by jurists and academic scholars of international law, and have been cited favorably by foreign courts – including

---

1252 The State of Israel, *Gaza Operation Investigations: An Update*, *supra* note 1198, paras. 26-28.

1253 The State of Israel, *The Operation in Gaza: Factual and Legal Aspects*, *supra* note 1, para. 298.

1254 § 440(I)(a) and (b) Israel Military Justice Law.

the Supreme Court of Canada, the House of Lords in the United Kingdom and the European Court of Justice[1255].

3.1.1.3. The IDF investigation procedure regarding alleged violations of the Law of Armed Conflict

Once the MAG receives a complaint concerning an alleged violation of the Law of Armed Conflict, the following procedure takes place: (i) The MAG reviews the complaint and refers it either for a command investigation or – when there is an allegation of *per se* criminal behavior – for a criminal investigation, (ii) with regard to those complaints referred for a command investigation, the MAG reviews the record and findings of the investigation, along with other available material, in order to determine whether there is a suspicion of a criminal act – in which case the complaint is referred for a criminal investigation – or whether to recommend disciplinary proceedings, (iii) following a criminal investigation, the MAG reviews the entire evidentiary record to determine whether or not to file an indictment or to recommend disciplinary proceedings[1256].

3.1.1.3.1. Sources of complaints

The consistent policy of the IDF has been to investigate alleged violations of the Law of Armed Conflict, regardless of the source of the allegations[1257]. Information on alleged misconduct of soldiers reaches the IDF authorities in various ways, including: Formal or informal complains by alleged victims or family members; complaints by commanders or soldiers who witnessed an incident; reports by non-governmental organizations and the news media; complaints or letters by non-governmental organizations, journalists, embassies or international organizations; and complaints forwarded to or filed directly with the MAG by the Israeli Police and other law enforcement agencies. Any person may file a complaint with the Military Police at any civilian police station regarding alleged misconduct by IDF soldiers. Gaza residents can file complaints directly in writing (in Hebrew, Arabic or English), through a non-governmental organization acting on their behalf or through the Military Liaison that works directly with the Palestinian civilian population. Regardless of the source, the IDF evaluates each complaint based on the circumstances of the case and the evidence available[1258].

1255 The State of Israel, *Gaza Operation Investigations: An Update*, *supra* note 1198, paras. 34-40; See *supra* notes 885-887.

1256 The State of Israel, *Gaza Operation Investigations: An Update*, *supra* note 1198, para. 44.

1257 *Ibid.*, para. 41.

1258 *Ibid.*, paras. 47-49.

3.1.1.3.2. MAG screening and referral

The MAG – in particular the military prosecution – plays a major role in the IDF's system of investigating alleged violation of the Law of Armed Conflict. Such investigations are considered extremely important and the Military Advocate General is personally involved in the examination of many cases. The military prosecution receives all complaints of IDF misconduct for screening and review, and directly refers any complaint that alleges *per se* criminal behavior to the MPCID for criminal investigation. With regard to the other complaints, which, depending on the specific circumstances, may or may not constitute a criminal offense, the MAG must first determine whether the evidence raises a suspicion of criminal activity and warrants a referral to the MPCID. In making its decision, the MAG evaluates the complaints themselves, along with the record of evidence developed during military command investigations (also known as operational debriefings) and other materials.

Some of Israel's critics have misunderstood the nature of these investigative tracks and incorrectly assumed that all complaints must first proceed through the command investigation stage, thereby delaying criminal proceedings for months[1259]. This premise is, however, wrong. The military prosecution has full authority to initiate direct criminal investigations of those complaints alleging conduct that is clearly criminal in nature. With respect to other complaints, which are first subject to command investigations, there is no requirement that the military prosecution await a final report from the command investigator before making a criminal referral. At any point, when there is a reasonable suspicion of criminal misconduct, the military prosecution may launch a criminal investigation[1260].

3.1.1.3.3. Command investigations

Under Israel's Military Justice Law, a command investigation is an "inquiry held in the army, in accordance with IDF orders, regarding an event which occurred during training or operational activity, or in relation to them"[1261]. The longstanding practice of the IDF is to conduct a command investigation in the field following any kind of military action. Such an investigation normally focuses on examining the performance of the forces and identifying aspects of an operation to preserve and to improve, but may also focus on specific problems

---

1259 Goldstone Report, *supra* note 28, paras. 1830, 1831.

1260 The State of Israel, *Gaza Operation Investigations: An Update*, *supra* note 1198, paras. 50-53.

1261 § 539(A)(a) Israel Military Justice Law.

that occurred. By undertaking this review, the IDF seeks to reduce future operational errors, including those potentially resulting in civilian casualties.

In addition to these routine post-operation investigations, when a complaint is filed with the MAG, which does not allege *per se* criminal behavior, the MAG requests a command investigation, in order to compile an evidentiary record and make a preliminary assessment of the complaint. If warranted, the command investigation will also recommend remedial measures, such as disciplinary action (which can result in prison sentences). Under IDF Supreme Command Order 2.0702, the command investigator must transmit the complete record of a command investigation to the MAG upon request or automatically in certain types of cases – in particular whenever a civilian has been killed or seriously injured. Thus, the investigation of specific complaints as part of a command investigation serves not merely as a means to improve military performance, but also as a preliminary inquiry on behalf of the MAG into potential military misconduct. Furthermore, the IDF's Chief of General Staff has the authority to initiate special (also called "expert") command investigations for exceptionally complex cases. This type of investigation is conducted by a commanding officer who is outside the relevant chain of command.

According to IDF law: (i) The command investigator shall not be limited by the rules of evidence, (ii) a soldier who is inquired in the course of a command investigation shall not be represented by a lawyer, (iii) a soldier cannot refuse a demand by a command investigator to provide information, by testimony or by other means – even if he/she is entitled not to provide it to an investigating entity, since it might incriminate him/her, and (iv) all evidence obtained during a command investigation must be preserved – in particular exhibits, maps, photos, etc.[1262].

Contrary to some criticism[1263], command investigations do not substitute *de jure* or *de facto* for criminal investigations. They serve as a means of compiling an evidentiary record for the MAG, which enables it to determine whether there is a factual basis to open a criminal investigation. The review by the MAG, not the command investigation, lies at the heart of the system[1264].

1262 IDF Supreme Command Order 2.0702.

1263 Goldstone Report, *supra* note 28, para. 1819.

1264 The State of Israel, *Gaza Operation Investigations: An Update*, *supra* note 1198, paras. 54-62.

3.1.1.3.4. Criminal investigations and prosecutions

As noted above, the MAG (military prosecution) automatically refers any complaint alleging *per se* criminal conduct to the MPCID for direct criminal investigation. With respect to other complaints, the MAG initiates a criminal investigation once a reasonable suspicion of criminal activity has been found. The military prosecution notifies the complainant of its decision whether to open a criminal investigation – including the underlying reasons therefor. This decision can be appealed by the complainant both to the Attorney General and the Israeli Supreme Court.

Once the MPCID completes its criminal investigation, the military prosecution reviews the evidence and decides whether to file an indictment (prosecutorial discretion). Once again, the complainant retains the right to appeal a decision of the military prosecution, which prosecutorial discretion in individual cases is subject to review by both the Attorney General and the Supreme Court.

Historically, the MAG has aggressively prosecuted cases of soldier misconduct towards Palestinian civilians. From January 2002 through December 2008, there have been 1,467 criminal investigations into such alleged misconduct by IDF soldiers, leading to 140 indictments. Of these indictments, as of December 2008, 103 defendants were convicted and ten cases are still pending[1265].

3.1.2. Israeli investigations of misconduct allegations following the Gaza armed conflict

According to the Israeli Government, following the Gaza armed conflict, Israel took several concrete steps to reaffirm its commitment to thoroughly investigate – and where appropriate – prosecute alleged violations of the Law of Armed Conflict by its military forces during the Gaza conflict[1266].

3.1.2.1. The launch of five special (expert) command investigations

On 20 January 2009 – two days after the cessation of hostilities – IDF Chief of General Staff, Lt. General Gabi Ashkenazi, ordered the launch of five special command investigations into a range of allegations raised by international and non-governmental organizations and various news media. To head the investigations, Lt. General Ashkenazi appointed five Colonels with substantial field and command expertise, who were not directly involved with the incidents investigated or in the direct chain of command. The mandate focused on five types of alleged violations of the Law of Armed Conflict, encompassing 30 individual

---

1265 *Ibid.*, paras. 63-70.
1266 *Ibid.*, para. 90.

incidents: (i) Incidents, in which a large number of civilians not directly participating in the hostilities were harmed, (ii) incidents where UN and international facilities were fired upon and damaged, (iii) incidents involving shooting at medical facilities, buildings, vehicles and crews, (iv) destruction of private property and infrastructure by ground forces, and (v) the use of weaponry containing phosphorus[1267].

The clear focus of these investigations was to assess specific incidents of harm to civilians and protected persons or facilities. The mandates directed the command investigators to conduct detailed inquiries into, *inter alia*, the orders and instructions given in the IDF – at different levels, before and during the operation – regarding the avoidance of harm, including instructions regarding avoidance of disproportionate harm to civilians not taking part in the hostilities and safety ranges for the use of different weapons from such civilians in different circumstances[1268].

In accordance with standard IDF procedures for command investigations, the investigators operated independently and had access to all available materials as well as the freedom to question any relevant IDF personnel. They interviewed numerous soldiers and officers, and gathered relevant documents and other materials from external sources. They reviewed operational logs, video footage and photographs from aerial vehicles, relevant rules of engagement and operational plans, and volumes of other relevant materials[1269].

Upon completion of the five special command investigations, the investigators presented their findings to the IDF Chief of General Staff, who adopted their recommendations[1270]. The latter also ordered the IDF to implement lessons learned on a broad range of matters, by: (i) Highlighting or clarifying certain standing orders, (ii) establishing further guidelines on the use of various munitions, and (iii) taking steps to improve coordination with humanitarian organizations and entities[1271].

1267 Israel Ministry of Foreign Affairs, *Israeli Investigations into Allegations regarding the Gaza Operation – Status Report* (2009).

1268 The State of Israel, *Gaza Operation Investigations: An Update*, *supra* note 1198, para. 97.

1269 *Ibid.*, para. 98; The State of Israel, *The Operation in Gaza: Factual and Legal Aspects*, *supra* note 1, para. 319.

1270 Israel Defense Forces, *Conclusion of Investigations into Central Claims and Issues in Operation Cast Lead* (2009).

1271 The State of Israel, *Gaza Operation Investigations: An Update*, *supra* note 1198, para. 101.

The Military Advocate General also received the findings and evidentiary record of each of the special command investigations as a source of factual information to assist in the analysis of the relevant allegations[1272].

3.1.2.2. The sixth special (expert) command investigation

In addition to the original five special command investigations, the Military Advocate General recommended that the Chief of General Staff establish an additional special command investigation to assess certain allegations discussed in the Goldstone Report. The Chief of General Staff agreed and on 10 November 2009, the additional command investigation was established. The purpose of the additional special command investigation was to focus on three sets of allegations from the Goldstone Report: (i) The Al-Samouni residence, where the IDF attack allegedly caused the injury and death of several dozen civilians who were seeking shelter there, (ii) the alleged mistreatment of Palestinian detainees by IDF forces, and (iii) the IDF's alleged attack on the Al-Maquadme Mosque[1273].

3.1.2.3. Other command investigations

In addition to the above discussed special command investigations, the MAG referred complaints regarding approximately 90 incidents for command investigation. These incidents generally involved allegations of civilian injuries / deaths and destruction of civilian property[1274].

3.1.2.4. Criminal investigations

By January 2010, the MAG has referred 36 separate incidents for criminal investigation. Of these, 19 involved alleged shootings towards civilians; 12 of the 19 were referred by the MAG directly (without requesting a command investigation or awaiting the results of one) for criminal investigation. The remaining 17 incidents involved allegations of using civilians as human shields, mistreatment of detainees and civilians, and pillage and theft. All of these cases were referred by the MAG directly for criminal investigation[1275].

Between January and July 2010, Israel has launched 11 additional criminal investigations into IDF conduct during the Gaza operations, bringing the total number to 47 (out of which 34 were referred directly for criminal investigation)[1276]. Some of these criminal investigations have resulted in criminal indict-

---

1272 *Ibid.*, para. 102.

1273 *Ibid.*, paras. 124, 125.

1274 *Ibid.*, para. 128.

1275 *Ibid.*, paras. 131-135.

1276 The State of Israel, *Gaza Operation Investigations: Second Update*, *supra* note 1196, paras. 23, 24.

ments and trials, several others have resulted in military disciplinary actions and the rest have been closed after concluding that the Law of Armed Conflict or IDF procedures have not been violated[1277].

Between July 2010 and May 2011, Israel opened five additional criminal investigations, bringing the total number to 52[1278].

3.1.3. Changes to IDF operational guidelines as a result of the investigations

Israel recognizes that, despite IDF extensive efforts to avoid such results, its military operation in Gaza resulted in numerous deaths and injuries to Palestinian civilians and considerable damage to private property[1279]. The Israeli Government emphasizes that the effort to protect civilians and avoid damage to civilian property is, and shall always remain, a core concern of its armed forces. Accordingly, following the investigation of the events of the Gaza conflict, the IDF issued two new orders designed to further increase the protection of civilians and civilian property in future armed conflicts[1280].

3.1.3.1. New written procedures regarding the protection of civilians in urban warfare

Following the Gaza armed conflict, the IDF has adopted important new written procedures and doctrine designed to enhance the protection of civilians in urban warfare by (i) further emphasizing that the protection of civilians is an integral part of a commander's mission, (ii) requiring increased attention to civilian matters in operational planning, and (iii) specifying steps to better insulate the civilian population from combat operations and to limit unnecessary damage to civilian property and infrastructure by improving the identification and marking of civilian sites and infrastructure in advance.

In addition, the new written procedures mandate the planning of a number of additional provisions aimed at safeguarding the civilian population by: Creating safe havens and evacuation routes for civilians to take refuge and safely escape the combat area; providing medical treatment for civilians; improving existing

---

1277 *Ibid.*, paras. 10-12.

1278 Committee of Independent Experts in International Humanitarian and Human Rights Laws to Monitor and Assess any Domestic, Legal or other Proceedings Undertaken by both the Government of Israel and the Palestinian Side (hereinafter "Davis Committee"), *Updated Report*, UN Doc. A/HRC/16/24 (5 May 2011), para. 24.

1279 The State of Israel, *Gaza Operation Investigations: Second Update*, *supra* note 1196, paras. 146, 147.

1280 *Ibid.*, paras. 148, 149.

methods of communication with the civilian population; and ensuring humanitarian access to combat zones during curfews, closure and other limitations of movement.

Finally, the new written procedures require the assignment of a Humanitarian Affairs Officer to each combat unit – beginning at the battalion level – responsible for advising the commanding officer and educating the soldiers with regard to the protection of civilians, civilian property and infrastructure, and the planning and coordination of humanitarian assistance and movement.

Although the majority of these issues were already addressed in various operational orders and guidelines in existence prior to the Gaza armed conflict, the new revised procedures are very important, as they are comprehensive and applicable to all stages of military operations – in particular the crucial stage of planning[1281].

3.1.3.2. New order regulating the destruction of private property for military purposes

In the aftermath of Operation "Cast Lead", the destruction of private property and infrastructure by ground forces was the subject of one of the five special command investigations ordered by the IDF Chief of General Staff. One of the main lessons learned from this investigation was that there should be a set of clear rules and guidelines to assist commanders when making decisions in such situations. Accordingly, upon the instructions of the Chief of General staff, a new Standing Order on Destruction of Private Property for Military Purposes was formulated. The new Standing Order, which entered into force in October 2009, addresses in clear terms when and under what circumstances civilian structures and agricultural infrastructure may legitimately be demolished in circumstances of imperative military necessity. Furthermore, it clarifies the applicable legal criteria and limitations, and allocates specific command responsibility and hierarchical authority for decision-making in this regard[1282].

3.1.4. The Turkel Commission

Following the maritime incident of 31 May 2010[1283], the Government of Israel established on 14 June 2010 an independent public commission to examine var-

1281 *Ibid.*, paras. 150-153.

1282 *Ibid.*, paras. 154, 155.

1283 In this incident, the IDF raided six ships of the "Gaza Freedom Flotilla" organized by the Free Gaza Movement and the Turkish Foundation for Human Rights and Freedoms and Humanitarian Relief (IHH). The ships were raided in international waters of the

ious aspects of the actions taken by the IDF during said incident. In addition, the commission was also asked to determine:

> [W]hether the examination and investigation process for complaints and allegations raised with regard to violations of the [Law of Armed Conflict], as generally practiced in Israel [. . .], is consistent with the obligations of the State of Israel pursuant to the rules of international law[1284].

The commission is headed by retired Supreme Court Justice Jacob Türkel, joined by Professor Shabtai Rosenne (died during the work of the commission in September 2010 and was not replaced) and Amos Horev, a retired general and former president of the Technion – Israel Institute of Technology. Two foreign experts were also appointed to act as observers: Nobel Peace Prize Laureate Lord William David Trimble of Northern Ireland and former Canadian Judge Advocate General Kenneth Watkin[1285]. The Turkel Commission has not yet published the second part of its final report, which will include the commission's conclusions regarding the above mentioned question.

The Israeli Government sees the Turkel Commission as additional proof for Israel's genuine commitment to ensure that its military forces operate within the limits of international law, as in addition to thoroughly investigating alleged violations of the Law of Armed Conflict by IDF forces during the Gaza conflict, Israel wishes to guarantee that its examination and investigation mechanisms are of the highest international standard[1286].

3.2. The view of the international community regarding the Israeli investigations

On 5 November 2009, the UN General Assembly (i) endorsed the Goldstone Report, and (ii) called upon the Government of Israel to investigate the serious violations and allegations mentioned in said report in a manner, which is inde-

---

Mediterranean Sea due to their intention to reach the Gaza Strip and break the Israeli-Egyptian blockade thereon.

1284 Public Commission to Examine the Maritime Incident of 31 May 2010 – The Turkel Commission, *Report – Part One* (2010), para. 4.

1285 *Ibid.*; The State of Israel, *Gaza Operation Investigations: Second Update*, *supra* note 1196, para. 159.

1286 Israel Ministry of Foreign Affairs, *Israeli Investigations into Allegations regarding the Gaza Operation – Status Report*, *supra* note 1267; The State of Israel, *The Operation in Gaza: Factual and Legal Aspects*, *supra* note 1, para. 14; The State of Israel, *Gaza Operation Investigations: Second Update*, *supra* note 1196, para. 161.

pendent, credible and in conformity with international standards[1287]. After the UN Secretary-General received Israel's first update regarding its investigation of the IDF's conduct during the Gaza armed conflict in January 2010, the UN General Assembly reiterated – on 26 February 2010 – its call upon the Government of Israel to investigate the allegations made against its armed forces in an independent and credible manner[1288, 1289].

On 25 March 2010 the UN Human Rights Council – which established the United Nations Fact-Finding Mission on the Gaza Conflict and endorsed its findings (the Goldstone Report) on 16 October 2009[1290] – decided:

> [I]n the context of the follow-up to the [Goldstone Report], to establish a committee of independent experts in international humanitarian and human rights laws to monitor and assess any domestic, legal or other proceedings undertaken by both the Government of Israel and the Palestinian side [. . .], including the independence, effectiveness, genuineness of these investigations and their conformity with international standards[1291].

The committee of independent experts in international humanitarian and human rights laws (the "Davis Committee"[1292]) submitted its report on 23 September 2010 and the updated version thereof on 5 May 2011. The documents included the following findings:

(i) The Davis Committee welcomed certain steps that have resulted from Israel's investigations into the conduct of the IDF during the Gaza armed conflict. These include: The adoption of new written procedures for the protection of civilians in urban warfare, the establishment of a "humanitarian officer" for every combat battalion with responsibility for handling the civilian population in the combat zone, the formulation of the new Standing Order on Destruction of Private Property for Military Purposes, the establishment of a clear doctrine and strict orders regarding the use of munitions

---

1287 See *supra* note 258.

1288 UN General Assembly Resolution 64/254 (26 February 2010).

1289 In both cases the UN General Assembly also urged the Palestinian side to conduct similar investigations – based on the findings of the Goldstone Report.

1290 See *supra* note 257.

1291 UN Human Rights Council Resolution 13/9 (25 March 2010).

1292 Mary McGowan Davis, a former Justice of the Supreme Court of the State of New York, was, at first, a member of the committee (Chaired by Professor Christian Tomuschat) and later was appointed as Chair thereof.

containing white phosphorus, and the establishment of the Turkel Commission[1293];

(ii) The Davis Committee had reservations as to whether Israeli investigations were sufficiently prompt. The Committee noted that many Palestinian witnesses were interviewed only at the very end of 2009, while many allegations of International Humanitarian Law violations were reported almost immediately after the end of the Gaza conflict or, at the latest, in September 2009 with the publication of the Goldstone Report. The Committee expressed concern about the fact that some investigations into allegations made in the Goldstone Report were still ongoing, as such significant delays could result in the loss of crucial evidence and accurate testimonies[1294];

(iii) The Davis Committee did, in general terms, get the impression that Israel's military justice system has certain built-in mechanisms to preserve its independence – based, in particular, on the fact that the Israeli Minister of Defense, rather than the Chief of General Staff, appoints the Military Advocate General and that the decisions of the latter are subject to review by the Israeli Attorney General and Supreme Court[1295]. Nevertheless, despite the structural guarantees of independence built into the military justice system, the dual responsibilities of the MAG in the specific context of the Israeli investigations raised concerns regarding lack of impartiality. The Military Advocate General is legal adviser to the Chief of General Staff and other military authorities. Yet, at the same time, he/she is the supervisor of disciplinary law in the military. Although the combination of the advisory and supervisory functions in one office does not automatically lead to a conflict of interest or a lack of impartiality, the situation in the case at hand is complicated by the fact that many of the allegations of serious violations reported in the Goldstone Report directly link to advice provided to IDF units by the MAG. According to the Davis Committee, the fact that the Israeli investigation of the 36 serious incidents reported in the Goldstone Report led thus far to: 21 cases of no violation or discontinuation of proceedings for various reasons; 6 cases of unclear results; 3 cases, in which disciplinary action was taken; 1 indictment and 5 ongoing criminal investigations,

---

1293 Committee of Independent Experts in International Humanitarian and Human Rights Laws to Monitor and Assess any Domestic, Legal or other Proceedings Undertaken by both the Government of Israel and the Palestinian Side (hereinafter "Davis Committee"), *Report*, UN Doc. A/HRC/15/50 (23 September 2010), para. 42.

1294 *Ibid.*, para. 51; Davis Committee, *Updated Report*, *supra* note 1278, paras. 82, 83.

1295 Davis Committee, *Report*, *supra* note 1293, para. 52; Davis Committee, *Updated Report*, *supra* note 1278, para. 40.

shows that the military investigations produced very little – which does not support the claim in favor of MAG impartiality[1296];

(iv) The Davis Committee concluded that the lack of any IDF standard process of informing Palestinian complainants about the progress and results of investigations led to a lack of transparency, which had a negative effect on the perception of justice and the confidence of victims in the Israeli military justice system[1297];

(v) Israel has not conducted investigations into decisions made at the highest levels regarding the design and implementation of the Gaza Operations. A core finding in the Goldstone Report was that the responsibility for the systematic and deliberate nature of the destruction in Gaza "lies in the first place with those who designed, planned, ordered and oversaw the operations"[1298]. Since such serious alleged violations go far beyond individual criminal responsibility at the level of combatants and even commanders, the Davis Committee concluded that Israel's official inquiry must be conducted by a truly independent body – not affected by the obvious conflict inherent in the military examining its own conduct and, therefore, able to effectively investigate allegations against decision makers higher up the chain of command[1299];

(vi) As a result of the lack of cooperation from Israeli authorities, the Davis Committee did not have sufficient information to conclusively determine whether the investigations, which Israel has conducted and reported about to the international community, met international standards in terms of independence, effectiveness, thoroughness and genuineness[1300].

3.3. Analysis

While Art. 17 Rome-Statute requires a focus on the handling of a particular case, it will almost inevitably be necessary to consider the broader context, laws, procedures, practices and standards of the state concerned when assessing the admissibility of the particular case. Furthermore, one may credibly draw infer-

---

1296 Davis Committee, *Report*, *supra* note 1293, paras. 53-55, 91; Davis Committee, *Updated Report*, *supra* note 1278, para. 77.

1297 Davis Committee, *Report*, *supra* note 1293, paras. 57, 58, 60; Davis Committee, *Updated Report*, *supra* note 1278, paras. 45, 46, 81.

1298 Goldstone Report, *supra* note 28, para. 1895.

1299 Davis Committee, *Report*, *supra* note 1293, paras. 64, 95; Davis Committee, *Updated Report*, *supra* note 1278, paras. 41, 79.

1300 Davis Committee, *Report*, *supra* note 1293, paras. 44, 48-50, 89.

ences from the general to the particular. Where a system is shown to be independent, impartial and meeting standards of genuineness, this may contribute to an inference of genuineness in the particular case. Conversely, where a system shown to be plagued with political interference, scripted trials and unwillingness to pursue certain groups of offenders or offences, this may contribute to an inference of a lack of genuineness in the particular case[1301]. Consequently, the following analysis of Israel's (general) investigatory response to the allegations made against the conduct of the IDF during the Gaza conflict in light of Art. 17 Rome-Statute, can apply to the admissibility of any specific case / incident the Prosecutor may consider to examine more closely.

3.3.1. Sufficient gravity – Art. 17(1)(d) Rome-Statute

Before the more controversial issue of admissibility can be discussed, the question whether the Prosecutor is expected to decide that the case at hand fulfills the "gravity requirement" under Art. 17(1)(d) and 53(1)(c) Rome-Statute should be addressed. Although the term "sufficient gravity" is not explicitly defined in the Rome-Statute, the decision whether a certain case is of sufficient gravity can be made based on factors, such as the degree and magnitude of the wrongdoing, the extent to which the crimes were planned or part of a policy, the effect the crimes had / still have on the victims, and the overall responsibility of high-level individuals[1302].

Should the Prosecutor decide to follow the prevailing opinion within the international community – reflected in the Goldstone Report and a number of other reports prepared by non-governmental organizations following the Gaza conflict – he is expected to have little doubt regarding the "gravity requirement", as the IDF was accused of (i) willful killing; torture and inhumane treatment; willfully causing great suffering or serious injury to body or health; and extensive destruction of property, not justified by military necessity and carried out unlawfully and wantonly[1303], (ii) committing said crimes in a widespread manner, as part of a policy[1304], and (iii) causing the victims in the Gaza Strip severe and long-term suffering as a direct result of the trauma experienced during the attacks, the hardship of life and the fear of future attacks[1305]. In addition, the re-

1301 ICC Office of the Prosecutor, *Informal Expert Paper: The Principle of Complementarity in Practice* (2003), para. 35.

1302 See *supra* notes 1234, 1237.

1303 See *supra* notes 435, 450, 458, 460.

1304 Goldstone Report, *supra* note 28, paras. 1891, 1921.

1305 *Ibid.*, para. 1881.

sponsibility for these alleged crimes goes beyond individual criminal responsibility at the level of combatants and even commanders, and lies with those who designed, planned, ordered and oversaw their execution[1306].

3.3.2. Admissibility – Art. 17 Rome-Statute

With regard to the possibility of cases related to the alleged conduct of the IDF during the Gaza armed conflict being admissible before the ICC, Art. 17(1)(a) and (b) Rome-Statute provide that such cases shall be inadmissible if they (i) are being investigated or prosecuted by the Israeli military justice system, or (ii) have been investigated by the Israeli military justice system, which has decided not to prosecute the person or people concerned – unless it has been determined that said justice system is unwilling or unable to genuinely carry out the investigation / prosecution.

The above described investigations Israel has conducted / is conducting into the allegations made against the conduct of the IDF in Gaza undoubtedly fulfill the first part of Art. 17(1)(a) and (b) Rome-Statute, so that cases related to said IDF conduct can be admissible before the ICC only if it is determined that the "unwilling / unable exception" is applicable in the case at hand[1307].

3.3.2.1. Inability – Art. 17(3) Rome-Statute

The comprehensive analysis of (i) the system currently in place in Israel for investigating allegations of international law violations by the IDF, and (ii) the investigatory steps taken by Israel in accordance with said system, leaves no doubt regarding the full functionality of the Israeli military justice system, so that under no circumstances can it be considered unavailable or to have totally / substantially collapsed. Therefore, the possibility of the Israeli military justice system being "unable", in accordance with Art. 17(3) Rome-statute, must be ruled out.

3.3.2.2. Unwillingness – Art. 17(2) Rome-Statute

In contrast to the above, the possibility of the Israeli military justice system being "unwilling" is much less straight forward, as in this regard the Davis Committee had serious doubts and concerns with respect to certain aspects of the Israeli investigations, which could constitute "unwillingness" in accordance with Art. 17(2) Rome-Statute.

1306 *Ibid.*, para. 1895; Davis Committee, *Report*, *supra* note 1293, para. 64.

1307 Admissibility under Art. 17(1)(c) Rome-Statute is less relevant in the case at hand, as claims concerning possible "unwillingness" in the Israeli military justice system pertain only to the investigation / prosecution phase, not the trial phase – as discussed below.

First, the fact that by May 2011 approximately one third of the serious incidents featured in the Goldstone Report were still unresolved or unclear, resulted in the Davis Committee having "strong reservations" regarding the ability of Israel's military justice system to investigate allegations of wrongdoing during military operations in a sufficiently prompt manner – which is a central and significant characteristic of an effective justice system[1308]. This finding could constitute "unwillingness" in the form of an "unjustified delay [. . .] which in the circumstances is inconsistent with an intent to bring the person concerned to justice", in accordance with Art. 17(2)(b) Rome-Statute, as one could claim that (i) the proceedings pertaining to the unresolved / unclear serious allegations have taken considerably longer than other similar proceedings conducted by the Israeli military justice system, (ii) the delays were avoidable, but not prevented – at least in most cases, and (iii) the impaired effectiveness of such slow-moving investigations, resulting from the loss of crucial evidence and accurate testimonies over time, significantly reduces the prospect of ultimately achieving accountability and justice – which is inconsistent with a genuine state interest in bringing the person concerned to justice.

Second, the Davis Committee raised serious concerns regarding the impartiality of the MAG given its dual responsibility in the IDF – according to which the Military Advocate General is legal adviser to the Chief of General Staff and other IDF units, and, at the same time, the supervisor of disciplinary law in the IDF. According to the Committee, the fact that MAG members are responsible for investigating IDF conduct, which directly links to advice given to various IDF units by other MAG members, constitutes a clear conflict of interest and thus a lack of impartiality[1309].

Numerous Israeli and international non-governmental organizations support the Davis Committee's concerns regarding MAG impartiality and, in addition, claim that the MAG cannot be considered independent under the current Israeli military justice system. Such claims are based on the fact that despite the MAG's complete independence in interpreting the law, it is an integral part of the IDF in all other matters and, as such, fully depends on the military system for budgets, personnel, promotions, etc.[1310].

1308 See *supra* note 1294.

1309 See *supra* note 1296.

1310 FIDH – International Federation for Human Rights, *Shielded From Accountability – Israel's Unwillingness to Investigate and Prosecute International Crimes* (2011), pp. 2-3.

The subordination of the investigative body of war crimes allegations to the authority of the MAG, despite its clear connection to the military units against which such allegations have been made, creates a situation, in which the MAG is neither subjectively free of personal prejudice or bias, nor impartial from an objective point of view[1311]. This, in addition to the fact that the MAG is not independent from the military hierarchy in all non-legal matters and, therefore, could be subject to outside pressures[1312], confirms the claim made by many in this regard that "[n]o system can investigate itself"[1313] in a manner, which is completely impartial and independent.

Consequently, Israel's current system for investigating misconduct allegations could constitute "unwillingness" in accordance with Art. 17(2)(c) Rome-Statute, which requires that investigations conducted within such system were / are not being conducted impartially or independently. This conclusion is not affected by the fact that the military justice system is subject to civilian supervision, as intervention by Israel's Attorney General or Supreme Court occurs only in extremely exceptional cases[1314], so that these cannot be considered an ordinary part of Israel's investigation system.

Third, the Davis Committee criticized the fact that Israel's investigative efforts did not pertain to the country's senior decision makers during Operation "Cast Lead" who, according to the Goldstone Report, bear the overall responsibility for the conduct of the IDF during the conflict. In addition, the Committee concluded that the investigation of such senior decision makers must be conducted by an external body, as the system / structure currently in place in Israel does not allow for independent and effective investigations on that level of the chain of command[1315]. Although the Davis Committee does not mention this possibility, Israeli and international non-governmental organizations argue that the current Israeli investigation system serves the purpose of shielding Israel's senior political and military decision makers from criminal responsibility for international crimes. According to these organizations, when considering the structural deficiencies of the current Israeli system, no other conclusion is possible, as:

(i) A situation, in which the MAG would be responsible for investigating the role of high-level political leaders in the alleged commission of interna-

---

1311 See *supra* note 1226.

1312 See *supra* note 1225.

1313 B'Tselem – The Israeli Information Center for Human Rights in the Occupied Territories, *Israel's Report to the UN Misstates the Truth* (2010).

1314 *Ibid.*; FIDH – International Federation for Human Rights, *supra* note 1310, pp. 3-4.

1315 See *supra* note 1299.

tional crimes, would offend the very governmental structures that subject the military to the political echelon. Furthermore, the fact that most military policy decisions in Israel are made by the political leadership, creates a very close relationship between the military and the political leadership, which does not allow the former to independently and effectively investigate the latter;

(ii) Command investigations are classified inquiries within a specific army unit with the purpose of drawing operational conclusions. They are neither suitable nor relevant to the criminal investigation, let alone prosecution, of war crimes allegations; on the contrary, their use may harm or even completely disrupt criminal investigations. Furthermore, in the exceptional cases, in which command investigations lead to criminal prosecution, these mostly involve low-rank soldiers who violated military orders on their own initiative, whereby senior officers are usually submitted to disciplinary – i.e. not criminal – proceedings. Accordingly, an investigation system, which is designed to focus on the operational, rather than the policy, aspect of military operations and, therefore, almost never questions the conduct of the most senior decision makers, must be regarded as shielding the latter[1316].

Accordingly, Israel's continued use of an investigation system, which is designed to focus on the most serious crimes, but not on the most responsible[1317], could constitute "unwillingness" in accordance with Art. 17(2)(a) Rome-Statute.

4. Conclusion

Based on the above, it seems the Prosecutor should have no doubt with regard to the question whether cases related to the alleged conduct of the Israeli military during the Gaza armed conflict would be admissible under Art. 17 Rome-Statute.

Nevertheless – in light of the complementarity regime's main objective of protecting state sovereignty and allowing ICC intervention only as a last resort – one must bear in mind that despite its concerns and doubts, the Davis Committee:

(i) Found that "Israel has dedicated significant resources to investigate over 400 allegations of operational misconduct in Gaza reported by the United

1316 FIDH – International Federation for Human Rights, *supra* note 1310, pp. 6-7.
1317 See *supra* note 1221.

Nations Independent Fact-Finding Mission on the Gaza Conflict and others"[1318];

(ii) Noted the work of the Turkel Commission – both as an independent mechanism to assess / investigate "high-level operational and legal decisions concerning the execution of the military operation in Gaza"[1319] and with regard to its purpose of reviewing "the ability of the military justice system to investigate promptly allegations of wrongdoing during military operations"[1320].

Thus, the Davis Committee chose to convey its impression that Israel was serious about (i) investigating the allegations made against the IDF – within Israel's current investigation system, and (ii) ensuring that said system fully complied with international standards. Since this completely contradicts possible Israeli "unwillingness" under Art. 17(2) Rome-Statute, the Prosecutor is not expected to consider cases related to the conduct of the IDF in Gaza admissible under Art. 17 Rome-Statute before the Turkel Commission submits the second part of its final report and the Israeli Government has a chance to study and implement the relevant recommendations. However, should this process fail to significantly improve the deficits in Israel's current investigation system, pointed out by the Davis Committee and others, the Prosecutor may, very well, conclude that cases related to Operation "Cast Lead" are admissible under Art. 17 Rome-Statute.

1318 Davis Committee, *Updated Report*, *supra* note 1278, para. 77.
1319 *Ibid.*, para. 80.
1320 *Ibid.*, para. 82.

SUMMARY AND CONCLUSION

Returning to the purpose of the research stated in the Introduction, this thesis has provided an in-depth procedural analysis of the possibility of Israel / Israelis facing legal consequences before the ICJ or the ICC, based on the serious allegations made against the conduct of the IDF during the Gaza armed conflict of 2008/2009. The conclusions reached during said analysis can be summarized as follows:

1. ICJ jurisdiction over the Gaza armed conflict

The first question regarding possible ICJ jurisdiction over the events of the Gaza conflict pertained to the Court's contentious jurisdiction – i.e. the possibility of litigation between the State of Israel and another state(s) before the ICJ concerning possible violations of international law by Israeli military forces during the conflict in Gaza. This possibility was rejected in Chapter One as a result of:

(i) The consent requirement, according to which the ICJ derives its jurisdiction from the definite consent of the states that are party to each case, so that no state can be made a party to contentious proceedings against its express will;

(ii) The fact that the State of Israel explicitly rejects the ICJ's contentious jurisdiction with respect to any element of the Israeli-Palestinian conflict.

The second possibility analyzed in Chapter One was that of possible ICJ advisory jurisdiction in the case at hand. The main conclusion reached in this analysis was that should the ICJ be requested to provide an advisory opinion regarding possible Israeli violations of international law during the Gaza conflict, the Court would have the jurisdiction to do so. Such an advisory jurisdiction would have no binding effect upon the requesting organ or the state to which it pertains; however, the substantive authority attached to a legal opinion given by the principal judicial organ of the UN and the highest international tribunal in the world could have great influence on (i) the international community's approach towards the events and aftermath of the Gaza armed conflict and, in turn, (ii) Israeli policy and actions going forward.

2. ICC jurisdiction over the Gaza armed conflict

In order to determine whether the ICC could investigate / prosecute Israeli military personnel and government officials following the Gaza armed conflict, the first question dealt with in Chapter Two pertained to the ICC's subject-matter jurisdiction – i.e. whether the allegations made against the conduct of the IDF in the case at hand would fall within such jurisdiction. This was answered positively after concluding that a number of said allegations fulfill the substantive requirements of crimes against humanity and war crimes defined in the Rome Statute. This was followed by the examination of whether the ICC would have personal jurisdiction over Israeli military commanders and government officials, who took part in the Gaza conflict – which was also concluded positively.

Chapter Two then provided an analysis of three additional jurisdictional elements, which were all concluded negatively, due to the fact that none of the parties involved in the Gaza armed conflict became States Parties either prior, during or after the conflict:

(i) ICC temporal jurisdiction – rejected in accordance with Art. 11(1) and (2) Rome-Statute;
(ii) ICC nationality based jurisdiction – rejected in accordance with Art. 12(2)(b) Rome-Statute;
(iii) ICC territorial jurisdiction – rejected in accordance with Art. 12(2)(alt. 1)(a) Rome-Statute.

Consequently, *ad hoc* acceptance of ICC territorial jurisdiction, in accordance with Art. 12(2)(alt. 2)(a) and (3) Rome-Statute, remained the final option for the ICC to acquire jurisdiction over the events of the Gaza armed conflict – apart from the (highly) unlikely possibility of a UN Security Council referral under Art. 13(b) Rome-Statute[1321].

On 21 January 2009, the Palestinian Authority declared its *ad hoc* acceptance of ICC jurisdiction in accordance with Art. 12(3) Rome-Statute, which requires that (only) "States" make such declarations. The analysis of the highly significant and controversial question of whether the Palestinian Authority's declaration of 21 January 2009 fulfilled said requirement constitutes the "heart" of this research and was concluded by rejecting the possibility of the Palestinian Authority making use of Art. 12(3) Rome-Statute, as:

(i) The Palestinian Authority did not constitute a full-fledged state: Despite coming very close to fulfilling the requirements of statehood, according to both the declarative and constitutive theories, the Palestinian Authority

1321 See *supra* note 872.

chose not to claim that a State of Palestine already exists. Until it does so, the Palestinian Authority cannot be considered a full-fledged state, regardless of the situation on the ground;

(ii) The Palestinian Authority did not constitute a quasi-state for the purpose of the Rome Statute only: Despite its undisputable quasi-state features, the Palestinian Authority possessed only one of the three characteristics of adequate "government capacity" to delegate criminal jurisdiction to the ICC, namely, the capacity to exercise criminal jurisdiction over Palestinians. With regard to the additional two characteristics, the Oslo Accords, the legal instrument which created the Palestinian Authority and defined its legal and jurisdictional powers, deprived the latter from exercising criminal jurisdiction over Israelis and seriously restricted its ability to conduct foreign relations.

Chapter Two concluded by examining the effect (i) official capacity and immunity, and (ii) individual criminal responsibility could have on if / how the ICC takes action against individual Israeli government officials and military commanders. This question has been examined despite the conclusion reached above, as the scenario of the ICC acquiring jurisdiction over the events of the Gaza armed conflict as a result of (i) the Prosecutor reaching a different conclusion than the one presented in this research, or (ii) a UN Security Council referral in accordance with Art. 13(b) Rome-Statute, remains unlikely yet possible.

3. Admissibility of cases related to the Gaza conflict before the ICC

Chapter Three completed the analysis of possible ICC action against Israeli officials by examining whether cases related to the Gaza armed conflict would be admissible under Art. 17 Rome-Statute – a question relevant only in the unlikely case that the events of the Gaza conflict reach The Hague (see above). The conclusion reached in this regard consisted of two main findings:

(i) Certain aspects of the Israeli investigations into the allegations made against the conduct of the IDF during the Gaza conflict and the system, within which such investigations have been conducted, could constitute "unwillingness" in accordance with Art. 17(2) Rome-Statute. Such aspects include: First, the unjustified delay in the investigation of numerous serious allegations made against the IDF, which significantly reduces the effectiveness of such investigations and the prospect of achieving accountability and justice. Second, the dual responsibility of the MAG in the IDF, which (especially under the circumstances of the case at hand) could constitute a clear conflict of interest, leading to a lack of impartiality and independence of the proceedings. Third, the subordination of the investigative body of war crimes allegations to the authority of the MAG does not allow for higher-level investigations that focus on the policy, rather the operational, aspect of military operations – a fact which could constitute the shielding of the most senior decision makers from criminal responsibility;

(ii) Despite the above, Israel is genuinely interested in ensuring that all investigations of allegations made against the conduct of the IDF in Gaza are conducted internally and that the system, within which such investigations are conducted, complies with international standards.

Therefore, cases related to the Gaza armed conflict could be admissible under Art. 17 Rome-Statute only if the steps and actions to be taken by the State of Israel, in order to fulfill its intent, are not able to persuade the international community / the Prosecutor that the above mentioned deficits in the Israeli investigations and overall system have been dealt with sufficiently.

BIBLIOGRAPHY AND SOURCES

Books and Book Chapters

Amr, Mohamed Sameh M., *The Role of the International Court of Justice as the Principal Judicial Organ of the United Nations*, The Hague: Kluwer Law International (2003).

Bassiouni, M. Cherif, *Introduction to International Criminal Law*, Ardsley: Transnational Publishers, Inc. (2003).

Bassiouni, M. Cherif, *The Legislative History of the International Criminal Court*, Volume 1, Ardsley: Transnational Publishers, Inc. (2005).

Benvenuti, Paolo, "Complementarity of the International Criminal Court", in: Ellis, Mark S. and Richard J. Goldstone (eds.), *The International Criminal Court: Challenges to Achieving Justice and Accountability in the 21st Century*, New York: International Debate Education Association (2008).

Boot, Machteld, *Genocide, Crimes Against Humanity, War Crimes: Nullum Crimen Sine Lege and the Subject Matter Jurisdiction of the International Criminal Court*, Antwerp: Intersentia (2002).

Cassese, Antonio, Paola Gaeta and John R.W.D. Jones (eds.), *The Rome Statute of the International Criminal Court: A Commentary*, Volumes 1 and 2, Oxford: Oxford University Press (2002).

Crawford, James, *The Creation of States in International Law*, 2nd edition, Oxford: Oxford University Press (2006).

Elsea, Jennifer, *International Criminal Court: Overview and Selected Legal Issues*, New York: Novinka Books (2003).

Eyffinger, Arthur, *The International Court of Justice, 1946 - 1996*, The Hague: Kluwer Law International (1996).

Fitzmaurice, Gerald, *The Law and Procedure of the International Court of Justice*, Volume 1, Cambridge: Grotius Publications Limited (1986).

Gadirov, Javid, *Mapping International Justice: Immunity of State Officials and Individual Criminal Responsibility*, Budapest: CEU, Budapest College (2008).

Gardiner, Richard K., *Treaty Interpretation*, Oxford: Oxford University Press (2008).

Gerding, Marc, "Völkerstrafrecht vor internationalen Strafgerichten", in: Kühne, Hans-Heiner, Robert Esser and Marc Gerding (eds.), *Völkerstrafrecht*, Osnabrück: Julius Jonscher Verlag (2007).

Greig, D. W., *International Law*, 2nd edition, London: Butterworths (1976).

Henckaerts, Jean-Marie and Louise Doswald-Beck, *Customary International Humanitarian Law*, Volume 1, Cambridge: Cambridge University Press (2009).

Hillier, Tim, *Sourcebook on Public International Law*, London: Cavendish Publishing Limited (1998).

Khalil, Asem, *Which Constitution for the Palestinian Legal System?*, Roma: Pontificia Università Lateranense (2003).

Kim, Young Sok, *The Law of the International Criminal Court*, Buffalo: William S. Hein & Co., Inc. (2007).

Lauterpacht, Elihu (ed.), *International Law – Being the Collected Papers of Hersch Lauterpacht*, Volume 3, Cambridge: Cambridge University Press (1977).

Lee, Roy S. (ed.), *The International Criminal Court – Elements of Crimes and Rules of Procedure and Evidence*, Ardsley: Transnational Publishers, Inc. (2001).

Oppenheim, Lassa, *International Law – A Treatise*, 7th edition, Volume 1, London: Longmans, Green and Co. Ltd. (1952).

Rosenne, Shabtai, *The Law and Practice of the International Court, 1920 - 2005*, Volume 1, Leiden: Martinus Nijhoff Publishers (2006).

Rosenne, Shabtai, *The World Court – What it is and How it Works*, 2nd edition, Leyden: A.W.Sythoff (1963).

Sadat, Leila Nadya, *The International Criminal Court and the Transformation of International Law: Justice for the New Millennium*, Ardsley: Transnational Publishers, Inc. (2002).

Schabas, William A., *An Introduction to the International Criminal Court*, 1st edition, Cambridge: Cambridge University Press (2001).

Schabas, William A., *An Introduction to the International Criminal Court*, 3rd edition, Cambridge: Cambridge University Press (2007).

Schabas, William A., *The International Criminal Court: A Commentary on the Rome Statute*, Oxford: Oxford University Press (2010).

Schiff, Benjamin N., *Building the International Criminal Court*, Cambridge: Cambridge University Press (2008).

Shehadeh, Raja, *Occupier's Law: Israel and the West Bank*, Washington: Institute for Palestine Studies (1985).

Sinclair, Ian, *The Vienna Convention on the Law of Treaties*, 2nd edition, Manchester: Manchester University Press (1984).

Singh, Nagendra, *The Role and Record of the International Court of Justice*, Dordrecht: Martinus Nijhoff Publishers (1989).

Stone, Julius, *Israel and Palestine: Assault on the Law of Nations*, Baltimore: Johns Hopkins University Press (1981).

Sugihara, Takane, "The Judicial Function of the International Court of Justice with Respect to Disputes Involving Highly Political Issues", in: Muller, A.S, D. Raič and J.M. Thuránszky (eds.), *The International Court of Justice – Its Future Role after Fifty Years*, The Hague: Martinus Nijhoff Publishers (1997).

Triffterer, Otto (ed.), *Commentary on the Rome Statute of the International Criminal Court – Observers' Notes, Article by Article*, 2nd edition, Munich: C.H.Beck (2008).

Watson, Geoffrey R., *The Oslo Accords – International Law and the Israeli-Palestinian Peace Agreements*, Oxford: Oxford University Press (2000).

Werle, Gerhard, *Principles of International Criminal Law*, 2nd edition, The Hague: T.M.C. Asser Press (2009).

Zimmermann, Andreas, Christian Tomuschat and Karin Oellers-Frahm (eds.), *The Statute of the International Court of Justice – A Commentary*, Oxford: Oxford University Press (2006).

Journal Articles

Abizadeh, Arash, "Introduction to the Rome Statute of the International Criminal Court", *World Order* 34.2 (2003), pp. 19-27.

Akande, Dapo, "International Law Immunities and the International Criminal Court", *American Journal of International Law* 98 (2004), pp. 407-433.

Akande, Dapo, "The Jurisdiction of the International Criminal Court over Nationals of Non-Parties: Legal Basis and Limits", *Journal of International Criminal Justice* 1 (2003), pp. 618-650.

Alexandrov, Stanimir A., "The Compulsory Jurisdiction of the International Court of Justice: How Compulsory is it?", *Chinese Journal of International Law* 5.1 (2006), pp. 29-38.

Alvarez, Jose E., "The New Dispute Settlers: (Half) Truths and Consequences", *Texas International Law Journal* 38 (2003), pp. 405-444.

Ambos, Kai, "General Principles of Criminal Law in the Rome Statute", *Criminal Law Forum* 10 (1999), pp. 1-32.

Baker, Alan, "The International Criminal Court: Israel's Unique Dilemma", *Justice Magazine* 18 (1998), pp. 19-25.

Benoliel, Daniel and Ronen Perry, "Israel, Palestine, and the ICC", *Michigan Journal of International Law* 32 (2010), pp. 73-127.

Benvenisti, Eyal, "The Israeli-Palestinian Declaration of Principles: A Framework for Future Settlement", *European Journal of International Law* 4 (1993), pp. 542-554.

Benzing, Markus, "The Complementarity Regime of the International Criminal Court: International Criminal Justice between State Sovereignty and the

Fight against Impunity", *Max Planck Yearbook of United Nations Law* 7 (2003), pp. 591-632.
Bingbin, Lu, "Reform of the International Court of Justice – A Jurisdictional Perspective", *Perspectives* 5.2 (2004), pp. 22-31.
Bisharat, George E., *et al.*, "Israel's Invasion of Gaza in International Law", *Denver Journal of International Law and Policy* 38.1 (2009), pp. 41-114.
Blumenthal, Daniel A., "The Politics of Justice: Why Israel Signed the International Criminal Court Statute and what the Signature Means", *Georgia Journal of International and Comparative Law* 30 (2002), pp. 593-615.
Boyle, Francis A., "The Creation of the State of Palestine", *European Journal of International Law* 1 (1990), pp. 301-306.
Brown, Nathan J., "The Hamas-Fatah Conflict: Shallow but Wide", *Fletcher Forum of World Affairs* 34.2 (2010), pp. 37-51.
Brubacher, Matthew R., "Prosecutorial Discretion within the International Criminal Court", *Journal of International Criminal Justice* 2.1 (2004), pp. 71-95.
Coleman, Andrew, "War Crimes and the ICJ's Advisory Jurisdiction", *Alternative Law Journal* 26 (2001), pp. 32-35.
Crawford, James, "The Creation of the State of Palestine: Too Much Too Soon?", *European Journal of International Law* 1 (1990), pp. 307-313.
Cryer, Robert, "Prosecuting the Leaders: Promises, Politics and Practicalities", *Göttingen Journal of International Law* 1.1 (2009), pp. 45-75.
Dajani, Omar M., "Stalled Between Seasons: The International Legal Status of Palestine During the Interim Period", *Denver Journal of International Law and Policy* 26.1 (1997), pp. 27-92.
Elagab, Omer Y., "The Darfur Situation and the ICC: An Appraisal", *Journal of Politics and Law* 1.3 (2008), pp. 43-60.
Eyffinger, Arthur, "Legal and Political Acrobats – The Fate and Future of the International Court of Justice", *Harvard International Review* 27.1 (2005), pp. 84-85.
Freeland, Steven, "How Open Should the Door Be? – Declarations by non-States Parties under Article 12(3) of the Rome Statute of the International Criminal Court", *Nordic Journal of International Law* 75 (2006), pp. 211-241.
Gallant, Kenneth S., "Jurisdiction to Adjudicate and Jurisdiction to Prescribe in International Criminal Courts", *Villanova Law Review* 48 (2003), pp. 763-842.
Gallant, Kenneth S., "The International Criminal Court in the System of States and International Organizations", *Leiden Journal of International Law* 16.3 (2003), pp. 553-591.

Gioia, Federica, "State Sovereignty, Jurisdiction, and 'Modern' International Law: The Principle of Complementarity in the International Criminal Court", *Leiden Journal of International Law* 19 (2006), pp. 1095-1123.

Greenawalt, Alexander K.A., "Justice Without Politics? Prosecutorial Discretion and the International Criminal Court", *NYU Journal of International Law and Politics* 39 (2007), pp. 583-673.

Halevy, Efraim, "Israel's Hamas Portfolio", *Israel Journal of Foreign Affairs* 2.3 (2008), pp. 41-47.

Kattan, Victor, "Operation Cast Lead: Use of Force Discourse and *jus ad bellum* Controversies", *Palestine Yearbook of International Law* 15 (2009), pp. 95-118.

Keith, Kenneth, "The Advisory Jurisdiction of the International Court of Justice: Some Comparative Reflections", *Australian Yearbook of International Law* 17 (1996), pp. 39-58.

Kreß, Claus, "Reflections on the *Iudicare* Limb of the Grave Breaches Regime", *Journal of International Criminal Justice* 7 (2009), pp. 789-809.

Lapidoth, Ruth, "The Advisory Opinion and the Jewish Settlements", *Israel Law Review* 38 (2005), pp. 292-297.

Lenk, Arthur, "International Justice – Political Misuses of International Law: The Development of the 'Crime' of Population Transfer in International Criminal Court", *Eyes on the ICC* 1.1 (2004), pp. 71-85.

Levy, Ayelet, "Israel Rejects its own Offspring: The International Criminal Court", *Loyola of Los Angeles International & Comparative Law Review* 22 (1999), pp. 207-249.

Malanczuk, Peter, "Some Basic Aspects of the Agreements Between Israel and the PLO from the Perspective of International Law", *European Journal of International Law* 7.4 (1996), pp. 485-500.

Mari, Mustafa, "The Israeli Disengagement from the Gaza Strip: An End of the Occupation?", *Yearbook of International Humanitarian Law* 8 (2005), pp. 356-368.

Mckinney, Kathryn M., "The Legal Effects of the Israeli-PLO Declaration of Principles: Steps Towards Statehood for Palestine", *Seattle University Law Review* 18 (1994), pp. 93-128.

Oda, Shigeru, "The Compulsory Jurisdiction of the International Court of Justice: A Myth? – A Statistical Analysis of Contentious Cases", *International and Comparative Law Quarterly* 49 (2000), pp. 251-277.

Orkand, Seth Benjamin, "Coming Apart at the Seamline – The Oslo Accords and Israel's Security Barrier: A Missed Opportunity at the International Court of Justice and the Israeli Supreme Court", *Gonzaga Journal of International Law* 10 (2007), pp. 390-436.

Pellet, Alain, "The Palestinian Declaration and the Jurisdiction of the International Criminal Court", *Journal of International Criminal Justice* 8 (2010), pp. 981-999.

Philipp, Christiane E., "The International Criminal Court – A Brief Introduction", *Max Planck Yearbook of United Nations Law* 7 (2003), pp. 331-339.

Pichon, Jakob, "The Principle of Complementarity in the Cases of the Sudanese Nationals *Ahmad Harun* and *Ali Kushayb* before the International Criminal Court", *International Criminal Law Review* 8 (2008), pp. 185-228.

Power, Susan, "War, Invasion, Occupation? A Problem of Status on the Gaza Strip", *Trinity College Law Review* 12 (2009), pp. 25-39.

Prince, James L., "The International Legal Implications of the November 1988 Palestinian Declaration of Statehood", *Stanford Journal of International Law* 25 (1989), pp. 681-708.

Quigley, John, "David v. Goliath: Humanitarian and Human Rights Law in Light of the Palestinian Right of Self-Determination and Right to Recapture Territory Taken by Force", *NYU Journal of International Law and Politics* 21 (1989), pp. 489-525.

Quigley, John, "The Israel-PLO Interim Agreements: Are they Treaties?", *Cornell International Law Journal* 30 (1997), pp. 717-740.

Ronen, Yaël, "ICC Jurisdiction over Acts Committed in the Gaza Strip – Article 12(3) of the ICC Statute and Non-state Entities", *Journal of International Criminal Justice* 8 (2010), pp. 3-27.

Ronen, Yaël, "Superior Responsibility of Civilians for International Crimes Committed in Civilian Settings", *Vanderbilt Journal of Transnational Law* 43 (2010), pp. 313-356.

Sacouto, Susana and Katherine Cleary, "The Gravity Threshold of the International Criminal Court", *American University International Law Review* 23 (2008), pp. 807-854.

Samson, Elizabeth, "Is Gaza Occupied?: Redefining the Status of Gaza Under International Law", *American University International Law Review* 25 (2010), pp. 915-967.

Scheffer, David J., "A Negotiator's Perspective on the International Criminal Court", *Military Law Review* 167 (2001), pp. 1-19.

Scheffer, David J., "Article 98(2) of the Rome Statute: America's Original Intent", *Journal of International Criminal Justice* 3 (2005), pp. 333-353.

Scheffer, David J., "How to Turn the Tide Using the Rome Statute's Temporal Jurisdiction", *Journal of International Criminal Justice* 2 (2004), pp. 26-34.

Scheffer, David J., "The United States and the International Criminal Court", *American Journal of International Law* 93.1 (1999), pp. 12-22.

Shany, Yuval, "Binary Law Meets Complex Reality: The Occupation of Gaza Debate", *Israel Law Review* 41 (2008), pp. 68-86.

Shany, Yuval, "Farawy, so Close: The Legal Status of Gaza After Israel's Disengagement", *Yearbook of International Humanitarian Law* 8 (2005), pp. 369-383.

Shany, Yuval, "In Defence of Functional Interpretation of Article 12(3) of the Rome Statute – A Response to Yaël Ronen", *Journal of International Criminal Justice* 8 (2010), pp. 329-343.

Stahn, Carsten, Mohamed M. El Zeidy and Héctor Olásolo, "The International Criminal Court's Ad Hoc Jurisdiction Revisited", *American Journal of International Law* 99.2 (2005), pp. 421-431.

Stahn, Carsten, "Why Some Doors may be Closed Already: Second Thoughts on a 'Case-by-Case' Treatment of Article 12(3) Declarations", *Nordic Journal of International Law* 75 (2006), pp. 243-248.

Tunks, Michael A., "Diplomats or Defendants? Defining the Future of Head-of-State Immunity", *Duke Law Journal* 52 (2002), pp. 651-682.

van der Vyver, Johan D., "Personal and Territorial Jurisdiction of the International Criminal Court", *Emory International Law Review* 14 (2000), pp. 1-103.

Weiner, Justus R., "Hard Facts Meet Soft Law – The Israel-PLO Declaration of Principles and the Prospects for Peace: A Response to Katherine W. Meighan", *Virginia Journal of International Law* 35 (1995), pp. 931-970.

Weiner, Justus R., "Peace and its Discontents: Israeli and Palestinian Intellectuals who Reject the Current Peace Process", *Cornell International Law Journal* 29 (1996), pp. 501-535.

Worster, William Thomas, "Law, Politics, and the Conception of the State in State Recognition Theory", *Boston University International Law Journal* 27 (2009), pp. 115-171.

Yang, Lijun, "On the Principle of Complementarity in the Rome Statute of the International Criminal Court", *Chinese Journal of International Law* 4.1 (2005), pp. 121-132.

NGO / Other Reports, Publications and Legal Opinions

Airports Council International – Asia-Pacific Region, *Dateline – the Official Newsletter of the Asia-Pacific Region of Airports Council International*, Volume 14, Number 1 (2006), available at <http://www.airports.org/aci/ACIAPAC/File/Dateline/DateLine_J UNE06 (FINAL).pdf>.

Al-Haq, *Position Paper on Issues Arising from the Palestinian Authority's Submission of a Declaration to the Prosecutor of the International Criminal Court under Article 12(3) of the Rome Statute* (2009), available at <http://www.icc-cpi.int/NR/rdonlyres/D3C77FA6-9DEE-45B1-ACC0-B41706BB41E5/281874/OTPAlHaqpositionpapericc14December20091.pdf>.

Al Mezan Centre for Human Rights, *Cast Lead Offensive in Numbers – Statistical Report on: Persons Killed and Property Damaged or Destroyed in the Gaza Strip by the Israeli Occupation Forces during Operation Cast Lead, 27 December 2008 - 18 January 2009* (2009), available at <http://www.mezan.org/upload/8941.pdf>.

Amnesty International, *Israel/Gaza – Operation 'Cast Lead': 22 Days of Death and Destruction* (2009), available at <http://www.amnesty.org/en/library/asset/MDE15/015/2009/en/8f299083-9a74-4853-860f0563725e633a/mde -150152009en.pdf>.

Anti-Defamation League, *The United Nations and Palestinian Statehood: Scenarios and Realities* (2011), available at <http://www.adl.org/peace-process/print-faq.pdf>.

Benvenisti, Eyal, *The Law on the Unilateral Termination of Occupation*, Tel Aviv University Law School (2008), available at <http://law.bepress.com/taulwps/fp/art93/>.

Brown, Nathan J., *The Palestinian Reform Agenda*, United States Institute of Peace, Peaceworks No. 48 (2002), available at <http://www.usip.org/files/resources/pwks48.pdf>.

B'Tselem – The Israeli Information Center for Human Rights in the Occupied Territories, *Guidelines for Israel's Investigation into Operation Cast Lead, 27 December 2008 - 18 January 2009* (2009), available at <http://www.btselem.org/download/200902_operation_cast_lead_position_paper_eng.pdf>.

Cordesman, Anthony H., *The "Gaza War": A Strategic Analysis*, Center for Strategic & International Studies (2009), available at <http://csis.org/files/media/csis/pubs/090202_gaza_war.pdf>.

Davenport, David, Kenneth Anderson, Samuel Estreicher, Eugene Kontorovich, Julian G. Ku and Abraham D. Sofaer, *The Palestinian Declaration and ICC Jurisdiction* (2009), available at <http://www.icc-cpi.int/NR/rdonlyres/D3C77FA6-9DEE-45B1-ACC0-B41706BB41E5/281873/Paldeclandiccjurisd1.pdf>.

European Centre for Law and Justice, *Legal Memorandum in Opposition to the Palestinian Authority's January 2009 Attempt to Accede to ICC Jurisdiction over Alleged Acts Committed on Palestinian Territory Since 1 July 2002* (2009), available at <http://www.icc-cpi.int/NR/rdonlyres/D3C77FA6-9DEE-45B1-ACC0-B41706BB41E5/281869/OTPlegalmemorandum1.pdf>.

FIDH – International Federation for Human Rights, *Shielded From Accountability – Israel's Unwillingness to Investigate and Prosecute International Crimes* (2011), available at <http://www.fidh.org/IMG/pdf/report_justice_israel-final-3-2.pdf>.

Gold, Dore and Diane Morrison, *Discussion on Whether the Declaration Lodged by the Palestinian Authority Meets Statutory Requirements: Historical and Diplomatic Considerations* (2010), available at <http://www.icc-cpi.int/NR/rdonlyres/553F5F08-2A84-43E9-8197-6211B5636FEA/282527/DoreGold1.pdf>.

Gowlland-Debbas, Vera, *Note on the Legal Effects of Palestine's Declaration under Article 12(3) of the ICC Statute* (2010), available at <http://www.icc-cpi.int/NR/rdonlyres/56368E8B-2FBB-4CFB-88AB-98D105F2C56F/282610/PalestineGowllandDebbas.pdf>.

Macedo, Stephen, *et al.*, *The Princeton Principles on Universal Jurisdiction*, Princeton University, Program in Law and Public Affairs (2001), available at <http://lapa.princeton.edu/hosteddocs/unive_jur.pdf>.

Mendes, Errol, *Statehood and Palestine for the Purpose of Article 12(3) of the ICC Statute* (2010), available at <http://www.icc-cpi.int/NR/rdonlyres/D3C77FA6-9DEE-45B1-ACC0-B41706BB41E5/281876/OTPErrolMendesNewSTATEHOODANDPALESTINEFORTHEPURPOS.pdf>.

Oxford Public Interest Lawyers, *Legal Consequences of Israel's Construction of a Separation Barrier in the Occupied Territories*, University of Oxford (2004), available at <http://www.nad-plo.org/userfiles/file/Reports/wallrelated1.pdf>.

Palestinian Centre for Human Rights, *Targeted Civilians – A PCHR Report on the Israeli Military Offensive against the Gaza Strip, 27 December 2008 - 18 January 2009* (2009), available at <http://www.pchrgaza.org/files/Reports/English/pdf_spec/gaza%20war%20report.pdf>.

Private Sector Coordination Council Gaza Governorates, *Gaza Private Sector Post-War Status and Needs* (2009), available at <http://www.met.gov.ps/MneModules/epapers/PostWarStatusNeed.pdf>.

Public Commission to Examine the Maritime Incident of 31 May 2010 – The Turkel Commission, *Report – Part One* (2010), available at <http://www.jewishvirtuallibrary.org/jsource/Society_&_Culture/TurkelCommission.pdf>.

Quigley, John, *Memorandum Concerning the Posted Submissions in Regard to Palestine's Declaration* (2010), available at <http://www.icc-cpi.int/NR/rdonlyres/D3C77FA6-9DEE-45B1-ACC0-B41706BB41E5/281978/Quigleyadditionalsubmission1.pdf>.

Shaw, Malcolm N., *In the Matter of the Jurisdiction of the International Criminal Court with regard to the Declaration of the Palestinian Authority* (2010), available at <http://www.icc-cpi.int/NR/rdonlyres/553F5F08-2A84-43E9-8197-6211B5636FEA/283164/OTP2010000035449SupplementaryOpinionMalcolmShaw2.PDF>.

Sonntag, Michael, *Der IGH als Hauptrechtsprechungsorgan der UNO*, Johannes Kepler Universität Linz, Institut für Völkerrecht und Internationale Beziehungen (1998), available at <http://www.sonntag.cc/teaching/IGH/IGH.pdf>.

The Independent Fact Finding Committee on Gaza to the League of Arab States, *No Safe Place* (2009), available at <http://www.emro.who.int/palestine/reports%5Cadvocacy_HR%5Chuman_rights%5CReport%20on%20the%20findings%20of%20the%20Fact%20Finding%20Mission%20in%20gaza%20-%20Gaza%20April%2009.pdf>.

The International Centre for Criminal Law Reform and Criminal Justice Policy, *International Criminal Court – Manual for the Ratification and Implementation of the Rome Statute*, 3rd edition (2008), available at <http://www.icclr.law.ubc.ca/Publications/Reports/ICC%203rd%20Ed%20Manual%20for%20Website.pdf>.

Government Documents and Publications

Commission of the European Communities, *Commission Staff Working Paper, European Neighbourhood Policy – Country Report: Palestinian Authority of the West Bank and Gaza Strip* (2004), available at <http://ec.europa.eu/world/enp/pdf/country/pa_enp_country_report_2004_en.pdf>.

Council of the European Union, *Council Joint Action 2005/797/CFSP on the European Union Police Mission for the Palestinian Territories* (2005), available at <http://eur-lex.europa.eu/LexUriServ/LexUriServ.do?uri=OJ:L:2005:300:0065:0069:EN:PDF>.

European Union Coordinating Office for Palestinian Police Support and the Palestinian National Authority – Ministry of Interior, *Factsheet*, available at <http://www.consilium.europa.eu/uedocs/cmsUpload/EUCOPPShandoutFeb2006.pdf>.

Israel Defense Forces, *Conclusion of Investigations into Central Claims and Issues in Operation Cast Lead* (2009), available at <http://idfspokesperson.com/2009/04/22/idf-announcement-findings-from-cast-lead-investigations/>.

Israel Defense Forces, *Majority of Palestinians Killed in Operation Cast Lead: Terror Operatives* (2009), available at <http://dover.idf.il/IDF/English/News/today/09/03/2602.htm>.

Israel Ministry of Foreign Affairs, *IDF Operation in Gaza: Cast Lead* (2009), available at <http://www.mfa.gov.il/MFA/Terrorism-+Obstacle+to+Peace/Terrorism+and+Islamic+Fundamentalism-/Aerial_strike_weapon_development_center+_Gaza_28-Dec-2008.htm>.

Israel Ministry of Foreign Affairs, *Israeli Investigations into Allegations regarding the Gaza Operation – Status Report* (2009), available at <http://www.mfa.gov.il/MFA/Government/Law/Legal+Issues+and+Rulings/Israeli_investigations_Gaza_Operation-Status_Report-sept_2009.htm>.

Israel Ministry of Foreign Affairs, *Israel - PLO Recognition: Exchange of Letters between PM Rabin and Chairman Arafat* (1993), available at <http://www.mfa.gov.il/MFA/Peace+Process/Guide+to+the+Peace+Process/Israel-PLO+Recognition+-+Exchange+of+Letters+betwe.htm>.

Israel Ministry of Foreign Affairs, *Israel's Settlements – Their Conformity with International Law* (1996), available at <http://www.mfa.gov.il/MFA/Archive/Peace+Process/1996/ISRAEL-S%20SETTLEMENTS%20-%20THEIR%20CONFORMITY%20WITH%20INTER>.

Israel Ministry of Foreign Affairs, *Operation Cast Lead: Israel Strikes Back Against Hamas Terror in Gaza* (2009), available at <http://www.mfa.gov.il/MFA/Terrorism-+Obstacle+to+Peace/Hamas+war+against+Israel/Israel_strikes_back_against_Hamas_terror_infrastructure_Gaza_27-Dec-2008.htm>.

Israel Ministry of Foreign Affairs, *Security Cabinet Declares Gaza Hostile Territory* (2007), available at <http://www.mfa.gov.il/MFA/Government/Communiques/2007/Security+Cabinet+declares+Gaza+hostile+territory+19-Sep-2007.htm>.

Palestinian National Authority – Ministry of Justice, *Declaration Recognizing the Jurisdiction of the International Criminal Court* (21 January 2009), available at <http://www.icc-cpi.int/NR/rdonlyres/74EEE201-0FED-4481-95D4-C8071087102C/279777/20090122PalestinianDeclaration2.pdf>.

The State of Israel, *Gaza Operation Investigations: An Update* (2010), available at <http://www.mfa.gov.il/NR/rdonlyres/8E841A98-1755-413D-A1D2-8B30F64022BE/0/GazaOperationInvestigationsUpdate.pdf>.

The State of Israel, *Gaza Operation Investigations: Second Update* (2010), available at <http://www.mfa.gov.il/NR/rdonlyres/1483B296-7439-4217-933C-653CD19CE859/0/GazaUpdateJuly2010.pdf>.

The State of Israel, *The Operation in Gaza, 27 December 2008 - 18 January 2009: Factual and Legal Aspects* (2009), available at <http://www.mfa.gov.il/NR/rdonlyres/E89E699D-A435-491B-B2D0-017675DAFEF7/0/GazaOperationwLinks.pdf>.

The State of Israel, *Written Statement on Jurisdiction and Propriety concerning the Request of the International Court of Justice for an Advisory Opinion on "the legal consequences arising from the construction of the wall by Israel"* (2004), available at <http://www.jewishvirtuallibrary.org/jsource/Peace/israelbrief.pdf>.

International Organizations Documents and Publications

Committee of Independent Experts in International Humanitarian and Human Rights Laws to Monitor and Assess any Domestic, Legal or other Proceedings Undertaken by both the Government of Israel and the Palestinian Side, *Report*, UN Doc. A/HRC/15/50 (23 September 2010), available at <http://www2.ohchr.org/english/bodies/hrcouncil/docs/15session/A.HRC.15.50_en.pdf>.

Committee of Independent Experts in International Humanitarian and Human Rights Laws to Monitor and Assess any Domestic, Legal or other Proceedings Undertaken by both the Government of Israel and the Palestinian Side, *Updated Report*, UN Doc. A/HRC/16/24 (5 May 2011), available at <http://daccess-dds-ny.un.org/doc/UNDOC/GEN/G11/130/75/PDF/G1113075.pdf?OpenElement>.

Executive Office of the Secretary-General, Protocol and Liaison Service, *Permanent Missions to the United Nations – No. 301* (March 2011), available at <http://www.un.int/protocol/bluebook/bb301.pdf>.

ICC, *About the Court*, available at <http://www.icc-cpi.int/Menus/ICC/About+the+Court/>.

ICC, *Chronology of the International Criminal Court*, available at <http://www2.icc-cpi.int/Menus/ICC/About+the+Court/ICC+at+a+glance/Chronology+of+the+ICC.htm>.

ICC, *Declarations Art. 12(3)*, available at <http://www.icc-cpi.int/Menus/ICC/Structure+of+the+Court/Registry/Declarations.htm>.

ICC, *Establishment of the Court*, available at <http://www2.icc-cpi.int/Menus/ICC/About+the+Court/ICC+at+a+glance/Establishment+of+the+Court.htm>.

ICC Office of the Prosecutor, *Draft Policy Paper on Preliminary Examinations* (2010), available at <http://www.icc-cpi.int/NR/rdonlyres/E278F5A2-A4F9-43D7-83D2-6A2C9CF5D7D7/282515/OTP_Draftpolicypaperonpreliminaryexaminations04101.pdf>.

ICC Office of the Prosecutor, *Informal Expert Paper: The Principle of Complementarity in Practice* (2003), available at <http://www.icc-cpi.int/iccdocs/doc/doc654724.pdf>.

ICC Office of the Prosecutor, *Paper on some Policy Issues before the Office of the Prosecutor* (2003), available at <http://www.amicc.org/docs/OcampoPolicyPaper9_03.pdf>.

ICC Office of the Prosecutor, *Situation in Palestine – Summary of Submissions on whether the Declaration Lodged by the Palestinian National Authority Meets Statutory Requirements* (2010), available at <http://uclalawforum.com/media/background/gaza/2010-05-03_ICC_OTP-Summary_of_Submissions.pdf>.

ICC Office of the Prosecutor, *Visit of the Palestinian National Authority Minister of Foreign Affairs, Mr. Riad al-Malki, and Minister of Justice, Mr. Ali Khashan, to the Prosecutor of the ICC* (13 February 2009), available at <http://www.icc-cpi.int/NR/rdonlyres/4CC08515-D0BA-454D-A594-446F30289EF2/280869/PNAMFA130209.pdf>.

ICC Registrar, *Acknowledgment of Receipt of the Palestinian Authority's Correspondence of 21 January 2009* (23 January 2009), available at <http://www.icc-cpi.int/NR/rdonlyres/74EEE201-0FED-4481-95D4-C8071087102C/279778/20090123404SALASS2.pdf>.

ICC, *Structure of the Court*, available at <http://www.icc-cpi.int/Menus/ICC/Structure+of+the+Court/>.

ICJ Information Department, *Questions & Answers About the Advisory Procedure* (2010), available at <http://www.icj-cij.org/presscom/en/kos_faq_en.pdf>.

ICRC, *Working Paper to Assist the Preparatory Commission in its Work to Establish the Elements of Crimes for the International Criminal Court* (1999), available at <http://www.iccnow.org/documents/ICRCWorkPaperArticle8Para2b.pdf>.

UNESCO Executive Board, *Report by the Director-General on Appropriate Ways and Means of Giving Effect to Paragraph 8(a) of 131 EX/Decision 9.4* (29 September 1989), available at <http://unesdoc.unesco.org/images/0008/000837/083783EO.pdf>.

UN General Assembly Resolution 37/123 (16 December 1982).

UN General Assembly Resolution 43/160 A (9 December 1988).

UN General Assembly Resolution 43/177 (15 December 1988).

UN General Assembly Resolution 52/250 (7 July 1998).

UN General Assembly Resolution 54/42 (1 December 1999).

UN General Assembly Resolution 63/3 (8 October 2008).

UN General Assembly Resolution 64/10 (5 November 2009).

UN General Assembly Resolution 64/254 (26 February 2010).

UN General Assembly Resolution 181 (II), 29 November 1947.

UN General Assembly Resolution 260 (III), 9 December 1948.

UN General Assembly Resolution 377 A (3 November 1950).

UN General Assembly Resolution 2625 (XXV), 24 October 1970.

UN General Assembly Resolution 3210 (XXIX), 14 October 1974.
UN General Assembly Resolution 3236 (XXIX), 22 November 1974.
UN General Assembly Resolution 3237 (XXIX), 22 November 1974.
UN Human Rights Council Resolution 13/9 (25 March 2010).
UN Human Rights Council Resolution S-12/1 (16 October 2009).
United Nations Fact-Finding Mission on the Gaza Conflict, *Human Rights in Palestine and Other Occupied Arab Territories*, UN Doc. A/HRC/12/48 (25 September 2009), available at <http://www2.ohchr.org/english/bodies/hrcouncil/docs/12session/a-hrc-12-48.pdf>.
United Nations, *Yearbook of the International Law Commission 1966*, Volume 2, UN Doc. A/CN.4/SER.A/1966/Add. 1 (1967).
UN Security Council Resolution 9 (15 October 1946).
UN Security Council Resolution 1397 (12 March 2002).
UN Security Council Resolution 1850 (16 December 2008).
UN Security Council Resolution 1860 (8 January 2009).

Electronic Resources

Al-bab – An Open Door to the Arab World, *Speech by Yasser Arafat at the Arab Summit in Beirut, 27 - 28 March 2002*, available at <http://www.al-bab.com/arab/docs/league/arafat02.htm>.
Ash, Robert Weston, *Is Palestine a "State"? A Response to Professor John Quigley's Article, "The Palestine Declaration to the International Criminal Court: The Statehood Issue"*, Rutgers Law Record (2009), available at <http://lawrecord.com/files/36_Rutgers_L_Rec_186.pdf>.
Baker, Alan, *Reasons not to Join the International Criminal Court in The Hague*, Jerusalem Center for Public Affairs (2010), available at <http://www.globallawforum.org/ViewBlog.aspx?ArticleId=48>.
Bassiouni, M. Cherif, *Comment on the Gaza Question: "Does the Prosecutor of the ICC have the Authority to Open an Investigation into Alleged Crimes Committed in the 2008-2009 Gaza Conflict?"*, UCLA School of Law, Human Rights & International Criminal Law Online Forum (2010), available at <http://uclalawforum.com/forum/permalink/859>.
B'Tselem – The Israeli Information Center for Human Rights in the Occupied Territories, *B'Tselem Publishes Complete Fatality Figures from Operation Cast Lead* (2009), available at <http://www.btselem.org/press_releases/20090909>.

B'Tselem – The Israeli Information Center for Human Rights in the Occupied Territories, *Israel's Report to the UN Misstates the Truth* (2010), available at <http://www.btselem.org/gaza_strip/20100204_israels_report_to_un>.

Diker, Dan, *The Palestinians' Unilateral "Kosovo Strategy": Implications for the PA and Israel*, Jerusalem Center for Public Affairs (2010), available at <http://www.jcpa.org/JCPA/Templates/ShowPage.asp?DBID=1&LNGID=1&TMID=111&FID=443&PID=0&IID=3271>.

Dugard, John, *Take the Case*, The New York Times (2009), available at <http://www.nytimes.com/2009/07/23/opinion/23iht-eddugard.html>.

Fletcher, George P., *No Jurisdictional Basis for an Investigation Pursuant to the Palestinian Declaration*, UCLA School of Law, Human Rights & International Criminal Law Online Forum, available at <http://uclalawforum.com/gaza#Fletcher>.

Gold, Dore, *Countdown to September: Israel, the Palestinians, and the UN General Assembly*, Jerusalem Center for Public Affairs (2011), available at <http://www.jcpa.org/JCPA/Templates/ShowPage.asp?DBID=1&LNGID=1&TMID=111&FID=443&PID=0&IID=6969>.

Gradstein, Linda, *Palestinians to Push for UN Recognition as Independent State*, AOL News (2011), available at <http://www.aolnews.com/2011/01/10/palestinians-to-push-for-un-recognition-as-independent-state/>.

Horovitz, Sigall, *Accountability of the Hamas under International Humanitarian Law*, Jerusalem Center for Public Affairs (2009), available at <http://www.globallawforum.org/ViewPublication.aspx?ArticleId=99>.

Hussein, Adam, *Israel and the International Criminal Court: The United Nations Fact-Finding Mission on the Gaza Conflict and its Role in the Arab-Israeli Conflict* (2010), available at <http://works.bepress.com/adam_hussein/1/>.

Iliopoulos, Katherine, *Will Anyone be Held Accountable for War Crimes in Gaza?*, The Crimes of War Education Project (2009), available at <http://www.crimesofwar.org/commentary/will-anyone-be-held-accountable-for-war-crimes-in-gaza/>.

International Committee of the Red Cross ("ICRC"), *Commentary on the Geneva Conventions and the Additional Protocols*, available at <http://www.icrc.org/ihl.nsf/CONVPRES?OpenView>.

Israel Ministry of Foreign Affairs, *Statement by Judge Eli Nathan – Head of the Delegation of Israel to the Rome Conference* (1998), available at <http://www.mfa.gov.il/mfa/mfaarchive/1990_1999/1998/7/judge%20eli %20nathan%20at%20un%20diplomatic%20conference%20of%20pl>.

Kearney, Michael, *It is Imperative that in Considering the Issue at Hand, the Correct Question be Asked, and that Palestinian Jurisdiction over Crimes set out in the Rome Statute be Acknowledged as Giving the ICC the Ability to Accept the PA Declaration*, UCLA School of Law, Human Rights & International Criminal Law Online Forum, available at <http://uclalawforum.com/gaza#Kearney>.

Lapidoth, Ruth, *Should the International Court of Justice Give an Advisory Opinion on Israel's Separation Fence?*, Jerusalem Center for Public Affairs (2004), available at <http://www.jcpa.org/JCPA/Templates/ShowPage.asp?DBID=1&LNGID =1&TMID= 111&FID=378&PID=1857&IID=704>.

Office of the Legal Adviser to the Israeli Ministry of Foreign Affairs, *Israel and the International Criminal Court* (2002), available at <http://www.mfa.gov.il/MFA/MFAArchive/2000_2009/2002/6/Israel%20 and%20the%20International%20Criminal%20Court>.

Permanent Observer Mission of Palestine to the United Nations, *Statement on the Occasion of the International Day of Solidarity with the Palestinian People* (2008), available at <http://www.un.int/wcm/content/site/palestine/pid/11804>.

Quigley, John, *The ICC Prosecutor has Authority to Investigate, and the ICC has Jurisdiction, because the Prosecutor has in Hand a Consent Declaration from the State on whose Territory the Alleged Crimes were Committed*, UCLA School of Law, Human Rights & International Criminal Law Online Forum, available at <http://uclalawforum.com/gaza#Quigley>.

Quigley, John, *The Palestine Declaration to the International Criminal Court: The Statehood Issue*, Rutgers Law Record (2009), available at <http://lawrecord.com/files/35_Rutgers_L_Rec_1.pdf>.

Scheinert, Josh, *A Just Dilemma – Does the International Criminal Court Have Anything to Offer Israel?*, The Jerusalem Post (2008), available at <http://www.jpost.com/Features/Article.aspx?id=109228>.

Schneider, Howard, *Palestinian Premier Sets Timeline for Establishing State, Asks Constituents to 'Roll Up Their Sleeves'*, The Washington Post (2009), available at <http://www.washingtonpost.com/wp-dyn/content/article/2009/06/22/AR 2009062202962.html>.

The European Parliament, Press Release: *Mahmoud Abbas at the European Parliament* (2009), available at <http://www.europarl.europa.eu/sides/getDoc.do?language=en&type=IM-PRESS&reference=20090203IPR48164>.

The Telegraph, *Mahmoud Abbas Signals Intent to Bid for UN Recognition for Palestinian Statehood* (2012), available at <http://www.telegraph.co.uk/news/worldnews/middleeast/palestinianauthority/8600134/Mahmoud-Abbas-signals-intent-to-bid-for-UN-recognition-for-Palestinian-statehood.html>.

Treaties and Conventions

Additional Protocol I to the Geneva Conventions of 12 August 1949, relating to the Protection of Victims of International Armed Conflicts (8 June 1977).

Additional Protocol II to the Geneva Conventions of 12 August 1949, relating to the Protection of Victims of Non-International Armed Conflicts (8 June 1977).

First Geneva Convention for the Amelioration of the Condition of the Wounded and Sick in Armed Forces in the Field (12 August 1949).

Fourth Geneva Convention relative to the Protection of Civilian Persons in Time of War (12 August 1949).

Israel - Palestine Liberation Organization: Declaration of Principles on Interim Self-Government Arrangements (13 September 1993).

Israel - Palestine Liberation Organization: Interim Agreement on the West Bank and the Gaza Strip (28 September 1995).

Second Geneva Convention for the Amelioration of the Condition of Wounded, Sick and Shipwrecked Members of Armed Forces at Sea (12 August 1949).

The 1920 Treaty of Sèvres.

The 1923 Treaty of Lausanne.

The 1933 (entry into force 1934) Convention on Rights and Duties of States.

The 1945 (entry into force 1945) Charter of the United Nations.

The 1948 Universal Declaration of Human Rights.

The 1948 (entry into force 1951) Convention on the Prevention and Punishment of the Crime of Genocide.

The 1961 (entry into force 1964) Vienna Convention on Diplomatic Relations.

The 1963 (entry into force 1967) Vienna Convention on Consular Relations.

The 1966 (entry into force 1976) International Covenant on Civil and Political Rights.

The 1969 (entry into force 1980) Vienna Convention on the Law of Treaties.

The 1969 (entry into force 1985) Convention on Special Missions.

The 1972 (entry into force 1972) Convention on International Liability for Damage Caused by Space Objects.

The 1980 (entry into force 1983) United Nations Convention on Prohibitions or Restrictions on the Use of Certain Conventional Weapons which may be Deemed to be Excessively Injurious or to have Indiscriminate Effects as amended on 21 December 2001.

The 1982 (entry into force 1994) United Nations Convention on the Law of the Sea.

The 1984 (entry into force 1987) Convention against Torture and other Cruel, Inhumane or Degrading Treatment or Punishment.

The 1992 (entry into force 1994) United Nations Framework Convention on Climate Change.

The 1997 (entry into force 2001) International Convention for the Suppression of Terrorist Bombings.

The 1998 (entry into force 2002) Rome Statute of the International Criminal Court.

The 2006 (entry into force 2008) Convention on the Rights of Persons with Disabilities.

Third Geneva Convention relative to the Treatment of Prisoners of War (12 August 1949).

CASES, DECISIONS, JUDGMENTS AND ADVISORY OPINIONS

ICC

Situation in the Democratic Republic of the Congo, Judgment on the Prosecutor's Appeal against the Decision of Pre-Trial Chamber I entitled "Decision on the Prosecutor's Application for Warrants of Arrest, Article 58", ICC Appeals Chamber, No. ICC-01/04 (13 July 2006).

The Prosecutor v. Germain Katanga and Mathieu Ngudjolo Chui, ICC Pre-Trial Chamber I, No. ICC-01/04-01/07 (30 September 2008).

The Prosecutor v. Jean-Pierre Bemba Gombo, ICC Pre-Trial Chamber II, No. ICC-01/05-01/08 (15 June 2009).

The Prosecutor v. Omar Hassan Ahmad Al Bashir, ICC Pre-Trial Chamber I, No. ICC-02/05-01/09 (4 March 2009).

The Prosecutor v. Thomas Lubanga Dyilo, ICC Pre-Trial Chamber I, No. ICC-01/04-01/06 (24 February 2006).

The Prosecutor v. Thomas Lubanga Dyilo, ICC Pre-Trial Chamber I, No. ICC-01/04-01/06 (29 January 2007).

ICJ Advisory Opinions

Application for Review of Judgement No. 158 of the United Nations Administrative Tribunal (12 July 1973).

Certain Expenses of the United Nations (Article 17, Paragraph 2, of the Charter), 20 July 1962.

Interpretation of Peace Treaties with Bulgaria, Hungary and Romania (30 March 1950).

Interpretation of the Agreement of 25 March 1951 between the WHO and Egypt (20 December 1980).

Legal Consequences for States of the Continued Presence of South Africa in Namibia (South West Africa) Notwithstanding Security Council Resolution 276 (1970), 21 June 1971.

Legal Consequences of the Construction of a Wall in the Occupied Palestinian Territories (9 July 2004).

Legality of the Threat or Use of Nuclear Weapons (8 July 1996).

Reservations to the Convention on the Prevention and Punishment of the Crime of Genocide (28 May 1951).

Western Sahara (16 October 1975).

ICJ Contentious Cases

Case Concerning Application of the Convention on the Prevention and Punishment of the Crime of Genocide (*Bosnia and Herzegovina v. Serbia and Montenegro*), 26 February 2007.

Case Concerning Military and Paramilitary Activities in and Against Nicaragua (*Nicaragua v. United States of America*), 26 November 1984.

Case Concerning the Arrest Warrant of 11 April 2000 (*Democratic Republic of the Congo v. Belgium*), 14 February 2002.

Case Concerning the Northern Cameroons (*Cameroon v. United Kingdom*), 2 December 1963.

Case Concerning United States Diplomatic and Consular Staff in Teheran (*United States of America v. Iran*), 24 May 1980.

Case of the Monetary Gold Removed from Rome in 1943 – Preliminary Question (*Italy v. France, United Kingdom of Great Britain and Northern Ireland and United States of America*), 15 June 1954.

North Sea Continental Shelf Cases (*Federal Republic of Germany v. Denmark; Federal Republic of Germany v. Netherlands*), 20 February 1969.

ICTY

The Prosecutor v. Dario Kordic and Mario Cerkez, ICTY Appeals Chamber, Nr. IT-95-14/2-A (17 December 2004).

The Prosecutor v. Dragoljub Kunarac, et al., ICTY Appeals Chamber, No. IT-96-23 and IT-96-23/1-A (12 June 2002).

The Prosecutor v. Dusko Tadic, ICTY Appeals Chamber, No. IT-94-1-A (15 July 1999).

The Prosecutor v. Dusko Tadic, ICTY Appeals Chamber, No. IT-94-1-T (2 October 1995).

The Prosecutor v. Dusko Tadic, ICTY Trial Chamber, No. IT-94-1-T (7 May 1997).

The Prosecutor v. Miroslav Kvocka, et al., ICTY Appeals Chamber, No. IT-98-30/1-A (28 February 2005).

The Prosecutor v. Radislav Krstic, ICTY Appeals Chamber, No. IT-98-33-A (19 April 2004).

The Prosecutor v. Radislav Krstic, ICTY Trial Chamber, No. IT-98-33-T (2 August 2001).

The Prosecutor v. Tihomir Blaskic, ICTY Appeals Chamber, No. IT-95-14 (29 October 1997).

The Prosecutor v. Tihomir Blaskic, ICTY Trial Chamber, No. IT-95-14-T (3 March 2000).

The Prosecutor v. Zdravko Mucic, et al., ICTY Trial chamber, No. IT-96-21-T (16 November 1998).

ICTR

The Prosecutor v. Jean-Paul Akayesu, ICTR Chamber I, No. ICTR-96-4-T (2 September 1998).

Israel Supreme Court

Jaber Al-Bassiouni Ahmed and others v. The Prime Minister of Israel, HCJ 9132/07 (30 January 2008).

Mara'abe v. Prime Minister of Israel, HCJ 7957/04 (15 September 2005).

Physicians for Human Rights v. OC Southern Command, HCJ 8990/02 (27 April 2003).

The Public Committee against Torture in Israel v. The Government of Israel, HCJ 769/02 (13 December 2006).

Others

A and others v. Secretary of State for the Home Department, UK House of Lords, No. EWCA Civ 1123 (8 December 2005).

Application under s. 83.28 of the Criminal Code, Supreme Court of Canada, File No. 29872 (23 June 2004).

France et al. v. Goering et al., 22 International Military Tribunal (Nuremberg), 1 October 1946.

France v. Commission of the European Communities, European Court of Justice, No. C-482/99 (16 May 2002).

Morris v. The United Kingdom, European Court of Human Rights, Application No. 38784/97 (26 February 2002).

Salim Ahmed Hamdan v. Donald Rumsfeld, et al., Supreme Court of the United States, No. 05-184 (29 June 2006).

Status of Eastern Carelia, PCIJ Advisory Opinion (23 July 1923).

The Attorney General v. Adolf Eichmann, District Court of Jerusalem, Criminal Case 40/61 (December 1961).

Yassin Abdullah Kadi v. Council of the European Union and Commission of the European Communities, European Court of Justice, No. C-402/05 P (2008).

INDEX

J

L

M

N

O

P

Q

R

Internationales und Europäisches Strafverfahrensrecht

Herausgegeben von Hans-Heiner Kühne und Robert Esser

Band 1 Sibyl Stein: Zum europäischen *ne bis in idem* nach Artikel 54 des Schengener Durchführungsübereinkommens. Zugleich ein Beitrag zur rechtsvergleichenden Auslegung zwischenstaatlich geltender Vorschriften. 2004.

Band 2 Friederike Charlotte Grube: Richter ohne Robe. Laienrichter in Strafsachen im deutschen und anglo-amerikanischen Rechtskreis. Eine rechtsgeschichtliche und rechtsvergleichende Untersuchung unter besonderer Berücksichtigung verfassungsrechtlicher Aspekte. 2005.

Band 3 Christiane Paul: Das Abwesenheitsverfahren als rechtsstaatliches Problem. Rechtsvergleichende Untersuchung deutscher, englischer, französischer, niederländischer und österreichischer Regelungen angesichts der Rechtsprechung des Europäischen Gerichtshofs für Menschenrechte. 2007.

Band 4 Kai Peter Hecheltjen: Der Richtervorbehalt im kartellrechtlichen Nachprüfungsverfahren der Europäischen Kommission. 2007.

Band 5 Martina Werwie-Haas: Die Umsetzung der strafrechtlichen Entscheidungen des Europäischen Gerichtshofs für Menschenrechte in Deutschland, Österreich, der Schweiz und im Vereinigten Königreich. 2008.

Band 6 Vera Warnking: Strafprozessuale Beweisverbote in der Rechtsprechung des Europäischen Gerichtshofs für Menschenrechte und ihre Auswirkungen auf das deutsche Recht. 2009.

Band 7 Christian Mülfarth: Grundlagen und Grenzen von Beweiserhebung und Beweisverwertung im spanischen Strafverfahren. Eine rechtsvergleichende Untersuchung. 2009.

Band 8 Daniel Joachim Hußung: Der Tatbegriff im Artikel 54 des Schengener Durchführungsübereinkommens. 2011.

Band 9 Johannes Stalberg: Zum Anwendungsbereich des Art. 50 der Charta der Grundrechte der Europäischen Union (ne bis in idem). 2013.

Band 10 Oded Friedmann: The Possibility of the ICJ and the ICC Taking Action in the Wake of Israel's Operation “Cast Lead” in the Gaza Strip. A Jurisdiction and Admissibility Analysis. 2013.

www.peterlang.de